Materialist Shakespeare

V

Materialist Shakespeare

A History

Edited by

IVO KAMPS

VERSO

London · New York

First published by Verso 1995
© This collection Verso 1995
© Individual contributions the contributors 1995
All rights reserved

Verso
UK: 6 Meard Street, London W1V 3HR
USA: 180 Varick Street, New York NY 10014-4606

Verso is the imprint of New Left Books

ISBN 0 86091 463 1
ISBN 0 86091 674 X (pbk.)

British Library Cataloguing in Publication Data
A catalogue record for this book is available from the British Library

Library of Congress Cataloging-in-Publication Data
Materialist Shakespeare : an introduction / edited by Ivo Kamps.
   p.   cm.
Includes index.
ISBN 0–86091–463–1 — ISBN 0–86091–674–X (pbk.)
   1. Shakespeare, William, 1564–1616—Political and social views.
2. Literature and society—England—History—16th century.
3. Literature and society—England—History—17th century.
4. Historical criticism (Literature)   5. Materialism in literature.
6. Marxist criticism.   I. Kamps, Ivo.
PR3024.M38   1995
822.3′3—dc20   94–45797
                                                               CIP

Typeset by Solidus (Bristol) Limited
Printed and bound in Great Britain by Biddles Ltd., Guildford and King's Lynn

For Michael Sprinker,
friend and teacher

Contents

Acknowledgements

The editor gratefully acknowledges permission of various journals, presses and individuals to reprint the following materials: Paul Delany, '*King Lear* and the Decline of Feudalism.' *PMLA* 92 (1977): 429–40; Walter Cohen, '*The Merchant of Venice* and the Possibilities of Historical Criticism', *ELH* 49 (1982): 765–89; Louis Adrian Montrose, '"The Place of a Brother" in *As You Like It*: Social Process and Comic Form', *Shakespeare Quarterly* 32 (1981): 28–54; Stephen Greenblatt, 'Martial Law in the Land of Cockaigne', *Shakespearean Negotiations* (Berkeley and Los Angeles: Univ. of California Press, 1988), pp. 129–64; Alan Sinfield, '*Macbeth*: History, Ideology, and Intellectuals', *Critical Quarterly* 28, 1/2 (spring/ summer 1986): 63–77; Katharine Eisaman Maus, 'Proof and Consequences: Inwardness and Its Exposure in the English Renaissance', *Representations* 34 (1991): 29–52; Michael D. Bristol, 'Charivari and the Comedy of Abjection in *Othello*', *Renaissance Drama* 21 (1990): 3–22; Robert Weimann, 'Representation and Performance: The Uses of Authority in Shakespeare's Theatre', *PMLA* 107 (1992): 497–510; James R. Andreas, 'Othello's African American Progeny', *South Atlantic Review* 57 (1992): 39–57; Lynda E. Boose, 'Scolding Brides and Bridling Scolds: Taming the Woman's Unruly Member', *Shakespeare Quarterly* 42 (1991): 179–213; Graham Holderness, '"What Ish My Nation": Shakespeare and National Identities', *Textual Practice* 5:1 (1991): 74–93; Claire McEachern, '*Henry V* and the Paradox of the Body Politic', *Shakespeare Quarterly* 45.1 (1994): 33–56; John Drakakis, '"Fashion It thus": *Julius Caesar* and the Politics of Theatrical Representation', *Shakespeare Survey* 44 (1992): 65–73. I would like to thank Dana and Greg Carpenter for their help in proofing the text.

Materialist Shakespeare: An Introduction
Ivo Kamps

Over the last decade and a half, we have witnessed the rapid ascendancy of materialist Shakespearean criticism in Great Britain and the United States. When we look back on the sundry approaches – structuralism, political feminism, semiotics, deconstruction, psychoanalysis, New Criticism – which vied for the critical limelight in the 1970s, it becomes clear that materialist criticism has fared disproportionately well. There are several reasons for this meteoric rise. First, materialism, which until the early to mid 1970s basically meant traditional Marxism, has managed to diversify into various types of criticism, most notably cultural materialism, materialist feminism, and new historicism (or cultural poetics). This diversification was greatly enabled by the advent of poststructuralist theory, vital aspects of which materialist criticism embraced,[1] making it possible for so-called 'vulgar' Marxism to rethink the relationship between principles of determination, human agency, and the creation and reception of works of art. Secondly, since many of today's outstanding materialist critics were trained during the heyday of the New Criticism and the latter days of the 'old' historicism, we often find that their work not only utilizes valuable close-reading skills but also addresses critically questions and concerns voiced by approaches which dominated academic discourse until quite recently. The result of these changes is that a relatively homogeneous Marxist criticism (which languished in the academic margins of Shakespeare studies in the 1950s and 1960s) has been transformed into an omnipresent and thriving mix of materialist practices. The essays included in this anthology, all of them published after 1976, bear witness both to the rise of materialist criticism in the late 1970s, 1980s and early 1990s, and to the heterogeneous proliferation of its methods and practices.

Each particular offshoot of materialist practice has its own rich and complex history within the discipline of materialist criticism; we are fortunate to possess by now a substantial and insightful body of work that analyses and historicizes their development, and brings into focus the conspicuous differences between them.[2] These differences – which will be rehearsed shortly – foreground methodological and political contrasts within materialist practice. For a volume like this one, whose essays offer the reader a broad range of materialist practices, but whose table of contents also implies a provisional diachronic account of how materialist criticism of Shakespeare has fared over roughly the last twenty years, it is important to highlight what the different approaches have in common.

Common Ground

Whatever the current points of divergence among new historicism, cultural materialism and materialist feminism, they share a common origin. The term 'materialism' of course has a long and complex history dating back as far as the pre-Socratic philosophers, but even if we start with Marx, with whom the term has become most closely associated in this century, it becomes clear that the basic concept allows for enormous flexibility when it comes to generating theories of literature. Let me begin here by outlining briefly four salient features of materialist practice that have a direct bearing on literary theory and criticism. Historical materialism, the type of materialism most pertinent to literary forms,[3] posits, in Engels's words, that 'the ultimate causes of social changes and political revolutions are to be sought, not in the minds of men ... but in the *economics* of the epoch concerned'.[4] One crucial consequence of Engels's materialist dictum is a radical break with Western philosophical idealism from Plato to Hegel. Materialist thought rejects notions of both the autonomy and the primacy of *ideas* in social life. Secondly, the materialist economist is concerned with ways in which human praxis or, more specifically, human labour and its organization transform physical nature into products and mediates social relations. The materialist literary critic adheres to these same principles but emphasizes the relation between human praxis and socio-economic formations and their joint production of various literary forms (and/or genres) and meanings. More recently, however, materialists have also adopted the difficult concept (prominent in the thought of Althusser) of the superstructure's 'relative autonomy' vis-à-vis the base.[5] Fourthly, critics espousing a materialist conception of history and literature share a methodological commitment to rigorous and concrete historical research.

An indispensable feature enveloping these aspects of materialist practice is of course ideological critique. Materialist analysis, even at its most scientific, remains ideological in nature, and relentlessly critiques the network of ideologies that obscures people's real relation to the relations of production. Materialism's ideological thrust, however, is often poorly understood. For instance, we are now told by conservative critics that the last decade and a half has been witness to a needless, malicious and destructive 'politicization' of Shakespeare studies in both Britain and the United States. Critics like Anne Barton, Graham Bradshaw, Richard Levin and Brian Vickers have asserted that materialist criticism has reduced the meaning of Shakespeare's plays to Leftist ideology. To describe what has taken place in Shakespeare studies as a 'politicization' is, however, at the very least misleading and at worst an outright mischaracterization. As used by conservative critics, the term means to make political something that is (or was) not political. But this is absurd. What the 'politicization' – if we must use that word – of Shakespeare studies really signals is a recognition that literary criticism is an activity inescapably replete with ideological values, which is quite different from merely *reducing* literature to a monolithic ideology that exists only in the mind of the materialist critic.[6]

Of course there was a political criticism of Shakespeare long before the rise of feminism, neo-Marxism and the new historicism. The materialist critics who came to the fore in the 1980s did not invent political Shakespeare. Even conservative commentators understood that Shakespeare held political beliefs, and that it might be worthwhile to identify them; but this kind of search for an author's politics is, of course, not the same as recognizing that the *way* in which that search is conducted is itself fraught with the ideologies (however complex and difficult to articulate) of the investigator's 'interpellation' (to use Althusser's term) by his or her educational, cultural and professional milieu. Except for a handful of early Marxist Shakespeareans like Aleksadr Smirnov, Sidney Shanker, Michael Folsom and Paul Siegel, influential mainstream political critics like E.M.W. Tillyard, Lily Beth Campbell and L.C. Knights believed they were engaging with Shakespeare's politics only, not their own.[7]

From the mid 1970s on, however, it has become increasingly self-evident to Shakespeareans that interpretation implies an at least twofold ideological operation: an encounter with the text's ideologies, which is in turn mediated by the reader's own ideological make-up. To use Terry Eagleton's well-known formulation, 'Reading is an ideological decipherment of an ideological product'.[8] The critic's task, as it is currently defined, is therefore a difficult and paradoxical one: to study a distant past that is shrouded in/by the present moment.

Differences

These commitments, then, to (1) a patterned relationship between cultural/ aesthetic forms and social relations of production; (2) to literature's relative autonomy; (3) to a programme of historical research; and (4) to ideological critique, are manifest across the spectrum of materialist criticism. But there are also notable points of divergence among Marxism, cultural materialism, materialist feminism and new historicism.

Traditional Marxism and its poststructuralist offshoots part ways on the question of economic determination. Cultural materialists, feminist materialists, and new historicists decline to analyse literary texts (which *are*, in some sense, the product of 'the minds of men') in terms of Engels's fierce emphasis on economic determination. They do so for sound reasons. When Engels speaks of the inefficacy of 'the minds of men' in bringing about social change he sounds, as later commentators have noted, more pessimistic than he really was.[9] In a well-known letter to Joseph Bloch, Engels writes:

> According to the materialist conception of history, the *ultimately* determining element in history is the production and reproduction of real life. More than this neither Marx nor I have ever asserted. Hence if somebody twists this into saying that the economic element is the *only* determining one, he transforms that proposition into a meaningless, abstract, senseless phrase. The economic situation is the basis, but the various elements of the superstructure – political forms of the class struggle and its results, to wit: constitutions established by the victorious class after a successful battle, etc., judicial forms, and even the reflexes of all these actual struggles in the brains of the participants, political, juristic, philosophical theories, religious views and their further developments into systems of dogma – also exercise their influence upon the course of historical struggles and in many cases preponderate in determining their *form*.

Following Marx, Engels here draws on the familiar base–superstructure model to link *causally* the world of ideas, philosophies, religions, etc. to the material base of society, thereby making it objectionable for anyone ever again to discuss religion or myth or idealist philosophy without having to view them in the context of the material conditions that produced them, and that, in turn, these discourses seek to rationalize or naturalize. The question as to what the precise balance ought to be between the impact of base and superstructure in the analysis of literary texts has not yet been, and may never be, answered definitively. Indeed, each essay in this collection approaches the question slightly differently. Nonetheless it is clear that despite Althusser's forceful insistence on the economy as the determinant in the last instance,[10] most materialist literary scholarship has been much more successful in analysing texts in terms of the cultural and ideological moment of their production (and reception) than in explaining a determinate relationship between the means of production and a certain turn of phrase or rhythm or particular meaning in, for instance, a short lyric poem. As the evocative examples in the second chapter of Terry Eagleton's *Criticism and Ideology* indicate, the latter mode of criticism is not unthinkable; but it is, practically speaking, also a Herculean labour, since it exacts from the critic the identification of an unbroken chain of analysis of the reciprocal causality between the General Mode of Production, the Literary Mode of Production, and the minutiae of a certain rhyme, pun, irony, or interpreted meaning. The volatile and ever-changing nature of the interactions between these categories hampers materialism's desire for microscopic analysis.

The traditional strength of Marxist criticism lies in macroscopic analysis, in explaining epochal shifts and their impact on literary form. In this volume, two essays are exemplary of such readings. Walter Cohen construes *The Merchant of Venice* 'as a response to a conflict between two modes of production', whereas Paul Delany's essay on *King Lear* and the decline of feudalism, which first appeared in *PMLA* in 1977, is an outstanding and sophisticated instance of Marxism's axiomatic concern with the link between literature and the decline and emergence of historical epochs. Despite these important early successes, materialist critics today often eschew the base in favour of the superstructure.[11] In Shakespearean criticism we increasingly witness the construction of a Renaissance historical context or 'cultural system' – to use Louis Montrose's phrase – through a selective consideration of dominant and marginal ideologies (both Renaissance and contemporary), class, Renaissance political and religious doctrines, and everyday material practices. The literary text is treated as an enactment or production (as opposed to 'reflection' or 'reproduction') of that context or 'cultural system'.

The move toward a concept of 'cultural systems' marks not merely a difference between traditional Marxist materialism and neo-Marxist materialism; it also distinguishes Marxist materialism in general from new historicism. Traditionally Marxist criticism has insisted on the text's intrinsically ideological, formal, or generic features, something with which some new historicists have been less concerned. The idea is that Marxists resist allowing the literary text to fade into the 'cultural system' to the point where the 'literary' text ceases and is reborn as 'cultural' text. This resistance is rooted in the classical Marxist premise that literary form and genre are themselves a product of a complex network of social, economic and ideological forces: 'the true bearers of ideology in art are the very forms, rather than the abstractable content, of the work itself' (Eagleton, *Marxism* p. 24).[12] Hence, the particularity of literary form should be studied rather than effaced. It has been suggested that some new historicists, in search of the grand text of culture, have been less interested in the individuation of specific literary texts; but, increasingly, new historicists have begun to address this type of criticism. Louis Montrose, for example, has acknowledged that his widely influential essay on *A Midsummer Night's Dream* probably makes too little of the generic differences between and specific contexts of the various texts – Forsman's dream recorded in his diary, a Shakespeare play, the journal of the French ambassador, and a Spenser epic – which aid in the essay's construction of shaping Elizabethan fantasies.[13] And new historicist Leonard Tennenhouse, in his essay on Shakespeare's history plays, works in a time-honoured Marxist tradition when he explores the demise of the Elizabethan heroic history play genre in Jacobean times in terms of the changing political strategies for idealizing political authority.[14]

But there are perhaps deeper differences between new historicism and cultural materialism. Historian Hayden White observes that although both new historicism and cultural materialism aim to understand the literary text in its socio-cultural field, new historicist practice has a distinctly synchronic emphasis, whereas Marxist materialism is also concerned with the '"diachronic" aspects of the relationship between literature and the "cultural system"' (p. 293). New historicism, White argues apropos of Louis Montrose, reorients the focus of historical criticism along 'the axis of intertextuality' (p. 293). In practice this means that new historicism links a number of roughly contemporaneous 'texts' ('dreams, popular or aristocratic festivals, denunciations of witchcraft, sexual treatises, diaries and autobiographies, descriptions of clothing, reports of disease, birth and death records, accounts of insanity')[15] into 'the *synchronic* text of a cultural system' (White, p. 299), which sometimes spans a cultural space wide enough to enclose Shakespeare's *Twelfth Night* and tales of cross-dressing and transvestism in the French towns of Chaumont-en-Bassigni and Rouen.[16] From the neo-Marxist vantage point, the advantage of a synchronic approach is that it accents historical difference, but its handicap is that it 'does not explain historical change' (Cohen, p. 33).

A pivotal and often recognized difference between American new historicist and British cultural materialist practice is the latter's more pressing interest in the 'uses to which an historical *present* puts its own version of the English past' (Montrose, p. 27). The work of writers like Graham Holderness, Catherine Belsey, Jonathan Dollimore, Alan Sinfield, John Drakakis, and Kathleen McLuskie is often sprinkled with references to Thatcherism, the British educational system, the institution of the theatre, and contemporary political events. Cultural materialism defines itself as an oppositional criticism; that is, it strongly asserts that both literary texts and literary criticism subvert the contemporary cultural hegemony. In extreme cases such as Terry Eagleton's tongue-in-cheek reading of *Macbeth*, the emphasis on the play's ability to serve as an intervention in contemporary British culture causes the subject of Renaissance history to drop from the analysis completely.[17]

American new historicist Louis Montrose, following a line of exegesis similar to Walter Cohen's (pp. 31–2), plausibly explains this preoccupation with current affairs by arguing that in Britain's still rigid class society 'the study and performance of Shakespeare, the National Poet ... readily becomes the site of a struggle over the definition of national problems and priorities, a struggle to shape and reshape national identity and collective consciousness' (p. 27). Graham Holderness's '"What Ish My Nation?": Shakespeare and National Identities', included in this volume, is a searching meditation on the cultural reproduction of nationalism and patriotism as mediated by Kenneth Branagh's recent film of *Henry V*. In the United States, by contrast, Montrose notes, 'ethnic and social diversity, [a] lack of both a clearly articulated class structure and a strong tradition of radical politics and culture, immensely complex and decentralized cultural and educational institutions, and [a] relatively large, prosperous and secure professoriate [make] the presence and direction of such ideological processes ... perhaps less easily discernible, and sometimes less comfortably acknowledged ...' (p. 27). Montrose offered this insight in 1989, but Walter Cohen made an even stronger claim in 1987: American Marxist critics do not even address 'the issue that British Marxists have successfully begun to explore: the contemporary institutional force and social function of Shakespeare' (p. 32). In 1994, the situation has not changed radically, yet recent materialist studies by Michael Bristol and Hugh Grady not only track the production and reception of Shakespeare in past cultural moments but also in our own, interrogating recent and contemporary ideologies shaping 'Shakespeare' in the process.[18]

A notorious locus of difference between British materialist and American new historical criticism is the subject/structure problematic, something with which practitioners of both 'schools' have seriously grappled. Cultural materialists, feminist materialists and new historicists unequivocally reject the myth of the subject as 'The Individual', 'the freely self-creating and world-creating Individual of so-called bourgeois humanism' (Montrose, p. 21); they also agree that the subject is – to use Althusser's term again – interpellated, by a complex network of social, economic, ideological forces which, in its totality, extends beyond the subject's intellectual grasp or command. However, there arises a principal disagreement both between *and* among new historicists and cultural materialists on the precise nature of the subject/structure relationship, especially with regard to the subject's (in)ability to impact or subvert the social structure. Most Marx-inspired critics today try to avoid mechanical materialism, also known as 'vulgar' Marxism, in favour of a more flexible historical materialism. Following Marx's credo that people *do* make their own history (though not under conditions of their own choosing), materialist critics hold out for at least a limited form of human agency able effectively to contest the cultural and ideological hegemony. But this does not mean it is an easy task to start the revolution. Cultural materialist Jonathan Dollimore, for example, argues that 'We need to recognize . . . how a writer can be intellectually radical without necessarily being politically so. In the individual writer, or text, subversive thought and political conservativism may seem to be harmonized in a way which belies the fact that historically the two things relate dialectically: the former relates to the latter in ways which are initially integral to it yet eventually contradict it'.[19] Along these lines, Alan Sinfield, in an essay included here, argues that *Macbeth*, a play often thought to compliment and validate James I's absolutist notion of kingship, contains contradictory notions of absolutism. The play's ideological field accommodates arguments (those that can be found, for instance, in James's own writings) that favour absolutism, but it also includes conflicting references to the writings of Scotsman George Buchanan, whose *De jure regni* and *History of Scotland* express a theory of kingship that is 'the virtual antithesis of James's'. That Buchanan's subversive views, allowing for the deposition of tyrants, would go unnoticed by a whole theatre audience indoctrinated by James's theories is apparently contradicted by the fact that the 'Gunpowder Plotters were manifestly unconvinced by the king's arguments'.

Because of its radical potential due to its contradictory character as a social institution, the theatre was, John Drakakis argues in his study of *Julius Caesar*, a congenial locale for subjects to challenge aspects of the social structure. Located in the suburbs, outside the legal control of the city fathers, the theatre was very much a liminal institution, one that, as Steven Mullaney observes, 'could not be contained within the strict or proper bounds of the community'.[20] Moreover, in a cultural moment blighted by an anti-theatrical prejudice, the Renaissance theatre simultaneously enjoyed support from the Crown and the censorship of the Queen's Master of the Revels; it catered to a heterogeneous audience while also striving for respectability and patronage. These factors, Drakakis points out, made the theatre a place of 'relative "openness" to the production of contradictory cultural meanings'. Specifically, in *Julius Caesar*, Drakakis argues, Shakespeare enacts the cultural tension between 'those who would oppose theatrical representation [and those who] continued to insist upon the power of the theatrical image itself. . . .'

Stephen Greenblatt, on the other hand, richly influenced by the work of Michel Foucault on the question of containment, has argued in 'Invisible Bullets' and elsewhere that effective subversion is a myth.

'[S]ubversive' is for us a term used to designate those elements in Renaissance culture that contemporary authorities tried to contain or, when containment seemed impossible, to destroy and that now conform to our own sense of truth and reality. That is, we locate as 'subversive' in the past precisely those things that are *not* subversive to ourselves, that pose no threat to the order by which we live and allocate resources.... What we find in Harriot's *Brief and True Report* can best be described by adapting a remark about the possibility of hope that Kafka once made to Max Brod: There is subversion, no end to subversion, only not for us.

(*Shakespearean Negotiations*, p. 39)

Critics of new historicism have argued that this particular view of containment described less a Renaissance process than a kind of 'leftist disillusionment' (Cohen, p. 36) felt by a generation of American scholars whose hopes for social change were raised in the 1960s and dashed in the Reagan–Bush era. Recently, however, in his 1988 introduction to a book that contains the 'Invisible Bullets' essay, Greenblatt pulls back somewhat from the notion of 'totalizing power' and argues that 'Even those literary texts that sought most ardently to speak for a monolithic power could be shown to be the sites of institutional and ideological contestation' (*Shakespearean Negotiations*, p. 3). Here subversion should not be understood as *coup d'état*, but as a way of slowly corroding the principles that prop up authority. This last point is amply illustrated in Greenblatt's contribution to this volume. In 'Martial Law in the Land of Cockaigne', he reveals brilliantly how certain techniques of 'arousing and manipulating [salutary] anxiety' practised by representatives of the state for the purpose of securing a subject's obedience are cunningly practised by *Measure for Measure*'s Duke Vincentio and *The Tempest*'s Prospero, and turn out to be 'crucial techniques in the representational technologies of the Elizabethan and Jacobean theatre'.

Montrose, whose overall practice tends to accent the Marxist dimensions of new historicism, has gone so far as to suggest that the opposition between 'containment' and 'subversion', perhaps the most visible schism between new historicism and cultural materialism, is so 'reductive, polarized, and undynamic as to be of little conceptual value' (Montrose, p. 22). Instead, Montrose calls for a more 'heterogeneous and unstable, permeable and processual' concept of ideology that would ensure 'that an ideological dominance is qualified by the specific conjunctures of professional, class, and personal interests of individual cultural producers (such as poets and playwright) ...' (p. 22). Here Montrose's position is virtually identical with Dollimore and Sinfield's. For these British cultural materialists, the paradox of power producing its own subversion and depending upon that subversion for its continued existence 'disappears when we speak not of a monolithic power structure producing its effects but of one made up of different, often competing elements, and these not merely producing culture but producing it through appropriations'.[21]

Feminist Materialism

Recently, Walter Cohen has suggested that although new historicism's 'recurrent concern with gender aligns it with feminism, its subordination of gender to power leads it away from characteristically feminist concerns' (p. 33). A similar charge has routinely been levelled against a Marxism that maintains that the category of class takes precedence over gender. These opposite impulses may have kept feminism separate from materialist criticism in Shakespeare studies in the early to mid 1980s, but recent theoretical innovations have made possible a productive rapprochement between the two.[22]

In 1987, Cohen pointed out that early feminist criticism of Shakespeare arguably concerned itself primarily with 'the images of women' (p. 22). Enabled by, amongst other things, the tools of New Criticism, psycho-analysis, and a cogent feminist political stance, the critics included in the landmark anthology *The Woman's Part: Feminist Criticism of Shakespeare* sought to 'liberate Shakespeare's women from the stereotypes to which they have too often been confined; they examine[d] women's relations to each other; they analyze[d] the nature and effects of patriarchal structures; and they explore[d] the influence of genre on the portrayal of women'.[23] The powerful legacy of this critical programme is chronicled not only in *The Woman's Part* but in other major feminist studies like Coppélia Kahn's *Man's Estate* (1981), Irene Dash's *Wooing, Wedding, and Power: Women in Shakespeare's Plays* (1981), Linda Bamber's *Comic Women, Tragic Men* (1982), and Carol Thomas Neely's *Broken Nuptials in Shakespeare's Plays* (1985). Although these 'first phase' feminist critics put feminist criticism permanently on the academic agenda and syllabi – it also became clear that they made 'inadequate use of historical materials' (Cohen, p. 24). Feminist criticism's initial inability to engage in concrete historical research – in part because 'women's history [was] so new a field that both basic information and theoretical models [were] often lacking' (Cohen, p. 25) – more often than not led to essentialist modes of criticism, which were inevitably reductive in their representation of Renaissance women.

The key materialist insight opening up new avenues of investigation for feminist criticism was, as Rosemary Hennesy notes, a redefining of 'subjectivity' as 'discursively constructed'. This move has made possible the analysis of the 'intersections of gender and class' and unites traditionally feminist and Marxist concerns into a new mode of ideological critique (Hennesy, p. xii). Without having to abandon traditional women's issues and a strong feminist politics,[24] materialist feminism scrutinizes texts for fissures or gaps in 'narrative coherence' and studies them 'as signs of the disease that infects the social imaginary'. This enables materialist feminism to historicize 'these gaps and read them as displacements of ...

broad-ranging [social] contradictions....' One obvious advantage of a materialist–feminist alliance, Jonathan Dollimore observes, is that feminism need no longer co-opt or write off Shakespeare but can follow the 'unstable constructions of ... gender and patriarchy back to the contradictions of their historical moment'.[25] In this volume, Lynda Boose situates *The Taming of the Shrew* in a Renaissance context that links the ideology labelling women who transgress social norms as 'scolds' or 'shrews' with the material devices (such as bridles and cucking stools) designed to punish and rehabilitate them. (The companion volume to the present anthology, *Shakespeare and Gender: A History*,[26] along with *The Matter of Difference: Materialist Feminist Criticism of Shakespeare*, edited by Valerie Wayne, also include exemplary studies bridging the concerns and methods of materialism and gender studies.)

Theory and Practice

In theoretical (rather than practical) terms, Marxist literary criticism, in the current poststructuralist climate, appears to withdraw further and further from any notion of history as stable, dependable, and accessible. If there ever was a time a Marxist critic could embrace an innocent theory of mimesis and talk about literature expressing or reflecting history or culture, that time is long gone. The highly influential work of Fredric Jameson and Terry Eagleton, for instance, identifies so complex a network of mystifying mediatory negotiations between the artist, the work of art, and the moment of production, that what we conventionally call 'knowledge of history' becomes unobtainable by literary historical analysis. The historical 'Real' falls beyond the materialist critic's reach. In Fredric Jameson's words: 'history – Althusser's "absent cause," Lacan's "Real" – is *not* a text, for it is fundamentally non-narrative and non-representational; ... history is inaccessible to us except in textual form, or in other words, ... it can be approached only by way of prior (re)textualization'.[27] Or, as Eagleton couches it, 'History – certainly enters the text...; but it enters it precisely *as ideology*, as a presence determined and distorted by its measurable absences. This is not to say that real history is present in the text but in disguised form ... It is rather that history is "present" in the text in the form of a *double-absence*' (*Criticism*, p. 72). The type of historical *knowledge* available to the materialist critic, therefore, is of an indirect sort: what is available for inspection is the process of the text, 'the process whereby ideology produces the forms which produce it [i.e. the text]' (Eagleton, p. 84). This process does, in Jameson's words, 'draw the Real into its texture' (p. 81), but in a way that makes it twice hidden: first it is concealed in 'the phenomenal categories (commodity, wage-relations, exchange-

value and so on)', and secondly, it is made 'empirically imperceptible' by
the fact that the ideology of the text usually seeks to conceal or 'naturalize'
those categories (Eagleton, p. 85). As Eagleton puts it, 'what ideology does
to history the literary work raises to the second power, producing as
"natural" the significations by which history naturalizes itself; but the work
simultaneously reveals (to criticism, if not to the casually inspecting
glance) how that naturalness is the effect of a particular production. If the
text displays itself [its form or its substance] as "natural", it manifests itself
equally as constructed artifice; and it is in this duality that its relation to
ideology can be discerned' – and where 'knowledge' is to be harvested
(Eagleton, p. 85).[28]

Of course, these theoretical manoeuvrings are not really a withdrawal
from history but rather a more nuanced description of literature's
relationship to history. Nonetheless, to *do* historical criticism with the kind
of rigour and sophistication called for in this theory is a testing labour.
Hence, it appears that a gap between materialist theory and practice has
come into existence. Many materialist scholars of Shakespeare today,
acutely aware of the various layers of ideology that envelop them as well
as the textual objects of their inquiries, self-consciously confess the
epistemological limitations of their labours.[29] However, as noted above, it
is primarily the British materialists who forthrightly acknowledge and
valourize the study of the past as a simultaneous investigation of the
present. That said, it is quite obvious that upon making their confessions
most materialist critics plunge head-first into history in search of, if not the
unobtainable historical real, certainly for its substitute real: patriarchal
structures, royal authority, the legal system, and so forth. The reason that
critics uncover and explore what Eagleton terms the 'phenomenal categories' that precisely conceal the 'empirically imperceptible real' and
make it into a substitute real, is that they are ultimately uncomfortable
performing a precarious dance on a razor's edge balancing between
historical relativism and historical positivism. 'I began with a desire to
speak with the dead' – the rhapsodic opening sentence of Stephen
Greenblatt's *Shakespearean Negotiations* – is a determined effort to steer
clear of the poststructuralist abyss of endlessly deferred meaning and
historical absence. Yet it is hard to believe that Greenblatt actually believes
he can carry on a literal conversation with the past. While listening to the
dead, Greenblatt confesses, 'It was true that I could only hear my own
voice, but my own voice was the voice of the dead, for the dead contrived
to leave textual traces of themselves, and those traces make themselves
heard in the voices of the living' (p. 1). This peculiar fusion of dead and
living voices (who is talking when and saying what?) hardly constitutes a
rigorous materialist program,[30] yet it does fairly describe what most of us
who are engaged in materialist criticism actually *do*.

*

One of this book's chief purposes is to make available for classroom use a single volume charting the recent history of materialist critical practice since the late 1970s. Given this historical frame, I considered choosing articles that would confirm a strong narrative of materialist criticism's development. Reading through the various journals in search of suitable essays, it became increasingly clear to me that the category 'materialism' is far too broad and multifaceted a practice to be reduced to a uniform, teleological narrative. Indeed, even when we dissect materialist criticism into its various 'schools' the fact still remains that within the schools themselves there are significant methodological differences: Jonathan Dollimore differs from Graham Holderness, Louis Montrose from Stephen Greenblatt, and Lisa Jardine from Lynda Boose.[31] The connections between these critics do not yield any strict genealogy or homogeneity, rather they reveal differing degrees of influence, of a shared subject matter and of a common (though differently interpreted) reading list of primary and theoretical texts. Although I have conceived this anthology as a historical survey, I have shied away from seeking to transform the chronology of the essays into a succinct, purposive narrative. Instead, I have endeavoured to cull from the immense corpus of materialist Shakespeare criticism essays that are not only of exemplary quality but also typical of specific kinds and, collectively, suggestive of the broad range of materialist practices in Shakespeare studies (although limits of space prevented an exhaustive representation of all varieties of materialist critical practices).

In keeping with the familiar seminar format that combines a Shakespeare play with one or more pieces of criticism, several of the essays offered here are sustained readings of single plays. Again responding to the needs of seminar students and teachers, the articles selected cover the whole range of Shakespeare's writings, both generically and historically, while focusing for the most part on the most frequently taught plays.

Present and Future

It is difficult to divine where materialist criticism of Shakespeare will go from here. New historicism and neo-Marxism have produced fruitful models for synchronic and diachronic study of literature in its historical context. Increasingly, materialist scholars produce concrete historical research based on primary sources. With marvellous results, feminist and gender scholarship have joined in and expanded the materialist project. Overall, materialism has been an extraordinarily enabling practice for critics who, tired of relying on the interpretative principles of an earlier generation and simply rearranging the same pieces of evidence to arrive at marginally different conclusions, desired to put literature to new uses. Clearly, materialism's urgent sense of literature as an overdetermined ideological act has made possible radically new understandings of well-known plays, understandings that mark a sharp conceptual and methodological break with earlier modes of interpretation. Louis Montrose's influential early study of *As You Like It* is an excellent example. Rejecting then (in 1981) still popular views of literature as a freestanding object or as a passive reflector of society, Montrose proposes a view of literature as enactment of certain cultural tensions. Specifically, he argues that *As You Like It* participates in the Renaissance controversy over primogeniture, 'a structural principle of Elizabethan personal, family and social life'. Radically reversing traditional critical vantage points, which accounted the play's opening scenes, steeped in societal tension and sibling rivalry, a mere device to get the characters and the audience into the magical forest as soon as possible, Montrose cogently shows how 'Shakespeare uses the machinery of pastoral romance to remedy the lack of fit between deserving and having, between Nature and Fortune'. The essay presents a remarkable shift in the *kinds* of questions a critic can ask of a so-called pastoral love comedy.

Over the last two decades, then, materialists have reread Shakespeare's plays starting from a new set of premises. Older interpretations have been overhauled or displaced; the theoretical underpinnings of new critical and 'old' historicist interpretations have been analysed and critiqued; and, most recently, sweeping studies of Shakespeare's critical and cultural reception have demonstrated the socially constructed character of the Shakespeare phenomenon and canon. A broader awareness of identity and literature as socially and materially constructed has furthermore made possible an exciting rapprochement between materialist criticism and categories of gender and race (heretofore restricted to relatively isolated branches of criticism such as feminism, gay studies, and ethnic studies). A cluster of three essays on *Othello* is included here to illustrate the current range of materialist practices vis-à-vis a single Shakespearean text. James R. Andreas's 'Othello's African American Progeny', for instance, interprets Derrida's maxim that 'There is no racism without language' to mean that 'racism is a cultural virus' that lives and reproduces in language: 'the names, the jokes, the plays, the speeches, the casual exchanges, the novels'. For Andreas, '*Othello* – along with the many African American texts it has inspired – provides a running record of Western civilization's attempt to confront what Paul Robeson called "the problem of my own people."' *Othello* is the play whose racist 'nightmare of biracial sexual relations' has 'traumatized African American literature'. However, if racism is verbally transmitted in history, then 'its antidote must ... be verbally administered as well'. Consequently, Andreas examines not only race relations in *Othello* but also in three of its progenic texts – Richard Wright's *Native Son*, Ralph Ellison's *Invisible Man*, and Amiri Baraka's *The Dutchman* – all of which attempt to rewrite the racist's myth.

Equally interested in questions of race, Michael Bristol reads *Othello* as a carnivalesque text of great significance in 'the historical constitution both of racist sensibility and of racist political ideology'. Bristol asks us to withdraw momentarily our 'empathy' for or 'identification' with the play's main characters. Nor should we view them as unified subjects; instead Bristol asks us to regard these characters – Othello, Desdemona and Iago – 'as components in a carnivalesque "wardrobe" that is inscribed within the text, [and which] assigns them the roles of clown, transvestite, and "scourge of marriage" in a charivari'. These readings by Bristol and Andreas are not only novel but, if brought into the classroom, they should have a real impact on how students come to understand literature's function in the formation of race relations.

Similar progress has been made toward the rehistoricizing of Renaissance ideas about individuality and/or interiority. If Bristol deliberately brackets the question of subjectivity, Katharine Eisaman Maus, in her piece on 'Inwardness and Its Exposure in the English Renaissance', precisely foregrounds it, arguing that a notion of Renaissance 'psychological interiority' (a concept rejected by most materialist critics) need *not* result in 'a naive essentialism about "human nature"'. Maus examines the 'affinities between English legal and theatrical rituals' and 'the quasijudicial discovery of inwardness' in *Othello*, and makes a compelling case that 'there *is* that within which passes show'.

Focusing on the figure of the ruler, Claire McEachern's '*Henry V*: The Paradox of the Body Politic' displays close affinities with Maus's subject, yet approaches the issue of individuality with a different set of questions. She moves away from a protracted critical tradition preoccupied with the personality of Henry V and asks how it is that 'the play and its location in Elizabethan culture so repeatedly generate *personableness* as the currency of our response'. McEachern's answer is twofold: she argues that the representation of power in the play 'derives from a similar inflection in Elizabethan discourses of personality', and, secondly, that Henry's 'person-ality' and the 'Elizabethan personification of the crown' share the same 'tropes of subjectivity used to produce a particular Elizabethan political affect – that of corporate identity, of what we might call "the nation"'.

In addition to rereading the plays, rehistoricizing them, and constructing the history of their reception, materialist criticism has also launched itself into other areas of Shakespeare scholarship. A wonderful recent essay by Margreta de Grazia and Peter Stallybrass confirms that materialist concerns are now also being brought to bear on the process of textual editing.[32] What is more, materialist studies of Renaissance theatrical practices and the conditions of performance have begun to complement and partially replace traditional histories of the theatre.[33] A pioneer in the field of materialist performance studies, Robert Weimann, whose 1992 *PMLA* essay is reprinted here, offers the potent postulate that Shakespeare's theatre 'interrogate[d] not only the institutionalized authority of office, law and penalty but the internalized authority of "epistemic" or "moral" credentials'. Such interrogations are possible because of the 'crisis in authority' prompted by the Protestant Reformation's penchant for transferring the basis of authority from 'external and public modes ... to internal and private ones'. 'This is, and is not Cressid', Troilus despairs, having been confronted with 'a division between godlike reason and sensory perception'. Like Drakakis and Steven Mullaney, who also stress the theatre's liminal position in both a geographical and cultural sense, Weimann argues that in a geographical sense the theatre is 'secure enough to defy the authority of the city and [hence able] to complement the representation of the signs of authority with a self-authorization of signs and significations through which the needs and perspectives of the theatre asserted themselves'. In exploring this theatrical 'self-authorization', Weimann is especially concerned with a 'residue' that is 'the act of performance itself', and that escapes containment by 'the textual representation of dramatic fiction'. In the theatre's 'divided space', performance (and by performance Weimann means the 'irreducible investment of the non-representational energy, labour, needs, and exhaustion of the actors' minds and bodies') was able either to close the gaps or to destabilize the links 'between what was represented and what was representing or, to shift the emphasis somewhat, between the forms of fiction and the force of performance'.

In short, materialist criticism has successfully entered virtually all aspects of Shakespeare studies. So what is still to be done? In his well-known essay 'Contradiction and Overdetermination', written in the early 1960s, Althusser noted that when Marx gave us the structure of the (economic) base and superstructure, he handed us 'the two ends of the chain', of which 'the economy is the determinant ... *in the last instance*' (*For Marx*, p. 112); but he also 'told us to find out what goes on between them' (p. 111). The essays contained here, which are only a small part of a larger like-minded materialist corpus of Shakespeare criticism, suggest that Shakespeareans have successfully begun to respond to Marx's invitation, even if hard-core economic analyses are not yet the order of the day. On this last score materialist criticism may need to improve. Yet cultural materialist criticism's and especially new historicism's increasingly scrupulous forays into the microscopic and idiosyncratic 'infinity of effects' or 'accidents' whirling through the superstructure seem aimed at making accessible that part of history which Engels deemed epistemologically (though of course not actually) non-existent (Althusser, in *For Marx*, p. 118). The greatest challenge remains to link this infinity of effects causally to the *forms* of the superstructure that produced them in the first place. This means that along with the ongoing and increasingly penetrating practical criticism, we need to develop theories that can account for the interpretative moves we make. In the meantime, one thing is for certain: over the last two decades materialist criticism has permanently changed the way Shakespeare is read. It now seems most unlikely that Shakespeare studies can ever return to the comfortable pieties of their idealist past.

Notes

1. The names of theoretical innovators like Michel Foucault, Pierre Bourdieu, Michel de Certeau, Clifford Geertz, Jacques Derrida, Luce Irigaray, Julia Kristeva, E.P. Thompson, Fredric Jameson, Louis Althusser, Raymond Williams, Terry Eagleton grace the bibliographies of notable Shakespeareans like Graham Holderness, Jonathan Dollimore, Alan Sinfield, Kathleen McLuskie, Walter Cohen, Stephen Grenblatt, Louis Montrose, Leonard Tennenhouse, Christopher Pye and Catherine Belsey.

2. Walter Cohen, 'Political Criticism of Shakespeare', *Shakespeare Reproduced: The Text in History and Ideology*, eds Jean E. Howard and Marion O'Connor (New York: Methuen, 1987), p. 34; Hayden White, 'New Historicism: A Comment', in H. Aram Veeser, *The New Historicism* (New York and London: Routledge, 1989), p. 299; and Louis Montrose, 'Professing the Renaissance: The Poetics and Politics of Culture', in Veeser, p. 22.

3. The other main forms of materialism are philosophical materialism, which possesses 'ontological', 'epistemological' and 'practical' branches, and scientific materialism.

4. Friedrich Engels, *Anti-Dühring* in *Reader in Marxist Philosophy*, ed. Howard Selsam and Harry Martel (New York: International Publishers, 1980), p. 219.

5. See Hayden White's discussion of this feature shared by new historicism and cultural materialism, 'New Historicism: A Comment', in Veeser, p. 299; also see Louis Montrose, 'Professing the Renaissance', in Veeser, p. 22.

6. See, for instance, Richard Levin, 'The Poetics and Politics of Bardicide', *PMLA* 105 (1990): 491–504; Graham Bradshaw, *Misrepresentations: Shakespeare and the Materialists* (Ithaca, NY: Cornell UP, 1993); and Brian Vickers, *Appropriating Shakespeare: Contemporary Critical Quarrels* (New Haven and London: Yale UP, 1993), pp. 214–71, 372–416. Why is 'politicization' such a dirty word to some (neo-)conservative critics? The obvious answer is that the politics that currently pervade Shakespeare studies are not their politics. This said, I do want to stress that the Left and the Right should be treated with equal respect. Materialist readers who reduce the text to their politics or who deliberately mystify ideological aspects of interpretation are just as much in the wrong as conservatives who peddle their readings as being natural or commonsensical or wholly objective (see 'Introduction: Ideology and its Discontents', *Shakespeare Left and Right*, ed. Ivo Kamps (New York and London: Routledge, 1991), pp. 1–14.

7. See E.W.M. Tillyard's *The Elizabethan World Picture* (New York: Vintage, n.d.; first published in 1943) and *Shakespeare's History Plays* (New York: Collier Books, 1962 (1944)); Lily B. Campbell, *Shakespeare's 'Histories': Mirrors of Elizabethan Policy* (San Marino, CA: 1947); and L.C. Knights, 'Shakespeare and Political Wisdom', *Sewanee Review* 61 (1953): 43–55.

8. Terry Eagleton, *Criticism and Ideology: A Study in Marxist Literary Theory* (London: Verso, 1976), p. 62.

9. Raymond Williams, *Marxism and Literature* (Oxford and New York: Oxford UP, 1977), pp. 75–82.

10. Louis Althusser, *For Marx* (1965), trans. Ben Brewster (London: Verso, 1982), pp. 111ff.

11. See Perry Anderson, *Considerations on Western Marxism* (London: New Left Books, 1976). He argues that 'Western Marxism' has been, from Gramsci on, 'the Marxism of the superstructure', a left *Kulturkritik*, hopelessly weak on institutional advocacy, and led by philosophers and literary critics, not economists and political leaders of large working-class movements.

12. See V. Voloshinov, 'Discourse in Life and Discourse in Poetry: Questions of Sociological Poetics' (1926), trans. John Richmond, in *Russian Poetics in Translation*, ed. Ann Shukman and L.M. O'Toole (Oxford: RPT Publications, 1983), pp. 5–29; Terry Eagleton, *Marxism and Literary Criticism* (Berkeley and Los Angeles: Univ. of California Press, 1976), p. 24; and Fredric Jameson, *Marxism and Form: Twentieth-Century Dialectical Theories of Literature* (Princeton: Princeton UP, 1971), pp. 401ff.

13. Louis Montrose, '"Shaping Fantasies": Figuration of Gender and Power in Elizabethan Culture', *Representing the English Renaissance*, ed. Stephen Greenblatt (Berkeley, Los Angeles, London: Univ. of California Press, 1988), pp. 31–64.

14. Leonard Tennenhouse, 'Strategies of State and Political Plays: *A Midsummer Night's Dream, Henry IV, Henry V, Henry VIII*', in Jonathan Dollimore and Alan Sinfield, eds, *Political Shakespeare: New Essays in Cultural Materialism* (Ithaca, NY: Cornell UP, 1985).

15. Cohen, 'Political Criticism of Shakespeare', in *Shakespeare Reproduced*, p. 34.

16. See Stephen Greenblatt, 'Fiction and Friction', *Shakespearean Negotiations: The Circulation of Social Energy in Renaissance England* (Berkeley and Los Angeles: Univ. of California Press, 1988), pp. 66–93.

17. Terry Eagleton, *William Shakespeare* (Oxford and New York: Blackwell, 1986), pp. 1–8. From a Marxist materialist point of view, there is something supremely irresponsible yet audacious in the claim that 'The witches are the heroines' of the play (p. 2), even though neither Shakespeare nor his 'contemporary audience' would have recognized this. Indeed, Eagleton glibly asserts, only the 'unprejudiced reader' (p. 1) would be able to recognize the witches' true status in the play. Eagleton continues by arguing that the witches 'figure as the "unconscious" of the drama, that which must be exiled and repressed as dangerous but which is always likely to return with a vengeance' (p. 2). An investigation into the social position of witches in English Renaissance culture (there is a considerable amount of information on the subject) could potentially verify Eagleton's shrewd reading of the play; but he never bothers, preferring to read the play in the context of certain unsubstantiated generalizations about the displacement of counter-hegemonic social values onto a small group of socially marginalized creatures – the witches.

18. Michael Bristol, *Shakespeare's America, America's Shakespeare* (London and New York: Routledge, 1990); Hugh Grady, *Modernist Shakespeare: Critical Texts in a Material World* (Oxford: Clarendon Press, 1991). See my review of Bristol in *MLN* (1990) 1088–90, and of Grady in 'Shakespeare Criticism: "It is a kind of history"', *College English* 56 (1994): 339–43.

19. Jonathan Dollimore, *Radical Tragedy: Religion, Ideology and Power in the Drama of Shakespeare and his Contemporaries* (Chicago: Univ. of Chicago Press, 1984), p. 22.

20. Steven Mullaney, *The Place of the Stage: License, Play and Power in the English Renaissance* (Chicago and London: Univ. of Chicago Press, 1988), p. 9, quoted by Drakakis, this volume.

21. Jonathan Dollimore, 'Introduction', in Dollimore and Sinfield, eds, p. 12.

22. For general discussion of this rapprochement see Donna Landry and Gerald MacLean, *Materialist Feminisms* (Cambridge, MA and Oxford: Blackwell, 1993) and Rosemary Hennesy, *Materialist Feminism and the Politics of Discourse* (New York and London: Routledge, 1993). In Shakespeare studies, see Kathleen McLuskie, 'The Patriarchal Bard: Feminist Criticism and Shakespeare: *King Lear* and *Measure for Measure*' in Dollimore and Sinfield, eds, pp. 88–108; Catherine Belsey, *The Subject of Tragedy: Identity and Difference in Renaissance Drama* (London and New York: Methuen, 1985); Valerie Wayne, ed., *The Matter of Difference: Materialist Feminist Criticism of Shakespeare* (Ithaca, NY: Cornell UP, 1993).

23. Caroline Ruth Swift Lenz, Gayle Greene and Carol Thomas Neely, eds, *The Woman's Part: Feminist Criticism of Shakespeare* (Urbana, Ill.: Univ. of Illinois Press, 1980), p. 4.

24. See Catherine Belsey, 'A Future for Materialist Feminist Criticism?' in 'The Matter of Difference', ed. Valerie Wayne, p. 264.

25. Jonathan Dollimore, 'Shakespeare, Cultural Materialism and the New Historicism', in Dollimore and Sinfield, eds, p. 11.

26. Ivo Kamps and Deborah E. Barker, eds (London: Verso, 1995).

27. Fredric Jameson, *The Political Unconscious: Narrative as a Socially Symbolic Act* (Ithaca, NY: Cornell UP, 1981), p. 82.

28. For an early, highly lucid, text-book example of a materialist analysis of the way ideology conceals or mystifies economic and ideological categories, see Raymond Williams's reading of Ben Jonson's 'To Penshurst', in *The Country and the City* (New York: Oxford UP, 1973), pp. 26–34.

29. See for instance, Bristol, p. 4, and Phyllis Rackin, *Stages of History: Shakespeare's English Chronicles* (Ithaca, NY: Cornell UP, 1990), p. ix.

30. Greenblatt goes on to outline extremely useful and more rigorous categories of analysis (pp. 9–12).

31. Some very astute attempts by Cohen; Greenblatt, 'Towards a Poetics of Culture' in Veeser, pp. 1–14; and Montrose, 'Professing the Renaissance', have of course been made to historicize materialist practices.

32. Margreta de Grazia and Peter Stallybrass, 'The Materiality of the Shakespearean Text', *Shakespeare Quarterly* 44 (1993): 255–83.

33. Two outstanding recent materialist studies are Mullaney's *The Place of the Stage* and Jean E. Howard's *The Stage and Social Struggle in Early Modern England* (London and New York: Routledge, 1994).

2

King Lear and the Decline of Feudalism

Paul Delany

Modern criticism of *King Lear* has emphasized that it is the most metaphysical of Shakespeare's tragedies. The main characters each have their own theory about their place in the world, the meaning of their experience, and the relation between man and the higher powers; the play's action is thus subjected to continuous philosophical scrutiny by those who take part in it. Critics have been much concerned with this intricate debate about human destiny, which is carried on through the play both explicitly and by the implications of dramatic action. Ultimately, it is argued, the play makes a 'statement' about life, though there has been scant agreement on what the statement is. At one pole, Bradley and the neo-Christians have claimed that the play asserts the redemptive value of suffering; at the other, Jan Kott makes of it an absurdist drama about the *loss* of value that anticipates the modern apotheosis of the mode in the grotesque farces of Samuel Beckett.[1]

It would be obtuse to deny the importance of this metaphysical preoccupation in *King Lear*; obviously the play does explore the universal significance of individual experiences of pain or loss. But critical discussion will remain unproductive and unresolvable so long as it limits the play's metaphysics to a separate and self-contained mode of discourse. We need to remember that the first quarto of *King Lear* (1608) calls it a 'True Chronicle Historie' (i.e., a play based on matter from Holinshed or other early chronicles) and that it has much in common with Shakespeare's earlier works in the genre, especially the tetralogy that begins with *Richard II*. Its 'philosophy' becomes clearer when approached by way of the contemporary meaning, for Shakespeare and his audience, of the political struggle that it dramatizes. My aim in this paper will be to present a reading of *King Lear* grounded on the premises of dialectical materialism and to suggest some implications for a general assessment of Shakespeare's political outlook. In a single article I can only sketch the salient features of a complex historical situation; the close examination of the various divisions and crosscurrents within the class structure of Tudor England must be left to studies of wider scope.[2]

The analysis will take as its point of departure Marx's view of the English Renaissance as a transitional stage between the dominance of the feudal aristocracy and that of the commercial bourgeoisie, which consolidated its power over England's destiny in 1688. My concern will be with the effects of this transition on social and personal relations: that is, with shifts in consciousness that pertain to the cultural 'superstructure' rather than to the direct results of changes in the mode of production. Since economic relations are readily quantifiable their evolution can be charted with some precision, even in earlier periods of history; but social relations, always more mixed and indefinite, adapt neither smoothly nor rapidly to economic change. It does not lie in our power to change our personalities overnight, except in rare instances of conversion; psychological conflict must therefore be endemic in a dynamic society. Traditional styles of relationship will be continuously undermined by the forces of change, but the personality structure appropriate for new kinds of social organization can evolve only gradually. By the time it has become 'second nature', it will have been outmoded by further change. The resultant instability and uncertainty will be perceived differently by various social groups according to the effect of economic change on their fortunes: what are symptoms of decline for one class may be portents of liberation and fresh opportunity for another.

Shakespeare lived at a time when an uncertain balance had been struck in the transition from the feudal-aristocratic society of medieval England to the emergent bourgeois state. The aristocracy and the bourgeoisie were a rough match for each other in power, cohesion, and self-confidence; each had its characteristic moral values and style of life, and each claimed that its own way constituted 'human nature': the personality typical of a particular class was elevated to a norm that all mankind should recognize. *King Lear* pits these rival concepts of human nature against each other in sharp and mutually exclusive opposition. In such a conflict, one would expect Marx's sympathies to be given wholeheartedly to the historically progressive energies of the bourgeoisie; but his discussion of it in *The Communist Manifesto* is in fact strongly ambivalent:

> The bourgeoisie, wherever it has got the upper hand, has put an end to all feudal, patriarchal, idyllic relations. It has pitilessly torn asunder the motley feudal ties that bound man to his 'natural superiors', and has left remaining no other nexus between man and man than naked self-interest, than callous 'cash-payment'. It has drowned the most heavenly ecstasies of religious fervour, of chivalrous enthusiasm, of philistine sentimentalism, in the icy water of egotistical calculation. It has resolved personal

worth into exchange value, and in place of the numberless indefeasible chartered freedoms, has set up that single, unconscionable freedom – Free Trade.[3]

In this elegy for a dying culture Marx seems dismayed by the human costs of the breakup of the feudal order and appalled by the moral nihilism of those who destroyed it. Elsewhere, in more splenetic moods, he may delight in consigning some losing cause to the 'rubbish heap of history'; but the achievement of feudalism he finds too appealing to be thus summarily dismissed. No matter how greedy, inefficient, and exploitive the feudal church and aristocracy may have been, their fervent idealism sustained man's sense of his own worth and of his right to his allotted place in the social hierarchy. The new order, however, having set up cash payment as the only measure of social obligation, ruthlessly attacks all customary bonds that impede the development of production and trade:

> Constant revolutionising of production, uninterrupted disturbance of all social conditions, everlasting uncertainty and agitation distinguish the bourgeois epoch from all earlier ones. All fixed, fast-frozen relations, with their train of ancient and venerable prejudices and opinions, are swept away, all new-formed ones become antiquated before they can ossify. All that is solid melts into air, all that is holy is profaned, and man is at last compelled to face, with sober senses, his real conditions of life, and his relations with his kind.
>
> (*Manifesto*, p. 35)

In his appreciation of feudal values Marx revealed the chivalric idealism that still lingered from his adolescence and also, perhaps, his pride at having won the aristocratic Jenny von Westphal as his bride. His curiously nostalgic account of the decline of feudalism probably also reflects the influence of a man of kindred temperament, but opposite allegiance: Thomas Carlyle. *Past and Present* (1843) professes a devotion to the corporate society of medieval England and a horror of the moral vacuity of laissez-faire that are remarkably close in tone and diction to the analysis given five years later in *The Communist Manifesto*:

> All this dire misery, therefore; all this of our poor Workhouse Workmen, of our Chartisms, Trades-strikes, Corn-Laws, Toryisms, and the general downbreak of Laissez-faire in these days, – may we not regard it as a voice from the dumb bosom of Nature, saying to us: Behold! Supply-and-demand is not the one Law of Nature; Cash-payment is not the sole nexus of man with man, – how far from it. Deep, far deeper than Supply-and-demand, are Laws, Obligations sacred as Man's Life itself: these also, if you will continue to do work, you shall now learn and obey.[4]

In *King Lear* Shakespeare displays a similar attachment to traditional and aristocratic values, combined with a distaste and fear of the acquisitive, unscrupulous bourgeois values (as they appear to him) that are taking their place. His view of the class conflict of his time is conditioned by that basic division in his temperament that is dramatized in his plays as the opposition of the Lion and the Fox.[5] The Lion, or man of passion, Shakespeare usually represents as an aristocrat of the old style: noble, open, and generous, but flawed by his devotion to the formal ceremony and the quixotic gesture. His honourable simplicity ensures his defeat by the Fox, the cunning and ruthless devotee of Machiavellian *realpolitik*. In his history plays, Shakespeare inclines to a more sceptical view of the Lion's virtues. For the good of the kingdom, the rash and histrionic Lion must be supplanted by the politic Fox: thus Bolingbroke prevails over Richard, Hal over Hotspur. But in the tragedies, the Lion's credulity is intrinsic to his noble nature, whereas the Fox's cunning is savage and nihilistic: Othello is overthrown by Iago, Lear and Gloucester by Regan, Goneril, and Edmund.

The social meaning of this recurrent opposition of character types has already been explored by critics, though usually from the somewhat nostalgic viewpoint of Christian humanism. E.M.W. Tillyard, for example, defines the action of *Richard II* as the superseding of Richard's world of 'medieval refinement' by the more realistic, modern-minded statesmanship of Bolingbroke.[6] John F. Danby takes a similar approach to *King Lear*, attributing Lear's faith in 'Benignant Nature' to the ordered medieval world view of Bacon and Hooker, while seeing in Edmund's 'Malignant Nature' an anticipation of Hobbes's concept of primitive culture as a war of all against all. Danby's premises are neo-Christian rather than Marxist – he says the play 'is at least as Christian as the *Divine Comedy*'[7] – but his analysis is based on the same class opposition in Elizabethan society that I have described above. So, where a Marxist might single out Edmund as typifying the new bourgeois ethic of irreverent, individualist acquisitiveness, Danby sees a person:

[who] is not a co-operative member of a grand community.... Edmund is the careerist on the make, the New Man laying a mine under the crumbling walls and patterned streets of an ageing society that thinks it can disregard him.

For the two Natures and two Reasons imply two societies. Edmund belongs to the new age of scientific inquiry and industrial development, of bureaucratic organization and social regimentation, the age of mining and merchant-venturing, of monopoly and Empire-making, the age of the sixteenth century and after: an age of competition, suspicion, glory. He hypostatizes those trends in man which guarantee success under the new conditions. (pp. 45–6)

Edmund is determined to strike off all shackles that might inhibit the free play of his energies. He therefore denies the inherited medieval standards of Elizabethan society insofar as they assume (in Danby's words) 'a co-operative, reasonable decency in man, and respect for the whole as being greater than the part: "God to be worshipped, parents to be honoured, others to be used by us as we ourselves would be by them"' (p. 46).

Danby's description of the dialectical opposition in *Lear* is useful and convincing, even if one does not share his idealization of medieval social values. Like many modern conservatives, he laments the shift of Western culture from *Gemeinschaft* to *Gesellschaft*, from organic community to atomistic state. Indeed, by the time he wrote *Lear* Shakespeare himself seems to have been of this party, though his adherence to it was qualified by the self-division that counts as an asset to the dramatist. Kenneth Burke has already pointed out this double vision in Shakespeare's treatment of social issues:

> This 'tragic ambiguity' whereby a growing trend is at once recommended and punished, is present also in Shakespeare's treatment of Macbeth, who represents the new bourgeois concepts of ambition in grotesque guise. In confronting the emergent capitalist standards, Shakespeare retained many conservative, feudal norms of value. The result, made by the incongruous juxtaposition of both conservative and revolutionary frames, was a 'tragic ambiguity' whereby he gave expression to the rising trends, but gave them the forbidding connotations of criminality.[8]

I shall assume, therefore, that the opposition between the party of Lear and the party of Regan, Goneril, and Edmund is not merely a conflict between good and evil persons; it conveys also a social meaning that derives from the contemporary historical situation as Shakespeare understood it.[9] However, the reflection of social reality in *Lear* is neither simple nor direct, and the Marxist critic who aspires to do more than simply proclaim his own sympathies must refine his methods of analysis to cope with the complexities of Shakespeare's dramatic representation of the underlying issues. An important complication in *Lear* derives from its setting in time: not in the England of Shakespeare but in an archaic, pre-Christian realm that mingles history and folklore. The play therefore omits such essential elements of the transition from feudalism to the mercantile economy as the great increase in the use of money. The all-pervasive 'cash nexus' of Marx and Carlyle is insignificant in *Lear*, since power is determined by one's ability to command personal loyalty, and payments are made in kind rather than in cash.[10] Edmund schemes for possession of Edgar's land, not his money, and when Lear abdicates he divides land rather than liquid assets.

King Lear, then, represents the neocapitalist economy of the Renaissance, not directly, but rather through an exploration of the philosophical concepts and moral values that are typically associated with that economy. The most imaginative interpreter of such intellectual derivatives of the Renaissance economic transition has been Lucien Goldmann. He suggests that the Renaissance bourgeoisie, as it comes to equal or dominate the aristocracy economically, elaborates a corresponding rationalist doctrine of empirical individualism that supersedes the earlier Aristotelian and animist world views. The concepts of the organic community and the bounded universe are replaced by those of the reasonable individual and infinite space; the idea of social hierarchy yields to that of the collectivity of isolated, free, and equal individuals.[11] The tragic consciousness of the late Renaissance derives from a nostalgic sense of loss and division: it combines intellectual comprehension of the new rationalist position with a 'radical refusal to accept this world as man's only hope and only perspective' (p. 43). Lear and Gloucester, we observe, are racked by the contrast between their immediate perception of man as no more than a 'poor, bare, forked animal' (III.iv.110) and their longing for intervention by the 'justicers above', who seem to have withdrawn their care for mankind. Their plight corresponds to that of the protagonist described by Lukács in his 'Metaphysics of Tragedy':

> he hopes that from the struggle of opposing forces will come a Divine judgment, a pronouncement of ultimate truth. But the world around him goes its own way, indifferent to both questions and answers. All things have become dumb and the combats distribute arbitrarily, with indifference, triumph, or defeat. The clear words of God's judgment will never resound again in the march of destiny; it was their voice that awakened everything into life, now he must live alone, for himself; the voice of the judge has fallen silent for ever.[12]

That Lear and Gloucester suffer such a crisis of faith is evident; but it does not stem from purely intellectual doubts, since the opening scenes of the play show them in moods of senile complacency. Their crisis is the direct result of having their settled views of the cosmos and society challenged by Edmund, Regan, and Goneril. The challenge first arises in the recurrent explorations of the meaning of a *bond*. Lear's party appeal to the traditional bonds – between parent and child, master and servant, lord and vassal – that knit together the elements of feudal society. So, for Gloucester, 'the bond crack'd 'twixt son and father' (I.ii.113) is but one symptom of a general disorder: 'in cities, mutinies; in countries, discord; in palaces, treason'. That he should blame it all on 'late eclipses in the sun and moon' (I.ii.106) merely shows his ignorance of the real forces of change at work in the kingdom. There is a similarly ironic ignorance in

Lear's loss of insight and control in the division scene: he is seduced by Goneril's rhetoric, which denies all order and limit in claiming to love him 'Dearer than eyesight, space and liberty', whereas he scorns Cordelia's modest pledge to love him 'According to [her] bond; no more nor less' (I.i.56,93). For Edmund the word has an opposite meaning: the individual's obligations to society he brushes aside as no more than 'the plague of custom' (I.ii.3). His own views he slyly attributes to Edgar, in the forged letter, which complains of 'an idle and fond bondage in the oppression of aged tyranny, who sways, not as it hath power, but as it is suffer'd' (I.ii.50). Casting off any allegiance to his actual rulers, whom he finds restrictive and arbitrary, he declares his fealty to the only superior that can accommodate his limitless ambition: 'Thou, Nature, art my goddess; to thy law / My services are bound' (I.ii.1–2). This 'heroic vitalism'[13] of Edmund's looks back to Machiavelli, forward to such ideologies as laissez-faire and Social Darwinism. 'Legitimacy' he derides as a principle that serves only to prop up a moribund status quo; he sets against it his vision of a society of achieved rather than ascribed status, where his restless opportunism could flourish unimpeded. To his mind, the social and natural orders would then be homologous, and would recognize only the one sovereignty of Nature herself. His ideas scarcely differ in principle from the main line of development of bourgeois social theory over the next three centuries; but for Lear, and apparently for Shakespeare also, an open society such as Edmund envisions represents simply the triumph of crime.[14]

Edmund, Regan, and Goneril extend their political ruthlessness to the personal realm by espousing a strict and often brutal functionalism in social life; their opponents, on the other hand, are addicted to precedent and ceremony, whatever the cost in efficiency. The contrast is most evident in the struggle over Lear's claim to his retinue of a hundred knights.[15] The text of the play leaves in question the actual qualities of these men. For Lear, naturally, they are 'men of choice and rarest parts, / That all particulars of duty know', and an indispensable element of 'all th' addition to a king' (I.iv.272–3; I.i.136). But Goneril hates them, for two reasons. First, they put in hazard the very sovereignty that she and her sister have just won. They 'hourly carp and quarrel, breaking forth / In rank and not-to-be-endured riots' (I.iv.211–12), and so long as he is surrounded by such a menacing bodyguard Lear cannot be written off as a political force. Second, it offends her ascetic concern for domestic orderliness to be overrun by this band of ruffians:

> Men so disorder'd, so debosh'd, and bold,
> That this our court, infected with their manners,
> Shows like a riotous inn: epicurism and lust

Makes it more like a tavern or a brothel
Than a grac'd palace.

(I.iv.250–54)

There is a tinge of puritanism in her distaste for the moral laxity of the
ancien régime – a laxity made prominent at the very start of the play by
Gloucester's lustful reminiscences. Like Philo in the opening scene of
Antony and Cleopatra, she sees the health of the state threatened by vice
and luxury in high places. Of course, it is also true that Goneril's own later
actions will be far more vicious than anything that might have passed
muster in the mildly licentious atmosphere of Lear's court. As in the case
of Malvolio, or of Angelo in *Measure for Measure*, Shakespeare mistrusts
puritanical attitudes because he believes they conceal a hidden desire to
indulge in what they most condemn.

Whether or not Lear's retainers are as troublesome as Regan and Goneril
claim will have little effect on the struggle over their fate, for, however
they behave, Lear is as stubbornly committed to keeping them in his
service as his daughters are to dismissing them. This conflict may be
interpreted as a small-scale and symbolic representation of the long Tudor
controversy over 'maintenance': the right of a peer to support an armed and
uniformed (liveried) body of retainers and be escorted by them in public.[16]
Such private armies were an implicit challenge to the power of the throne
and to the civil order; the Tudor monarchs carried on a long struggle to
restrict and finally abolish maintenance, a struggle that was part of their
broad policy of limiting the claims of assertive aristocrats and subordinating their powers to the throne. The execution of Essex in 1601, after his
abortive challenge to Elizabeth's authority, brought this conflict to a
dramatic climax. By the end of the sixteenth century maintenance of a
liveried retinue, especially in London, had become a token of an
aristocrat's devotion to an archaic style of conspicuous consumption rather
than a credible gesture of independence from central authority. But even as
late as the 1570s the second Earl of Southampton (father of Shakespeare's
patron) continued to affect a style of feudal autarchy in proceeding through
the streets:

> bravely attended and served by the best gentlemen of those countries
> wherein he lived; his muster roll never consisted of four lackeys and a
> coachman, but of a whole troop of at least a hundred well mounted
> gentlemen and yeomen; he was not known in the streets by guarded
> liveries but by gold chains; not by painted butterflies ever running as if
> some monster pursued them, but by tall goodly fellows that kept a
> constant pace both to guard his person and to admit any man to their Lord
> which had serious business.[17]

The contemporary commentator stresses not just the number but also the dignity and quality of Southampton's retinue. They are men of substance in their own right who yet are proud to be part of Southampton's household. In this they swim against the current, for at this time the great aristocratic households were shrinking, and the status of those who remained in them was declining. Even the richest peers could no longer afford to support hundreds of retainers, as they had done in the Middle Ages, nor did they need them for local warfare; at the same time, young gentlemen were ceasing to consider it honourable to provide personal service to an aristocrat. By the mid-eighteenth century, Lawrence Stone observes, domestic service had acquired the social stigma that it still bears, so that 'it was generally accepted that "a livery suit may indeed fitly be called a badge of servility"' (p. 214). Where the feudal ethic had exalted service to a superior as the most honourable of human bonds, the bourgeois era regarded it as an intrinsic violation of individual dignity.[18]

Around 1600 these contradictory notions of service were both still current; they are evident in the instinctive hostility between Kent and Oswald. Though Kent is an earl in his own right, when cast out of favour he feels it most honourable to serve Lear still, as a poor but honest subject who tells the King that he recognizes 'that in your countenance which I would fain call master' (I.iv.30).[19] But because the choice is his own he retains his integrity and status. He despises Oswald as a jumped-up 'eater of broken meats' who must be 'super-serviceable' to his mistress's vices because he is no more than a parasite. The bitterest pill, for Kent, is that Oswald can claim the prerogatives of a gentleman despite his lack of birth or breeding, merely by pandering to Regan: 'That such a slave as this should wear a sword, / Who wears no honesty' (II.ii.73–74). Kent's outrage is that of a member of a hereditary class that sees its privileges devalued and its ideals of loyalty superseded.

The argument over 'service' in the play, therefore, mingles issues of status, power, and economics. The last of these is brought out in Regan's distaste for the sheer wastefulness of Lear's entourage,[20] and the bad example they set – she suggests that it is the influence of the 'riotous knights' that has incited Edgar to depose his father, in the hope of enjoying 'th' expense and waste of his revenues' (II.i.100). We see here another aspect of Shakespeare's characteristic opposition of the man of passion to the man of calculation: the former spends freely, if not always wisely, whereas the latter husbands his financial resources in the same manner as his emotional ones. In the *Richard II* tetralogy a balance is finally struck on the side of the savers. Richard's squandering of England's wealth justifies his overthrow by the more prudent Bolingbroke; later in the cycle Falstaff must be dismissed lest Bolingbroke's 'unthrifty son' appear to be another wastrel monarch. In Sonnet 94 Shakespeare passes an enigmatic judgement on the underlying issue of personal temperament: he gives credit to the men of restraint who 'husband nature's riches from expense', but his praise is tinged with mistrust. Elsewhere in the sequence he continually exhorts his aristocratic 'lovely boy' to give himself more freely in emotional relationships and to become a father so that he will not have lived only for himself.

One can trace this debate back to the medieval poem 'Winnere and Wastoure', and beyond, but for Shakespeare it is far more than a mere literary trope. It reflects his personal distillation of the historical dialectic defined earlier in this paper: the opposition between a feudal aristocratic ethic that promotes display, generosity and conspicuous consumption, and a bourgeois ethic that values thrift because it promotes the accumulation rather than the dissipation of capital. Though in his personal life Shakespeare was a prudent saver and investor, he seems to have admired the more dashing aristocratic style of expenditure; certainly when he criticized it he did so only halfheartedly, whereas he is venomous in his portrayals of the usurer Shylock, and of Regan and Goneril. Not only does he imply that financial and emotional meanness are but two aspects of an identical underlying disposition, he also associates these traits with a murderous callousness toward man's actual necessities of subsistence. This attitude is eloquently expressed in Lear's outburst when told that there is no economic need for him to have any servants of his own:

O! reason not the need; our basest beggars
Are in the poorest thing superfluous:
Allow not nature more than nature needs,
Man's life is cheap as beast's.

(II.iv.266–9)

He then lapses into incoherent rage and goes out into the storm rather than submit to being dependent on his daughters' household. Though the moving quality of his plea has often been praised, it is really a debater's point. His daughters are only proposing, as they have done before in the argument over his retinue, to apply a standard of economic rationality to Lear's expenses; whereas it is precisely the idea that he should be 'reasonable' in his expectations that drives him mad. He cannot bear that his royal dignity should be measured by the scale of the countinghouse.[21] But the Fool well knows the difference between a beggar's life and that of a court dependent, even if his master does not.

When Lear goes to the heath, the argument over how the kingdom should be managed ceases to be such a pressing issue. In the brute struggle for power that ensues, long-run policy becomes irrelevant. Lear and Gloucester, suddenly cast on their own resources, must make their agonized passage through the lower depths of their country and of their own consciousness. Under the stress of this journey they state a social doctrine that may seem to contradict the thesis of this paper about the play's fundamental oppositions and that therefore requires careful examination.

We have, first, parallel expressions of regret by Lear and Gloucester for their previous callousness toward the poor. When Lear is exposed to the storm, he realizes for the first time what 'poor naked wretches' must ordinarily suffer from the elements:

> O! I have ta'en
> Too little care of this. Take physic, Pomp;
> Expose thyself to feel what wretches feel,
> That thou mayst shake the superflux to them,
> And show the Heavens more just.

(III.iv.32–36)

Gloucester, later, gives his purse to Poor Tom and takes comfort that his own suicidal misery may at least benefit a humble beggar:

> Here, take this purse, thou whom the heav'ns' plagues
> Have humbled to all strokes: that I am wretched
> Makes thee the happier: Heavens, deal so still!
> Let the superfluous and lust-dieted man,
> That slaves your ordinance, that will not see
> Because he does not feel, feel your power quickly;
> So distribution should undo excess,
> And each man have enough.

(IV.i.64–71)

Certainly such sentiments mark an advance from Lear's previous ego-centric outburst about 'Reason not the need'; he and Gloucester now see that so long as the poor are hungry and cold the self-indulgence of the rich is an offence against divine justice. Nevertheless, they still view social inequality from the traditional perspective of Christian charity, with its ideal of an organic, hierarchical state in which all are linked together in brotherly love. The remedy for the sufferings of the poor is that the rich should treat them better, not that they should demand redress of their own initiative. So long as they remain the 'deserving poor' – long-suffering peasants or devoted menials – Shakespeare usually presents them sym-pathetically; but if they should resort to direct action on their own behalf they mutate into that old standby the mindlessly destructive Shakespearean mob. The underlying bias is the classic syndrome of 'Tory radicalism', wherein the highest and lowest orders of society – aristocracy and peasants – are exhorted to unite against the middle.[22] Though at best the aims of this party may be humanistic and its commitment to social justice genuine, it

argues from quite different premises than those of either bourgeois or
socialist revolutionaries.

In his second great mad scene Lear progresses to a much more radical
critique of the social hierarchy, when he muses on the example of a hungry
beggar being driven off by a farmer's dog:

> There thou might'st behold
> The great image of Authority:
> A dog's obey'd in office.
> Thou rascal beadle, hold thy bloody hand!
> Why dost thou lash that whore? Strip thine own back;
> Thou hotly lusts to use her in that kind
> For which thou whipp'st her. The usurer hangs the cozener.
> Thorough tatter'd clothes small vices do appear;
> Robes and furr'd gowns hide all. Plate sin with gold,
> And the strong lance of justice hurtless breaks;
> Arm it in rags, a pigmy's straw does pierce it.
> None does offend, none, I say, none; I'll able 'em:

(IV.vi.159–70)

Passages like this have been cited by Soviet critics to support their view
of Shakespeare as a 'Writer of the People', a progressive artist 'whose
work embodies the revolutionary essence of the Renaissance'.[23] But Lear's
contempt for Authority requires closer examination. First, it is not just
logic-chopping to note that he is at this point intermittently mad; the
Elizabethan stage madman was expected to make pungent criticisms of the
way of the world, but this did not mean that the audience expected society
to be reordered in accordance with the madman's insights. Still, Lear
presents a bitter and cogent indictment of the powers that be: the judges are
themselves criminals at heart, and they apply a double standard to rich and
poor, since sin ceases to be sin when plated with gold. He reacts, in part,
as a Christian radical. The beadle who lusts after the whore he punishes
recalls the gospel story of the woman taken in adultery, and Lear takes a
Christian view of political corruption both in concluding that where all
offend, none offends, and in recommending to Gloucester that 'Thou must
be patient' (IV.vi.180). But another equally logical response alternates with
Christian resignation in Lear's mind, to steal upon his enemies and 'kill,
kill, kill, kill, kill, kill!' (IV.vi.189). Soviet critics applaud the trenchant
cynicism of Lear's social analysis, but fail to see that he draws no
conclusions that deserve to be called progressive; he merely vacillates
between saying 'resist not evil' and revelling in the prospect of a war of
all against all. Indeed, if he had any rational scheme of social reconstruction there would be less occasion for him to rave at the prevalence of
injustice. That in coming to know himself he has become incompetent to
resume power is, ironically, a large part of his tragedy; that he will not even

be allowed to retire from office unmolested is what completes it.

The last movement of the play begins with Lear's vision of himself and Cordelia becoming 'Gods' spies'; now, like Leir in the *True Chronicle*, he wants only to lead a life of religious meditation, caring nothing for the kingdom that Edmund has won. After he and Cordelia are led away, the triple call of the trumpet that brings Edgar to trial by combat with Edmund leads us to expect a secular last judgement, in which traditional moral values and chivalric decorum will be reasserted. But any consolation we may draw from Edgar's victory is swept away in its dreadful sequel. In the shadow of this loss, Edgar's accession to the throne seems only a partial restoration of order – as compared, say, with the ending of *The Tempest*, where the old ruler and his daughter are reinvested with full power and fertility. Kent's prescience that he will soon die and the haziness of England's future under Edgar confirm that although Edmund, Regan, and Goneril lie dead they have succeeded in their original aim of tearing down the old order they so much despised.

How does a Marxist interpretation of *King Lear* affect its status as a tragedy? George Steiner, in *The Death of Tragedy,* claims that 'the Marxist world view, even more explicitly than the Christian, admits of error, anguish, and temporary defeat, but not of ultimate tragedy'.[24] A progressive and determinist theory of history, he says, cannot accommodate the classic tragic situation of a noble hero overcome by a blind and malignant fate; and he quotes Marx's dictum that 'Necessity is blind only in so far as it is not understood' (p. 4). Steiner's scheme, however, does not do justice to the complexity of the issue. It is true that Stalin's directives on 'Socialist Realism' called for one-dimensional proletarian heroes and happy endings; but Roland Barthes has argued convincingly that such literary dogmas incorporated the norms of petty-bourgeois popular writing, instead of seeking to express a genuinely dialectic sense of reality.[25] So far as Marx's denial of 'blind necessity' is concerned, Steiner fails to distinguish between the Marxist (or any other) theory of history, which is based on a *retrospective analysis* of events, and the way in which people experience those events *as they happen*. Though Oedipus grapples blindly with his fate, the audience does not share his blindness – and the tragic effect is created by just this disparity.

Marx himself had a definite theory of tragedy; though not fully developed, it was a sophisticated one based on a deep knowledge and appreciation of the whole Western literary tradition (each year, for example, he read through Aeschylus in the original). He saw the essence of tragedy as a disharmony or disproportion between the hero's ambitions and the time in which he lives. His main application of this scheme occurs in comments on the tragedy *Franz von Sickingen*, which was written by his comrade Ferdinand Lassalle in 1859. The 'tragic conflict' of the play, according to Engels, was that between 'the historically necessary postulate' – the liberation of the German peasantry – and 'the practical impossibility of its realization' by von Sickingen, who in 1522–23 led a revolt of the German knights against the higher nobility.[26] Without going into the details of Marx's analysis of von Sickingen's fate, we may simply note that in his terms the play counts as a 'progressive' tragedy, wherein the hero takes up the cause of a particular class *too soon*, that is, before historical conditions offer any possibility that the cause will prevail. What is more surprising is that Marx also admitted the validity of the opposite kind of tragedy: one in which a class (or individuals representing it) fails to recognize that the time has come when it must yield to those whom history has brought forward to supersede it. The relevant passage, from an article of 1843 criticizing Hegel's philosophy of law, is noteworthy for its free movement between the concepts of history as literature and literature as history:

> The history of the *Ancien Régime* [i.e., in eighteenth-century France] was *tragic* so long as it was the established power in the world, while freedom on the other hand was a personal notion – in short, so long as it believed and had to believe in its own validity. As long as the *Ancien Régime* as an existing world order struggled against a world that was just coming into being, there was on its side a historical but not a personal error. Its downfall was therefore tragic....
>
> The modern *Ancien Régime* [i.e., the rule of Frederick William IV of Prussia] is merely the *comedian* in a world whose *real heroes* are dead. History is thorough and goes through many phases as it conducts an old form to the grave. The final phase of a world-historical form is *comedy*. The Greek gods, already tragically and mortally wounded in Aeschylus' *Prometheus Bound*, had to die again comically in Lucian's dialogues. Why this course of history? So that mankind may part from its past *happily*.[27]

When the weakness of a declining class becomes evident to all, the appropriate tone for literary representation of its experience will fall in the range between pathos and comedy: for example, Chekhov's *The Cherry Orchard* or *Don Quixote* – which Marx greatly admired as 'the epic of a dying-out chivalry whose virtues were ridiculed and scoffed at in the emerging bourgeois world'.[28] But in *King Lear* we have a tragic hero who is at first utterly confident of his own 'validity' and correspondingly unconscious of how badly he had managed the destiny of his country. He is even more out of touch with reality than his historical counterpart Richard II; but in that play the rising man, Bolingbroke, is moved by a genuine grievance and by a deep concern for the condition of England. In

Lear, however, Edmund embodies no hope of the future, but only the most destructive aspects of the new era of bourgeois transformation. Though Lear has let the garden of England run to seed, it is clear that Edmund, Regan, and Goneril have no interest in restoring it to its proper condition. The struggle between the old order and the new is therefore bound to be a tragic one, whose outcome is too dark and bloody to be redeemed by the vapidly moralistic Edgar.

I shall conclude with a few general comments on the sources and implications of Shakespeare's class loyalties, in the hope that my analysis of *King Lear* may make some contribution to a Marxist interpretation of its author's whole career. His origins were in the provincial bourgeoisie; at the time of his birth his father was prosperous and respected, though he later suffered financial reverses and lost status in Stratford – a childhood experience similar to the early social humiliations of Dickens and Joyce. By moving to London, perhaps because of an imprudent marriage, Shakespeare distanced himself from his class birthright; and by making a career in the theatre he joined himself to an institution whose status and prosperity depended on aristocratic patrons, since it was under attack by the London bourgeoisie, already deeply tinged with puritan mistrust of the stage. The Ovidian hedonism of his first published works (*Venus and Adonis, The Rape of Lucrece*) and their dedication to the Earl of Southampton established a commitment to aristocratic styles and values that remained prominent throughout his literary career. Yet, as economic man, Shakespeare was a shrewd and cautious bourgeois investor, mainly in real estate. He steadily improved his financial position and eventually gained the right to call himself 'Gent.', despite having got his start as an actor, a socially dubious profession (see Sonnet 111). Like Oswald he acquired a sword, the appurtenance of a gentleman.[29] His monetary success as a playwright reflected his sensitivity to the tastes of a mass audience: his aristocratic predilections never became so extreme as to make him a self-consciously opaque and elitist writer like Chapman.

The apparent inconsistency between Shakespeare's values as a writer and those reflected in his personal business may perhaps be resolved by considering his orientation toward the audience of Elizabethan theatre. At the start of his career the success of *Tamburlaine the Great* and *The Spanish Tragedy* gave a clear indication of audience taste: it wanted dramatic characters to be noble, magniloquent, and exotic, the very opposite qualities to the thrift and calculation that were the bywords of the mercantile bourgeoisie. The hero must display his personality in large and lavish gesture, even at the risk of being pulled down from his eminence by lesser men; so Shakespeare usually made him some kind of aristocrat. This seems to have been in part a personal trait: he surely attributed special qualities of glamour and seductiveness to the well-born, a susceptibility most clearly revealed in his quasi-sexual infatuation with the 'lovely boy' of the sonnets. But his private inclinations were complementary to his artistic aims, for only aristocratic dignity and grandiloquence could provide adequate correlatives to the intensity of inner passion that he wished to show forth on the stage – as D.H. Lawrence has already observed:

> I think it is a final criticism against *Madame Bovary* that people such as Emma Bovary and her husband Charles simply are too insignificant to carry the full weight of Gustave Flaubert's sense of tragedy. Emma and Charles Bovary are a couple of little people. Gustave Flaubert is not a little person. But, because he is a realist and does not believe in 'heroes,' Flaubert insists on pouring his own deep and bitter tragic consciousness into the little skins of the country doctor and his uneasy wife. . . .
>
> The great tragic soul of Shakespeare borrows the bodies of kings and princes – not out of snobbism, but out of natural affinity. You can't put a great soul into a commonplace person.[30]

Unable to foresee the future monuments of bourgeois art, Shakespeare was concerned to uphold, and to perfect, the established grand style of innate authority and emotional display. For those attached to the old order the shift to a new mode of social organization will always seem to bring with it a dilution or demeaning of personal relations; and, indeed, there will be an inevitable time lag before the network of human connections in the new order can become as intricate and laden with historical significance as it had been under the old. Moreover, radical innovations in literary genre will usually be required to accommodate the full expression of the new sensibility. The close explorations of inner life that are the special achievements of the early bourgeois era, such as Pepys's *Diary, Robinson Crusoe*, and *Clarissa*, could never be represented on the stage: their relentless introspection, their minute examination of psychological detail, can make a gradual impression only on the consciousness of a persistent and solitary reader, not on that of a vibrant mass audience.

As a man of the theatre, Shakespeare was inclined to attribute meanness of stature to such introverted and calculating bourgeois types; yet at the same time he recognized their contribution to the new and effective style of power in his age. In the earlier stages of his career, especially in the history plays, he was inclined to accept the Tudor compromise as the best guarantee of both England's grandeur and its prosperity: Hal, by the end of *II Henry IV*, has come to synthesize the best qualities of the old England and the new, so that he can take the throne as an ideal ruler who heals his country's divisions. He is capable of dispassionate political calculation, but also of warlike vigour – as in his defeat of Hotspur – and of simple good humour with his boon companions of the tavern. Many critics, it is true, have proved reluctant to accept this ideal Hal, the benevolent Machiavel with the common touch; he fails to win our affection, they argue, because Shakespeare is, at heart, of Falstaff's party. Whatever the truth of this question, it seems evident that in his later tragedies – *Othello* (1604) and those following – Shakespeare no longer envisions any union of the Lion and the Fox, but only their instinctive opposition to each other. The aristocratic protagonist is undermined by a naïve confidence in the potency of his magnanimous imaginings; becoming more histrionic as he loses touch with the realities of power, he is finally reduced, like Lear, Antony, and Coriolanus, to a solipsistic willfulness as superb as it is ineffectual. Meanwhile his emotionally frigid opponent, master of the situation and of himself, entangles his victim in the coils of his own excess.

This, then, is the basic mode in which Shakespeare apprehends the crisis of the aristocracy in his time and the decline of feudal-heroic values. Unable to reconcile himself with the emerging bourgeois forces, he either associates their predominance with the tragic decay of the old order or else opposes to them a mystical countervailing force: Cordelia's redemptive grace, the patriarchical magic of Prospero. His art may indeed still embody a 'life-affirming humanism', as the Soviet critic Anisimov claims;[31] but, in the later plays, at least, it is neither an optimistic nor a progressive humanism – rather one whose essence is nostalgia, whose glory is that of the setting sun.

Notes

1. A.C. Bradley, *Shakespearean Tragedy* (London: Macmillan, 1905); Jan Kott, *Shakespeare Our Contemporary* (London: Methuen, 1967). Apart from specific works cited later, I shall make no effort to survey the vast body of writings about the play. Citations of *King Lear* will be to the revised Arden Edition by Kenneth Muir (Cambridge, Mass.: Harvard Univ. Press, 1957).

2. The following would make good starting points for the Marxist interpretation of Shakespeare and his time (though I am not always in agreement with them): Paul N. Siegel, *Shakespearean Tragedy and the Elizabethan Compromise* (New York: New York Univ. Press, 1957); *Shakespeare in His Time and Ours* (Notre Dame: Univ. of Notre Dame Press, 1968); Arnold Kettle, ed., *Shakespeare in a Changing World* (New York: International, 1964); Roman Samarin and Alexander Nikolyukin, eds, *Shakespeare in the Soviet Union* (Moscow: Progress, 1966).

3. Karl Marx and Frederick Engels, *Manifesto of the Communist Party* (1848; rpt. Moscow: Progress, 1971), pp. 34–5.

4. *Past and Present* (London: Chapman & Hall, 1843), pp. 250–51.

5. The seminal, though eccentric, treatment of this theme is by Wyndham Lewis, *The Lion and the Fox: The Role of the Hero in the Plays of Shakespeare* (New York: Barnes & Noble, n.d.).

6. *Shakespeare's History Plays* (New York: Collier, 1962), pp. 278–99.

7. *Shakespeare's Doctrine of Nature: A Study of King Lear* (London: Faber & Faber, 1961), p. 205.

8. *Attitudes toward History* (Los Altos, Calif.: Hermes, 1959), p. 29.

9. After a previous version of this paper was completed, my attention was drawn to Rosalie Colie's 'Reason and Need: *King Lear* and the "Crisis" of the Aristocracy', in *Some Facets of King Lear: Essays in Prismatic Criticism*, ed. R. Colie and F.T. Flahiff (Toronto & Buffalo: Univ. of Toronto Press, 1974). The late Colie analyses the play's social oppositions along lines similar to mine; she draws illustrations, as I do, from Lawrence Stone's magisterial *The Crisis of the Aristocracy 1558–1641* (Oxford: Clarendon, 1965). Our conclusions, however, differ radically in that she views Shakespeare as taking an evenhanded, detached stance toward the social struggles of his time: 'Like Shakespeare's other great plays', she observes, '*King Lear* deals in problems and problematics: neither way of life is sanctified, neither is regarded as an unqualified success' (p. 196).

10. There are minor, anachronistic exceptions, such as Kent's denunciation of Oswald as a 'hundred-pound . . . knave' (II.ii.15). Marx's famous disquisition on 'The Power of Money in Bourgeois Society' takes the form of a commentary on Timon's address to gold as the 'common whore of mankind' (*Tim. Ath.* IV.iii.42): *Economic and Philosophic Manuscripts of 1844* (New York: International, 1964), pp. 165–9.

11. Goldmann, *Le Dieu caché: Etude sur la vision tragique dans les Pensées de Pascal et dans le théâtre de Racine* (Paris: Gallimard, 1955), pp. 35–8. Quotations from this work are in my own translation.

12. Georg Lukacs, *Die Seele und die Formen* (Berlin: Fleischel, 1911), p. 332; quoted in Goldman, p. 45.

13. I borrow this apt term from Eric Bentley's *A Century of Hero-Worship* (Boston: Beacon, 1957), where it defines the tradition of Carlyle, Nietzsche, Shaw, and D.H. Lawrence.

14. This point has already been touched on by Edwin Muir in his brief but suggestive study *The Politics of King Lear* (Glasgow: Jackson, 1947), p. 19. On the later development and legitimization of Edmund's opportunistic premises, see the standard treatment by C.B. Macpherson, *The Political Theory of Possessive Individualism: Hobbes to Locke* (Oxford: Clarendon, 1962).

15. The issue of Lear's retinue is apparently Shakespeare's invention; in his probable major source, the anonymous 1605 work *The True Chronicle History of King Leir*, ed. Sidney Lee (London: Chatto & Windus, 1909), Leir lives unaccompanied in religious retirement with Gonorill.

16. My account of maintenance is based on Lawrence Stone, pp. 201–17, and sources there cited.

17. Gervase Markham, *Honour in His Perfection* (London, 1624), p. 20; quoted in Stone, p. 214. 'Guarded liveries': frilly, overornate costumes. 'Painted butterflies': cf. Lear's reference to 'gilded butterflies' (V.iii.13). The spendthrift seventeenth Earl of Oxford, a contemporary of Southampton's, also sported a retinue of '100 tall yeomen in livery' (Stone, p. 211).

18. Goneril's use of the word implies a further contrast between service as recognition of a legitimate authority and as mere opportunism: 'To thee [i.e., Edmund] a woman's services are due: / My Fool usurps my body' (IV.ii.27–28). She wishes to serve (in more senses than one) the virile Edmund, rather than her squeamish lawful husband.

19. Cf. Orlando's praise of Adam, the old servant in *As You Like It*, who serves 'for duty, not for need' (II.iii.58).

20. Shakespeare reverses the situation in *The True Chronicle History*, where Leir irritates Gonorill by criticizing her spendthrift tastes in food and clothing.

21. Cf. the argument of the like-minded Troilus against any abatement of Priam's absolutism: 'Weigh you the worth and honour of a king, / So great as our dread father, in a scale / Of common ounces? Will you with counters sum / The past-proportion of his infinite?' (*T&C* II.ii.26–29).

22. In English political history, such coalitions have often been based on an alleged community of rural interests against urban commercialism or, later, against manufacturers. This was the basic division of forces in the Civil War: the more economically developed

south-eastern part of England for Parliament, the more archaic and feudal North and West for the King.

23. Phrases by Maxim Gorky and Alexander Anikst: *Shakespeare in the Soviet Union*, pp. 12, 113. Compare Swinburne's comment: 'A poet of revolution he is not, as none of his country in that generation could have been: but . . . the author of *King Lear* avowed himself in the only good and rational sense of the words a spiritual if not a political democrat and socialist' (*A Study of Shakespeare*, London: Chatto & Windus, 1902, p. 175).

24. *The Death of Tragedy* (New York: Knopf, 1963), p. 342.

25. *Le Degré zéro de l'écriture* (Paris: Seuil, 1953), section on 'Ecriture et révolution'.

26. Engels, letter to Lassalle of 18 May 1859; quoted in Lee Baxandall and Stefan Morawski, eds, *Marx and Engels on Literature and Art* (St Louis: Telos, 1973), p. 110. Marx's analysis of the play, which is similar to Engels's, is given in a letter to Lassalle of 19 April 1859.

27. 'Toward the Critique of Hegel's Philosophy of Law: Introduction', in *Writings of the Young Marx on Philosophy and Society*, ed. Loyd Easton and Kurt Guddat (Garden City, N.Y.: Anchor-Doubleday, 1967), pp. 253–4.

28. Baxandall and Morawski, p. 150.

29. It is listed among the bequests in his will.

30. *Phoenix* (London: Heinemann, 1936), p. 226.

31. *Shakespeare in the Soviet Union*, p. 140.

3

'The Place of a Brother' in *As You Like It*: Social Process and Comic Form*

Louis Adrian Montrose

As You Like It creates and resolves conflict by mixing what the characters call Fortune and Nature – the circumstances in which they find themselves, as opposed to the resources of playfulness and boldness, moral virtue and witty deception, with which they master adversity and fulfil their desires.

The romantic action is centred on the meeting, courtship, and successful pairing of Rosalind and Orlando. This action is complicated, as Leo Salingar reminds us, by

> a cardinal social assumption ... (which would have been obvious to ... Shakespeare's first audiences) – that Rosalind is a princess, while Orlando is no more than a gentleman. But for the misfortune of her father's exile, they might not have met in sympathy as at first; but for the second misfortune of her own exile, as well as his, they could not have met in apparent equality in the Forest.[1]

The personal situations of Rosalind and Orlando affect, and are affected by, their relationship to each other. Rosalind's union with Orlando entails the weakening of her ties to her natural father and to a cousin who has been closer to her than a sister; Orlando's union with Rosalind entails the strengthening of his ties to his elder brother and to a lord who becomes his patron. Orlando's atonements with other men – a natural brother, a social father – precede his atonement with Rosalind. They confirm that the disadvantaged young country gentleman is worthy of the princess, by 'nature' and by 'fortune'. The atonement of earthly things celebrated in Hymen's wedding song incorporates man and woman within a process that reunites man with man. This process is my subject.

As the play begins, Orlando and Adam are discussing the terms of a paternal will; the first scene quickly explodes into fraternal resentment and envy, hatred and violence. By the end of the second scene, the impoverished youngest son of Sir Rowland de Boys finds himself victimized by 'a tyrant Duke' and 'a tyrant brother' (I.iii.278).[2] The compact early scenes expose hostilities on the manor and in the court that threaten to destroy both the family and the state. Although modern productions have shown that these scenes can be powerful and effective in the theatre, modern criticism has repeatedly downplayed their seriousness and significance. They are often treated merely as Shakespeare's mechanism for propelling his characters – and us – into the forest as quickly and efficiently as possible. Thus Harold Jenkins, in his influential essay on the play, writes of 'the inconsequential nature of the action' and of 'Shakespeare's haste to get ahead'; for him, the plot's interest consists in Shakespeare's ability to get 'most of it over in the first act'.[3] If we *reverse* Jenkins' perspective, we will do justice to Shakespeare's dramaturgy and make better sense of the play. What happens to Orlando at home is not Shakespeare's contrivance to get him into the forest; what happens to Orlando in the forest is Shakespeare's contrivance to remedy what has happened to him at home. The form of *As You Like It* becomes comic in the process of resolving the conflicts that are generated within it; events unfold and relationships are transformed in accordance with a precise comic teleology.

Jaques sententiously observes that the world is a stage; the men and women, merely players; and one man's time, a sequence of acts in which he plays many parts. Shakespeare's plays reveal many traces of the older drama's intimate connection to the annual agrarian and ecclesiastical cycles. But more pervasive than these are the connections between Shakespearean comic and tragic forms and the human life cycle – the sequence of acts performed in several ages by Jaques's social player. Action in Shakespearean drama usually originates in combinations of a few basic kinds of human conflict: conflict among members of different families, generations, sexes, and social classes. Shakespeare tends to focus dramatic action precisely *between* the social 'acts', between the sequential 'ages', in the fictional lives of his characters. Many of the plays turn upon points of transition in the life cycle – birth, puberty, marriage, death – where discontinuities arise and where adjustments are necessary to basic interrelationships in the family and in society. Such dramatic actions are analogous to rites of passage. Transition rites symbolically impose markers upon the life cycle and safely conduct people from one stage of life to the next; they give a social shape, order, and sanction to personal existence.[4]

In *As You Like It*, the initial conflict arises from the circumstances of inheritance by primogeniture. The differential relationship between the first born and his younger brothers is profoundly augmented at their father's death: the eldest son assumes a paternal relationship to his siblings; and the potential for sibling conflict increases when the relationship between brother and brother becomes identified with the relationship between father and son. The transition of the father from life to death both fosters and obstructs the transition of his sons from childhood to manhood. In *As You Like It*, the process of comedy accomplishes successful passages between ages in the life cycle and ranks in the social hierarchy. By the end of the play, Orlando has been brought from an impoverished and powerless adolescence to the threshold of manhood and marriage, wealth and title.

A social anthropologist defines inheritance practices as 'the way by which property is transmitted between the living and the dead, and especially between generations'.

> Inheritance is not only the means by which the reproduction of the social system is carried out ... it is also the way in which interpersonal relationships are structured. ...
>
> The linking of patterns of inheritance with patterns of domestic organization is a matter not simply of numbers and formations but of attitudes and emotions. The manner of splitting property is a manner of splitting people; it creates (or in some cases reflects) a particular constellation of ties and cleavages between husband and wife, parents and children, sibling and sibling, as well as between wider kin.[5]

As Goody himself concedes, the politics of the family are most powerfully anatomized, not by historians or social scientists, but by playwrights. Parents and children in Shakespeare's plays are recurrently giving or withholding, receiving or returning, property and love. Material and spiritual motives, self-interest and self-sacrifice, are inextricably intertwined in Shakespearean drama as in life.

Lear's tragedy, for example, begins in his division of his kingdom among his daughters and their husbands. He makes a bequest of his property to his heirs before his death, so 'that future strife / May be prevented now' (I.i.44–45). Gloucester's tragedy begins in the act of adultery that begets an 'unpossessing bastard' (II.i.67). Edmund rails against 'the plague of custom ... the curiosity of nations' (I.ii.3–4); he sees himself as victimized by rules of legitimacy and primogeniture. *As You Like It* begins with Orlando remembering the poor bequest from a dead father and the unnaturalness of an elder brother; he is victimized by what he bitterly refers to as 'the courtesy of nations' (I.i.45–6). Rosalind dejectedly remembers 'a banished father' (I.ii.4) and the consequent loss of her own preeminent social place. Celia responds to her cousin with naive girlhood loyalty: 'You know my father hath no child but I, nor none is like to have; and truly when he dies, thou shalt be his heir; for what he hath taken away from thy father perforce, I will render thee again in affection' (I.ii.14–19). The comic action of *As You Like It* works to atone elder and younger brothers, father and child, man and woman, lord and subject, master and servant. Within his play, Rosalind's magician-uncle recreates situations that are recurrent sources of ambiguity, anxiety, and conflict in the society of his audience; he explores and exacerbates them, and he resolves them by brilliant acts of theatrical prestidigitation.

The tense situation which begins *As You Like It* was a familiar and controversial fact of Elizabethan social life. Lawrence Stone emphasizes that 'the prime factor affecting all families which owned property was ... primogeniture'; that 'the principle and practice of primogeniture ... went far to determine the behaviour and character of both parents and children, and to govern the relationship between siblings'.[6] In the sixteenth and seventeenth centuries, primogeniture was more widely and rigorously practised in England – by the gentry and lesser landowners, as well as by the aristocracy – than anywhere else in Europe. The consequent hardships, frequent abuses, and inherent inequities of primogeniture generated a 'literature of protest by and for younger sons' that has been characterized as 'plentiful,' 'vehement' in tone, and 'unanimous' in its sympathies.[7]

Jaques was not the only satirist to 'rail against all the first-born of Egypt' (II.v.57–8). John Earle included the character of a 'younger Brother' in his *Micro-Cosmographie* (1628):

> His father ha's done with him, as *Pharaoh* to the children of Israel, that would have them make brick, and give them no straw, so he taskes him to bee a Gentleman, and leaves him nothing to maintaine it. The pride of his house has undone him, which the elder Knighthood must sustaine, and his beggery that Knighthood. His birth and bringing up will not suffer him to descend to the meanes to get wealth: but hee stands at the mercy of the world, and which is worse of his brother. He is something better then the Servingmen; yet they more saucy with him, then hee bold with the master, who beholds him with a countenance of sterne awe, and checks him oftner then his Liveries.... Nature hath furnisht him with a little more wit upon compassion; for it is like to be his best revenew.... Hee is commonly discontented, and desperate, and the forme of his exclamation is, that Churle my brother.[8]

As a class, the gentry experienced a relative rise in wealth and status during this period. But the rise was achieved by inheriting eldest sons at the expense of their younger brothers. As Earle and other contemporaries clearly recognized, the gentry's drive to aggrandize and perpetuate their estates led them to a ruthless application of primogeniture; this left them without the means adequately to provide for their other offspring. The psychological and socio-economic consequences of primogeniture for younger sons (and for daughters) seem to have been considerable:

downward social mobility and relative impoverishment, inability to marry or late marriage, and fewer children.

In 1600, about the time *As You Like It* was first performed, Thomas Wilson wrote a valuable analysis of England's social structure. His description of gentlemen reveals a very personal involvement:

> Those which wee call Esquires are gentlemen whose ancestors are or have bin Knights, or else they are the heyres and eldest of their houses and of some competent quantity of revenue fitt to be called to office and authority in their Country. . . . These are the elder brothers.
>
> I cannot speak of the number of yonger brothers, albeit I be one of the number myselfe, but for their estate there is no man hath better cause to knowe it, nor less cause to praise it; their state is of all stations for gentlemen most miserable. . . . [A father] may demise as much as he thinkes good to his younger children, but such a fever hectick hath custome brought in and inured amongst fathers, and such fond desire they have to leave a great shewe of the stock of their house, though the branches be withered, that they will not doe it, but my elder brother forsooth must be my master. He must have all, and all the rest that which the catt left on the malt heape, perhaps some smale annuytye during his life or what please our elder brother's worship to bestowe upon us if wee please him.[9]

The foregoing texts characterize quite precisely the situation of Orlando and his relationship to Oliver at the beginning of *As You Like It*. They suggest that Shakespeare's audience may have responded with some intensity to Orlando's indictment of 'the courtesy of nations'.

In his constitutional treatise, *De Republica Anglorum* (written ca. 1562; printed 1583), Sir Thomas Smith observes that 'whosoever studies the laws of the realm, who studies at the universities, who professes liberal sciences and to be short, who can live idly and without manual labour, and will bear the port, charge and countenance of a gentleman ... shall be taken for a gentleman'.[10] The expected social fate of a gentleborn Elizabethan younger son was to lose the ease founded upon landed wealth that was the very hallmark of gentility. Joan Thirsk suggests that, although there were places to be had for those who were industrious and determined to make the best of their misfortune,

> the habit of working for a living was not ingrained in younger sons of this class, and no amount of argument could convince them of the justice of treating them so differently from their elder brothers. The contrast was too sharp between the life of an elder son, whose fortune was made for him by his father, and who had nothing to do but maintain, and perhaps augment it, and that of the younger sons who faced a life of hard and

continuous effort, starting almost from nothing. Many persistently
refused to accept their lot, and hung around at home, idle, bored, and
increasingly resentful.[11]

At the beginning of *As You Like It*, Orlando accuses Oliver of enforcing his
idleness and denying him the means to preserve the gentility which is his
birthright: 'My brother Jaques he keeps at school, and report speaks
goldenly of his profit; for my part, he keeps me rustically at home, or, to
speak more properly, stays me here at home unkept; for call you that
keeping for a gentleman of my birth, that differs not from the stalling of
an ox? ... [He] mines my gentility with my education' (I.i.5–10, 20–21).
Orlando is 'not taught to make anything' (l.30); and his natural virtue is
marred 'with idleness' (ll.33–4). When Adam urges him to leave the family
estate, Orlando imagines his only prospects to be beggary and highway
robbery (II.iii.29–34). He finally agrees to go off with Adam, spending the
old labourer's 'youthful wages' in order to gain 'some settled low content'
(II.iii.67–8).

Shakespeare's opening strategy is to plunge his characters and his
audience into the controversy about a structural principle of Elizabethan
personal, family, and social life. He is not merely using something topical
to get his comedy off to a lively start: the expression and resolution of
sibling conflict and its social implications are integral to the play's form
and function. The process of comedy works against the seemingly
inevitable prospect of social degradation suggested at the play's beginning,
and against its literary idealization in conventions of humble pastoral
retirement. In the course of *As You Like It*, Orlando's gentility is preserved
and his material well-being is enhanced. Shakespeare uses the machinery
of pastoral romance to remedy the lack of fit between deserving and
having, between Nature and Fortune. Without actually violating the
primary Elizabethan social frontier separating the gentle from the base, the
play achieves an illusion of social levelling and of unions across class
boundaries. Thus, people of every rank in Shakespeare's socially heterogeneous audience might construe the action as they liked it.

Primogeniture is rarely mentioned in modern commentaries on *As You
Like It*, despite its obvious prominence in the text and in the action.[12]
Shakespeare's treatment of primogeniture may very well have been a vital
– perhaps even the dominant – source of engagement for many in his
Elizabethan audience. The public theatre brought together people from all
the status and occupational groups to be found in Shakespeare's London
(except, of course, for the poorest labourers and the indigent). Alfred
Harbage points out that the two groups 'mentioned again and again in
contemporary allusions to the theatres' are 'the students of the Inns of
Court and the apprentices of London'.[13] In addition to these youthful

groups, significant numbers of soldiers, professionals, merchants, shop-keepers, artisans, and household servants were also regular playgoers. The careers most available to the younger sons of gentlemen were in the professions – most notably the law, but also medicine and teaching – as well as in trade, the army, and the church.[14] Thus, Shakespeare's audience must have included a high proportion of gentleborn younger sons – adults, as well as the youths who were students and apprentices. Among these gentleborn younger sons, and among the baseborn youths who were themselves socially subordinate apprentices and servants, it is likely that Orlando's desperate situation was the focus of personal projections and a catalyst of powerful feelings. 'During the sixteenth century', Thirsk concludes, 'to describe anyone as "*a younger son*" was a short-hand way of summing up a host of grievances. . . . *Younger son* meant an angry young man, bearing more than his share of injustice and resentment, deprived of means by his father and elder brother, often hanging around his elder brother's house as a servant, completely dependent on his grace and favour'.[15] Youths, younger sons, and all Elizabethan playgoers who felt that Fortune's benefits had been 'mightily misplaced' (II.i.33–4) could identify with Shakespeare's Orlando.

It is precisely in the details of inheritance that Shakespeare makes one of the most significant departures from his source. Sir John of Bordeaux is on his deathbed at the beginning of Lodge's *Rosalynde*; he divides his land and chattels among his three sons:

> Unto thee *Saladyne* the eldest, and therefore the chiefest piller of my house, wherein should be ingraven as well the excellence of thy fathers qualities, as the essentiall forme of his proportion, to thee I give foureteene ploughlands, with all my Mannor houses and richest plate. Next unto *Fernadyne* I bequeath twelve ploughlands. But unto *Rosader* the youngest I give my Horse, my Armour and my Launce, with sixteene ploughlands: for if inward thoughts be discovered by outward shadowes, *Rosader* will exceed you all in bountie and honour.[16]

The partible inheritance devised by Lodge's Sir John was an idiosyncratic variation on practices widespread in Elizabethan society among those outside the gentry.[17] Saladyne, the eldest born, inherits his father's authority. Rosader receives more land and love – he is his father's joy, although his last and least. Saladyne, who becomes Rosader's guardian, is deeply resentful and decides not to honour their father's will: 'What man thy Father is dead, and hee can neither helpe thy fortunes, nor measure thy actions: therefore, burie his words with his carkasse, and bee wise for thy selfe' (p. 391).

Lodge's text, like Thomas Wilson's, reminds us that primogeniture was not a binding law but rather a flexible social custom in which the propertied sought to perpetuate themselves by preserving their estates intact through successive generations. Shakespeare alters the terms of the paternal will in Lodge's story so as to alienate Orlando from the status of a landed gentleman. The effect is to intensify the differences between the eldest son and his siblings, and to identify the sibling conflict with the major division in the Elizabethan social fabric: that between the landed and the unlanded, the gentle and the base. (Within half a century after Shakespeare wrote *As You Like It*, radical pamphleteers were using 'elder brother' and 'younger brother' as synonyms for the propertied, enfranchised social classes and the unpropertied, unenfranchised social classes.) Primogeniture complicates not only sibling and socio-economic relationships but also relationships between generations: between a father and the eldest son impatient for his inheritance; between a father and the younger sons resentful against the 'fever hectic' that custom has inured among fathers.

Shakespeare's plays are thickly populated by subjects, sons and younger brothers who are ambivalently bound to their lords, genitors, and elder siblings – and by young women moving ambivalently between the lordships of father and husband. If this dramatic proliferation of patriarchs suggests that Shakespeare had a neurotic obsession, then it was one with a social context. To see father-figures everywhere in Shakespeare's plays is not a psychoanalytic anachronism, for Shakespeare's own contemporaries seem to have seen father-figures everywhere. The period from the mid sixteenth to the mid seventeenth century in England has been characterized by Lawrence Stone as 'the patriarchal stage in the evolution of the nuclear family'.[18] Writing of the early seventeenth-century family as 'a political symbol and a social institution', Gordon J. Schochet documents that

> virtually all social relationships – not merely those between fathers and children and magistrates and subjects – were regarded as patriarchal or familial in essence. The family was looked upon as the basis of the entire social order. . . .
>
> So long as a person occupied an inferior status within a household – as a child, servant, apprentice, or even as a wife – and was subordinated to the head, his social identity was altogether vicarious. . . .
>
> Before a man achieved social status – if he ever did – he would have spent a great many years in various positions of patriarchal subordination.[19]

This social context shaped Shakespeare's preoccupation with fathers; and it gave him the scope within which to reshape it into drama, satisfying his own needs and those of his paying audience. His plays explore the difficulty or impossibility of establishing or authenticating a self in a rigorously hierarchical and patriarchal society, a society in which full social identity tends to be limited to propertied adult males who are the heads of households.

Shakespeare's Sir Rowland de Boys is dead before the play begins. But the father endures in the power exerted by his memory and his will upon the men in the play – his sons, Adam, the dukes – and upon their attitudes toward each other. The play's very first words insinuate that Orlando's filial feeling is ambivalent: 'As I remember, Adam, it was upon this fashion bequeathed me by will but poor a thousand crowns, and, as thou sayst, charged my brother on his blessing to breed me well; and there begins my sadness' (I.i.1–4). Orlando's diction is curiously indirect; he conspicuously avoids naming his father. Absent from Shakespeare's play is any expression of the special, compensatory paternal affection shown to Lodge's Rosader. There is an implied resentment against an unnamed father, who has left his son a paltry inheritance and committed him to an indefinite and socially degrading dependence upon his own brother. Ironically, Orlando's first explicit acknowledgement of his filial bond is in a declaration of personal *independence*, a repudiation of his bondage to his eldest brother: 'The spirit of my father, which I think is within me, begins to mutiny against this servitude' (I.i.21–3). Orlando's assertions of filial piety are actually self-assertions, directed against his father's eldest son. As Sir Rowland's inheritor, Oliver perpetuates Orlando's subordination within the patriarchal order; he usurps Orlando's selfhood.

In a private family and household, the eldest son succeeds the father as patriarch. In a royal or aristocratic family, the eldest son also succeeds to the father's title and political authority. Thus, when he has been crowned as King Henry V, Hal tells his uneasy siblings, 'I'll be your father and your brother too. / Let me but bear your love, I'll bear your cares' (*2 Henry IV*, V.ii.57–8). Like Henry, Oliver is simultaneously a father and a brother to his own natural sibling; he is at once Orlando's master and his peer. Primogeniture conflates the generations in the person of the elder brother and blocks the generational passage of the younger brother. What might be described dispassionately as a contradiction in social categories is incarnated in the play, as in English social life, in family conflicts and identity crises.[20]

Orlando gives bitter expression to his personal experience of this social contradiction: 'The courtesy of nations allows you my better in that you are the firstborn, but that same tradition takes not away my blood, were there twenty brothers betwixt us. I have as much of my father in me as you, albeit I confess that your coming before me is nearer his reverence' (I.i.45–51). Here Orlando asserts that all brothers are equally their father's sons. Oliver might claim a special paternal relationship because he is the first-born; but

Orlando's own claim actually to incorporate their father renders insubstantial any argument based on age or birth order. Thus, Orlando can indict his brother and repudiate his authority: 'You have trained me like a peasant, obscuring and hiding from me all gentlemanlike qualities. The spirit of my father grows strong in me, and I will no longer endure it' (I.i.68–71). Because the patriarchal family is the basic political unit of a patriarchal society, Orlando's protests suggest that primogeniture involves contradictions in the categories of social status as well as those of kinship. Orlando is subordinated to his sibling as a son to his father, and he is subordinated to a fellow gentleman as a peasant would be subordinated to his lord.

Orlando incorporates not only his father's likeness and name ('Rowland') but also his potent 'spirit' – his personal genius, his manliness, and his moral virtue. To Adam, Orlando is 'gentle, strong, and valiant' (II.iii.6). He is his father's gracious and virtuous reincarnation: 'O you memory of old Sir Rowland!' (II.iii.3–4). Adam challenges the eldest son's legal claim to be his father's heir by asserting that Oliver is morally undeserving, that he is *spiritually* illegitimate:

> Your brother, no, no brother, yet the son –
> Yet not the son, I will not call him son –
> Of him I was about to call his father.

(II.iii.19–21)

Orlando's claim to his spiritual inheritance leads immediately to physical coercion: Oliver calls him 'boy' and strikes him. Orlando responds to this humiliating form of parental chastisement not with deference but with rebellion: he puts his hands to Oliver's throat. Orlando's assertion of a self which 'remembers' their father is a threat to Oliver's patriarchal authority, a threat to his own social identity: 'Begin you to grow upon me?' (I.i.85). The brothers' natural bond, in short, is contaminated by their ambiguous social relationship.

Because fraternity is confused with filiation – because the generations have, in effect, been collapsed together – the conflict of elder and younger brothers also projects an Oedipal struggle between father and son. In the second scene, the private violence between the brothers is displaced into the public wrestling match. Oliver tells Charles, the Duke's wrestler, 'I had as lief thou didst break [Orlando's] neck as his finger' (I.i.144–5). Sinewy Charles, the 'general challenger' (I.ii.159), has already broken the bodies of 'three proper young men' (l.lll) before Orlando comes in to try 'the strength of [his] youth' (l.161). In a sensational piece of stage business, Orlando and Charles enact a living emblem of the generational struggle. When Orlando throws Charles, youth is supplanting age, the son is supplanting the father. This contest is preceded by a remarkable exchange:

CHA. Come, where is this young gallant that is so desirous to lie with his
      mother earth?
ORL. Ready sir, but his will hath in it a more modest working.

(I.ii.188–91)

Charles's challenge gives simultaneous expression to a filial threat of
incest and a paternal threat of filicide. In this conspicuously motherless
play, the social context of reciprocal father–son hostility is a male struggle
for identity and power fought between elders and youths, first-born and
younger brothers.[21]

Orlando's witty response to Charles suggests that he regards neither his
fears nor his threats. Orlando's 'will' is merely to come to man's estate and
to preserve the status of a gentleman. At the beginning of *As You Like It*,
then, Shakespeare sets himself the problem of resolving the consequences
of a conflict between Orlando's powerful assertion of identity – his
spiritual claim to be a true inheritor – and the social fact that he is a
subordinated and disadvantaged younger son. In the forest, Oliver will be
spiritually reborn and confirmed in his original inheritance. Orlando will
be socially reborn as heir apparent to the reinstated Duke. Orlando will
regain a brother by 'blood' and a father by 'affinity'.

Orlando is not only a younger son but also a youth. And in its language,
characterization, and plot, *As You Like It* emphasizes the significance of age
categories. Most prominent, of course, is Jaques's disquisition on the seven
ages of man. But the play's *dramatis personae* actually fall into the three
functional age groups of Elizabethan society: youth, maturity, and old age.
Orlando's youth is referred to by himself and by others some two dozen
times in the first two scenes: he is young; a boy; a youth; the youngest son;
a younger brother; a young fellow; a young gallant; a young man; a young
gentleman. Social historians have discredited the notion that adolescence
went unexperienced or unacknowledged in early modern England. Lawrence Stone, for example, emphasizes that in Shakespeare's time there was
'a strong contemporary consciousness of adolescence (then called
"youth"), as a distinct stage of life between sexual maturity at about fifteen
and marriage at about twenty-six'.[22] Shakespeare's persistent epithets
identify Orlando as a member of the group about which contemporary
moralists and guardians of the social order were most obsessively
concerned. The Statute of Artificers (1563) summarizes the official
attitude: 'Until a man grow unto the age of twenty-four years he ... is wild,
without judgement and not of sufficient experience to govern himself'.[23]
The youthful members of an Elizabethan household – children, servants,
and apprentices – were all supposed to be kept under strict patriarchal
control. Stone points out that 'it was precisely because its junior members

were under close supervision that the state had a very strong interest in encouraging and strengthening the household.... It helped to keep in check potentially the most unruly element in any society, the floating mass of young unmarried males'.[24] Orlando is physically mature and powerful, but socially infantilized and weak.

That Shakespeare should focus so many of his plays on a sympathetic consideration of the problems of youth is not surprising when we consider that perhaps half the population was under twenty, and that the youthfulness of Shakespeare's society was reflected in the composition of his audience.[25] In his richly documented study, Keith Thomas demonstrates that

> So far as the young were concerned, the sixteenth and seventeenth centuries are conspicuous for a sustained drive to subordinate persons in their teens and early twenties and to delay their equal participation in the adult world. This drive is reflected in the wider dissemination of apprenticeship; in the involvement of many more children in formal education; and in a variety of measures to prolong the period of legal and social infancy.[26]

Elizabethan adolescence seems to have been characterized by a high degree of geographical mobility: youths were sent off to school, to search for work as living-in servants, or to be apprenticed in a regional town or in London. Alan Macfarlane has suggested that, 'at the level of family life', this widespread and peculiarly English custom of farming out adolescent children was 'a mechanism for separating the generations at a time when there might otherwise have been considerable difficulty'. 'The changes in patterns of authority as the children approached adulthood would ... be diminished.' He speculates further that, at the collective level, 'the whole process was a form of age ritual, a way of demarcating off age-boundaries by movement through space'.[27]

The family was a source of social stability, but most families were short-lived and unstable. Youth was geographically mobile, but most youths were given no opportunity to enjoy their liberty. In schools and in households, the masters of scholars, servants, and apprentices were to be their surrogate fathers. Thomas stresses that, 'though many children left home early and child labour was thought indispensable, there was total hostility to the early achievement of economic independence'.[28] The material basis of that hostility was alarm about the increasing pressure of population on very limited and unreliable resources. One of its most significant results was delayed marriage: 'Combined with strict prohibition on alternative forms of sexual activity, late marriage was the most obvious way in which youth was prolonged. For marriage was the surest test of adult status and on it hinged crucial differences in wages, dress, and economic independence.'[29] Most

Elizabethan youths and maidens were in their mid or late twenties by the time they entered Hymen's bands.[30] When Touchstone quips that 'the forehead of a married man [is] more honourable than the bare brow of a bachelor' (III.iii.53–5), he is giving a sarcastic twist to a fundamental mark of status. And when, late in his pseudo-mock-courtship of Ganymede, Orlando remarks ruefully that he 'can live no longer by thinking' (V.ii.50), he is venting the constrained libido of Elizabethan youth. One of the critical facts about the Elizabethan life cycle – one not noted in Jaques's speech – was that a large and varied group of codes, customs, and institutions regulated 'a separation between physiological puberty and social puberty'.[31] 'Youth', then, was the Elizabethan age category separating the end of childhood from the beginning of adulthood. It was a social threshold whose transitional nature was manifested in shifts of residence, activity, sexual feeling and patriarchal authority.

The dialectic between Elizabethan dramatic form and social process is especially conspicuous in the triadic romance pattern of exile and return that underlies As You Like It. Here the characters' experience is a fictional analogue of both the theatrical and the social experiences of its audience. 'The circle of this forest' (V.iv.34) is equivalent to Shakespeare's Wooden O. When they enter the special space-time of the theatre, the playgoers have voluntarily and temporarily withdrawn from 'this working-day world' (I.iii.12) and put on 'a holiday humour' (IV.i.65–6). When they have been wooed to an atonement by the comedy, the Epilogue conducts them back across the threshold between the world of the theatre and the theatre of the world. The dramatic form of the characters' experience corresponds, then, not only to the theatrical experience of the play's audience but also to the social process of youth in the world that playwright, players, and playgoers share. In a playworld of romance, Orlando and Rosalind experience separation from childhood, journeying, posing and disguising, altered and confused relationships to parental figures, sexual ambiguity, and tension. The fiction provides projections for the past or ongoing youthful experiences of most of the people in Shakespeare's Elizabethan audience. The forest sojourn conducts Orlando and Rosalind from an initial situation of oppression and frustration to the threshold of interdependent new identities. In one sense, then, the whole process of romantic pastoral comedy – the movement into and out of Arden – is what Macfarlane calls 'a form of age ritual, a way of demarcating off age-boundaries by movement through space'. The characters' fictive experience is congruent with the ambiguous and therefore dangerous period of the Elizabethan life cycle that is betwixt and between physical puberty and social puberty.

Not only relationships between offspring and their genitors, or between youths and their elders, but any relationship between subordinate and superior males might take on an Oedipal character in a patriarchal society. Orlando is perceived as a troublemaker by Oliver and Frederick; his conflicts are with the men who hold power in his world, with its insecure and ineffectual villains. 'The old Duke is banished by his younger brother the new Duke' (I.i.99–100). Old Adam has served Orlando's family 'from seventeen years, till now almost fourscore' (II.iii.71), but under Oliver he must endure 'unregarded age in corners thrown' (1.42). It is precisely the elders abused by Frederick and Oliver who ally themselves to Orlando's oppressed youth.[32] Adam gives to Orlando the life savings that were to have been the 'foster-nurse' (II.iii.40) of his old age; he makes his 'young master' (1.2) his heir. The idealized relationship of Orlando and his old servant compensates for the loss or corruption of Orlando's affective ties to men of his own kin and class. But Adam's paternity is only a phase in the reconstitution of Orlando's social identity. In the process of revealing his lineage to the old Duke, Orlando exchanges the father-surrogate who was his own father's servant for the father-surrogate who was his own father's lord.

> If that you were the good Sir Rowland's son,
> As you have whisper'd faithfully you were,
> And as mine eye doth his effigies witness
> Most truly limn'd and living in your face,
> Be truly welcome hither. I am the duke
> That lov'd your father.
>
> (II.vii.194–9)

The living son replaces his dead father in the affections of their lord. The Duke, who has no natural son, assumes the role of Orlando's patron, his social father: 'Give me your hand / And let me all your fortunes understand' (ll.202–3). Orlando's previous paternal benefactor has been supplanted: Adam neither speaks nor is mentioned again.

The reunion of the de Boys brothers is blessed by 'the old Duke'; the circumstance which makes that reunion possible is Oliver's expulsion by 'the new Duke'. In Lodge's *Rosalynde*, the two kings are not kin. Shakespeare's departure from his immediate source unifies and intensifies the conflicts in the family and the polity. The old Duke who adopts Orlando in the forest has been disinherited by his own younger brother in the court; Frederick has forcibly made himself his brother's heir. In the course of the play, fratricide is attempted, averted, and repudiated in each sibling relationship. Tensions in the nuclear family and in the body politic are miraculously assuaged within the forest. The Duke addresses his first words to his 'co-mates and brothers in exile' (II.i.1). The courtly decorum of hierarchy and deference may be relaxed in the forest, but it has not been abrogated; the Duke's 'brothers in exile' remain courtiers and servants attendant upon his grace. An atmosphere of charitable community has been created among those who have temporarily lost or abandoned their normal social context; the sources of conflict inherent in the social order are by no means genuinely dissolved in the forest, but rather are translated into a quiet and sweet style. In the forest, the old usurped Duke is a co-mate and brother to his loyal subjects and a benevolent father to Orlando. The comedy establishes *brotherhood* as an ideal of social as well as sibling male relationships; at the same time, it reaffirms a positive, nurturing image of *fatherhood*. And because family and society are a synecdoche, the comedy can also work to mediate the ideological contradiction between spiritual fraternity and political patriarchy, between social communion and social hierarchy.[33]

Like Richard of Gloucester, Claudius, Edmund, and Antonio, Frederick is a discontented younger brother whom Shakespeare makes the malevolent agent of his plot. Frederick generates action in *As You Like It* by banishing successively his elder brother, his niece, and his subject. Like his fellow villains, Frederick is the effective agent of a dramatic resolution which he himself does not intend; the tyrant's perverted will subserves the comic dramatist's providential irony. Frederick enforces the fraternal bond between Orlando and Oliver by holding Oliver responsible for Orlando on peril of his inheritance, forcing Oliver out to apprehend his brother. By placing Oliver in a social limbo akin to that suffered by Orlando, Frederick unwittingly creates the circumstances that lead to the brothers' reunion:

DUKE F.   Thy lands and all things that thou dost call thine,
          Worth seizure, do we seize into our hands,
          Till thou canst quit thee by thy brother's mouth
          Of what we think against thee.
OLI.   O that your Highness knew my heart in this!
          I never lov'd my brother in my life.
DUKE F.   More villain thou.

                             (III.i.9–15)

Oliver has abused the letter and the spirit of Sir Rowland's will: 'It was ... charged my brother on his blessing to breed me well' (I.i.3–4). Frederick is Oliver's nemesis.

In the exchange I have just quoted, Frederick's attitude toward Oliver is one of *moral* as well as political superiority. His judgement of Oliver's villainy is sufficiently ironic to give us pause. Is the usurper in Frederick projecting onto Oliver his guilt for his own unbrotherliness? Or is the younger brother in him identifying with Orlando's domestic situation? In seizing Oliver's lands and all things that he calls his until Oliver's (younger) brother can absolve him, Frederick parodies his own earlier usurpation of his own elder brother. Frederick's initial seizure takes place before the play begins; its circumstances are never disclosed. We do better to observe Frederick's dramatic function than to search for his unconscious motives. Frederick actualizes the destructive consequences of younger brothers' deprivation and discontent, in the family and in society at large. The first scenes demonstrate that such a threat exists within Orlando himself. The threat is neutralized as soon as Orlando enters the good old Duke's comforting forest home; there his needs are immediately and bountifully gratified:

DUKE SEN. What would you have? Your gentleness shall force,
           More than your force move us to gentleness.
ORL.   I almost die for food, and let me have it.
DUKE SEN. Sit down and feed, and welcome to our table.
ORL.   Speak you so gently? Pardon me, I pray you.
           I thought that all things had been savage here,
           . . .
           Let gentleness my strong enforcement be;
           In the which hope, I blush, and hide my sword.
                                        (II.vii.102–7, 118–19)

What is latent and potential within Orlando is displaced onto Frederick and realized in his violence and insecurity, his usurpation and tyranny.

Frederick sustains the role of villain until he too comes to Arden:

Duke Frederick hearing how that every day
Men of great worth resorted to this forest,
Address'd a mighty power, which were on foot
In his own conduct, purposely to take
His brother here, and put him to the sword.
And to the skirts of this wild wood he came,
Where, meeting with an old religious man,
After some question with him, was converted
Both from his enterprise and from the world,
His crown bequeathing to his banish'd brother
And all their lands restor'd to them again
That were with him exil'd.
                                        (V.iv.153–64)

Like Orlando, Frederick finds a loving father in the forest. And his conversion is the efficient cause of Orlando's elevation. In the denouement of Lodge's *Rosalynde*, the reunited brothers, Rosader and Saladyne, join the forces of the exiled King Gerismond; the army of the usurping King Torismond is defeated, and he is killed in the action. With striking formal and thematic economy, Shakespeare realizes his change of plot as a change *within* a character; he gets rid of Frederick not by killing him off but by morally transforming him. Frederick gives all his worldly goods to his natural brother and goes off to claim his spiritual inheritance from a heavenly father.

The reunion of the de Boys brothers is narrated retrospectively by a reborn Oliver, in the alien style of an allegorical dream romance:

> ... pacing through the forest,
> Chewing the food of sweet and bitter fancy,
> Lo what befell! He threw his eye aside,
> And mark what object did present itself.
> Under an old oak, whose boughs were moss'd with age
> And high top bald with dry antiquity,
> A wretched ragged man, o'ergrown with hair,
> Lay sleeping on his back.
>
> (IV.iii.100–107)

These images of infirm age and impotence, of regression to wildness and ruin through neglect, form a richly suggestive emblem. Expounded in the context of the present argument, the emblem represents the precarious condition into which fratricidal feeling provoked by primogeniture has brought these brothers and their house: 'Such a fever hectic hath custome brought in and inured among fathers, and such fond desire they have to leave a great shewe of the *stock* of their house, though the *branches* be *withered*, that ... my elder brother forsooth must be my master'.[34] Orlando, whose 'having in beard is a younger brother's revenue' (III.ii.367–8), confronts a hairy man asleep amidst icons of age and antiquity. The description suggests that, in confronting 'his brother, his elder brother' (IV.iii.120), young Orlando is confronting a personification of his patriline and of the patriarchal order itself. The brothers find each other under an *arbor consanguinitatis*, at the de Boys 'family tree'.[35]

Agnes Latham suggests that the snake and the lioness which menace Oliver are metaphors for his own animosities: as the snake 'slides away, Oliver's envy melts, and his wrath goes with the lion'.[36] The text suggests that it is Orlando who undergoes such an allegorical purgation. When it sees Orlando, the snake slips under the bush where the lioness couches.

> OLI.   This seen, Orlando did approach the man,
>   And found it was his brother, his elder brother.
>   . . .
> ROS.   But to Orlando. Did he leave him there,
>   Food to the suck'd and hungry lioness?
> OLI.   Twice did he turn his back, and purpos'd so.
>   But kindness, nobler ever than revenge,
>   And nature, stronger than his just occasion,
>   Made him give battle to the lioness,

> Who quickly fell before him; in which hurtling
> From miserable slumber I awak'd.
>
> (IV.iii.119–20, 125–32)

In killing the lioness which threatens to kill Oliver, Orlando kills the impediment to atonement within himself. Oliver's narrative implies a causal relationship between Orlando's act of self-mastery and purgation and Oliver's own 'awakening'. When the brothers have been 'kindly bath'd' (IV.iii.140) in mutual tears, Oliver's 'conversion' (l.136) and his atonement with Orlando are consecrated by the Duke who loved their father. In the play's first words, Orlando remembered that Oliver had been charged, on his blessing, to breed him well. The Duke's bequest and injunction reformulate Sir Rowland's last will and testament:

> he led me to the gentle Duke,
> Who gave me fresh array and entertainment
> Committing me unto my brother's love.
>
> (IV.iii.142–4)

What has taken place offstage is a conversion of the crucial event that precipitated the fraternal conflict, the event 'remembered' in the very first words of the play.

At this point in the atonement, paternity and fraternity are reaffirmed as spiritual bonds rather than as bonds of blood and property. Brotherhood can now come to mean friendship freed from the material conflicts of kinship. Some remarks by Julian Pitt-Rivers illuminate the point:

> Kinship's nature ... is not free of jural considerations. Rights and duties are distributed differentially to kinsmen because kinship is a system, not a network of dyadic ties like friendship. Status within it is ascribed by birth.... Rules of succession and inheritance are required to order that which cannot be left to the manifestations of brotherly love.... A revealing assertion echoes through the literature on ritual kinship: 'Blood-brothers are like brothers,' it is said, then comes, 'in fact they are closer than real brothers.' The implication is troubling, for it would appear that true fraternity is found only between those who are not real brothers. Amity does not everywhere enjoin the same open-ended generosity, least of all between kinsmen, who quarrel only too often, in contrast to ritual kinsmen, who are bound by sacred duty not to do so.[37]

Before he goes to Arden, Orlando feels he has no alternative but to subject himself 'to the malice/Of a diverted blood and bloody brother' (II.iii.36–7). Shakespeare's task is to bring the relationship of Orlando and Oliver under the auspices of Hymen:

> Then is there mirth in heaven,

When earthly things made even
Atone together.

(V.iv.107–9)

In Touchstone's terms (V.iv.101–2), hostile siblings are brought to shake hands and swear their brotherhood by the virtue of comedy's If. The spiritual principle of 'brotherly love' is reconciled to the jural principle of primogeniture; 'real brothers' are made 'blood brothers' – as the napkin borne by Oliver so graphically testifies.[38]

Some commentators have seen the outlines of a Christian allegory of redemption in the play. They point to the presence of a character named Adam; the Duke's disquisition on 'the penalty of Adam'; the iconography of the serpent, the tree, and the *vetus homo*; the heroic virtue of Orlando; the comic rite of atonement.[39] Perhaps we do better to think of Shakespeare as creating resonances between the situations in his play and the religious archetypes at the foundations of his culture; as invoking what Rosalie Colie, writing of *King Lear*, calls 'Biblical echo'. What echoes deeply through the scenes I have discussed is the fourth chapter of Genesis, the story of Cain and Abel and what another of Shakespeare's fratricides calls 'the primal eldest curse .../A brother's murther' (*Hamlet*, III.iii.37–8). Adam's two sons made offerings to the Lord: 'and the Lord had respect unto Habel, and to his offering',

> But unto Kain and to his offring he had no regarde: wherefore Kain was exceding wroth, & his countenance fel downe.
>
> Then the Lord said unto Kain, Why art thou wroth? and why is thy countenence cast downe?
>
> If thou do wel, shalt thou not be accepted? and if thou doest not well, sinne lieth at the dore: also unto thee his desire *shal be subject*, and thou shalt rule over him.
>
> Then Kain spake to Habel his brother. And when they were in the field, Kain rose up against Habel his brother, and slewe him.
>
> Then the Lord said unto Kain, Where is Habel thy brother? Who answered, I canot tel. Am I my brothers keper?
>
> Againe he said, What hast thou done? the voyce of thy brothers blood cryeth unto me from the grounde.
>
> Now therefore thou art cursed from the earth, which hath opened her mouth to receive thy brothers blood from thine hand.[40]

The Geneva Bible glosses the italicized phrase in the seventh verse as a reference to the foundations of primogeniture: 'The dignitie of ye first borne is given to Kain over Habel'.

The wrath of Cain echoes in Oliver's fratricidal musings at the end of the first scene: 'I hope I shall see an end of him; for my soul – yet I know not why – hates nothing more than he. Yet he's gentle, never schooled and

yet learned, full of noble device, of all sorts enchantingly beloved, and
indeed so much in the heart of the world, and especially of my own people,
that I am altogether misprised. But it shall not be so long' (I.i.162–9).
Oliver feels humanly rather than divinely misprised; and it is his tyrannical
secular lord to whom he declares that he is not his brother's keeper.
Orlando sheds his own blood for his elder brother, which becomes the sign
of Oliver's conversion rather than the mark of his fratricidal guilt. Oliver
finds acceptance in the old Duke, who commits him to his brother's love.
Shakespeare is creating a resonance between his romantic fiction and
Biblical history, between the dramatic process of assuaging family conflict
in the atonements of comedy and the exegetical process of redeeming the
primal fratricide of Genesis in the spiritual fraternity of the Gospel:

> For brethren, ye have bene called unto libertie: onely use not *your* libertie
> as an occasion unto the flesh, but by love serve one another.
> For all the Law is fulfilled in one worde, which is this, Thou shalt love
> thy neighbour as thy self.
> If ye byte & devoure one another, take hede lest ye be consumed one
> of another.
> Then I say, walke in the Spirit, and ye shal not fulfil the lustes of the
> flesh.[41]
>
> (Galatians v. 13–16)

The rivalry or conflict between elder and younger brothers is a
prominent motif in the fictions of cultures throughout the world. Its typical
plot has been described as 'the disadvantaged younger sibling or orphan
child besting an unjust elder and gaining great fortune through the timely
intercession of a benevolent supernatural being'.[42] Cultural fictions of the
triumphs of younger siblings offer psychological compensation for the
social fact of the deprivation of younger siblings. Such fictions are
symbolic mediations of discrepancies between the social categories of
status and the claims of individual merit, in which the defeat and
supplanting of the elder sibling by the younger reconciles ability with
status: 'The younger outwits, displaces, and becomes the elder; the senior
position comes to be associated with superior ability'.[43]

The folk-tale scenario of sibling rivalry is clear in the fourteenth-century
tale of *Gamelyn*, to which Lodge's Rosader plot and Shakespeare's
Orlando plot are indebted.[44] The disinherited Gamelyn and his outlaw
cohorts sentence Gamelyn's eldest brother to death by hanging. Their
topsy-turvy actions are sanctioned and absorbed by the social order: the
King pardons Gamelyn, restores his inheritance, and makes him Chief
Justice. In *As You Like It*, Shakespeare's characters emphasize the
discrepancy between 'the gifts of the world' and 'the lineaments of Nature'

(I.ii.40–41), between social place and personal merit. The comedy's task is to 'mock the good hussif Fortune from her wheel, that her gifts may henceforth be bestowed equally' (I.ii.30–32). Shakespeare transcends *Gamelyn* and its folktale paradigm in a wholehearted concern not merely to eliminate social contradictions, but also to redeem and reconcile human beings.[45] Oliver is not defeated, eliminated, supplanted; he is converted, reintegrated, confirmed. In the subplot of *King Lear*, the unbrotherly struggle for mastery and possession is resolved by fratricide; the comic resolution of *As You Like It* depends instead upon an expansion of opportunities for mastery and possession.

In Lodge's *Rosalynde*, the crude heroic theme of *Gamelyn* is already fused with the elegant love theme of Renaissance pastorals. In constructing a romantic comedy of familial and sexual tension resolved in brotherhood and marriage, Shakespeare gives new complexity and cohesiveness to his narrative source. The struggle of elder and younger brothers is not simply duplicated; it is inverted. In the younger generation, the elder brother abuses the younger; in the older generation, the younger abuses the elder. The range of experience and affect is thereby enlarged, and the protest against primogeniture is firmly balanced by its reaffirmation. Myth, Scripture, and Shakespearean drama record 'the bond crack'd betwixt son and father' (*King Lear*, I.ii.113–14). Hostilities between elder and younger brothers and between fathers and sons are homologous: 'Yea, and the brother shal deliver the brother to death, and the father the sonne, and the children shal rise against their parents, and shal cause them to dye' (Mark xiii.14). Because in *As You Like It* the doubling and inversion of fraternal conflict links generations, the relationship of brother and brother can be linked to the relationship of father and son. In the process of atonement, the two families and two generations of men are doubly and symmetrically bound: the younger brother weds the daughter of the elder brother, and the elder brother weds the daughter of the younger brother. They create the figure of *chiasmus*. Whatever vicarious benefit *As You Like It* brings to younger brothers and to youths, it is not achieved by perverting or destroying the bonds between siblings and between generations, but by transforming and renewing them – *through marriage*.

In Arden, Orlando divides his time between courting Rosalind (who is played by Ganymede, who is played by Rosalind) and courting the old Duke who is Rosalind's father. Celia teases Rosalind about the sincerity of Orlando's passion, the truth of his feigning, by reminding her of his divided loyalties: 'He attends here in the forest on the Duke your father' (III.iv.29–30). Rosalind, who clearly resents that she must share Orlando's attentions with her father, responds: 'I met the Duke yesterday and had much question with him. He asked me of what parentage I was: I told him of as good as he, so he laughed and let me go. But what talk we of fathers, when there is such a man as Orlando?' (III.iv.31–5). Celia has already transferred her loyalties from her father to Rosalind; Rosalind is transferring hers from her father and from Celia to Orlando. But she withholds her identity from her lover in order to test and to taunt him. In the forest, while Orlando guilelessly improves his place in the patriarchal order, Rosalind wittily asserts her independence of it. Rosalind avoids her father's recognition and establishes her own household within the forest; Orlando desires the Duke's recognition and gladly serves him in his forest-court.

It is only after he has secured a place within the old Duke's benign all-male community that Orlando begins to play the lover and the poet: 'Run, run Orlando, carve on every tree/The fair, the chaste, and unexpressive she' (III.ii.9–10):

> *But upon the fairest boughs,*
> *Or at every sentence end,*
> *Will I Rosalinda write,*
> *Teaching all that read to know*
> *The quintessence of every sprite*
> *Heaven would in little show.*
> *Therefore Heaven Nature charg'd*
> *That one body should be fill'd*
> *With all graces wide-enlarg'd.*
> *Nature presently distill'd*
> *Helen's cheek, but not her heart,*
> *Cleopatra's majesty,*
> *Atalanta's better part,*
> *Sad Lucretia's modesty.*
> *Thus Rosalind of many parts*
> *By heavenly synod was devis'd,*
> *Of many faces, eyes, and hearts,*
> *To have the touches dearest priz'd.*
> *Heaven would that she these gifts should have,*
> *And I to live and die her slave.*

(ll.132–51)

The Petrarchan lover 'writes' his mistress or 'carves' her in the image of his own desire, incorporating virtuous feminine stereotypes and scrupulously excluding what is sexually threatening. The lover masters his mistress by inscribing her within his own discourse; he worships a deity of his own making and under his control. When Rosalind-Ganymede confronts this 'fancy-monger' (III.ii.354–5) who 'haunts the forest ... deifying the name of Rosalind' (ll.350, 353–4), she puts a question to him: 'But are you so much in love as your rhymes speak?' (l.386). Rosalind and Touchstone interrogate and undermine self-deceiving amorous rhetoric with bawdy wordplay and relentless insistence upon the power and inconstancy of physical desire. All the love-talk in the play revolves around the issue of mastery in the shifting social relationship between the sexes: in courtship, maidens suspect the faithfulness of their suitors; in wedlock, husbands suspect the faithfulness of their wives. The poems of feigning lovers and the horns of cuckolded husbands are the complementary preoccupations of Arden's country copulatives.

Consider the crucially placed brief scene (IV.ii) which is barely more than a song inserted between the betrothal scene of Orlando and Rosalind-Ganymede and the scene in which Oliver comes to Rosalind bearing the bloody napkin. In IV.i, Rosalind mocks her tardy lover with talk of an emblematic snail: 'He brings his destiny with him. . . . Horns – which such as you fain to be beholding to your wives for' (ll.54–5, 57–8). Touchstone has already resigned himself to the snail's destiny with his own misogynistic logic: 'As horns are odious, they are necessary. It is said, many a man knows no end of his goods. Right. Many a man has good horns and knows no end of them. Well, that is the dowry of his wife, 'tis none of his own getting' (III.iii.45–9). Now, in IV.ii, Jaques transforms Rosalind's jibes into ironic male self-mockery: 'He that killed the deer' is to have the horns set on his head 'for a branch of victory' (ll.1, 5). Jaques calls for a song – ' 'Tis no matter how it be in tune, so it makes noise enough' (ll.8–9). The rowdy horn song is a kind of charivari or 'rough music', traditionally the form of ridicule to which cuckolds and others who offended the community's moral standards were subjected.[46] This charivari, however, is also a song of consolation and good fellowship, for not only the present 'victor' but all his companions 'shall bear this burden' (ll.12–13).

> *Take thou no scorn to wear the horn,*
> *It was a crest ere thou wast born.*
> *Thy father's father wore it,*
> *And thy father bore it.*
> *The horn, the horn, the lusty horn,*
> *Is not a thing to laugh to scorn.*

(ll.14–19)

The play's concern with patriarchal lineage and the hallmarks of gentility is here transformed into an heraldic celebration of the horn – instrument of male potency and male degradation – which marks all men as kinsmen. Thus, although cuckoldry implies the uncertainty of paternity, the song celebrates the paradox that it is precisely the common destiny they share with the snail that binds men together – father to son, brother to brother. Through the metaphor of hunting (with its wordplays on 'deer' and 'horns') and the medium of song, the threat that the power of insubordinate women poses to the authority of men is transformed into an occasion for affirming and celebrating patriarchy and fraternity.

After the mock-marriage (IV.i) in which they have indeed plighted their troth, Rosalind-Ganymede exuberantly teases Orlando about the shrewishness and promiscuity he can expect from his wife. Naively romantic Orlando abruptly leaves his threatening Rosalind in order 'to attend the Duke at dinner' (IV.i.170). On his way from his cruel mistress to his kind patron, Orlando encounters his own brother. It is hardly insignificant that Shakespeare changes the details of the fraternal recognition scene to include an aspect of sexual differentiation wholly absent from Lodge's romance. He adds the snake which wreathes itself around Oliver's neck; and he makes it into an insidious female, 'who with her head, nimble in threats, approach'd/The opening of his mouth' (IV.iii.109–10). Furthermore, he changes Lodge's lion into a lioness whose nurturing and aggressive aspects are strongly and ambivalently stressed: 'a lioness, with udders all drawn dry' (l.114); 'the suck'd and hungry lioness' (l.126). Orlando has retreated in the face of Rosalind's verbal aggressiveness. He has wandered through the forest, 'chewing the food of sweet and bitter fancy' (l.101), to seek the paternal figure who has nurtured him. Instead, he has found Oliver in a dangerously passive condition, threatened by a double source of oral aggression.

Oliver's fantastic narrative suggests a transformation of the sexual conflict initiated by Rosalind when she teases Orlando in IV.i. Rosalind and the lioness are coyly linked in the exchange between the lovers at their next meeting:

> ROS. O my dear Orlando, how it grieves me to see thee wear thy heart in a scarf!
> ORL. It is my arm.
> ROS. I thought thy heart had been wounded with the claws of a lion.
> ORL. Wounded it is, but with the eyes of a lady.
>
> (V.ii.19–23)

The chain which Rosalind bestows upon Orlando at their first meeting ('Wear this for me' [I.ii.236]) is the mark by which Celia identifies him in the forest ('And a chain, that you once wore, about his neck' [III.ii.178]). The 'green and gilded snake' (IV.iii.108) encircling Oliver's neck is a demonic parody of the emblematic stage property worn by his brother throughout the play. The gynephobic response to Rosalind is split into the erotic serpent and the maternal lioness, while Orlando is split into his victimized brother and his heroic self. Orlando's mastery of the lioness ('Who quickly fell before him' [IV.iii.131]) is, then, a symbolic mastery of Rosalind's challenge to Orlando. But it is also a triumph of fraternal 'kindness' (l.128) over the fratricidal impulse. Relationships between elder and younger brothers and between fathers and sons are purified by what the text suggests is a kind of matricide, a triumph of men over female powers. Thus the killing of the lioness may also symbolize a repudiation of the consanguinity of Orlando and Oliver. If this powerful female – the carnal source of siblings – is destroyed, both fraternity and paternity can be reconceived as male relationships unmediated by woman, relationships of the spirit rather than of the flesh. Orlando's heroic act, distanced and framed in an allegorical narrative, condenses aspects of both the romantic plot and the sibling plot. And these plots are themselves the complementary aspects of a single social and dramatic process.

Before Orlando is formally married to Rosalind at the end of the play, he has reaffirmed his fraternal and filial bonds in communion with other men. Orlando's rescue of Oliver from the she-snake and the lioness frees the brothers' capacity to give and to receive love. Now Oliver can 'fall in love' with Celia; and now Orlando 'can live no longer by thinking' (V.ii.50) about Rosalind. Oliver asks his younger brother's consent to marry, and resigns to him his birthright: 'My father's house and all the revenue that was old Sir Rowland's will I estate upon you, and here live and die a shepherd' (ll.10–12).[47] Orlando agrees with understandable alacrity: 'You have my consent. Let your wedding be tomorrow (ll.13–14). Marriage, the social institution at the heart of comedy, serves to ease or eliminate fraternal strife. And fraternity, in turn, serves as a defense against the threat men feel from women.

Rosalind-as-Ganymede and Ganymede-as-Rosalind – the woman out of place – exerts an informal organizing and controlling power over affairs in the forest. But this power lapses when she relinquishes her male disguise and formally acknowledges her normal status as daughter and wife: 'I'll have no father, if you be not he. / I'll have no husband, if you be not he' (V.iv.121–2). In a ritual gesture of surrender, she assumes the passive role of mediatrix between the Duke and Orlando:

[*To the Duke*] To you I give myself, for I am yours.
[*To Orl.*] To you I give myself, for I am yours.

(V.iv.115–16)

The Duke's paternal bond to Orlando is not established through the natural fertility of a mother but through the supernatural virginity of a daughter: 'Good Duke receive thy daughter/Hymen from heaven brought her' (V.iv.110–11). The play is quite persistent in creating strategies for subordinating the flesh to the spirit, and female powers to male controls. Hymen's marriage rite gives social sanction to the lovers' mutual desire. But the atonement of man and woman also implies the social subordination of wife to husband. Rosalind's exhilarating mastery of herself and others has been a compensatory 'holiday humour', a temporary, inversionary rite of misrule, whose context is a transfer of authority, property, and title from the Duke to his prospective male heir. From the perspective of the present argument, the romantic love plot serves more than its own ends: it is also the means by which other actions are transformed and resolved. In his unions with the Duke and with Rosalind, Orlando's social elevation is confirmed. Such a perspective does not deny the comedy its festive magnanimity, it merely reaffirms that Shakespearean drama registers the form and pressure of Elizabethan experience. If *As You Like It* is a vehicle for Rosalind's exuberance, it is also a structure for her containment.[48]

Jaques de Boys, 'the second son of old Sir Rowland' (V.iv.151), enters suddenly at the end of the play. This Shakespearean whimsy fits logically into the play's comic process. As the narrator of Frederick's strange eventful history, Jaques brings the miraculous news that resolves the conflict between his own brothers as well as the conflict between the brother-dukes. As Rosalind mediates the affinity of father and son, so Jaques – a brother, rather than a mother – mediates the kinship of eldest and youngest brothers; he is, in effect, the incarnate middle term between Oliver and Orlando. The Duke welcomes him:

> Thou offer'st fairly to thy brothers' wedding;
> To one his lands withheld, and to the other
> A land itself at large, a potent dukedom.

> (V.iv.166–8)

Jaques's gift celebrates the wedding of his brothers to their wives and to each other. Solutions to the play's initial conflicts are worked out between brother and brother, father and son – among men. Primogeniture is reaffirmed in public and private domains: the Duke, newly restored to his own authority and possessions, now restores the de Boys patrimony to Oliver. The aspirations and deserts of the youngest brother are rewarded when the Duke acknowledges Orlando as his own heir, the successor to property, power, and title that far exceed Oliver's birthright. The eldest brother regains the authority due him by primogeniture at the same time that the youngest brother is freed from subordination to his sibling and validated in his claim to the perquisites of gentility.

With his patrimony restored and his marriage effected, Oliver legitimately assumes the place of a patriarch and emerges into full social adulthood; he is now worthy to be the son and heir of Sir Rowland de Boys. Orlando, on the other hand, has proved himself worthy to become son and heir to the Duke. Thomas Wilson, another Elizabethan younger brother, made the bitter misfortune of primogeniture the spur to personal achievement: 'This I must confess doth us good someways, for it makes us industrious to apply ourselves to letters or to armes, whereby many time we become my master elder brothers' masters, or at least their betters in honour and reputacion.'[49] Unlike Thomas Wilson, Shakespeare's Orlando is spectacularly successful, and his success is won more by spontaneous virtue than by industry. But like Wilson's, Orlando's accomplishments are those of a gentleman and a courtier. Unlike most Elizabethan younger sons, Orlando is not forced to descend to commerce or to labour to make his way in the world. He succeeds by applying himself to the otiose courtship of his mistress and his prince. Although the perfection of his social identity is deferred during the Duke's lifetime, Orlando's new filial subordination is eminently beneficent. It grants him by affinity what he has been denied by kinship: the social advancement and sexual fulfilment of which youths and younger sons were so frequently deprived. The de Boys brothers atone together when the eldest replaces a father and the youngest recovers a father.

Social and dramatic decorum require that, 'to work a comedy kindly, grave old men should instruct, young men should show the imperfections of youth.'[50] London's city fathers, however, were forever accusing the theatres and the plays of corrupting rather than instructing youth: 'We verely think plays and theatres to be the cheif cause ... of ... disorder & lewd demeanours which appear of late in young people of all degrees.'[51] Shakespeare's play neither preaches to youths nor incites them to riot. In the world of its Elizabethan audience, the form of Orlando's experience may indeed have functioned as a collective compensation, a projection for the wish-fulfilment fantasies of younger brothers, youths, and all who felt themselves deprived by their fathers or their fortunes. But Orlando's mastery of adversity could also provide support and encouragement to the ambitious individuals who identified with his plight. The play may have fostered strength and perseverance as much as it facilitated pacification and escape. For the large number of youths in Shakespeare's audience – first-born and younger siblings, gentle and base – the performance may have been analogous to a rite of passage, helping to ease their dangerous and prolonged journey from subordination to identity, their difficult transition from the child's part to the adult's.

My subject has been the complex interrelationship of brothers, fathers, and sons in As You Like It. But I have suggested that the play's concern with relationships among men is only artificially separable from its concern with relationships between men and women. The androgynous Rosalind – boy actor and princess – addresses Shakespeare's heterosexual audience in an epilogue: 'My way is to conjure you, and I'll begin with the women. I charge you, O women, for the love you bear to men, to like as much of this play as please you. And I charge you, O men, for the love you bear to women – as I perceive by your simpering none of you hates them – that between you and the women the play may please' (V.iv.208–14). Through the subtle and flexible strategies of drama – in puns, jokes, games, disguises, songs, poems, fantasies – *As You Like It* expresses, contains, and discharges a measure of the strife between the men and the women. Shakespeare's comedy manipulates the differential social relationships between the sexes, between brothers, between father and son, master and servant, lord and subject. It is by the conjurer's art that Shakespeare manages to reconcile the social imperatives of hierarchy and difference with the festive urges toward levelling and atonement. The intense and ambivalent personal bonds upon which the play is focused – bonds between brothers and between lovers – affect each other reciprocally and become the means of each other's resolution. And as the actions within the play are dialectically related to each other, so the world of Shakespeare's characters is dialectically related to the world of his audience. *As You Like It* is both a theatrical *reflection* of social conflict and a theatrical *source* of social conciliation.

Notes

*A much abbreviated version of this study was presented at the 1979 meeting of the Philological Association of the Pacific Coast (UCLA, 10 November 1979). My work on *As You Like It* has been stimulated and improved by the interest and criticism of Page du Bois, Phyllis Gorfain, and Ronald Martinez.

1. Leo Salingar, *Shakespeare and the Traditions of Comedy* (Cambridge: Cambridge Univ. Press, 1974), pp. 297–8. On the *topos*, see John Shaw, 'Fortune and Nature in *As You Like It*', *Shakespeare Quarterly*, 6 (1955), 45–50; *A New Variorum Edition of Shakespeare: 'As You Like It'*, ed. Richard Knowles, with Evelyn Joseph Mattern (New York: MLA, 1977), pp. 533–7.

2. *As You Like It* is quoted from the new Arden edition, ed. Agnes Latham (London: Methuen, 1975); all other plays are quoted from *The Riverside Shakespeare*, gen. ed. G. Blakemore Evans (Boston: Houghton Mifflin, 1974).

3. Harold Jenkins, '*As You Like It*', *Shakespeare Survey*, 8 (1955), 40–51; quotation from p. 41. There is an exception to this predominant view in Thomas McFarland, *Shakespeare's Pastoral Comedy* (Chapel Hill: Univ. of North Carolina Press, 1972), pp. 98–103.

4. The paradigm for transition rites – the triadic movement from separation through marginality to reincorporation – was formulated in Arnold Van Gennep's classic, *The Rites of Passage* (1909), trans. M.B. Vizedom and G.L. Caffee (Chicago: Univ. of Chicago Press, 1960). Among more recent discussions, see *Essays on the Ritual of Social Relations*, ed. Max Gluckman (Manchester: Manchester Univ. Press, 1962); Victor Turner, *Dramas, Fields, and Metaphors* (Ithaca: Cornell Univ. Press, 1974); and Edmund Leach, *Culture and Communication* (Cambridge: Cambridge Univ. Press, 1976). For further discussion of analogies to transition rites in Shakespearean drama and Elizabethan theatre, see Louis Adrian Montrose, 'The Purpose of Playing: Reflections on a Shakespearean Anthropology', *Helios*, New Series, 7 (Winter 1980), 51–74.

5. Jack Goody, 'Introduction', in *Family and Inheritance: Rural Society in Western Europe, 1200–1800*, ed. Jack Goody, Joan Thirsk, and E.P. Thompson (Cambridge: Cambridge Univ. Press, 1976), pp. 1,3.

6. Lawrence Stone, *The Family, Sex and Marriage in England 1500–1800* (New York: Harper & Row, 1977), pp. 87–8.

7. Joan Thirsk, 'Younger Sons in the Seventeenth Century', *History* (London), 54 (1969), 358–77; quotation from p. 359. Thirsk cites *As You Like It*, I.i, as part of that literature.

8. Ed. Edward Arber (1869; rpt., New York: AMS Press, 1966), pp. 29–30. I have modernized obsolete typographical conventions in quotations from this and other Renaissance texts.

9. Thomas Wilson, *The State of England Anno Dom. 1600*, ed. F.J. Fisher, Camden Miscellany, 16 (London: Camden Society, 1936), pp. 1–43; quotation from pp. 23–4.

10. Rpt. in *Social Change and Revolution in England 1540–1640*, ed. Lawrence Stone (New York: Barnes & Noble, 1965), p. 120.

11. Thirsk, 'Younger Sons', p. 368.

12. An exception is John W. Draper, 'Orlando, the Younger Brother', *Philological Quarterly*, 13 (1934), 72–7.

13. See Alfred Harbage, *Shakespeare's Audience* (New York: Columbia Univ. Press, 1941), pp. 53–91; quotation from p. 80.

14. See Thirsk, 'Younger Sons', pp. 363, 366–8.

15. Ibid., p. 360.

16. *New Variorum* ed. of *AYL*, p. 382; future page references will be to this text of *Rosalynde*, which follows the First Quarto (1590). On the relationship of *AYL* to *Rosalynde*, see *Narrative and Dramatic Sources of Shakespeare*, ed. Geoffrey Bullough (London: Routledge & Kegan Paul, 1958), II, 143–57; Marco Mincoff, 'What Shakespeare Did to *Rosalynde*', *Shakespeare Jahrbuch*, 96 (1960), 78–89; *New Variorum* ed. of *As You Like It*, pp. 475–83.

17. See Joan Thirsk, 'The European Debate on Customs of Inheritance, 1500–1700', in *Family and Inheritance*, pp. 177–91: 'The inheritance customs of classes below the gentry did not give rise to controversy: practices were as varied as the circumstances of families. Primogeniture in the original sense of advancing the eldest son, but nevertheless providing for the others, was common, perhaps the commonest custom among yeoman and below, but it did not exercise a tyranny. Among the nobility primogeniture was most common.... In general it did not cause excessive hardship to younger sons because the nobility had the means to provide adequately for all' (p. 186).

18. Stone, *Family, Sex and Marriage*, p. 218. *Contra* Stone, there is evidence to suggest that the nuclear family was in fact the pervasive and traditional pattern in English society outside the aristocracy; that the English family at this period was profoundly patriarchal remains, however, undisputed. The assumptions and conclusions of Stone's massive study have not found complete acceptance among his colleagues. See the important review essays on Stone's book by Christopher Hill, in *The Economic History Review*, 2nd. Ser., 31 (1978), 450–63; by Alan Macfarlane, in *History and Theory*, 18 (1979), 103–26; and by Richard T. Vann, in *The Journal of Family History*, 4 (1979), 308–14.

19. *Patriarchalism in Political Thought* (New York: Basic Books, 1975), pp. 65–6.

20. Orlando's predicament may be compared to Hamlet's: for each of these young Elizabethan heroes, the process of becoming himself involves a process of 'remembering' the father for whom he is named. But the generational passage of each is blocked by a 'usurper' of his spiritual inheritance, who mediates ambiguously between the father and the son: Oliver is a brother–father to Orlando; Claudius, himself the old King's younger brother, is an uncle–father to Hamlet.

21. Thus, I am not suggesting that the text and action of *As You Like It* displace a core fantasy about mother–son incest. My perspective is socio-anthropological rather than psychoanalytic: allusions to incest amplify the confusion between older and younger generations, kin and non-kin; they exemplify the tension inherent in the power relations between male generations in a patriarchal society. Perhaps one reason for Shakespeare's fascination with kingship as a dramatic subject is that it provides a paradigm for patriarchy and succession. Prince Hal's destiny is to replace his father as King Henry; his father's death is the legal condition for the creation of his own identity. A major aspect of comic form in the *Henry IV* plays is Hal's process of projecting and mastering his patricidal impulse until he comes into his kingdom legitimately.

22. Stone, *Family, Sex and Marriage*, p. 108.

23. Quoted in Keith Thomas, 'Age and Authority in Early Modern England', *Proceedings of the British Academy*, 62 (1976), 205–48; quotation from p. 217.

24. Stone, *Family, Sex and Marriage*, p. 27.

25. See Stone, *Family, Sex and Marriage*, p. 72; Thomas, 'Age and Authority', p. 212; Harbage, *Shakespeare's Audience*, p. 79.

26. Thomas, 'Age and Authority', p. 214.

27. Alan Macfarlane, *The Family Life of Ralph Josselin, A Seventeenth-Century Clergyman: An Essay in Historical Anthropology* (Cambridge: Cambridge Univ. Press, 1970), Appendix B: 'Children and servants: the problem of adolescence', pp. 205, 210.

28. Thomas, 'Age and Authority', p. 216.

29. Stone, *Family, Sex and Marriage*, p. 226.

30. See Peter Laslett, *The World We Have Lost*, 2nd edn (New York: Charles Scribner's Sons, 1973), pp. 85–6; Stone, *Family, Sex and Marriage*, pp. 46–54; Thomas, 'Age and Authority', pp. 225–7.

31. Thomas, 'Age and Authority', p. 225.

32. In his learned and suggestive study, Thomas shows that youths were regarded with suspicion and were subordinated, while the very old – unless they had wealth – were regarded with scorn and were ignored. (*King Lear* records the consequences of an old man's self-divestment.) Thomas notes that the trend to exclude the young and the aged from 'full humanity' was 'already implicit in the plea made to an Elizabethan archdeacon's court to disregard the evidence of two witnesses. One was a youth of eighteen, the other was a man of eighty. Both, it was urged, lacked discretion. The one was too young; the other too old' (p. 248).

33. On pastoral form and social order in *As You Like It*, see Charles W. Hieatt, 'The Quality of Pastoral in *As You Like It*', *Genre*, 7 (1974), 164–82; Harold Toliver, *Pastoral Forms and Attitudes* (Berkeley: Univ. of California Press, 1971), pp. 100–114; Judy Z. Kronenfield, 'Social Rank and the Pastoral Ideals of *As You Like It*', *Shakespeare Quarterly*, 29 (1978), 333–48. For an interesting discussion of the interplay between patriarchal and fraternal models of social relations in the sixteenth century, see Mary Ann Clawson, 'Early Modern Fraternalism and the Patriarchal Family', *Feminist Studies*, 6 (1980), 368–91.

34. Wilson, *State of England, 1600*, p. 24; italics mine.

35. Orlando and Oliver are sons of Sir Rowland de Boys, whose surname is a play on 'woods' and 'boys'. The tree is a heraldic emblem for Orlando, as well as for Oliver: in Arden, Celia tells Rosalind that she 'found him under a tree like a dropped acorn. . . . There lay he stretched along like a wounded knight' (III.ii.230–31, 236–7); we find him carving Rosalind's name 'on every tree' (l.9). If my interpretation of the emblematic reunion scene seems fanciful, the fancy is decidedly Elizabethan. Unprecedented social mobility created an obsessive concern with marks of status: 'One of the most striking features of the age was a pride of ancestry which now reached new heights of fantasy and elaboration. . . . Genuine genealogy was cultivated by the older gentry to reassure themselves of their innate superiority over the upstarts: bogus genealogy was cultivated by the new gentry in an effort to clothe their social nakedness' (Lawrence Stone, *The Crisis of the Aristocracy 1558–1641* (Oxford: Clarendon Press, 1965), p. 23). In the passage on primogeniture I have quoted in my text, Thomas Wilson's arboreal metaphors have a naturalness in their context that suggests that such metaphors were an integral part of Elizabethan thought patterns. Stone notes that in the sixteenth century the lengthy genealogies of the 'upper landed classes, the country gentry and nobility', tended 'to pay only cursory attention to collateral branches, and are mainly concerned with tracing the male line backward in time. Similarly, the growing complexity of coats of arms recorded alliances in the male line of the heir by primogeniture of the nuclear family, not kin connections. . . . The family mausoleums of the period contain the remains of the male heirs of the nuclear family and their wives from generation to generation, but only rarely adult younger children or kin relatives. The rule of primogeniture is clearly reflected in the disposal of the bodies after death' (*Family, Sex and Marriage*, p. 135). Orlando is in danger of becoming merely a withered branch of the old 'de Boys' stock.

36. Latham, Arden edn of *As You Like It*, p. xliii.

37. See Julian Pitt-Rivers, 'The Kith and the Kin', in *The Character of Kinship*, ed. Jack Goody (Cambridge Univ. Press, 1973), pp. 89–105; quotation from p. 101.

38. The histories of brotherhood and sisterhood follow opposite directions in the play. We are introduced to Rosalind and Celia as first cousins 'whose loves / Are dearer than the

natural bond of sisters' (I.ii.265–6); since childhood, they have been 'coupled and inseparable' (I.iii.72). In the course of the play, they are uncoupled and separated from each other and from their girlhoods by the intervention of sexual desire and the new emotional and social demands of marriage. All four female characters in the play are maidens on the threshold of wedlock. The inverse relationship between brotherhood and sisterhood within the play and the conspicuous absence of matronly characters are reflections of the male and patriarchal bias of Elizabethan family and social structures.

39. See Richard Knowles, 'Myth and Type in *As You Like It'*, *ELH*, 33 (1966), 1–22; René E. Fortin, '"Tongues in Trees": Symbolic Patterns in *As You Like It'*, *Texas Studies in Literature and Language*, 14 (1973), 569–82.

40. Genesis iv.4–11, in *The Geneva Bible* (1560), facsimile ed. (Madison: Univ. of Wisconsin Press, 1969). Italics in the original. All further references to the Bible from this source.

41. 'The flesh lusteth against the Spirit' (Galatians v.17) is glossed in the Geneva Bible: 'That is, the natural man striveth against ye Spirit of regeneration.' The spiritually regenerate Oliver marries the aptly named Celia; the socially regenerate Orlando marries a Rosalind brought 'from heaven' (V.iv.111) by Hymen.

42. Michael Jackson, 'Ambivalence and the Last-Born: Birth-order position in convention and myth', *Man*, New Series, 13 (1978), 341–61; quotation from p. 350. This anthropological essay, based on comparative ethnography of the Kuranko (Sierra Leone) and Maori (New Zealand), has clarified my thinking about the society of Arden.

43. Jackson, 'Ambivalence and the Last-Born', p. 354.

44. *New Variorum* ed. of *As You Like It*, pp. 483–7, provides a synopsis of the plot of *Gamelyn* and a digest of opinions about its direct influence on *As You Like It*.

45. Compare Lodge's address to the reader at the end of *Rosalynde*: 'Heere Gentlemen may you see ... that vertue is not measured by birth but by action; that younger brethren though inferiour in yeares, yet may be superiour to honours; that concord is the sweetest conclusion, and amitie betwixt brothers more forceable than fortune' (pp. 474–5).

46. On charivari and cuckoldry, see the masterful 1976 Neale Lecture in English History by Keith Thomas, 'The Place of Laughter in Tudor and Stuart England', published in *The Times Literary Supplement*, 21 January 1977, pp. 77–81. Students of Shakespearean comedy would do well to bear in mind Thomas's point that 'laughter has a social dimension. Jokes are a pointer to joking situations, areas of structural ambiguity in society itself, and their subject-matter can be a revealing guide to past tensions and anxieties'. From this perspective, 'Tudor humour about shrewish and insatiable wives or lascivious widows was a means of confronting the anomalies of insubordinate female behaviour which constantly threatened the actual working of what was supposed to be a male-dominated marital system. Hence the ... obsession with cuckoldry' (p. 77).

47. Of course, Oliver's gallant gesture of social and economic deference to his youngest brother (a spontaneous reversal of the primogeniture rule into the ultimogeniture rule) cannot be made good until there is a profound change in the society from which they have fled. Oliver's lands and revenues are no longer his to give to Orlando; it is because of Orlando that Frederick has confiscated them.

48. Several generations of critics – most of them men, and quite infatuated with Rosalind themselves – have stressed the exuberance and ignored the containment. Much the same may be said of some recent feminist critics (see, for example, Juliet Dusinberre, *Shakespeare and the Nature of Women* (London: Macmillan, 1975)), although they approach the character in another spirit. The 'feminism' of Shakespearean comedy seems to me more ambivalent in tone and more ironic in form than such critics have wanted to believe. *Contra* Dusinberre, Linda T. Fitz emphasizes that 'the English Renaissance institutionalized, where it did not invent, the restrictive marriage-oriented attitude toward women that feminists have been struggling against ever since.... The insistent demand for the right – nay, obligation – of women to be happily married arose as much in reaction against woman's intractable pursuit of independence as it did in reaction against Catholic ascetic philosophy' ('"What Says the Married Woman?" Marriage Theory and Feminism in the English Renaissance', *Mosaic*, 13, no. 2 [Winter 1980], 1–22; quotations from pp. 11, 18). A provocative Renaissance context for Shakespeare's Rosalind is to be found in the essay, 'Women on Top', in Natalie Zemon

Davis, *Society and Culture in Early Modern France* (Stanford: Stanford Univ. Press, 1975), pp. 124–51.

   49. Wilson, *State of England, 1600*, p. 24.

   50. George Whetstone, Epistle Dedicatory to *Promos and Cassandra* (1578), quoted in Madeleine Doran, *Endeavors of Art* (Madison: Univ. of Wisconsin Press, 1954), p. 220.

   51. From a document (1595) in the 'Dramatic Records of the City of London', quoted in Harbage, *Shakespeare's Audience*, p. 104.

4

The Merchant of Venice and the Possibilities of Historical Criticism
Walter Cohen

Traditional historical scholarship has not fared well with many contemporary literary theorists. Jonathan Culler concludes: 'The identification of historical sequences, while an inevitable and indispensable aspect of literary study, is not just open to oversimplification; it is itself an act of oversimplification.'[1] What is rhetorically striking in this passage is the comfortable coexistence of the author's characteristic moderation with the extremity of the position. Under the influence of the work of Louis Althusser in particular and of structuralism and post-structuralism in general, similar doubts have penetrated Marxism, long a bastion of historical interpretation. Terry Eagleton argues that 'Marx initiates a "genealogical" break with any genetic-evolutionist conception of the historical materialist method, and, indeed, of its object – "history" itself'. For Eagleton, 'history is not a classical narrative: for what kind of narrative is it that has always already begun, that has an infinitely deferred end, and, consequently, can hardly be spoken of as having a middle?'[2] Fredric Jameson (although he begins with the injunction 'Always historicize!') is at pains to demonstrate that Marxism 'is not a historical *narrative*'. And his own 'historicizing operation' presupposes a fundamental bifurcation:

> we are thus confronted with a choice between study of the nature of the 'objective' structures of a given cultural text (the historicity of its forms and of its content, the historical moment of emergence of its linguistic possibilities, the situation-specific function of its aesthetic) and something rather different which would instead foreground the interpretive categories or codes through which we read and receive the text in question.[3]

In partial opposition to these claims, I hope to show that it is possible to have it both ways, to combine history with structure and to connect 'the historical moment' with 'the interpretive categories' through which that moment has been understood. Such innovative critical strategies as symptomatic reading, metacommentary, and the elucidation of the ideology of form acquire their full force only when explicitly located within the larger framework provided by the Marxist notion of the mode of production. Jameson, in fact, comes close to this position in asserting that 'Marxism, ... in the form of the dialectic, affirms a primacy of theory which is at one and the same time a recognition of the primacy of History itself'.[4] The resulting procedure may also be viewed as a modified version of the approach recently proposed by Robert Weimann. More particularly, the present discussion proceeds from a detailed account of *The Merchant of Venice* to a brief look at broader issues. It concludes by reversing gears and summarily considering not the utility of contemporary theory for the study of Renaissance literature, but the implications of Renaissance literature for the development of theory.

The Merchant of Venice (1596) offers an embarrassment of socio-economic riches. It treats merchants and usurers, the nature of the law, and the interaction between country and city. But since it is also about the relationship between love and friendship, the meaning of Christianity, and a good deal more, a thematically minded critic, regardless of his or her persuasion, may be in for a bit of difficulty. In the most comprehensive and compelling study of the play yet produced, Lawrence Danson attempts to solve this problem by arguing that *The Merchant of Venice* dramatizes not the triumph of one set of values over another, but the transformation of conflicts into harmonies that incorporate what at the same time they transcend.[6] Shakespeare's procedure thus resembles both medieval figural and Hegelian dialectics.[7] Because the intellectual and structural design posited by Danson elegantly accommodates not only thematic diversity but also our ambivalent responses to both Shylock and the Christian characters, it is the appropriate object of a sceptical scrutiny of interpretation in *The Merchant of Venice*.

Shakespeare needs to be interpreted, it may be claimed, simply because of the antiquity and complexity of his art. Yet far from being ideologically neutral, such an enterprise, by juxtaposing an alternative and richer reality with our own, involves an implicit critique of the present. Even more, we may recall that Shakespeare's plays, despite their elaborateness, appealed to a broadly heterogeneous primary audience: an achievement that depended on a comparative social and cultural unity, long since lost, in the nation as well as the theatre. This underlying coherence emerges in the logical and, it would seem, inherently meaningful unfolding of the dramatic plot,[8] a strong example of which is provided by the rigorously interlocking, causal development of *The Merchant of Venice*. Presumably, then, the best criticism would deepen, rather than overturn, a sense of the play's meaning widely shared in space and in time.[9]

This is, however, precisely what we do not find in discussions of *The Merchant of Venice*. The play has been seen as the unambiguous triumph of good Christians over a bad Jew;[10] as the deliberately ambiguous triumph of the Christians;[11] as the unintentionally ambiguous, and hence artistically flawed, triumph of the Christians;[12] as the tragedy of Shylock, the bourgeois hero;[13] and as a sweeping attack on Christians and Jews alike.[14] No other Shakespearean comedy before *All's Well That Ends Well* (1602) and *Measure for Measure* (1604), perhaps no other Shakespearean comedy at all, has excited comparable controversy. Probably the most promising way out of this dilemma is to see the play as a new departure for Shakespeare; as his earliest comedy drawn from the Italian *novelle*; as the first of several not quite successful attempts to introduce more powerful characters, more complex problems of conduct, more realistic representation, and a more serious vision of life into a traditionally light genre.[15] Such a perspective is not without its drawbacks. Nonetheless, it has the virtue of suggesting that the play is by and large a romantic comedy; that it is partially flawed; that it calls for an unusual set of critical questions;[16] and, most important, that it requires us not so much to interpret as to discover the sources of our difficulty in interpreting, to view the play as a symptom of a problem in the life of late sixteenth-century England.

Critics who have studied *The Merchant of Venice* against the background of English history have justifiably seen Shylock, and especially his lending habits, as the embodiment of capitalism.[17] The last third of the sixteenth century witnessed a sequence of denunciations of the spread of usury. In *The Specvlation of Vsurie*, published during the year Shakespeare's play may first have been performed, Thomas Bell expresses a typical sense of outrage. 'Now, now is nothing more frequent with the rich men of this world, than to writhe about the neckes of their poore neighbours, and to impouerish them with the filthie lucre of Usurie.'[18] Behind this fear lay the transition to capitalism: the rise of banking; the increasing need for credit in industrial enterprises; and the growing threat of indebtedness facing both aristocratic landlords and, above all, small, independent producers, who could easily decline to working-class status.[19] Although the lower classes were the main victims, it may be as inadequate to describe opposition to usury in Shakespeare or elsewhere as popular in character, as it is misleading to argue that 'Elizabethan drama, even in its higher ranges, was not the expression of a "class" culture at all'.[20] Rather, we are confronted with the hegemonic position of the nobility, whose interests the ideology ultimately served. Artisans and peasant smallholders might fall into the proletariat, but once the majority of the traditional ruling class had adapted to capitalism, the issue of usury faded away.

This had not occurred by 1600, however, and *The Merchant of Venice* offers a number of specific parallels to the anti-usury campaign,[21] most notably in its contrasts between usury and assistance to the poor, and between usurers and merchants. Miles Mosse, for example, laments that 'lending upon *vsurie* is growne so common and usuall among men, as that free lending to the needie is utterly overthrowne'.[22] The distinction between merchants and usurers, also of medieval origin, could be drawn on the grounds that only the former operated for mutual benefit, as opposed to self-interest. Or it might be argued, in language recalling Shakespeare's high valuation of 'venturing', that the usurer does not, like 'the merchant that crosse the seas, adventure', receiving instead a guaranteed return on his money.[23]

A number of dubious consequences follow from concentrating too narrowly on the English background of *The Merchant of Venice*, however. From such a perspective, the play as a whole seems unproblematic, non-economic issues unimportant, and related matters like Shylock's religion or the Italian setting irrelevant.[24] Even explicitly economic concerns do not make adequate sense. An emphasis on the difference between trade and usury might imply that Antonio and his creator are resolutely medieval anti-capitalists.[25] But not only do Shakespeare's other plays of the 1590s show few signs of hostility to capitalism, *The Merchant of Venice* itself is quite obviously pro-capitalist, at least as far as commerce is concerned. It would be more accurate to say that Shakespeare is criticizing merely the worst aspects of an emerging economic system, rather than the system itself. In this respect, moreover, he deviates from the anti-usury tracts and from English reality alike. Writers of the period register both the medieval ambivalence about merchants and the indisputable contemporary fact that merchants were the leading usurers: suspicion of Italian traders ran particularly high.[26] It may be that Shakespeare intends a covert parallel between Shylock and Antonio. Yet no manipulation will convert a comedy in which there are no merchant-usurers and in which the only usurer is a Jew into a faithful representation of British economic life.

Similar trouble arises with Shylock, whom critics have at times allegorically Anglicized as a grasping Puritan.[27] The identification is unconvincing, however, partly because it is just as easy to transform him into a Catholic[28] and, more generally, because he is too complex and contradictory to fit neatly the stereotype of Puritan thrift. It is also unclear what kind of capitalist Shylock is. The crisis of the play arises not from his insistence on usury, but from his refusal of it. The contrast is between usury, which is immoral because it computes a charge above the principal from the moment of the loan, and interest, which is perfectly acceptable because it 'is never due but from the appointed day of payment forward'.[29] Antonio immediately recognizes that Shylock's proposal falls primarily into the latter category, and he responds appropriately, if naively: 'Content in faith, I'll seal to such a bond, / And say there is much kindness in the Jew.'[30]

In addition, the penalty for default on the bond is closer to folklore than to capitalism: stipulation for a pound of flesh, after all, is hardly what one would expect from *homo economicus*. To be sure, Shakespeare is literalizing the traditional metaphorical view of usurers.[31] Moreover, Shylock's desire for revenge is both motivated by economics and possessed of a large degree of economic logic (e.g., I.iii.39–40; and III.i.49, and 117–18). But when the grasping moneylender refuses to relent in return for any repayment – 'No not for Venice' – he goes beyond the bounds of rationality and against the practices of a ruthless modern businessman (IV.i.226).[32] In short, although it is proper to view *The Merchant of Venice* as a critique of early British capitalism, that approach fails even to account for all of the purely economic issues in the work. Can tolerable sense be made of the play's economics, or was Shakespeare merely being fanciful? To answer these questions, we need to take seriously the Venetian setting of the action.

To the English, and particularly to Londoners, Venice represented a more advanced stage of the commercial development they themselves were experiencing. G.K. Hunter's telling remark about the predilections of the Jacobean theatre – 'Italy became important to the English dramatists only when "Italy" was revealed as an aspect of England' – already applies in part to *The Merchant of Venice*.[33] Yet Venetian reality during Shakespeare's lifetime contradicted almost point for point its portrayal in the play. Not only did the government bar Jewish usurers from the city, it also forced the Jewish community to staff and finance low-interest, non-profit lending institutions that served the Christian poor. Funding was primarily derived from the involuntary donations of Jewish merchants active in the Levantine trade. The Jews of Venice thus contributed to the early development of capitalism not as usurers but as merchants involved in an international, trans-European economic network. Ironically, elsewhere in the Veneto, the public Christian banks on which the Jewish loan-houses of Venice were modelled drew most of their assets from interest-bearing deposits by the late sixteenth century.[34]

From a longer historical view of Italy and Venice, however, *The Merchant of Venice* assumes a recognizable relationship to reality. Between the twelfth and the early fourteenth centuries in Italy international merchant-usurers were often required by the church to make testamentary restitution of their profits from moneylending. Thereafter, this occupation decomposed into its constituent parts. Without changing their financial transactions, the merchants experienced a sharp rise in status, eventually evolving into the great philanthropical merchant princes of the Renaissance. The other descendants of the earlier merchant-usurers, the small, local usurer-pawnbrokers, suffered a corresponding decline in social position. This latter group, the main victim of ecclesiastical action against usury in the fifteenth and sixteenth centuries, increasingly consisted of immigrant Jews.[35]

Jewish moneylenders benefited the Venetian Republic in two principal ways. They provided a reliable, lucrative source of tax revenues and forced loans to finance the state's military preparations; and they also drove down interest rates for private citizens, rich and poor, underselling the Christian usurers, whom, consequently, they gradually replaced. The Christian banks referred to above, founded in the late fifteenth century, were designed not only to assist the poor but also to eliminate Jewish moneylenders by providing cheaper credit. Although never established in Venice itself, the *Monti di Pietà*, as they were called, were soon widespread in the cities and towns of the Republican mainland. They rarely succeeded in completely replacing Jewish pawnbrokers, however.[36]

This, then, is the other, Italian historical background to *The Merchant of Venice*. None of Shakespeare's probable sources refers to any prior enmity between merchant and usurer, much less to a comparable motive for the antagonism. English discussions of Italy, on the other hand, regularly mention both Jewish usury and Venetian charity,[37] while Bell, among others, speaks of the *mons pietatis*, a bank where the poor can 'borrow money in their neede, and not bee oppressed with usury'.[38] From this point of view, the hostility between Antonio, the open-handed Christian merchant, and Shylock, the tight-fisted Jewish usurer, represents not the conflict between declining feudalism and rising capitalism, but its opposite. It may be seen as a special instance of the struggle, widespread in Europe, between Jewish quasi-feudal fiscalism and native bourgeois mercantilism, in which the indigenous forces usually prevailed.[39] Both the characterization and the outcome of *The Merchant of Venice* mark Antonio as the harbinger of modern capitalism. By guaranteeing an honourable reputation as well as a secure and absolute title to private property, the exemption of the Italian merchant-financier from the stigma of usury provided a necessary spur to the expansion of the new system.[40] Shylock, by contrast, is a figure from the past: marginal, diabolical, irrational, archaic, medieval. Shakespeare's Jacobean tragic villains – Iago, Edmund, Macbeth and Augustus – are all younger men bent on destroying their elders. Shylock is almost the reverse, an old man with obsolete values trying to arrest the course of history.[41]

Obviously, however, the use of Italian materials in *The Merchant of Venice*, for all its historicity, remains deeply ideological in the bad sense, primarily because of the anti-Semitic distinction between vindictive Jewish usurer and charitable Christian merchant.[42] Shylock's defence of usury is not so strong as it could have been,[43] nor was Shakespeare's preference for an Italian merchant over a Jewish usurer universally shared at the time.[44] Indeed, the very contrast between the two occupations may be seen as a false dichotomy, faithful to the Renaissance Italian merchant's understanding of himself but not to the reality that self-conception was designed to justify.

We can understand the apparently contradictory implications of British and Italian economic history for *The Merchant of Venice* as a response to the intractability of contemporary life. The form of the play results from an ideological reworking of reality designed to produce precisely the intellectual and structural pattern described at the beginning of this discussion. The duality we have observed, especially in Shylock, is absolutely necessary to this end. Briefly stated, in *The Merchant of Venice* English history evokes fears of capitalism, and Italian history allays those fears. One is the problem, the other the solution, the act of incorporation, of transcendence, toward which the play strives.

A similar, if less striking, process of reconciliation is at work with Antonio, whose social significance varies inversely to Shylock's. As a traditional and conservative figure, he nearly becomes a tragic victim of economic change; as the embodiment of progressive forces, he points toward the comic resolution. But Antonio cannot be too progressive, cannot represent a fundamental rupture with the past. Giovanni Botero attributed his country's urban preeminence partly to the fact that 'the gentleman in *Italy* does dwell in Cities',[45] and indeed the fusion in the towns of nobility and bourgeoisie helped generate the Renaissance in Italy and, much later, in England as well. The concluding tripartite unity of Antonio, Bassanio, and Portia[46] enacts precisely this interclass harmony between aristocratic landed wealth and mercantile capital, with the former dominant. A belief that some such relationship provided much of the social foundation of the English monarchy accounts for Shakespeare's essentially corporatist defence of absolutism in the 1590s.

A brief consideration of Marx's views on Jews, on usurers, on merchants, and on *The Merchant of Venice* will enable us to restate these conclusions with greater theoretical rigour and to point toward additional, related issues. In the 'Contribution to the Critique of Hegel's *Philosophy of Right*: Introduction', Shylock is an exploiter of the lower classes. Characterizing the German historical school of law, Marx comments: 'A Shylock, but a servile Shylock, it swears upon its bond, its historical, Christian-Germanic bond, for every pound of flesh cut from the heart of the people.' The Second part of 'On the Jewish Question' basically equates Judaism with capitalism, a position that Volume One of *Capital* reasserts in a discussion of the efforts of nineteenth-century British manufacturers to force children to work long hours. 'Workmen and factory inspectors protested on hygienic and moral grounds, but Capital answered: "My deeds upon my head! I crave the law, / The penalty and forfeit of my bond." This Shylock-clinging to the letter of the law ...', Marx adds, 'was but to lead up to an open revolt against the same law'. But the extended discussion of usury in Volume Three of *Capital* implicitly reaches a very different conclusion. Usurer's capital, Marx claims, arises long before the capitalist system itself, its parasitic action weakening the precapitalist mode of production off which it lives. But unassisted it cannot generate a transition to capitalism. When that transition does occur, however, usury inevitably declines, partly as a result of the determined opposition of mercantile capital. Finally, commercial capital itself is, like usury, an early and primitive form of capital and, as such, ultimately compatible with precapitalist modes of production. Thus, Marx's comments in effect recapitulate our entire argument on the economics of *The Merchant of Venice*.[47]

In one instance, however, they lead beyond that argument. Up to now, we have been primarily concerned to show how dramatic form, as the product of an ideological reworking of history, functions to resolve those contradictions that prove irreconcilable in life. But, of course, many critics have been unable to feel a final coherence to *The Merchant of Venice*. In Volume One of *Capital*, after showing how industrial capital endangers the worker, 'how it constantly threatens, by taking away the instruments of labour, to snatch from his hands his means of subsistence', Marx quotes Shylock's reply to the Duke's pardon: 'You take my life / When you do take the means whereby I live.'[48] The passage implies exactly the opposite of what is suggested by the lines previously cited from the same volume. There, Shylock was identified with capital, the Christians with labour; here, the Christians represent capital, Shylock labour. Such a reversal cannot be assimilated to the dualisms we have already discussed: instead, Marx's use of selective quotation succeeds in capturing Shylock as both victimizer and victim.

As many critics have observed, the fact that Shylock is grand as well as pitiable does not in itself imply any structural flaw in *The Merchant of Venice*. Shakespeare needed an antagonist possessed of sufficient, though perhaps not 'mythical', stature to pose a credible threat.[49] The sympathy elicited by the Jewish usurer, often a consequence of his mistreatment by Christian characters who resemble him more than they would admit, also serves a plausible formal purpose in the overall movement toward mercy and harmony. In fact, by the end of the trial scene most of the Christian characters have fairly settled accounts with Shylock.[50] The trouble is that Christianity has not. Although the Christian characters in the play are better than Shylock, the Christian characters *not* in the play are not. In his famous 'Jew' speech and in his declamation on slavery to the court, Shylock adopts the strategy of equating Christian with Jew to justify his own murderous intentions (III.ii.47–66 and IV.i.89–103). But by the end of Act IV, his analogies are strictly irrelevant to most of the Christian characters in the play. They have either given up the practices that Shylock attributes to them, or they have never been guilty of them at all: certainly, we meet no Christian slaveholders in *The Merchant of Venice*. Yet Shylock's universalizing accusations are never challenged in word by his Christian auditors, nor can they be sufficiently answered in deed by the individual charitable acts with which the trial concludes. The devastating judgements, particularly of the second speech, are allowed to stand; and they tell us that although Shylock is defeated and then incorporated in the world of the play, in the world beyond the play his values are pervasive.

This bifurcation is a consequence of the fundamental contradiction in Shakespeare's social material. English history requires that the threat embodied in Shylock be generalized; Italian history, that it remain localized. Yet if Shakespeare had fully responded to both imperatives, *The Merchant of Venice* would have lapsed into incoherence. If the play revealed that merchants were as exploitative as usurers, that they were in fact usurers, then its entire thrust toward harmonious reconciliation could only be understood as a fiendishly oblique instance of ironic demystification. But if instead Shakespeare intended the movement toward transcendent unity to be taken at least as seriously as the dangers of nascent capitalism, he needed to present the latter in a way that would not undermine the former. He needed to transform materialist problems into idealist ones (Antonio cannot very well give up commerce, but he can learn to be more merciful) or to project them harmlessly away from the Christian characters in the play (some Christians whom we do not meet own and mistreat slaves). To achieve a convincing resolution, Shakespeare had to begin with a partly imaginary dilemma. But only partly. For had his premise been wholly imaginary, his treatment could easily have been relatively free of contradiction. That it is not is a testimony to both his strengths and his limitations.

Such a perspective enables us to understand and in a sense to justify the opposed responses to *The Merchant of Venice*, to see in its flaws not signs of artistic incompetence but manifestations of preformal problems. It also suggests answers to the questions with which we began. We need to interpret this play particularly because its formal movement – dialectical transcendence – is not adequate to the social conflict that is its main source of inspiration and one of its principal subjects. Some of the merit of *The Merchant of Venice* ironically lies in the failure of its central design to provide a completely satisfying resolution to the dilemmas raised in the course of the action. We have seen that one purpose of the form is to reconcile the irreconcilable. Similarly, one effect of interpretive methods that view explication as their primary end is a complicity of silence with the play, in which the ideology of the form is uncritically reproduced and the whole, *The Merchant of Venice* as we have it, is replaced by the part, Shakespeare's possible intention.

These inferences may be related to the debate on organic form and artistic totality that has troubled Marxist criticism since the 1930s. It would seem that the above argument aligns itself with those theories that see in the sense of closure or wholeness sometimes produced by a work of art an analogue to reactionary corporatist ideologies designed to suppress awareness of class conflict. An anti-organicist orientation, however, must deny in principle the possibility that the realm of aesthetics can deliver an experience of a contradictory totality or, for that matter, of demystification followed by retotalization.[51] Few plays if any completely accomplish so much: the achievement of *The Merchant of Venice* is oblique and partial. But it would be a mistake to overgeneralize from a single example: some of the greatest works of the early seventeenth-century theatre, most notably *King Lear*, do in fact approach this elusive ideal.

Nonetheless, our consideration of the ideology of form in *The Merchant of Venice* from the vantage point of economic history has primarily constituted an act of demystification. An exclusive preoccupation of this sort fails to do justice to the play, however. To locate the merit of the work in Shakespeare's inability to accomplish precisely what he intended hardly corrects the deficiency; it merely betrays the critic's wish that *The Merchant of Venice* were *The Jew of Malta*. The positive value of Shakespeare's comedy naturally includes the significant concerns that it voices, a prominent example of which is the problem of usury. But at least as important is the utopian dimension of the play: what may seem escapist from one perspective, from another becomes liberating. Although the effort of art to transcend the constraints of its time is not necessarily apparent, in *The Merchant of Venice* much of this tendency is right on the surface. For instance, the play persistently attempts to establish a congruence between economic and moral conduct, between outer and inner wealth; to depict a society in which human relationships are not exploitative. Such a vision, quite literally a fantasy, simultaneously distracts us from the deficiencies of our lives and reveals to us the possibility of something better. Utopian mystification and liberation are always inseparable and often, as here, strictly identical.

Similar lines of analysis could be extended to the other major issues in the play. Here, however, we need only suggest the outlines of such an inquiry. The supersession of justice by mercy, of the letter by the spirit, and of the Old Law by the New in the trial that occupies Act IV at once reveals the fairness of the legal system and the ethical premises of the entire plot.[52] Shakespeare's demonstration that the principle of equity is inherent in the rigour of the law is rooted 'in the adjustment of the common law to the practice of Equity in the Court of Chancery' during the sixteenth century.[53] Beginning in the 1590s, however, the officials of the old, comparatively popular common law courts and their counterparts on the newer, royally dominated courts like Chancery entered into a struggle that ultimately resulted in the common lawyers joining the militant opposition to the crown.[54] In this respect Shakespeare's ideological project represents an anticipatory and, in the event, futile attempt to reconcile absolutist values with popular, traditional, but ironically revolutionary institutions, so as to prevent civil war.[55] Another version of this compromise is implicit in Shylock's demand of his bond from the Duke: 'If you deny it, let the danger light / Upon your charter and your city's freedom!' (IV.i.38–9). On the one hand, the case acquires such political reverberations because Shakespeare assumes a feudal conception of law, in which justice is the central peacetime conduit of aristocratic power. On the other, Shylock's threat becomes so grave because the trial is based on a bourgeois commitment to binding contracts. Portia's integrative solution reveals the compatibility of rigour and freedom, of bourgeois self-interest and aristocratic social responsibility. But the profound allegiance to contractual law can make this ideological yoking seem either unjust or precarious, responses that indicate the tension between the limits of reality and the promises of utopia in *The Merchant of Venice*.

The relationship between country and city, perhaps the other major, overtly social issue raised by the action, situates the play in the tradition of Renaissance pastoral, a literary and theatrical reaction by the nobility to the two dominant trends of the age – the rise of capitalism and the partly complementary growth of absolutism. The construction of the pastoral world resolves the intractable dilemmas of aristocratic life in the city or at court: the form ideologically reconciles the socially irreconcilable.[56] Rather than representing a species of escapism, however, this enterprise is transformed into a fully conscious process in *The Merchant of Venice*. The strictly causal logic of the action, noted earlier, is identical to the interplay between Belmont and Venice. Because the multiple plot extends the social range of representation, the traditional ruling class, ensconced in the second or 'green' world, is tested and validated by its ability to master the deepest conflicts of the first world. Shakespeare's goal is thus, once again, to rebind what had been torn asunder into a new unity, under aristocratic leadership. The symbolic repository of value is the great country house, home not of reactionary seigneurial barons but, especially in England, of a rising class increasingly dependent for its revenues on capitalist agriculture and soon to align itself against the monarchy. The play, of course, remains oblivious of these developments: no one does any work at Belmont; there is no source of Portia's apparently endless wealth; and all comers are welcome to a communism of consumption, though not of production.[57] The aristocratic fantasy of Act V, unusually sustained and unironic even for Shakespearean romantic comedy, may accordingly be seen as a formal effort to obliterate the memory of what has preceded.

The treatment of love is also socially hybrid. The fairytale-like affair between Bassanio and Portia is constrained by the harsh will of a dead father, is motivated by a concern for property, and is premised upon the traditional sexual hierarchy. But largely for these very reasons, it produces a love match in which virtue counts for more than wealth or beauty, and the wife is, in practice at least, the equal of her husband. Shakespeare's typical synthesis here represents a response to the unsettled position of the late sixteenth-century aristocracy, whose practices and ideology were in the process of transition from a feudal to a bourgeois conception of marriage.[58] The striking characteristic of love in *The Merchant of Venice*, however, is that it is not unambiguously primary. For Leo Salingar, Shakespeare's comedies regularly enact an unresolved conflict in their author's mind 'over the claims of love and the claims of law in Elizabethan society'.[59] But in this play the controlling intellectual pattern requires what is partly a romantic and personal solution to a social problem. From this perspective, however, Act V may also be viewed as a playful and graceful effort by the aristocratic heroine to carry out the serious business of reestablishing the bourgeois assumptions of her marriage, assumptions endangered by the very romantic solution to a social problem that she has just provided.[60]

Since our discussion has been designed to complicate and at times to challenge a Christian interpretation, it is appropriate to conclude by examining directly the religious dimension of the action. The problem is not particularly the tendency of some critics to overemphasize the allegorical meaning of the plot's unfolding,[61] – although attempts to incorporate such moments as Shylock's anguished response to Jessica's sale of his ring or his forced, as opposed to his daughter's voluntary, conversion may seem a bit strained.[62] It is rather the difficulty of transforming the play into a paraphrasable meaning of any kind. Founding his argument upon the critical controversy over *The Merchant of Venice*, Norman Rabkin has questioned 'the study of meaning' and the 'bias towards rationality' in general, pronouncing 'all intellection ... reductive' because of 'its consistent suppression of the nature of aesthetic experi-ence'.[63] Although Rabkin's position is obviously opportunistic in its reliance on a notoriously hard case, it is quite true that 'aesthetic experience', especially when induced by more than words alone, cannot be adequately converted into argumentative meaning. At any rate, religious interpretation has proven symptomatically incapable of understanding the play as a comedy, except to the limited extent, suggested above, that romantic comedy and Christian myth share a common ritual movement.

On the other hand, as part of an effort to elucidate the overall significance of the work,[64] including its aesthetic value, a demystification of allegorical reading can specify the comic side of *The Merchant of Venice* in its integral relationship to the popular tradition in the theatre.

Allegory may be viewed as a utopian drive to assimilate alien experience, to create or restore unity where only incoherence and fragmentation are felt, to confer meaning upon a secular existence that seems intrinsically meaningless.[65] Shakespeare's intermittently quasi-allegorical mode in *The Merchant of Venice*, in its moving revelation of the correspondence between human agency and divine plan, represents the most profound version of the Christian Neoplatonism that flourished especially in the pastoral tragicomedy of the Counter Reformation court.[66] The providential pattern of Neoplatonism in turn moralizes the intrigue, a dramatic genre that at times confirms that Russian Formalist insistence on the primacy of form. When the intrigue serves as an end in itself, rather than merely as a means, issues are raised and then dropped not for their cognitive importance, but for their contribution to the plot, whose elegance is meant to point only to the playwright's ingenuity.[67] Ideologically, the intrigue, unlike Shakespearean comedy, proclaims that people are not responsible for their conduct, that social rules have no consequences, that things will work out, that the status quo is secure. But the intrigue itself actually domesticates a still more anarchic impulse toward misrule and liberation that returns us to the root of comedy. Today, literature often censors some fantasy about work;[68] in the Renaissance, however, when hierarchy was more open and alienated labour not yet the norm, dramatic form often submerged an aspiration toward freedom from social convention and constraint. Shakespeare's own religious interpretive strategy in *The Merchant of Venice* thus simultaneously constitutes an act of humane sophistication and a process of repressive concealment.

But the repression is incomplete, and the internal distancing produced by the subversive side of the play justifies our transformation of the learned surface, a comedy mainly in the Dantean sense, into a deep comic structure with affinities to popular festivity, folklore, and ritual. In general, Shakespeare's synthetic enterprise in an age of transition ran a considerable risk: the ultimately anti-absolutist implication, invisible to the playwright, of even a qualified allegiance to the country or to the common law is an obvious example. But these conflicts mainly concern the upper classes, and much of the material that we have considered and still more that could be cited place the work within the neoclassical literary and dramatic tradition. To understand the tensions generated within the synthesis by the popular heritage, to explore the consequences of what we will later identify as the inherent contradiction between artisanal base and absolutist superstructure in the public theatre for which Shakespeare wrote, we must attend to matters of stage position and of dramatic speech, to deviations from the norms of blank verse and Ciceronian prose.[69]

It is easy to demonstrate that the clown, Launcelot Gobbo, has an integral role in *The Merchant of Venice*, that, for example, his abandonment of Shylock for Bassanio foreshadows and legitimates Jessica's similar flight from Jew to Christian.[70] Nonetheless, his physical, social, ideological, and linguistic proximity to the audience comically challenges the primary mimetic action and intellectual design. Launcelot's function may first be illustrated by his penchant for malapropism. In seeking service with the understandably bewildered Bassanio, the socially mobile clown explains that 'the suit is impertinent to myself' (II.ii.130). Having somehow obtained the job, he revisits his old employer to invite him to dinner with his new one: 'I beseech you sir go, my young master doth expect your reproach'; to which Shylock replies, 'So do I his' (II.v.19–21). Shylock's recognition that the apparent misuse of 'reproach' for 'approach' is at some level intentional points to the linguistically and socially subversive connotations of young Gobbo's double meanings, to the 'impertinent' quality, again in two senses, of his speech and conduct.

In his final major appearance, Launcelot begins by expressing his theological concern for Jessica: 'I speak my agitation of the matter, therefore be o' good cheer, for truly I think you are damn'd – there is but one hope in it that can do you any good, and that is but a kind of bastard hope neither' (III.v.4–7). The confusion of 'agitation' and 'cogitation', the proposed response of 'good cheer' to the prospect of damnation, the ironic play on bastardy – all hopelessly jumble and thus demystify the serious religious issues of the plot. Later in the same scene the clown systematically and wittily misconstrues Lorenzo's apparently straightforward order that the kitchen staff 'prepare for dinner' (III.v.43). His quibbling replies range from an aggressive assertion that the servants, too, are hungry ('they have all stomachs!') to a pretended retreat into deferential humility ('I know my duty' [III.v.44 and 49]). In general, then, from his very first appearance, significantly in soliloquy, when 'the devil himself' prompts him to run from his master 'the Jew ... the very devil incarnation' (II.ii.25–6), Launcelot provides an alternative perspective on the related matters of Christian orthodoxy and social hierarchy. On the one hand, his nonsense parodically demystifies; on the other, it uniquely combines archaic memories and utopian vistas.

This complex vision is compatible with the disturbingly ambiguous implications of Shylock, himself a figure with important ancestors in the popular tradition.[71] Like the vice, he is associated with the devil; is the leading manipulator of the action; elicits from the audience fascination as well as revulsion, laughter as well as terror; functions as both homiletic foe of Christianity and incisive critic of Christian society; and, accordingly, ranges linguistically from rhetorically polished, mimetic dialogue to popular, self-expressive monologue. Thus, insofar as *The Merchant of Venice* combines a formally dominant, Christian, aristocratic ideology with that ideology's qualification by the alternative and partly oppositional conduct and values of other social classes, the play escapes standard categories of interpretation while strikingly embodying the central creative tension of Shakespearean drama.

The preceding comments rest on a number of assumptions that have not been explicitly stated. It may be useful, then, to sketch in some of the mediations between drama and society that make it plausible to think of *The Merchant of Venice* as a response to a conflict between two modes of production. I propose to move from the play to the form of romantic comedy; from there to the theatre as an institution; and from there, finally, to the larger contours of late Tudor England and of Renaissance Europe in general.

Any attempt to assimilate *The Merchant of Venice* to a conventional generic category like romantic comedy is bound to be problematic, however. The work stands apart from Shakespeare's other comedies of the 1590s, romantic or not, and, in addition, from most other comedies of the period, both in the gravity of its subject and in its socio-economic emphasis. Yet the play is entirely typical of comedy in its movement toward resolution and reconciliation, and typical of specifically romantic comedy in its reliance on married love as a means to those ends. Indeed, it is on the embattled terrain of the love-marriage that the ideological significance of the form of romantic comedy is to be located. On the one hand, married love represented a progressive step for women and men alike, consequent upon the relative liberation of women – at least in the realm of ideas – during the age of the Renaissance. On the other, the concluding matrimony of many a comedy may be viewed as a transference, defusing, or suppression of conflict. Romantic comedy, firmly founded on marital love, its climactic weddings presided over by great lords, dramatizes the adaptation of the nobility to a new social configuration, an acceptance of change inextricable from a reassertion of dominance.

The form carries out this function in self-consciously theatrical fashion. First, the characters' frequent recourse to disguise or acting is in part a response to the simultaneous instability and rigidity of the aristocracy's position. The improbable situations confronted by the protagonists are at once signs of uncertainty and insecurity, and preferred alternatives to the imposed constraints of daily life. Pastoral, intrigue, lower-class disguise, acting, the atmosphere of holiday or of release – all testify to a utopian impulse toward freedom and an extended range of self-expression. In the end, playing and pretence often help resolve the problems of the action: the main characters forego masquerade and return to the common conduct of a class whose collective sense of purpose has been renewed and reformed by their experience. Yet the conventional resolutions do not entirely negate the liberating moments that have preceded. From this perspective, it is possible to understand a distinctive feature of the form: that its power primarily resides not in social mimesis but in the representation of comic, anarchic freedom issuing in an ideal solution. It is from here, moreover, that its most enduring social criticism usually derives. As a rule, the festive side of a play is inversely proportional to both the social seriousness of the subject and the prominence of other, potentially antagonistic classes. Hence, *The Merchant of Venice*, by its very atypicality, reveals the formal and ideological limits of Renaissance romantic comedy.

At least in England, most such plays were performed in the permanent, public, commercial theatres that emerged in the last quarter of the sixteenth century. What was the character of this new institution? The monarchy, the nobility, the clergy, and the bourgeoisie all crucially shaped the cultural, political, social, and economic functioning of the theatre industry. Yet on matters of immediate production and consumption – actors and companies, stages and playhouses, playwrights and audiences – popular influences were paramount.[72] More precisely, the theatre combined widespread commercialization, relative absence of a proletariat and extensive regulation of the conditions of production. It most closely approximated, in other words, the postfeudal, precapitalist, fundamentally artisanal mode of economic organization known to some historians as petty commodity production.

As such, the public theatre constituted part of both the base and the superstructure, and its function in one conflicted with its role in the other. However aristocratic the explicit message of a play might be, the conditions of its production introduced alternative, lower-class effects. For members of the audience, a trip to the theatre was a festive occasion, a species of escape, a form of aspiration, an embodiment of an ideal. Romantic comedy in particular could evoke recollections of popular pagan ritual and thus inspire often legitimate upper-class fears of religious heterodoxy. The same interaction of dramatic form and theatrical mode of production generated socially subversive effects from the recurrent use of lower-class disguise as a means of aristocratic validation; yet stage performance also rationalized and contained such implications, not only by the specific resolution of the plot, but also by the channelling of anarchic instincts that is an inherent part of attendance at a play. The public theatre in this respect offered communal affirmation and social ratification, a means of confronting fear and anger in a manner that promoted reassurance about the existence and legitimacy of a new order. The theatre within the nation, like theatricality within the play, at least in part served to restore a stratified social unity.

That unity was ultimately guaranteed by an incomplete but stable absolutist state that had temporarily abandoned centralizing efforts after the unrest of the middle of the century and the still earlier era of initial national consolidation. Like the public theatre, though on a far grander scale, the monarchy both reinforced and depended on the relative cultural homogeneity of town and country, of upper class and lower. Its social basis was thus at least as complex as the stage's. We might note in particular the presence of an increasingly powerful ensemble of capitalist classes, whose crucial influence is unmistakable everywhere from the broadest issues of national policy to the narrowest details of a play such as *The Merchant of Venice*. But in the end, emphasis on the bourgeoisie or analogies between the state and the theatre are profoundly misleading. In England as elsewhere in Europe, absolutism served the interests of the neofeudal aristocracy against those of all other classes, in the epoch of western Europe's transition from feudalism to capitalism.[73] *The Merchant of Venice* is of a piece with this international pattern of development. An English play with an Italian setting, it attempts to come to terms with a stage in the process by which western Europe was undergoing an internal transformation that was soon to make it the dominant power on earth.

At this point, it may reasonably be asked what guarantees of validity are possessed by the interpretive categories and procedures that govern the present discussion. Metacommentary, for example, can obviously be turned against itself, opening up a process of infinite regress. The primacy claimed for modes of production would seem to be vulnerable to a similar, if not quite identical challenge. The reply to these objections, such as it is, is the traditional one: the validity of the overall argument offered above depends on that argument's explanatory power. Put another way, the organizing hypotheses are designed to provide a paradigm for, and thus to risk falsification across, the range of European drama of the sixteenth and seventeenth centuries, from Ariosto to Racine. Yet explanatory power is hardly a neutral or independent concept, inextricably bound as it is to such questions as what sort of knowledge is being sought and why. And the answers to these questions will ultimately be determined by the critic's sense of what matters most. The founding premise of this essay is – to quote Fredric Jameson once again, this time apparently contradicting his opposition between Marxism and historical narrative – that 'the human adventure is one; ... a single great collective story; ... for Marxism, the collective struggle to wrest a realm of Freedom from a realm of Necessity'.[74]

Finally, if we attempt to use *The Merchant of Venice* to interrogate literary theory, rather than the other way around, it will be evident from what already has been said that the play imposes upon us, in a particularly forceful fashion, the need to account for both its familiarity and its otherness. But it seems more profitable to ask instead what problems the work raises for the specific perspective adopted here. We may approach this matter by noting that Renaissance dramatic theory was fundamentally incapable of grasping the nature or significance of Renaissance dramatic practice, at least in England. This failure was largely a consequence of an inability to theorize the social heterogeneity, and especially the popular elements, that gave the drama its distinctive quality and that have always made it an attractive subject for a radical, activist-oriented criticism. Yet the distance between Renaissance and Marxist theory may not be as great as this formulation suggests. In both instances, the problem is the gap between theory and practice. Marxist theory, whatever its intentions, will tend to reproduce the defects of Renaissance theory whenever it remains isolated, as it currently does, from a now scarcely existent, larger, contemporary movement for social and political transformation capable of once again uniting learned and popular culture, and thereby both justifying a theoretical project like the present one and providing Shakespearean drama with its most resonant context at least since the early seventeenth century.

Notes

1. Jonathan Culler, *The Pursuit of Signs: Semiotics, Literature, Deconstruction* (Ithaca: Cornell Univ. Press, 1981), p. 65.
2. Terry Eagleton, *Walter Benjamin: Or, Towards a Revolutionary Criticism* (London: NLB, 1981), pp. 64 and 70.
3. Fredric Jameson, *The Political Unconscious: Narrative as a Socially Symbolic Act* (Ithaca: Cornell Univ. Press, 1981), pp. 9, 139, and 9, respectively.
4. Jameson, *The Political Unconscious*, p. 14.
5. Robert Weimann, *Structure and Society in Literary History: Studies in the History and Theory of Historical Criticism* (Charlottesville: Univ. Press of Virginia, 1976).
6. Lawrence Danson, *The Harmonies of* The Merchant of Venice (New Haven: Yale Univ. Press, 1978).
7. For figural interpretation, see Erich Auerbach, 'Figura', in *Scenes from the Drama of European Literature*, trans. Ralph Manheim (New York: Meridian Books, 1959), pp. 11–76. The dialectics of the trial scene are stressed by Danson, p. 70; the more general 'dialectical element in Shakespeare's comic structure' is noted by Northrop Frye, *A Natural Perspective: The Development of Shakespearean Comedy and Romance* (New York: Harcourt, Brace and World, 1956), p. 133.
8. For the social and ideological implications of the well-made plot in the novel, see Jameson, 'Metacommentary', *PMLA*, 86 (1971), 12–13. Sigurd Burckhardt, *Shakespearean Meanings* (Princeton: Princeton Univ. Press, 1968), pp. 206–36, offers a symbolic, modernist, self-referential analysis of the rigours of the plot in *The Merchant of Venice*.
9. For this argument, see Richard Levin, 'Refuting Shakespeare's Endings – Part II', *Modern Philology*, 75 (1977), 132–58.
10. See C.L. Barber, *Shakespeare's Festive Comedy: A Study of Dramatic Form and Its Relation to Social Custom* (Princeton: Princeton Univ. Press, 1959), pp. 163–91; Frank

Kermode, 'The Mature Comedies', in *Early Shakespeare*, ed. John Russell Brown and Bernard Harris, Stratford-upon-Avon Studies, no. 3 (New York: St Martin's Press, 1961), pp. 220–24; and Paul N. Siegel, 'Shylock, the Elizabethan Puritan, and Our Own World', in *Shakespeare in His Time and Ours* (Notre Dame: Univ. of Notre Dame Press, 1968), pp. 337–8.

11. Danson's argument is a sophisticated version of this approach.

12. See Madeleine Doran, *Endeavors of Art: A Study of Form in Elizabethan Drama* (Madison: Univ. of Wisconsin Press, 1954), pp. 318–19, 347, and 362–4.

13. Auerbach, *Mimesis: The Representation of Reality in Western Literature*, trans. Willard S. Trask (Princeton: Princeton Univ. Press, 1953), pp. 314–15, 316, 320, 325, and 328, offers elements of this reading, though also acknowledging that the resolution of the play precludes a tragic interpretation. The stage tradition described by Brown, 'The Realization of Shylock: A Theatrical Criticism', in *Early Shakespeare*, ed. Brown and Harris, pp. 187–209, seems to fall primarily into this category.

14. Anselm Schlösser, 'Dialectic in *The Merchant of Venice*', *Zeitschrift für Anglistik und Amerikanistik*, 23, 1975, 5–11; Marc Shell, 'The Wether and the Ewe: Verbal Usury in *The Merchant of Venice*', *Kenyon Review*, NS 1 (1979), 65–92; Burton Hatlen, 'Feudal and Bourgeois Concepts of Value in *The Merchant of Venice*', in *Shakespeare: Contemporary Critical Approaches*, ed. Harry R. Garvin (Lewisburg: Bucknell Univ. Press, 1980), pp. 91–105; and René Girard, '"To Entrap the Wisest": A Reading of *The Merchant of Venice*', in *Literature and Society*, ed. Edward W. Said, Selected Papers from the English Institute, 1978, NS 3 (Baltimore: Johns Hopkins Univ. Press, 1980), pp. 100–19. For a more detailed discussion of this debate over the play, see Danson, pp. 1–18.

15. Leo Salingar, *Shakespeare and the Traditions of Comedy* (Cambridge: Cambridge Univ. Press, 1974), pp. 298–325.

16. For a theoretical statement and practical application of this argument, see Ralph W. Rader, 'Fact, Theory, and Literary Explanation', *Critical Inquiry*, 1 (1974), 249–50 and 258–61.

17. John W. Draper, 'Usury in *The Merchant of Venice*', *Modern Philology*, 33 (1935), 37–47; E.C. Pettet, '*The Merchant of Venice* and the Problem of Usury,' *Essays and Studies*, 31 (1945), 19–33; and Siegel, 'Shylock'.

18. Thomas Bell, *The Specvlation of Vsurie* (London, 1596), A2r. For similar statements, see Thomas Lodge, *An Alarum Against Vsurers* (London, 1584), E1r, and Roger Fenton, *A Treatise of Vsurie* (London, 1611), B1r.

19. R.H. Tawney, Introd. to *A Discourse upon Usury by Way of Dialogue and Orations, for the Better Variety and More Delight of All Those That Shall Read this Treatise (1572)*, by Thomas Wilson (New York: Harcourt Brace, [1925]), pp. 1–172. See also Lawrence Stone, *The Crisis of the Aristocracy, 1558–1641* (Oxford: Clarendon Press, 1965), pp. 158, 183, and 541–3.

20. L.C. Knights, *Drama and Society in the Age of Jonson* (London: Chatto and Windus, 1937), p. 11. The same assumption governs Knights's comments on usury, pp. 127–30, 164–8, and passim.

21. Some of these are pointed out by Draper, pp. 45–6, and Pettet, pp. 26–7.

22. Miles Mosse, *The Arraignment and Conviction of Vsurie* (London, 1595), C3v. See also H.A. [Henry Arthington?], *Provision for the Poore, Now in Penurie* (London, 1597), C2v, and Philip Caesar, *A General Discovrse Against the Damnable Sect of Vsurers* (London, 1578), the title page of which refers to 'these / later daies, in which, Charitie being ba- / nished, Couetousnes hath got- / ten the vpper hande'.

23. *The Death of Vsvry, or the Disgrace of Vsvrers* (London, 1594), E1r. The contrary valuation of merchant and usurer may also be found in Nicolas Sanders, *A Briefe Treatise of Vsvrie* (Lovanii, 1568), D1r, and in Lodge and Thomas Greene's *A Looking Glasse for London and England* (1590), ed. Tetsumaro Hayashi (Metuchen, NJ: The Scarecrow Press, 1970), I.iii. and III.i. A sympathetic view of merchants is taken for granted – a position impossible at the time with regard to usurers – in John Browne, *The Marchants Avizo* (London, 1591), and in *A True Report of Sir Anthony Shierlies Iourney* (London, 1600).

24. Draper, pp. 46–7; Pettet, pp. 19, 29, and 32; and Siegel, 'Shylock', pp. 249 and 252.

25. Draper, p. 39, and Pettet, pp. 19, 22, 23, 27, and 29.

26. Bell, B4v and C3v, is again representative. Medieval attitudes toward merchants are surveyed by Tawney, *Religion and the Rise of Capitalism: A Historical Study*, Holland Memorial Lectures, 1922 (New York: New American Library, 1954), pp. 20–39. *A Discovery of the Great Svbtiltie and Wonderful Wisedom of the Italians* (London, 1591), B1r, partly attributes Italy's success in economically exploiting other nations to the country's vigorous trade.

27. Siegel, 'Shylock', and A.A. Smirnov, *Shakespeare: A Marxist Interpretation* (New York: Critics Group, 1936), p. 35.

28. Danson, pp. 78–80, and T.A., *The Massacre of Money* (London, 1602), C2v.

29. Mosse, F2r. Tawney, *Religion*, pp. 43–4, elaborates on this point, and W.H. Auden, *The Dyer's Hand and Other Essays* (New York: Vintage, 1968), pp. 227–8, notes that Shylock does not demand usury.

30. The Arden edition of *The Merchant of Venice*, ed. Brown (London: Methuen, 1955), I.iii.148–9. Subsequent references are noted in the text.

31. Barber, p. 169; *Whartons Dreame* (London, 1578), A3r; and for a striking theatrical anticipation, Robert Wilson, *The Three Ladies of London* (1581), ed. John S. Farmer (The Tudor Facsimile Texts, 1911), D4v.

32. Stephen J. Greenblatt, 'Marlowe, Marx, and Anti-Semitism', *Critical Inquiry*, 5 (1978), 291–307, emphasizes Shylock's irrationality, even madness. My discussion of *The Merchant of Venice* is generally indebted to this essay.

33. 'English Folly and Italian Vice: The Moral Landscape of John Marston', in *Jacobean Theatre*, ed. John Russell Brown and Bernard Harris, Stratford-upon-Avon Studies, No. 1 (London: Edward Arnold, 1960), p. 95. For reservations about conflating late Elizabethan and Jacobean Italianism, see pp. 91–4. For comments on Venetian trade, see Robert Johnson's translation of Giovanni Botero, *Relations of the Most Famovs Kingdoms and Common – weales thorovgh the World* (London, 1611), Gg2v–Gg3v, and George Sandys, *A Relation of a Iourney* (London, 1615), B1r.

34. Brian Pullan, *Rich and Poor in Renaissance Venice: The Social Institutions of a Catholic State, to 1620* (Oxford: Basil Blackwell, 1971), pp. 538–621, and Fernand Braudel, *The Mediterranean and the Mediterranean World in the Age of Philip II*, trans. Siân Reynolds (London: Collins, 1973), II. 817 and 823. Fynes Moryson, *Shakespeare's Europe: A Survey of the Conditions of Europe at the End of the Sixteenth Century; Being Unpublished Chapters of Fynes Moryson's 'Itinerary'* (1617), ed. Charles Hughes, 2nd edn (1903; rpt. New York: Benjamin Blom, 1967), p. 488, gives a reasonably accurate picture of the position of Italian Jews.

35. Benjamin N. Nelson, 'The Usurer and the Merchant Prince: Italian Businessmen and the Ecclesiastical Law of Restitution. 1100–1550', *Journal of Economic History*, Supp. 7 (1947), 104–22, an essay deeply aware of the parallels to *The Merchant of Venice*.

36. Pullan, pp. 431–537.

37. Wylliam Thomas, *The Historye of Italye* (London, 1549), U4v–X1r, Y2v, and Y3v; Lewes Lewkenor's translation of Gasparo Contarini, *The Commonwealth and Government of Venice* (London, 1599), T2r; and Moryson, *An Itinerary* (London, 1617), H1v–H2r.

38. D4v. See also Fenton, P4v, and, for background, Tawney, Introd., pp. 125–7, and *Religion*, p. 53; Draper, pp. 45–6; and Nelson, *The Idea of Usury: From Tribal Brotherhood to Universal Otherhood*, 2nd edn (Chicago: Univ. of Chicago Press, 1969), p. 73 n. 2. Greenblatt seems to be the only critic to suggest a parallel between Antonio and the Monti di Pietà.

39. For fiscalism versus mercantilism, see Immanuel Wallerstein, *The Modern World-System: Capitalist Agriculture and the Origins of the European World-Economy in the Sixteenth Century* (New York: Academic Press, 1974), pp. 137–8 and 149. For possible problems with this hypothesis, as applied to Italy, see Pullan, p. 451. Greenblatt employs Wallerstein's paradigm to help explain *The Merchant of Venice*, but he does not seem aware that his argument consequently contradicts the position of those scholars, whom he also cites, who rely on the antiusury tracts. See his n. 5.

40. Nelson, 'The Usurer and the Merchant Prince', 120–2.

41. For similar perceptions, see Barber, p. 191, and Frye, p. 98.

42. Curiously, Brown, Introd. to his edition of *The Merchant of Venice*, p. xxxix, denies

that the play is anti-Semitic.

43. Danson, pp. 148–50, argues that Shakespeare allows Shylock a fairly strong case, but Draper, pp. 43–4, seems more persuasive in taking the opposite position.

44. See, for example, *Three Ladies*, D3v.

45. Robert Peterson's translation of Botero, *A Treatise. Concerning the Causes of the Magnificencie and Greatnes of Cities* (London, 1606), 13v.

46. Danson, p. 55.

47. Marx's remarks may be found in 'Contribution to the Critique of Hegel's *Philosophy of Right*: Introduction', in *The Marx–Engels Reader*, ed. Robert C. Tucker, 2nd edn (New York: Norton, 1978), p. 55; 'On the Jewish Question', in the *Marx–Engels Reader*, pp. 47–52; *The Process of Capitalist Production*, trans. Samuel Moore and Edward Aveling, vol. I of *Capital: A Critique of Political Economy*, ed. Frederick Engels (New York: International Publishers, 1967), pp. 287–8; and *The Process of Capitalist Production As a Whole*, vol. III of *Capital*, ed. Engels (New York: International Publishers, 1967), pp. 593–610 and 323–38.

48. *Capital*, I, 487.

49. The term is from Brents Stirling, Intro. to his edition of *The Merchant of Venice*, in *William Shakespeare: The Complete Works*, gen. ed. Alfred Harbage (Baltimore: Penguin, 1969), p. 213.

50. This position is most fully developed by Danson. See especially pp. 123–5.

51. For an early and crucial stage of this debate, see Ernst Bloch, Georg Lukács, Bertolt Brecht, Walter Benjamin, and Theodor Adorno, *Aesthetics and Politics*, trans. and ed. Ronald Taylor, Afterword by Jameson (London: NLB, 1977). Contemporary positions appear in Louis Althusser, 'The "Piccolo Teatro": Bertolazzi and Brecht', in *For Marx*, trans. Ben Brewster (London: NLB, 1977), pp. 129–51; Terry Eagleton, *Criticism and Ideology: A Study in Marxist Literary Theory* (London: NLB, 1976), pp. 102–61; and Pamela McCallum, 'Ideology and Cultural Theory', *Canadian Journal of Political and Social Theory*, 3 (1979), 131–43.

52. A recent attempt to define the meaning of the plot in terms of Act IV is Alice N. Benston's 'Portia, the Law, and the Tripartite Structure of *The Merchant of Venice*', *Shakespeare Quarterly*, 30 (1979), 367–85. See also Brown, Introd., p. li, and Danson, pp. 82–96 and 118–25. On the relationship between trial and drama, see Herbert Lindenberger, *Historical Drama: The Relation of Literature to Reality* (Chicago: Univ. of Chicago Press, 1975), pp. 21–3.

53. W. Gordon Zeeveld, *The Temper of Shakespeare's Thought* (New Haven: Yale Univ. Press, 1974), pp. 141–2. Other discussions of the play against the background of common law and Chancery include Maxine MacKay, 'The Merchant of Venice: A Reflection of the Early Conflict between Courts of Law and Courts of Equity', *Shakespeare Quarterly*, 15 (1964), 371–5; George Williams Keeton, *Shakespeare's Legal and Political Background* (New York: Barnes and Noble, 1967), pp. 132–52; and E.F.J. Tucker, 'The Letter of the Law in *The Merchant of Venice*', *Shakespeare Survey*, 29 (1976), 93–101. For a general review of commentaries on the legal situation in the play, see O. Hood Philips, *Shakespeare and the Lawyers* (London: Methuen, 1972), pp. 91–118.

54. Stone, *The Causes of the English Revolution* (London: Routledge and Kegan Paul, 1972), pp. 62, 75, 97–8, 103–105, and 114.

55. Zeeveld, p. 154 n. 20, and Tucker, pp. 98–101, both emphasize that Portia's argument and solution occur wholly within the canons of common law. But this particular integration of letter and spirit would have been impossible without Chancery's influence. For the popular prefeudal bases of English law, see Perry Anderson, *Passages from Antiquity to Feudalism* (London: NLB, 1974), p. 160, and *Lineages of the Absolutist State* (London: NLB, 1974), pp. 115–16.

56. Noël Salomon, *Recherches sur le thème paysan dans la 'comedia' au temps de Lope de Vega* (Bordeaux: Féret et Fils, 1965), passim, esp. pp. 167–96, 222–3, and 451–73; Raymond Williams, *The Country and the City* (New York: Oxford Univ. Press, 1973), pp. 18–21; and Elliot Krieger, 'The Dialectics of Shakespeare's Comedies', *Minnesota Review*, 7 (1976), 85–8.

57. Stone, *Causes*, pp. 105–108, and Williams, pp. 22–34.

58. Stone, *Crisis*, pp. 589–671.

59. Salingar, p. 312.

60. On the special role of love in this play, see R.F. Hill, *'The Merchant of Venice* and the Pattern of Romantic Comedy', *Shakespeare Survey*, 28 (1975), 75–87. For the problem of marriage in Act V, see Shell, pp. 86–7.

61. This is the case in Barbara K. Lewalski's distinguished essay, 'Biblical Allusion and Allegory in *The Merchant of Venice'*, *Shakespeare Quarterly*, 13 (1962), 327–43.

62. See Danson's efforts, pp. 136–9 and 164–9.

63. 'Meaning and Shakespeare', in *Shakespeare 1971: Proceedings of the World Shakespeare Congress Vancouver, August 1971*, ed. Clifford Leech and J.M.R. Margeson (Toronto: Univ. of Toronto Press, 1971), pp. 89–106. The quoted passages appear on p. 100.

64. This distinction is pursued, for different purposes, by E.D. Hirsch, Jr., 'Introduction: Meaning and Significance', in *The Aims of Interpretation* (Chicago: Univ. of Chicago Press, 1976), pp. 1–13.

65. Jameson, 'Metacommentary', p. 10, and 'Criticism in History', in *Weapons of Criticism: Marxism in America and the Literary Tradition*, ed. Norman Rudich (Palo Alto, CA: Ramparts Press, 1976), pp. 41–2.

66. Louise George Clubb, 'La mimesi della realtà invisibile nel dramma pastorale italiano e inglese del tardo rinascimento', *Misure Critiche*, 4 (1974), 65–92.

67. On the intrigue, see Laura Brown, 'The Divided Plot: Tragicomic Form in the Restoration', *ELH*, 47 (1980), 67–79.

68. Jameson, 'Metacommentary', p. 17.

69. For Shakespeare and Ciceronian prose, see Jonas A. Barish, *Ben Jonson and the Language of Prose Comedy* (Cambridge: Harvard Univ. Press, 1960), pp. 1–40. Brian Vickers, 'Shakespeare's Use of Rhetoric', in *A New Companion to Shakespeare Studies*, ed. Kenneth Muir and S. Schoenbaum (Cambridge: Cambridge Univ. Press, 1971), pp. 83–98, demonstrates that classical rhetoric informs the language of high and low characters alike. The remainder of the present discussion is primarily indebted to Robert Weimann's *Shakespeare and the Popular Tradition in the Theater: Studies in the Social Dimension of Dramatic Form and Function*, ed. Robert Schwartz (Baltimore: Johns Hopkins Univ. Press, 1978).

70. Geoffrey Bullough, *Narrative and Dramatic Sources of Shakespeare*, I (London: Routledge and Kegan Paul, 1957), p. 457, and Frye, p. 97.

71. Frye, p. 93, sees the affinity between the two characters, though in somewhat different terms. Bernard Spivack, *Shakespeare and the Allegory of Evil: The History of a Metaphor in Relation to His Major Villains* (New York: Columbia Univ. Press, 1958), generally tends to exclude Shylock from the vice tradition, but he neglects most of the relevant evidence.

72. Although this conclusion rests on the work of a number of contemporary scholars, most of the relevant data may still be found in E.K. Chambers, *The Elizabethan Stage*, 4 vols. (Oxford: Clarendon Press, 1923).

73. Anderson, *Lineages of the Absolutist State*.

74. Jameson, *The Political Unconscious*, p. 19.

5

Macbeth: History, Ideology and Intellectuals

Alan Sinfield

It is often said that *Macbeth* is about 'evil', but we might draw a more careful distinction: between the violence which the State considers legitimate and that which it does not. Macbeth, we may agree, is a dreadful murderer when he kills Duncan. But when he kills Macdonwald – 'a rebel' (I.ii.10) – he has Duncan's approval:

> For brave Macbeth (well he deserves that name),
> Disdaining Fortune, with his brandish'd steel,
> Which smok'd with bloody execution,
> Like Valour's minion, carv'd out his passage,
> Till he fac'd the slave;
> which ne'er shook hands, nor bade farewell to him,
> Till he unseam'd him from the nave to th' chops,
> And fix'd his head upon our battlements.
> *Duncan.* O valiant cousin! worthy gentleman!

(I.ii.16–24)[1]

Violence is good, in this view, when it is in the service of the prevailing dispositions of power; when it disrupts them it is evil. A claim to a monopoly of legitimate violence is fundamental in the development of the modern state; when that claim is successful, most citizens learn to regard state violence as qualitatively different from other violence and perhaps they don't think of state violence as violence at all (consider the actions of police, army and judiciary as opposed to those of pickets, protesters, criminals and terrorists). *Macbeth* focuses major strategies by which the state asserted its claim at one conjuncture.

Generally in Europe in the sixteenth century the development was from feudalism to the absolutist state.[2] Under feudalism, the king held authority among his peers, his equals, and his power was often little more than nominal; authority was distributed also among overlapping non-national institutions such as the church, estates, assemblies, regions and towns. In

93

the absolutist state, power became centralized in the figure of the monarch, the exclusive source of legitimacy. The movement from one to the other was of course contested, not only by the aristocracy and the peasantry, whose traditional rights were threatened, but also by the gentry and urban bourgeoisie, who found new space for power and influence within more elaborate economic and governmental structures. Because of these latter factors especially, the absolutist state was never fully established in England. Probably the peak of the monarch's personal power was reached by Henry VIII; the attempt of Charles I to reassert that power led to the English Revolution. In between, Elizabeth and James I, and those who believed their interests to lie in the same direction, sought to sustain royal power and to suppress dissidents. The latter category was broad; it comprised aristocrats like the Earls of Northumberland and Westmorland who led the Northern Rising of 1569 and the Duke of Norfolk who plotted to replace Elizabeth with Mary Queen of Scots in 1571, clergy who refused the state religion, gentry who supported them and who tried to raise awkward matters in Parliament, writers and printers who published criticism of state policy, the populace when it complained about food prices, enclosures, or anything.

The exercise of state violence against such dissidents depended upon the achievement of a degree of legitimation – upon the acceptance by many people that state power was, at least, the lesser of two evils. A principal means by which this was effected was the propagation of an ideology of absolutism, which represented the English state as a pyramid, any disturbance of which would produce general disaster, and which insisted increasingly on the 'divine right' of the monarch. This system was said to be 'natural' and ordained by 'God'; it was 'good' and disruptions of it 'evil'. This is what some Shakespeareans have celebrated as a just and harmonious 'world picture'. Compare Perry Anderson's summary: 'Absolutism was essentially just this: *a redeployed and recharged apparatus of feudal domination*, designed to clamp the peasant masses back into their traditional social position.'[3]

The reason why the state needed violence and propaganda was that the system was subject to persistent structural difficulties. *Macbeth*, like very many plays of the period, handles anxieties about the violence exercised under the aegis of absolutist ideology. Two main issues come into focus. The first is the threat of a split between legitimacy and actual power – when the monarch is not the strongest person in the state. Such a split was altogether likely during the transition from feudalism to the absolutist state; hence the infighting within the dominant group in most European countries. In England the matter was topical because of the Essex rebellion in 1599: it was easy for the charismatic earl, who had shown at Cadiz that Englishmen could defeat Spaniards, to suppose that he would make a better ruler than the ageing and indecisive Elizabeth, for all her legitimacy. So Shakespeare's Richard II warns Northumberland, the kingmaker, that he is bound, structurally, to disturb the rule of Bolingbroke:

> thou shalt think,
> Though he [Bolingbroke] divide the realm and give thee half,
> It is too little, helping him to all.[4]

Jonathan Dollimore and I have argued elsewhere that the potency of the myth of Henry V in Shakespeare's play, written at the time of Essex's ascendancy, derives from the striking combination in that monarch of legitimacy and actual power.[5] At the start of *Macbeth* the manifest dependency of Duncan's state upon its best fighter sets up a dangerous instability (this is explicit in the sources). In the opening soliloquy of Act I scene vii Macbeth freely accords to Duncan entire legitimacy: he is Duncan's kinsman, subject and host, the king has been 'clear in his great office', and the idea of his deposition evokes religious imagery of angels, damnation and cherubims. But that is all the power the king has that does not depend upon Macbeth; against it is ranged 'Vaulting ambition', Macbeth's impetus to convert his actual power into full regal authority.

The split between legitimacy and actual power was always a potential malfunction in the developing absolutist state. A second problem was less dramatic but more persistent. It was this: what is the difference between absolutism and tyranny? – having in mind contemporary occurrences like the Massacre of St Bartholomew's in France in 1572, the arrest of more than a hundred witches and the torturing and killing of many of them in Scotland in 1590–91, and the suppression of the Irish by English armies. The immediate reference for questions of legitimate violence in relation to *Macbeth* is the Gunpowder Plot of 1605. This attempted violence against the state followed upon many years of state violence against Roman Catholics: the absolutist state sought to draw religious institutions entirely within its control, and Catholics who actively refused were subjected to fines, imprisonment, torture and execution. Consider the sentence passed upon Jane Wiseman in 1598:

> The sentence is that the said Jane Wiseman shall be led to the prison of the Marshalsea of the Queen's Bench, and there naked, except for a linen cloth about the lower part of her body, be laid upon the ground, lying directly on her back: and a hollow shall be made under her head and her head placed in the same; and upon her body in every part let there be placed as much of stones and iron as she can bear and more; and as long as she shall live, she shall have of the worst bread and water of the prison next her; and on the day she eats, she shall not drink, and on the day she drinks she shall not eat, so living until she die.[6]

This was for 'receiving, comforting, helping and maintaining priests', and refusing to reveal, under torture, who else was doing the same thing, and for refusing to plead. There is nothing abstract or theoretical about the state violence to which the present essay refers. Putting the issue succinctly in relation to Shakespeare's play, what is the difference between Macbeth's rule and that of contemporary European monarchs?

In *Basilikon Doron* (1599) King James tried to protect the absolutist state from such pertinent questions by asserting an utter distinction between 'a lawful good King' and 'an usurping Tyran':

> The one acknowledgeth himselfe ordained for his people, having received from God a burthen of government, whereof he must be countable: the other thinketh his people ordeined for him, a prey to his passions and inordinate appetites, as the fruites of his magnanimitie: And therefore, as their ends are directly contrarie, so are their whole actions, as meanes, whereby they preasse to attaine to their endes.[7]

Evidently James means to deny that the absolutist monarch has anything significant in common with someone like Macbeth. Three aspects of James's strategy in this passage are particularly revealing. First, he depends upon an utter polarization between the two kinds of ruler. Such antitheses are characteristic of the ideology of absolutism: they were called upon to tidy the uneven apparatus of feudal power into a far neater structure of the monarch versus the rest, and protestantism tended to see 'spiritual' identities in similarly polarized terms. James himself explained the function of demons like this: 'since the Devill is the verie contrarie opposite to God, there can be no better way to know God, then by the contrarie'.[8] So it is with the two kinds of rulers: the badness of one seems to guarantee the goodness of the other. Second, by defining the lawful good king against the usurping tyrant, James refuses to admit the possibility that a ruler who has *not* usurped will be tyrannical. Thus he seems to cope with potential splits between legitimacy and actual power by insisting on the unique status of the lawful good king, and to head off questions about the violence committed by such a ruler by suggesting that all his actions will be uniquely legitimate. Third, we may notice that the whole distinction, as James develops it, is in terms not of the *behaviour* of the lawful good king and the usurping tyrant, respectively, but in terms of their *motives*. This seems to render vain any assessment of the actual manner of rule of the absolute monarch. On these arguments, any disturbance of the current structure of power relations is against God and the people, and consequently any violence in the interest of the status quo is acceptable. Hence the legitimate killing of Jane Wiseman. (In fact, the distinction between lawful and tyrannical rule eventually breaks down even in James's analysis, as his commitment to the state leads him to justify even tyrannical behaviour in established monarchs.)[9]

It is often assumed that *Macbeth* is engaged in the same project as King James: attempting to render coherent and persuasive the ideology of the absolutist state. The grounds for a Jamesian reading are plain enough – to the point where it is often claimed that the play was designed specially for the king. At every opportunity Macbeth is disqualified ideologically and his opponents ratified. An entire antithetical apparatus of nature and supernature – the concepts through which a dominant ideology most commonly seeks to establish itself – is called upon to witness against him as usurping tyrant. 'Nature' protests against Macbeth (II.iv), Lady Macbeth welcomes 'Nature's mischief' (I.v.50) and Macbeth will have 'Nature's germens tumble all together, / Even till destruction sicken' (IV.i.59–60). Good and evil are personified absolutely by Edward the Confessor and the Witches, and the language of heaven and hell runs through the play; Lady Macbeth conjures up 'murth'ring ministers' (I.v.48) and Macbeth acknowledges 'The deep damnation of his [Duncan's] taking-off' (I.vii.20). It all seems organized to validate James's contention, that there is all the difference in this world and the next between a usurping tyrant and a lawful good king. The whole strategy is epitomized in the account of Edward's alleged curing of 'the Evil' – actually scrofula – 'A most miraculous work in this good King' (IV.iii.146–7). James himself knew that this was a superstitious practice, and he refused to undertake it until his advisers persuaded him that it would strengthen his claim to the throne in the public eye.[10] As Francis Bacon observed, notions of the supernatural help to keep people acquiescent (e.g. the man in pursuit of power will do well to attribute his success 'rather to divine Providence and felicity, than to his own virtue or policy').[11] *Macbeth* draws upon such notions more than any other play by Shakespeare. It all suggests that Macbeth is an extraordinary eruption in a good state – obscuring the thought that there might be any pronity to structural malfunctioning in the system. It suggests that Macbeth's violence is wholly bad, whereas state violence committed by legitimate monarchs is quite different.

Such manoeuvres are even more necessary to a Jamesian reading of the play in respect of the deposition and killing of Macbeth. Absolutist ideology declared that even tyrannical monarchs must not be resisted, yet Macbeth could hardly be allowed to triumph. Here the play offers two moves. First, the fall of Macbeth seems to result more from (super)natural than human agency: it seems like an effect of the opposition of good and evil ('Macbeth / Is ripe for shaking, and the Powers above / Put on their instruments' – IV.iii.237–9). Most cunningly, although there are material explanations for the moving of Birnam Wood and the unusual birth of Macduff, the audience is allowed to believe, at the same time, that these are (super)natural effects (thus the play works upon us almost as the Witches work upon Macbeth). Second, in so far as Macbeth's fall is accomplished by human agency, the play is careful to suggest that he is hardly in office before he is overthrown. The years of successful rule specified in the chronicles are erased and, as Paul points out, neither Macduff nor Malcolm has tendered any allegiance to Macbeth.[12] The action rushes along, he is swept away as if he had never truly been king. *Even so*, the contradiction can hardly vanish altogether. For the Jamesian reading it is necessary for Macbeth to be a complete usurping tyrant in order that he shall set off the lawful good king, and also, at the same time, for him not to be a ruler at all in order that he may properly be deposed and killed. Macbeth kills two people at the start of the play: a rebel and the king, and these are apparently utterly different acts of violence. That is the ideology of absolutism. Macduff also, killing Macbeth, is killing both a rebel and a king, but now the two are apparently the same person. The ultimate intractability of this kind of contradiction disturbs the Jamesian reading of the play.

Criticism has often supposed, all too easily, that the Jamesian reading of *Macbeth* is necessary on historical grounds – that other views of state ideology were impossible for Shakespeare and his contemporaries. But this was far from being so: there was a well-developed theory allowing for resistance by the nobility,[13] and the Gunpowder Plotters were manifestly unconvinced by the king's arguments. Even more pertinent is the theory of the Scotsman George Buchanan, as we may deduce from the fact that James tried to suppress Buchanan's writings in 1584 after his assumption of personal rule; in *Basilikon Doron* he advises his son to 'use the Law upon the keepers' of 'such infamous invectives' (p. 40). With any case so strenuously overstated and manipulative as James's, we should ask what alternative position it is trying to put down. Arguments in favour of absolutism constitute one part of *Macbeth*'s ideological field – the range of ideas and attitudes brought into play by the text; another main part may be represented by Buchanan's *De jure regni* (1579) and *History of Scotland* (1582). In Buchanan's view sovereignty derives from and remains with the people; the king who exercises power against their will is a tyrant and should be deposed.[14] The problem in Scotland is not unruly subjects, but unruly monarchs: 'Rebellions there spring less from the people than from the rulers, when they try to reduce a kingdom which from earliest times had always been ruled by law to an absolute and lawless despotism'.[15] Buchanan's theory is the virtual antithesis of James's; it was used eventually to justify the deposition of James's son.

Buchanan's *History of Scotland* is usually reckoned to be one of the sources of *Macbeth*. It was written to illustrate his theory of sovereignty and to justify the overthrow of Mary Queen of Scots in 1567. In it the dichotomy of true lawful king and usurping tyrant collapses, for Mary is the lawful ruler *and* the tyrant, and her deposers are usurpers *and yet* lawful also. To her are attributed many of the traits of Macbeth: she is said to hate integrity in others, to appeal to the predictions of witches, to use foreign mercenaries, to place spies in the households of opponents and to threaten the lives of the nobility; after her surrender she is humiliated in the streets of Edinburgh as Macbeth fears to be. It is alleged that she would not have shrunk from the murder of her son if she could have reached him.[16] This account of Mary as arch-tyrant embarrassed James, and that is perhaps why just eight kings are shown to Macbeth by the Witches (IV.i.119). Nevertheless, it was well established in protestant propaganda and in Spenser's *Faerie Queene*, and the Gunpowder Plot would tend to revivify it. Any recollection of the alleged tyranny of Mary, the lawful ruler, prompts awareness of the contradictions in absolutist ideology, disturbing the customary interpretation of *Macbeth*. Once we are alert to this disturbance, the Jamesian reading of the play begins to leak at every joint.

One set of difficulties is associated with the theology of good, evil and divine ordination which purports to discriminate Macbeth's violence from that legitimately deployed by the state. I have written elsewhere of the distinctive attempt of Reformation Christianity to cope with the para- doxical conjunction in one deity of total power and goodness, and will here only indicate the scope of the problem. *Macbeth*, in the manner of absolutist ideology and Reformation Christianity, strongly polarizes 'good' and 'evil', but, at the same time, also like the prevailing doctrine, it insists on complete divine control of all human events. This twin determination produces a deity that sponsors the 'evil' it condemns and punishes. Orthodox doctrine, which was Calvinist in general orientation, hardly flinched from this conclusion (for example, James said in his *Dæmonologie* that fallen angels are 'Gods hang-men, to execute such turnes as he employes them in').[17] Nevertheless, fictional reworkings of it often seem to point up its awkwardness, suggesting an unresolvable anxiety. Tradi- tional criticism registers this factor in *Macbeth* in its inconclusive debates about how far the Witches make Macbeth more or less excusable or in charge of his own destiny. The projection of political issues onto supposedly (super)natural dimensions seems to ratify the absolutist state but threatens also to open up another range of difficulties in contemporary ideology.

Macbeth also reveals a range of directly political problems to the reader rendered wary by Buchanan's analysis. They tend to break down the antithesis, upon which James relied, between the usurping tyrant and the legitimately violent ruler. Many of them have been noted by critics, though most commonly with the idea of getting them to fit into a single, coherent reading of the play. For a start, Duncan's status is in doubt: it is unclear how far his authority runs, he is imperceptive, and his state is in chaos well before Macbeth's violence against it (G.K. Hunter in the introduction to his Penguin edition (1967) registers unease at the 'violence and bloodthirstiness' of Macbeth's killing of Macdonwald (pp. 9–10)). Nor is Malcolm's title altogether clear, since Duncan's declaration of him as 'Prince of Cumberland' (I.iv.35–42) suggests what the chronicles indicate, namely that the succession was not necessarily hereditary; Macbeth seems to be elected by the thanes (II.iv.29–32).

I have suggested that *Macbeth* may be read as working to justify the overthrow of the usurping tyrant. Nevertheless, the *awkwardness* of the issue is brought to the surface by the uncertain behaviour of Banquo. In the sources he collaborates with Macbeth, but to allow that in the play would taint King James's line and blur the idea of the one monstrous eruption. Shakespeare compromises and makes Banquo do nothing at all. He fears Macbeth played 'most foully for't' (III.i.3) but does not even communicate his knowledge of the Witches' prophecies. Instead he wonders if they may 'set me up in hope' (III.i.10). If it is right for Malcolm and Macduff, eventually, to overthrow Macbeth, then it would surely be right for Banquo to take a clearer line.

Furthermore, the final position of Macduff appears quite disconcerting, once we read it with Buchanan's more realistic, political analysis in mind: Macduff at the end stands in the same relation to Malcolm as Macbeth did to Duncan in the beginning. He is now the king-maker on whom the legitimate monarch depends, and the recurrence of the whole sequence may be anticipated (in production this might be suggested by a final meeting of Macduff and the Witches).[18] For the Jamesian reading it is necessary to feel that Macbeth is a distinctively 'evil' eruption in a 'good' system; awareness of the role of Macduff in Malcolm's state alerts us to the fundamental instability of power relations during the transition to absolutism, and consequently to the uncertain validity of the claim of the state to the legitimate use of violence. Certainly Macbeth is a murderer and an oppressive ruler, but he is one version of the absolutist ruler, not the polar opposite.

Malcolm himself raises very relevant issues in the conversation in which he tests Macduff: specifically tyrannical qualities are invoked. At one point, according to Buchanan, the Scottish lords 'give the benefit of the doubt' to Mary and her husband, following the thought that 'more secret faults' may be tolerated 'so long as these do not involve a threat to the welfare of the state' (*Tyrannous Reign*, p. 88). Macduff is prepared to accept considerable threats to the welfare of Scotland:

                              Boundless intemperance
In nature is a tyranny; it hath been
Th' untimely emptying of the happy throne,
And fall of many kings. But fear not yet
To take upon you what is yours: you may
Convey your pleasures in a spacious plenty,
And yet seem cold – the time you may so hoodwink:
We have willing dames enough; there cannot be
That vulture in you, to devour so many
As will to greatness dedicate themselves,
Finding it so inclin'd.

                                                       (IV.iii.66–76)

Tyranny in nature means disturbance in the metaphorical kingdom of a
person's nature but, in the present context, one is likely to think of the
effects of the monarch's intemperance on the literal kingdom. Macduff
suggests that such behaviour has caused the fall not just of usurpers but of
kings, occupants of 'the happy throne'. Despite this danger, he encourages
Malcolm 'To take upon you what is yours' – a sinister way of putting it,
implying either Malcolm's title to the state in general or his rights over the
women he wants to seduce or assault. Fortunately the latter will not be
necessary, there are 'willing dames enough': Macduff is ready to mortgage
both the bodies and (within the ideology invoked in the play) the souls of
women to the monster envisaged as lawful good king. It will be all right,
apparently, because people can be hoodwinked: Macduff allows us to see
that the virtues James tries to identify with the absolutist monarch are an
ideological strategy, and that the illusion of them will probably be
sufficient to keep the system going.

    Nor is this the worst: Malcolm claims more faults, and according to
Macduff 'avarice / Sticks deeper' (lines 84–5): Malcolm may corrupt not
merely people but property relations. Yet this too is to be condoned. Of
course, Malcolm is not actually like this, but the point is that he well could
be, as Macduff says many kings have been, and that would all be
acceptable. And even Malcolm's eventual protestation of innocence cannot
get round the fact that he has been lying. He says 'my first false speaking
/ Was this upon myself' (lines 130–31) and that may indeed be true, but it
nevertheless indicates the circumspection that will prove useful to the
lawful good king, as much as to the tyrant. In Holinshed the culminating
vice claimed by Malcolm is lying, but Shakespeare replaces it with a
general and rather desperate evocation of utter tyranny (lines 91–100); was
the original self-accusation perhaps too pointed? The whole conversation
takes off from the specific and incomparable tyranny of Macbeth, but in the
process succeeds in suggesting that there may be considerable overlap
between the qualities of the tyrant and the true king.

*

Macbeth allows space for two quite different interpretive organizations: against a Jamesian illustration of the virtues of absolutism we may produce a disturbance of that reading, illuminated by Buchanan. This latter makes visible the way religion is used to underpin state ideology, and undermines notions that established monarchs must not be challenged or removed and that state violence is utterly distinctive and legitimate. It is commonly assumed that the function of criticism is to resolve such questions of interpretation – to go through the text with an eye to sources, other plays, theatrical convention, historical context and so on, deciding on which side the play comes down and explaining away contrary evidence. However, this is neither an adequate programme nor an adequate account of what generally happens.

Let us suppose, to keep the argument moving along, that the Jamesian reading fits better with *Macbeth* and its Jacobean context, as we understand them at present. Two questions then present themselves: what is the status of the disturbance of that reading, which I have produced by bringing Buchanan into view? And what are the consequences of customary critical insistence upon the Jamesian reading?

On the first question, I would make three points. First, the Buchanan disturbance *is in the play*, and inevitably so. Even if we believe that Shakespeare was trying to smooth over difficulties in absolutist ideology, to do this significantly he must deal with the issues which resist convenient inclusion. Those issues must be brought into visibility in order that they can be handled, and once exposed they are available for the reader or audience to seize and focus upon, as an alternative to the more complacent reading. A position tends to suppose an *op*position. Even James's writings are vulnerable to such analysis, for instance when he brings up the awkward fact that the prophet Samuel urgently warns the people of Israel against choosing a king because he will tyrannize over them. This prominent biblical instance could hardly be ignored, so James quotes it and says that Samuel was preparing the Israelites to be obedient and patient.[19] Yet once James has brought Samuel's pronouncement into visibility, the reader is at liberty to doubt the king's tendentious interpretation of it. It is hardly possible to deny the reader this scope: even the most strenuous closure can be repudiated as inadequate. We are led to think of the text not as propounding a unitary and coherent meaning which is to be discovered, but as handling a range of issues (probably intractable issues, for they make the best stories), and as unable to control the development of radically divergent interpretations.

Second, the Buchanan disturbance has been activated, in the present essay, as a consequence of the writer's scepticism about Jamesian ideological strategies and his concern with current political issues. It is conceivable that many readers of *Macbeth* will come to share this outlook. Whether this happens or not, the theoretical implication may be taken: if such a situation should come about, the terms in which *Macbeth* is customarily discussed would shift, and eventually the Buchanan disturbance would come to seem an obvious, natural way to consider the play. That is how notions of appropriate approaches to a text get established. We may observe the process, briefly, in the career of the Witches. For many members of Jacobean audiences, Witches were a social and spiritual reality: they were as real as Edward the Confessor, perhaps more so. As belief in the physical manifestation of supernatural powers, and especially demonic powers, weakened, the Witches were turned into an operatic display, with new scenes, singing and dancing, fine costumes and flying machines. In an adaptation by Sir William Davenant, this was the only stage form of the play from 1674 to 1744, and even after Davenant's version was abandoned the Witches' divertissements were staged, until 1888.[20] Latterly we have adopted other ways with the Witches – being still unable, of course, to contemplate them, as most of Shakespeare's audience probably did, as phenomena one might encounter on a heath. Kenneth Muir comments: 'with the fading of belief in the objective existence of devils, they and their operations can yet symbolize the workings of evil in the hearts of men' (New Arden *Macbeth*, p. lxx). Recent critical accounts and theatrical productions have developed all kinds of strategies to make the Witches 'work' for our time. These successive accommodations of one aspect of the play to prevailing attitudes are blatant, but they illustrate the extent to which critical orthodoxy is not the mere response to the text which it claims to be: it is *remaking* it within currently acceptable parameters.[21] The Buchanan disturbance may not always remain a marginal gloss to the Jamesian reading.

Third, we may assume that the Buchanan disturbance was part of the response of some among the play's initial audiences. It is in the nature of the matter that it is impossible to assess how many people inclined towards Buchanan's analysis of royal power. That there were such may be supposed from the multifarious challenges to state authority – culminating, of course, in the Civil War. *Macbeth* was almost certainly read against James by some Jacobeans. This destroys the claim to privilege of the Jamesian reading on the ground that it is historically valid: we must envisage diverse original audiences, activating diverse implications in the text. And we may demand comparable interpretive licence for ourselves. Initially the play occupied a complex position in its ideological field, and we should expect no less today.

With these considerations about the status of the Buchanan disturbance in mind, the question about the customary insistence on the Jamesian reading appears as a question about the politics of criticism. Like other kinds of cultural production, literary criticism helps to influence the way people think about the world; that is why the present essay seeks to make space for an oppositional understanding of the text and the state. It is plain that most criticism has not only reproduced but endorsed Jamesian ideology, so discouraging scrutiny, which *Macbeth* can promote, of the legitimacy of state violence. That we are dealing with live issues is shown by the almost uncanny resemblances between the Gunpowder Plot and the 1984 Brighton Bombing, and in the comparable questions about state and other violence which they raise. My concluding thoughts are about the politics of the prevailing readings of *Macbeth*. I distinguish conservative and liberal positions; both tend to dignify their accounts with the honorific term 'tragedy'.

The conservative position insists that the play is about 'evil'. Kenneth Muir offers a string of quotations to this effect: it is 'Shakespeare's "most profound and mature vision of evil"; "the whole play may be writ down as a wrestling of destruction with creation"; it is "a statement of evil"; "it is a picture of a special battle in a universal war ..."; and it "contains the decisive orientation of Shakespearean good and evil"'.[22] This is little more than Jamesian ideology writ large: killing Macdonwald is 'good' and killing Duncan is 'evil', and the hierarchical society envisaged in absolutist ideology is identified with the requirements of nature, supernature and the 'human condition'. Often this view is elaborated as a socio-political programme, allegedly expounded by Shakespeare and implicitly endorsed by the critic. So Muir writes of 'an orderly and closely-knit society, in contrast to the disorder consequent upon Macbeth's initial crime [i.e. killing Duncan, not Macdonwald]. The naturalness of that order, and the unnaturalness of its violation by Macbeth, is emphasized ...' (New Arden *Macbeth*, p. li). Irving Ribner says Fleance is 'symbolic of a future rooted in the acceptance of natural law, which inevitably must return to reassert God's harmonious order when evil has worked itself out'.[23]

This conservative endorsement of Jamesian ideology is not intended to ratify the modern state. Rather, like much twentieth-century literary criticism, it is backward-looking, appealing to an earlier and preferable supposed condition of society. Roger Scruton comments: 'If a conservative is also a restorationist, this is because he lives close to society, and feels in himself the sickness which infects the common order. How, then, can he fail to direct his eyes towards that state of health from which things have declined?'[24] This quotation is close to the terms in which many critics write of *Macbeth*, and their evocation of the Jamesian order which is allegedly restored at the end of the play constitutes a wistful gesture towards what they would regard as a happy ending for our troubled society. However, because this conservative approach is based on an inadequate analysis of political and social process, it gains no purchase on the main determinants of state power.

A liberal position hesitates to endorse any state power so directly, finding some saving virtue in Macbeth: 'To the end he never totally loses our sympathy'; 'we must still not lose our sympathy for the criminal'.[25] In this view there is a flaw in the state, it fails to accommodate the particular consciousness of the refined individual. Macbeth's imagination is set against the blandness of normative convention and for all his transgressions, perhaps because of them, Macbeth transcends the laws he breaks. In John Bayley's version: 'His superiority consists in a passionate sense for ordinary life, its seasons and priorities, a sense which his fellows in the play ignore in themselves or take for granted. Through the deed which tragedy requires of him he comes to know not only himself, but what life is all about.'[26] I call this 'liberal' because it is anxious about a state, absolutist or modern, which can hardly take cognizance of the individual sensibility, and it is prepared to validate to some degree the recalcitrant individual. But it will not undertake the political analysis which would press the case. Hence there is always in such criticism a reservation about Macbeth's revolt and a sense of relief that it ends in defeat: nothing could have been done anyway, it was all inevitable, written in the human condition. This retreat from the possibility of political analysis and action leaves the state virtually unquestioned almost as fully as the conservative interpretation.

Shakespeare, notoriously, has a way of anticipating all possibilities. The idea of literary intellectuals identifying their own deepest intuitions of the universe in the experience of the 'great' tragic hero who defies the limits of the human condition is surely a little absurd; we may sense delusions of grandeur. *Macbeth* includes much more likely models for its conservative and liberal critics in the characters of the two doctors. The English doctor has just four and a half lines (IV.iii.141–5) in which he says King Edward is coming and that sick people whose malady conquers the greatest efforts of medical skill await him, expecting a heavenly cure for 'evil'. Malcolm, the king to be, says 'I thank you, Doctor'. This doctor is the equivalent of conservative intellectuals who encourage respect for mystificatory images of ideal hierarchy which have served the state in the past, and who invoke 'evil', 'tragedy' and 'the human condition' to produce, in effect, acquiescence in state power.

The Scottish doctor, in V.i and V.iii, is actually invited to cure the sickness of the rulers and by implication the state: 'If thou couldst, Doctor, cast / The water of my land, find her disease ...' (V.iii.50–51). But this doctor, like the liberal intellectual, hesitates to press an analysis. He says: 'This disease is beyond my practice' (V.i.56), 'I think, but dare not speak' (V.i.76), 'Therein the patient / Must minister to himself' (V.iii.45–6), 'Were I from Dunsinane away and clear, / Profit again should hardly draw me here' (V.iii.61–2). He wrings his hands at the evidence of state violence and protects his conscience with asides. This is like the liberal intellectual who knows there is something wrong at the heart of the system but will not envisage a radical alternative and, to ratify this attitude, discovers in Shakespeare's plays 'tragedy' and 'the human condition' as explanations of the supposedly inevitable defeat of the person who steps out of line.

By conventional standards, the present essay is perverse. But an oppositional criticism is bound to appear thus: its task is to work across the grain of customary assumptions and, if necessary, across the grain of the text, as it is customarily perceived. Of course, literary intellectuals don't have much influence over state violence, their therapeutic power is very limited. Nevertheless, writing, teaching, and other modes of communicating all contribute to the steady, long-term formation of opinion, to the establishment of legitimacy. This contribution King James himself did not neglect. An oppositional analysis of texts like *Macbeth* will read them to expose, rather than promote, state ideologies.

Notes

1. *Macbeth* is quoted from the New Arden Shakespeare, 9th edn, ed. Kenneth Muir (London: Methuen, 1962).

2. See Nicos Poulantzas, *Political Power and Social Classes*, translation editor Timothy O'Hagan (London: New Left Books, 1973), pp. 157–68; Perry Anderson, *Lineages of the Absolute State* (London: New Left Books, 1974).

3. Anderson, *Lineages of the Absolute State*, p. 18. For further studies of the scope of absolutist ideology in England see V.G. Kiernan, 'State and Nation in Western Europe', *Past and Present*, 31 (1965), 20–38; W.T. MacCaffrey, 'England: The Crown and the New Aristocracy, 1540–1600', *Past and Present*, 30 (1965), 52–64; Alan Sinfield, 'Power and Ideology: An Outline Theory and Sidney's *Arcadia*', *English Literary History*, 52 (1985), 259–77. On attitudes to government and *Macbeth* see Michael Hawkins, 'History, Politics and *Macbeth*' in *Focus on 'Macbeth'*, ed. John Russell Brown (London: Routledge, 1982).

4. *King Richard II*, ed. Peter Ure, New Arden edn (London: Methuen, 1956), V.i.59–61.

5. Jonathan Dollimore and Alan Sinfield, 'History and Ideology: The Instance of *Henry V*', in *Alternative Shakespeares*, ed. John Drakakis (London: Methuen, 1985).

6. John Gerard, *The Autobiography of an Elizabethan*, trans. Philip Caraman (London: Longman, 1951), pp. 52–3.

7. *The Political Works of James I*, ed. Charles Howard McIlwain (New York: Russell and Russell, 1965), p. 18.

8. King James the First, *Dæmonologie (1597), Newes from Scotland (1591)* (London: Bodley Head, 1924), p. 55.

9. See James, *The Trew Law of Free Monarchies*, in *Political Works*, ed. McIlwain, pp. 56–61, 66.

10. Henry Paul, *The Royal Play of 'Macbeth'* (New York: Octagon Books, 1978), p. 373.

11. Francis Bacon, *Essays*, introduction by Michael J. Hawkins (London: Dent, 1972). See further Jonathan Dollimore, *Radical Tragedy* (Brighton: Harvester, 1984), specially ch. 5; Alan Sinfield, *Literature in Protestant England 1560–1660* (London: Croom Helm, 1983), ch. 7.

12. Paul, *The Royal Play of 'Macbeth'*, p. 196.

13. See W.D. Briggs, 'Political Ideas in Sidney's *Arcadia*', *Studies in Philology*, 28

(1931), 137–61, and 'Philip Sidney's Political Ideas', ibid., 29 (1932), 534–42.

14. See *The Tyrannous Reign of Mary Stewart, George Buchanan's Account*, trans. and ed. W.A. Gatherer (Edinburgh University Press, 1958), pp. 12–13; James E. Phillips, 'George Buchanan and the Sidney Circle', *Huntington Library Quarterly*, 12 (1948/9), 23–55; I.D. McFarlane, *Buchanan* (London: Duckworth, 1981), pp. 392–440.

15. *The Tyrannous Reign of Mary Stewart*, p. 49; see also p. 99.

16. *The Tyrannous Reign of Mary Stewart*, pp. 72, 86, 91, 111, 119, 145, 153; cf. *Macbeth*, III.i.48–56; V.vii.17–18; III.v.130–31; V.viii.27–9.

17. King James, *Dæmonologie*, p. 20. See further Sinfield, *Literature in Protestant England*, specially chapters 2, 6.

18. However, as Jim McLaverty points out to me, the play has arranged that Macduff will not experience temptation from his wife. In the chronicles Malcolm's son is overthrown by Donalbain; in Polanski's film of *Macbeth* Donalbain is made to meet the Witches.

19. *The Trew Law of Free Monarchies*, in *Political Works*, ed. McIlwain, pp. 56–61; referring to I Sam. 8:9–20.

20. See Hunter, *Macbeth*, Penguin edition, pp. 33–4; Dennis Bartholomeusz, *'Macbeth' and the Players* (Cambridge University Press, 1969). On the Witches and the ideological roles of women in the play see Peter Stallybrass, *'Macbeth* and Witchcraft', in Brown, ed., *Focus on 'Macbeth'*.

21. See further Jonathan Dollimore and Alan Sinfield, eds, *Political Shakespeare* (Manchester University Press, 1985), chs. 7, 9, 10.

22. Muir in the New Arden *Macbeth*, p. xlix, quoting G. Wilson Knight, L.C. Knights, F.C. Kolbe, Derek Traversi. See also Irving Ribner, *Patterns in Shakespearean Tragedy* (London: Methuen, 1960), p. 153; Robert Ornstein, *The Moral Vision of Jacobean Tragedy* (University of Wisconsin, 1965), p. 230; Hunter, Penguin edition, p. 7.

23. Ribner, *Patterns in Shakespearean Tragedy*, p. 159.

24. Roger Scruton, *The Meaning of Conservatism* (Harmondsworth: Penguin, 1980), p. 21.

25. A.C. Bradley, *Shakespearean Tragedy*, 2nd edn (London: Macmillan, 1965), p. 305; Wayne Booth, 'Macbeth as Tragic Hero', *Journal of General Education*, 6 (1951), revised for *Shakespeare's Tragedies*, ed. Laurence Lerner (Harmondsworth: Penguin, 1963), p. 186. See also Hunter, Penguin edition, pp. 26–9; Wilbur Sanders, *The Dramatist and the Received Idea* (Cambridge University Press, 1968), pp. 282–307.

26. John Bayley, *Shakespeare and Tragedy* (London: Routledge, 1981), p. 199; see also p. 193. I am grateful for the stimulating comments of Russell Jackson, Tony Inglis, Peter Holland and Jonathan Dollimore.

6

Martial Law in the Land of Cockaigne
Stephen Greenblatt

I want to begin this chapter with a sermon that Hugh Latimer, the great Protestant divine martyred during the reign of Mary Tudor, delivered before the Lady Catharine Bertie, duchess of Suffolk, in 1552. In the course of expounding his text, the Lord's Prayer, Latimer tells of something that happened many years before in Cambridge. He had gone with Thomas Bilney – the man who converted Latimer and who was himself martyred in the later years of Henry VIII's rule – to the town prison to urge the condemned to acknowledge their faults and to bear patiently their punishments. Among the prisoners was a pregnant woman who had been convicted of murdering one of her children. The woman claimed that the child had been sick for a year and had died of natural causes. Her husband being away, she alone witnessed the death. She went, she said, to her neighbours and friends to seek their help to prepare the child for burial, but it was harvest time and no one was at home. Therefore alone, 'in an heaviness and trouble of spirit', she made the necessary preparations and buried the dead. But when her husband returned home, he – who 'loved her not; and therefore ... sought means to make her out of the way' – accused her of murdering the child.[1] The accusation was believed by the Cambridge jury, and the woman was sentenced to be executed, the execution being delayed only until such time as she delivered her baby.

When Latimer spoke with her in prison, the woman steadfastly maintained her innocence, and after 'earnest inquisition' he came to believe her story. Immediately thereafter it chanced that he was called to Windsor to preach before Henry VIII. After the sermon the king graciously strolled with the minister in a gallery. Latimer knelt, told the woman's story, begged the king for a royal pardon on her behalf, and received it. He returned to Cambridge, pardon in hand, but he kept it hidden, exhorting the woman to confess the truth. She held fast to her professions of innocence.

In due time the woman had her baby, and Latimer consented to be its godfather. The moment had thus come for the woman's execution, and she was in an agony of apprehension. But she was fearful, Latimer found, not because she was about to die but because she would die without being 'churched' – that is, without the Catholic rite of purification based on the Jewish rituals traditionally held after childbirth (or menstruation) to cleanse the woman of the stain associated with any blood or discharge. 'For she thought,' writes Latimer, 'that she should have been damned, if she should suffer without purification.'

Latimer and Bilney then set about to disabuse her of this doctrinal error. They explained that the law of purification 'was made unto the Jews, and not unto us; and that women lying in child-bed be not unclean before God'. Significantly, Latimer opposed not the ritual of purification but only the belief that such a ritual cleanses women of sin, for women, he argues, 'be as well in the favour of God before they be purified as after'. Purification is not a theological but rather 'a civil and politic law, made for natural honesty sake; signifying, that a woman before the time of her purification, that is to say, as long as she is a green woman, is not meet to do such acts as other women, nor to have company with her husband: for it is against natural honesty, and against the commonwealth.' Only when the poor prisoner accepted this doctrinal point and agreed that she could go to her death unchurched and still receive salvation did Latimer produce the royal pardon and let her go.

I want to suggest that this little story reveals characteristic Renaissance beliefs and practices, and I propose to begin by noting some aspects of the gender relations it sketches.

First, we encounter the story as an allegorically charged but 'real-life' tale about a woman, a tale that Latimer relates in a sermon originally delivered before another woman. As such, perhaps it subtly suggests, in the presence of a social superior, Latimer's moral superiority and power and so reestablishes male dominance in a moment of apparent inferiority.[2]

Second, the story could perhaps have been told about a male prisoner in the grip of a comparable 'superstition' – let us imagine, for example, that he feared damnation if he did not have auricular confession and absolution prior to execution – but the prisoner's being female manifestly enhances its special symbolic charge. The woman's body after childbirth is polluted in 'nature' and in the commonwealth but not in the eyes of God: hence she can exemplify directly and in the flesh the crucial theological distinction between, on the one hand, the domain of law and nature and, on the other, the order of grace and salvation. The distinction applies to all of humanity, but the male body passes through no fully comparable moments of pollution.[3]

Third, the particular suitability of the woman's body for this theological allegory rests on an implied Pauline syllogism, conveniently reinforced by Latimer's saving of the woman: the woman is to the man as the man is to God. And this syllogism intersects with other implied analogical relations:

the woman is to the man as the simple peasant is to the gentleman and as the prisoner is to the free man.

Fourth, Latimer functions as part of a highly educated, male, professional elite that takes power over the woman away from her husband and lodges it in the punishing and pardoning apparatus of the state. The husband, as Latimer tells the story, had thought he could use that apparatus as an extension of his own power, but instead a gap is disclosed between patriarchal authority in the marital relation and patriarchal authority in the society at large.[4]

Fifth, the male professional elite, whether constituted as a body of jurists, theologians, or physicians, attempts to regulate the female body: to identify its periods of untouchability or pollution, to cleanse it of its stains, to distinguish between 'superstitious' practices and those conducive to public health. What we are witnessing is an instance of transcoding and naturalization: Latimer attempts to transfer the practice of purification from the religious to the civil sphere.[5] He goes out of his way to distinguish an appeal to 'natural honesty' – that is, the demands of cleanliness, decorum, and health – from 'superstition': thus he denies that before purification a woman sheds a malign influence on the objects about her and denounces those who 'think they may not fetch fire nor any thing in that house where there is a green woman'. Such folk beliefs are for Latimer part of the orbit of Catholicism and pose a threat to the commonwealth far greater than any posed by a 'green woman'. The religious rituals to ward off defilement are themselves defiling and must be cleansed by driving them out of the precinct of the sacred and into the realm of the secular.

Rituals of purification thus transcoded from the religious to the civil sphere serve to shape certain late sixteenth- and early seventeenth-century representations, in particular theatrical representations, of women. Thus, for example, Hermione in Shakespeare's *Winter's Tale* complains bitterly that her husband has denied her 'The child-bed privilege ... which 'longs/ To women of all fashion' (III.ii.103–4) and has brutally hurried her into 'th' open air, before' she has 'got strength of limit'. Leontes has denied his wife the 'child-bed privilege' because he believes that her adulterous body is defiled beyond redemption; she is, he is convinced, permanently and irreparably stained. Her sullying, as he perceives it, of the 'purity and whiteness' of his sheets threatens to defile him as well, and he imagines that he can save himself only by denouncing and destroying her. The secularized ritual is disrupted by a primal male nausea at the thought of the female body, the nausea most fully articulated in *King Lear*:

> But to the girdle do the gods inherit,
> Beneath is all the fiends': there's hell, there's darkness,
> There is the sulphurous pit, burning, scalding,

Stench, consumption. Fie, fie, fie! pah, pah!
Give me an ounce of civet; good apothecary,
Sweeten my imagination.

$$(IV.vi.126–131)^6$$

In *The Winter's Tale* this nausea appears to be awakened in some obscure way by Hermione's pregnancy, as if what it revealed was beyond the power of any ritual to cleanse. The play suggests that Leontes is horribly staining himself, and its last act movingly depicts a ceremony conducted by a woman, Paulina, to cleanse the king. *The Winter's Tale* then at once symbolically rehearses and reverses the ritual pattern that we glimpse in Latimer: the tainting of the female, her exclusion from the social contacts that normally govern her sex, and her ultimate reintegration into a renewed community.

We could go on to look at other instances of the 'green woman' and the tainted man in Renaissance drama, but for an understanding of the circulation of social energy the representational content of Latimer's story is less resonant than its strategic practice. Latimer and Bilney choose to leave the poor prisoner hanging, as it were, until she has accepted the doctrinal point: 'So we travailed with this woman till we brought her to a good trade; and at the length showed her the king's pardon and let her go.' A student of Shakespeare will immediately think of *Measure for Measure* where in the interest of moral reformation, Duke Vincentio, disguised as a holy friar, forces Claudio to believe that he is about to be executed – indeed forces virtually all of the major characters to face dreaded punishments – before he pardons everyone.

The resemblance between the tales arises not because Latimer's sermon is one of Shakespeare's sources but because Latimer is practising techniques of arousing and manipulating anxiety, and these techniques are crucial elements in the representational technology of the Elizabethan and Jacobean theatre.[7]

English dramatists developed extraordinary mastery of these techniques; indeed one of the defining characteristics of the dramaturgy of Marlowe and Shakespeare, as opposed to that of their medieval predecessors, is the startling increase in the level of represented and aroused anxiety. There is, to be sure, fear and trembling in the mysteries and moralities of the fifteenth and early sixteenth centuries, but a dread bound up with the fate of particular situated individuals is largely absent, and the audience shares its grief and joy in a collective experience that serves either to ward off or to absorb private emotions. Marlowe's *Faustus*, by contrast, though it appears conventional enough in its plot and overarching religious ideology, seems like a startling departure from everything that has preceded it precisely because the dramatist has heightened and individuated anxiety to an unprecedented degree and because he has contrived to implicate his audience as individuals in that anxiety.

Not all theatrical spectacles in the late sixteenth century are equally marked by the staging of anxiety: both civic pageantry and the masque are characterized by its relative absence. But in the public theatre the manipulation of anxiety plays an important part and is brought to a kind of perfection in Shakespeare. This is obviously and overwhelmingly the case in the tragedies: *Othello*, for example, remorselessly heightens audience anxiety, an anxiety focused on the audience's inability to intervene and stop the murderous chain of lies and misunderstandings. But it is equally the case, in a different register, in the comedies. The pleasures of love, courtship, music, dance, and poetry in these plays are continually seasoned by fear, grief, and the threat of shame and death. The comedy of *The Comedy of Errors*, for example, floats buoyantly on a sea of epistemological and ontological confusion that is represented as having potentially fatal consequences. The audience's anxiety at these consequences, and for that matter at its own confusion, is different from that in a tragedy but is nonetheless an important element in the aesthetic experience. We could argue that anxiety in the comedies is an emotion experienced only by the characters and not by the audience, that comic pleasure lies in contemplating the anxiety of others. But this Hobbesian account does not do justice to the currents of sympathy in the plays and overlooks Shakespeare's efforts to make us identify powerfully with the dilemmas that his characters face. A sardonic detachment, such as one feels in response to a play like Ben Jonson's *Every Man in His Humour*, is not called forth by *The Merchant of Venice* or *Twelfth Night*, plays in which the audience's pleasure clearly depends upon a sympathetic engagement with the characters' situation and hence the acceptance of a measure of anxiety.[8]

It is worth stressing, however, that the audience accepts theatrical anxiety for the sake of pleasure, since this pleasure enables us to make an important distinction between the manipulation of anxiety in the theatre and the comparable practice in Latimer.[9] The dramatist may have a palpable ideological purpose, generating anxiety, for example, to persuade women to submit to their husbands, or to warn men against paranoid suspicions of women, or to persuade subjects to obey even corrupt authority rather than risk rebellion. But in the public theatre such purposes are subordinated to the overriding need to give pleasure. Anxiety takes its place alongside other means – erotic arousal, the excitement of spectacle, the joys of exquisite language, the satisfaction of curiosity about other peoples and places, and so forth – that the players employ to attract and satisfy their customers. The whole point of anxiety in the theatre is to make it give such delight that the audience will pay for it again and again.[10] And this delight seems bound up with the marking out of theatrical anxiety as represented anxiety – not wholly real, either in the characters onstage or in the audience.[11]

Latimer, by contrast, insists that the anxiety in which he trafficks is real. He does not, as far as we can tell, withhold the prisoner's pardon to heighten her subsequent pleasure; his purpose rather is to use her anxiety as a tool to transform her attitude toward what he regards as superstition.[12] Why should anxiety be used for this purpose? The answer perhaps seemed too obvious for Latimer to articulate: anxiety, in the form of threats of humiliation and beating, had long been used as an educative tool. To be sure, the threat of hanging goes well beyond what Shakespeare's Duke Vincentio in *Measure for Measure* calls 'the threat'ning twigs of birch' (I.iii.24), but Latimer presumably believes that at moments of crisis, moments beyond hope itself, men and women have to face the truth; their defences are down, and they are forced to confront their salvation or perdition.[13] Latimer may also believe that we are all in effect under a death sentence from which we can be redeemed only by a mysterious and gratuitous act of pardon from God. The situation of the Cambridge prisoner is that of all mankind: hence the appropriateness of the story in a sermon on the Lord's Prayer. If he risked presumptuously casting himself or Henry VIII in the role of God, he could have appealed in good conscience to his certainty that he was God's humble servant. And if he seemed cruel, he could have told himself that he too would prefer death to doctrinal error. 'Be of good comfort, Master Ridley, and play the man,' Latimer was to say as the flames rose around his feet. 'We shall this day light such a candle, by God's grace, in England, as I trust shall never be put out.'

Latimer's last words, as the martyrologist Foxe reports them, move us beyond anxiety to the still point of absolute faith, but very few sixteenth-century Englishmen succeeded in reaching that point. (I doubt that many sixteenth-century Englishmen *wanted* to reach that point.) Those who governed the church had to be content that the faithful remain in a condition of what we may call salutary anxiety, and those who governed the state actively cultivated that condition. For the ruling elite believed that a measure of insecurity and fear was a necessary, healthy element in the shaping of proper loyalties, and Elizabethan and Jacobean institutions deliberately evoked this insecurity. Hence the church's constant insistence upon the fear and trembling, the sickness unto death, that every Christian should experience; hence too the public and increasingly spectacular character of the punishments inflicted by the state.

At his accession to the English throne, in response to a murky conspiracy known as the Bye Plot, James I staged a particularly elaborate display of the techniques of salutary anxiety. Two of the alleged conspirators – the priests Watson and Clarke – were tortured horribly, 'to the great discontent of the people,' writes one observer, 'who now think that matters were not so heinous as were made show of'.[14] As usual, the dismembered bodies were stuck on the city gates. A week later another conspirator, George Brooke, was executed, and then after several more days, the sheriff led to the scaffold Lords Grey and Cobham and Sir Gervase Markham, who had also been condemned to die. Markham, who had hoped for a reprieve, looked stunned with horror. After a delay, the sheriff told him that since he seemed ill-prepared to face death, he would be granted a two-hour reprieve; similar delays were granted to Grey and Cobham. The prisoners were then assembled together on the scaffold, 'looking strange one upon the other,' wrote Dudley Carleton, who witnessed the scene, 'like men beheaded, and met again in the other world'. At this point the sheriff made a short speech, asking the condemned if the judgements against them were just. When the wretches assented, he proclaimed that the merciful king had granted them their lives.[15]

The florid theatricality of the occasion was not lost on Carleton; the three men, he observed, were 'together on the stage as use is at the end of the play'. And in his letter granting the reprieve, James himself seems to confirm Carleton's perception. The king suggests that his clemency is in part a response to the 'hearty and general ... applause' given him on his entry into England, applause in which 'all the kin, friends, and allies' of the condemned participated.[16] The cheering had stopped after the first three executions, for if some anxiety is salutary, it may also go too far and evoke not obedience but a sullen withdrawal into discontented silence or even an outburst of rash rebellion. These scenarios are at most only partially and superficially in the control of the authorities; if at such times the prince seems to manipulate the anxieties of others, he inevitably discloses his own half-buried fears.[17] The executioner held up Brooke's severed head and cried, 'God save the king!' But the cry 'was not seconded', Carleton notes, 'by the voice of any one man but the sheriff'. The spectators to the display of royal clemency, on the other hand, once again found their voices, for their anxiety had been turned into gratitude: 'There was then no need to beg a *plaudite* of the audience,' remarks Carleton, 'for it was given with such hues and cries, that it went down from the castle into the town, and there began afresh.'[18] So too the audience may have cheered the flurry of pardons in the last act of *Measure for Measure*.

But why should Renaissance England have been institutionally committed to the arousal of anxiety? After all, there was plenty of anxiety without the need of such histrionic methods; like other European countries of the period, England had experienced a population growth that put a heavy strain on food supplies, and the struggle for survival was intensified by persistent inflation, unemployment, and epidemic disease. But perhaps precisely because this anxiety was pervasive and unavoidable, those in power wanted to incorporate it ideologically and manage it. Managed insecurity may have been reassuring both to the managers themselves and to those toward whom the techniques were addressed.

Public maimings and executions were designed to arouse fear and to set the stage for the royal pardons that would demonstrate that the prince's justice was tempered with mercy.[19] If there were only fear, the prince, it was said, would be deemed a tyrant; if there were only mercy, it was said that the people would altogether cease to be obedient. Similarly, religious anxiety was welcomed, even cultivated, as the necessary precondition of the reassurance of salvation. William Tyndale suggested that St Paul had written the Epistle to the Romans precisely to generate a suffering that could then be joyously relieved: 'For except thou have born the cross of adversity and temptation, and hast felt thyself brought unto the very brim of desperation, yea, and unto hell-gates, thou canst never meddle with the sentence of predestination without thine own harm.'[20]

What would be the harm? Why shouldn't the order of things be simply revealed without the prior generation of anxiety? Because, answers Tyndale, unless one is 'under the cross and suffering of tribulation', it is impossible to contemplate that order 'without secret wrath and grudging inwardly against God'; that is, 'it shall not be possible for thee to think that God is righteous and just'. Salutary anxiety, then, blocks the anger and resentment that would well up against what must, if contemplated in a secure state, seem an unjust order. And the great virtue of the technique is that it blocks *secret* wrath and *inward* grudging – that is, it does not merely suppress the expression of undesirable responses but represses those responses at their source, so that potential anger gives way to obedience, loyalty, and admiration.

Renaissance England had a subtle conception of the relation between anxiety and the fashioning of the individual subject, and its governing institutions developed discursive and behavioural strategies to implement this conception by arousing anxiety and then transforming it through pardon into gratitude, obedience, and love. These strategies were implicated from their inception in the management of spectacles and the fashioning of texts; that is, they are already implicated in cultural practices that are essential to the making and staging of plays. There was no need in this case for special modifications to adapt the techniques of salutary anxiety to the theatre. Indeed the theatre is a virtual machine for deploying these techniques in a variety of registers, from the comic anxiety that gives way to the clarification and release of marriage to the tragic anxiety that is at once heightened and ordered by the final solemnity of death. It is not surprising that the disguised duke of *Measure for Measure*, who fuses the strategies of statecraft and religion, has also seemed to many critics an emblem of the playwright.

This perception seems to me fundamentally correct, but it is complicated by what happens to the techniques of salutary anxiety when they are transferred to the stage. Even as it is evoked with extraordinary technical skill, salutary anxiety is emptied out in the service of theatrical pleasure. This emptying out through representation enables Shakespeare at once to identify the playwright with the mastery of salutary anxiety and to subject that mastery to complex ironic scrutiny. If Shakespeare in *Measure for Measure* seems to represent the protagonist's task as inflicting anxiety for ideological purposes, he also clearly calls that task into question. In a scene that particularly recalls Latimer's story, the disguised duke pays a pastoral visit to 'the afflicted spirits' in the town prison. 'Do me the common right,' he asks the provost,

> To let me see them, and to make me know
> The nature of their crimes, that I may minister
> To them accordingly.
>
> (II.iii.5–8)

'Repent you,' he asks the pregnant Juliet, who has been imprisoned for fornication, 'of the sin you carry?' The question, collapsing the sin and its fruit into one another, is a harsh one, but the prisoner replies serenely: 'I do; and bear the shame most patiently.' Sensing an unwelcome doctrinal slippage in the shift from sin to shame, Duke Vincentio proposes to teach the unfortunate Juliet

> how you shall arraign your conscience,
> And try your penitence, if it be sound,
> Or hollowly put on.

'I'll gladly learn,' Juliet replies, and the remainder of the short scene provides a revealing glimpse of the duke's methods and interests:

> DUKE: Love you the man that wrong'd you?
> JULIET: Yes, as I love the woman that wrong'd him.
> DUKE: So then it seems your most offenseful act
> Was mutually committed?
> JULIET: Mutually.
> DUKE: Then was your sin of heavier kind than his.
> JULIET: I do confess it, and repent it, father.
> DUKE: 'Tis meet so, daughter, but lest you do repent
> As that the sin hath brought you to this shame,
> Which sorrow is always toward ourselves, not heaven,
> Showing we would not spare heaven as we love it
> But as we stand in fear –
> JULIET: I do repent me as it is an evil,
> And take the shame with joy.
> DUKE: There rest.
> Your partner, as I hear, must die to-morrow,
> And I am going with instruction to him.

<pre>
              Grace go with you, *Benedicite*!
JULIET: Must die to-morrow? O injurious love,
              That respites me a life whose very comfort
              Is still a dying horror!
PROVOST: 'Tis pity of him.
</pre>

(II.iii.24–42)

The duke's questioning of the prisoner is based upon the medieval distinction between *attrition* and *contrition*. As one fourteenth-century theologian puts it, 'When the will of a man clinging to sin is overcome by fear and by consideration of the punishment owed for sin, and on account of this recoils from sin, he is said to be "attrite"; but when not only from fear of punishment, but also from love of eternal life he totally recoils from sin by fully detesting it, he is called "contrite." '[21] Juliet interrupts and in effect silences the duke's attempt to draw this doctrinal distinction: 'I do repent me as it is an evil,/And take the shame with joy.' These words may express a perfect contrition, but they may also signal a quiet rejection of the whole system for which the duke speaks. 'I do repent me as it is an evil' – but is it an evil? The provost had remarked of Claudio that he was 'a young man/More fit to do another such offence/Than die for this' (II.iii.13–15). 'And take the shame with joy': earlier Juliet referred to her unborn child as 'the shame'. If she is still doing so, then her words affirm not repentance but love for her child. In either case, Juliet's words here and throughout the exchange are remarkable for their tranquillity. Each of Duke Vincentio's questions would seem to be an attempt to awaken an instructive anxiety, but the attempt appears to fail.

In response to Juliet's words the duke can only reply, 'There rest.' But as if this 'rest' contradicts his own interest in arousing rather than allaying anxiety, he immediately continues by casually informing Juliet that the man she loves will be executed the next day. Her response provides ample evidence of anxiety, but that anxiety does not appear to serve an orthodox ideological purpose:

<pre>
          O injurious love,
    That respites me a life whose very comfort
    Is still a dying horror!
</pre>

Again the words are ambiguous (and emendations have been proposed), but Juliet appears either to be calling into question the divine love about which the duke has just been lecturing her or the human love whose fruit – the baby she carries in her womb – has presumably afforded her a 'respite' from the execution to which her conviction for fornication would have doomed her. In either case, the anxiety she is expressing simply brushes aside the theological categories the duke has taken it upon himself to instill in her.

None of the duke's other attempts to awaken anxiety and to shape it into what he regards as a proper attitude has the desired effect. When Claudio voices what sounds like an admirable acceptance of his situation – 'I have hope to live, and am prepar'd to die' – Duke Vincentio replies, 'Be absolute for death: either death or life/Shall thereby be the sweeter' (III.i.4–6). Here the duke would appear to be moulding Claudio's emotions into philosophical detachment, but the strategy fails since Claudio almost immediately abandons his detachment and frantically sues for life. We may say that the duke has succeeded in raising Claudio's anxiety level, but the moral purpose for which he set out to do so seems to have collapsed.

The duke had embarked on his course because Vienna seemed insufficiently anxious in the presence of authority:

> Now, as fond fathers,
> Having bound up the threat'ning twigs of birch,
> Only to stick it in their children's sight
> For terror, not to use, in time the rod
> Becomes more mock'd than fear'd; so our decrees,
> Dead to infliction, to themselves are dead,
> And liberty plucks justice by the nose;
> The baby beats the nurse, and quite athwart
> Goes all decorum.

> (I.iii.23–31)

But at the close of the play, society at large seems singularly unaffected by the renewed exercise in anxiety. The magnificent emblems of indifference are the drunken Barnadine and the irrepressible Lucio: if they are any indication, the duke's strategy has not changed the structure of feeling or behaviour in Vienna in the slightest degree. All that it has done is to offer the spectators pleasure in the spectacle. But that pleasure is precisely Shakespeare's professional purpose, and his ironic reflections on salutary anxiety do not at all diminish his commitment to it as a powerful theatrical technique.

When near the close of his career Shakespeare reflected upon his own art with still greater intensity and self-consciousness than in *Measure for Measure*, he once again conceived of the playwright as a princely creator of anxiety. But where in *Measure for Measure* disguise is the principal emblem of this art, in *The Tempest* the emblem is the far more potent and disturbing power of magic. Prospero's chief magical activity throughout *The Tempest* is to harrow the other characters with fear and wonder and then to reveal that their anxiety is his to create and allay. The spectacular storm in the play's first scene gives way to Miranda's empathic agitation: 'O! I have suffered/With those that I saw suffer.... O, the cry did knock/

Against my very heart.' 'The direful spectacle of the wrack,' replies Prospero,

> which touch'd
> The very virtue of compassion in thee,
> I have with such provision in mine art
> So safely ordered that there is no soul –
> No, not so much perdition as an hair
> Betid to any creature in the vessel
> Which thou heardst cry, which thou saw'st sink.

(I.ii.26–32)

Miranda has been treated to an intense experience of suffering and to a still more intense demonstration of her father's power, the power at once to cause such suffering and to cancel it. Later in the play the threat of 'perdition' – both loss and damnation – will be concentrated against Prospero's enemies, but it is important to recall that at the start the management of anxiety through the 'provision' of art is practised upon Prospero's beloved daughter. Her suffering is the prelude to the revelation of her identity, as if Prospero believes that this revelation can be meaningful only in the wake of the amazement and pity he artfully arouses. He is setting out to fashion her identity, just as he is setting out to refashion the inner lives of his enemies, and he employs comparable disciplinary techniques.

With his daughter, Prospero's techniques are mediated and softened: she suffers at the sight of the sufferings of unknown wretches. With his enemies the techniques are harsher and more direct – the spectacle they are compelled to watch is not the wreck of others but of their own lives. In one of the play's most elaborate scenes, Prospero stands above the stage, invisible to those below him, and conjures up a banquet for Alonso, Antonio, Sebastian, and their party; when they move toward the table, Ariel appears like a Harpy and, with a clap of his wings and a burst of thunder and lightning, makes the table disappear. Ariel then solemnly recalls their crimes against Prospero and sentences the guilty in the name of the powers of Destiny and Fate:

> Thee of thy son, Alonso,
> They have bereft; and do pronounce by me
> Ling'ring perdition (worse than any death
> Can be at once).

(III.iii.75–8)

Prospero is delighted at Ariel's performance:

> My high charms work,
> And these, mine enemies, are all knit up
> In their distractions. They now are in my pow'r.

(III.iii.88–90)

To compel others to be 'all knit up/In their distractions', to cause a paralysing anxiety, is the dream of power, a dream perfected over bitter years of exile.[22] But as we have already seen, the artful manipulation of anxiety is not only the manifestation of aggression; it is also a strategy for shaping the inner lives of others and for fashioning their behaviour. Hence we find Prospero employing the strategy not only upon those he hates but upon his daughter and upon the man whom he has chosen to be his daughter's husband. Ferdinand and Miranda fall in love instantly – 'It goes on, I see,/As my soul prompts it' (I.ii.420–21), remarks Prospero – but what is missing from their love is precisely the salutary anxiety that Prospero undertakes to impose: 'this swift business/I must uneasy make, lest too light winning/Make the prize light' (I.ii.451–3). To Miranda's horror, he accuses Ferdinand of treason and employs his magic charms once again to cause a kind of paralysis: 'My spirits,' exclaims Ferdinand, 'as in a dream, are all bound up' (I.ii.487). The rituals of humiliation and suffering through which Prospero makes Ferdinand and Miranda pass evidently have their desired effect: at the end of the play the couple displayed to the amazed bystanders are revealed to be not only in a state of love but in a state of symbolic war. The lovers, you will recall, are discovered playing chess, and Miranda accuses Ferdinand of cheating. The deepest happiness is represented in this play as a state of playful tension.

Perhaps the supreme representation of this tension in *The Tempest* is to be found not in Prospero's enemies or in his daughter and son-in-law but in himself. The entire action of the play rests on the premise that value lies in controlled uneasiness, and hence that a direct reappropriation of the usurped dukedom and a direct punishment of the usurpers has less moral and political value than an elaborate inward restaging of loss, misery, and anxiety. Prospero directs this restaging not only against the others but also – even principally – against himself. That is, he arranges for the reenactment in a variety of registers and through different symbolic agents of the originary usurpation, and in the play's most memorable yet perplexing moment, the princely artist puts himself through the paralysing uneasiness with which he has afflicted others. The moment to which I refer is that of the interrupted wedding masque. In the midst of the climactic demonstration of Prospero's magical powers, the celebration of the paradisal 'green land' where spring comes at the very end of harvest, Prospero suddenly starts, breaks off the masque, and declares that he had 'forgot that foul conspiracy/Of the beast Caliban and his confederates/Against my life' (IV.i.139–41).

In recalling the conspiracy, Prospero clearly exhibits signs of extreme distress: Ferdinand is struck by the 'passion/That works him strongly', and Miranda says that 'never till this day' has she seen him 'touch'd with anger, so distemper'd' (IV.i.143–5). Noticing that Ferdinand looks 'in a mov'd sort', as if he were 'dismay'd', Prospero tells him to 'be cheerful' and informs him that 'Our revels now are ended.' The famous speech that follows has the effect of drastically evacuating the masque's majestic vision of plenitude. 'Let me live here ever,' the delighted Ferdinand had exclaimed, enchanted by the promise of an aristocrat's equivalent of the Land of Cockaigne:

> Honor, riches, marriage-blessing,
> Long continuance, and increasing,
> Hourly joys be still upon you!
>
> (IV.i.106–8)

But Prospero now explains that the beneficent goddesses 'Are melted into air, into thin air' (IV.i.150). What had seemed solid is 'baseless'; what had seemed enduring ('the great globe itself')

> shall dissolve,
> And like this insubstantial pageant faded
> Leave not a rack behind.
>
> (IV.i.154–6)

Prospero offers this sublime vision of emptiness to make Ferdinand feel 'cheerful' – secure in the consciousness that life is a dream. It is difficult to believe in the effectiveness of these professed attempts at reassurance: like Duke Vincentio's religious consolations in *Measure for Measure*, they seem suited more to heighten anxiety than to allay it. The ascetic security Prospero articulates has evidently not stilled his own 'beating mind':

> Sir, I am vex'd;
> Bear with my weakness, my old brain is troubled.
> Be not disturb'd with my infirmity.
>
> (IV.i.158–60)

Since Prospero's art has in effect created the conspiracy as well as the defence against the conspiracy, and since the profession of infirmity comes at the moment of his greatest strength, we may conclude that we are witnessing the practice of salutary anxiety operating at the centre of the play's world, in the consciousness of Prospero himself, magician, artist, and prince. This does not mean that Prospero's anxiety about the conspiracy, about his enemies and servants and daughter, about his own inward state is not genuinely felt, nor does it mean that he is in absolute, untroubled control either of the characters whom he has brought onto the island or of himself. Rapt in his own magical vision of bounteousness, he has forgotten a serious threat to his life: 'The minute of their plot/Is almost come' (IV.i.141–2). But it is important to take seriously his deep complicity in his present tribulations, for only by actively willing them can he undo the tribulations that he unwillingly and unwittingly brought about years before. At that time, absorbed in his occult studies, he had been unaware of the dangers around him; now as the condition of a return to his dukedom, he himself brings those dangers to the centre of his retreat. This centre, whether we regard it as emblematic of the dominant religious, aesthetic, or political institution, is not the still point in a turbulent world but the point at which the anxieties that shape the character of others are screwed up to their highest pitch. Precisely from that point – and as a further exemplification of the salutary nature of anxiety – reconciliation and pardon can issue forth. This pardon is not a release from the power in which Prospero holds everyone around him but, as with Latimer and James I, its ultimate expression.[23]

Shakespeare goes beyond Latimer and James, however, in envisaging a case in which anxiety does not appear to have its full redeeming effect, a case in which the object of attention refuses to be fashioned inwardly, refuses even to acknowledge guilt, and yet is pardoned. The generosity of the pardon in this instance is inseparable from a demonstration of supreme force. 'For you, most wicked sir,' Prospero says to his brother Antonio,

> whom to call brother
> Would even infect my mouth, I do forgive
> Thy rankest fault – all of them; and require
> My dukedom of thee, which perforce, I know
> Thou must restore
>
> (V.i.130–34)

Antonio's silence at this point suggests that he remains unrepentant, but it also expresses eloquently the paralysis that is the hallmark of extreme anxiety. It has been argued convincingly that the truculence of the villains at the close of the play marks the limit of Prospero's power – as Prospero's failure to educate Caliban has already shown, the strategy of salutary anxiety cannot remake the inner life of everyone – yet at the very moment the limit is marked, the play suggests that it is relatively inconsequential. It would no doubt be preferable to receive the appropriate signs of inward gratitude from everyone, but Prospero will have to content himself in the case of Antonio with the full restoration of his dukedom.[24]

What I have been describing here is the theatrical appropriation and staging of a sixteenth- and seventeenth-century social practice. But the strategy of salutary anxiety is not simply reflected in a secondhand way by the work of art, because the practice itself is already implicated in the artistic traditions and institutions out of which this particular representation, *The Tempest*, has emerged. Latimer may have been indifferent or hostile to the drama and to literature in general, but his tale of the Cambridge prisoner seems shaped by literary conventions, earlier tales of wronged innocence and royal pardons. And if the practice he exemplifies helps to empower theatrical representations, fictive representations have themselves helped to empower his practice.[25] So too Dudley Carleton, watching men about to go to their deaths, thinks of the last act of a play, and when a pardon is granted, the spectators applaud. This complex circulation between the social dimension of an aesthetic strategy and the aesthetic dimension of a social strategy is difficult to grasp because the strategy in question has an extraordinarily long and tangled history, one whose aesthetic roots go back at least as far as Aristotle's *Poetics*. But we may find a more manageable, though still complex, model in the relation between *The Tempest* and one of its presumed sources, William Strachey's account of the tempest that struck an English fleet bound for the fledgling colony at Jamestown.[26]

Strachey's account, with its bravura description of a violent storm at sea and its tale of Englishmen providentially cast ashore on an uninhabited island rumoured to be devil haunted, is likely, along with other New World materials, to have helped shape *The Tempest*. The play was performed long before Strachey's narrative was printed in Purchas's *Pilgrims* as 'A true reportory of the wrack, and redemption of Sir Thomas Gates Knight,' but scholars presume that Shakespeare read a manuscript version of the work, which takes the form of a confidential letter written to a certain 'noble lady'.[27] My interest is not the particular verbal echoes, which have been painstakingly researched since Malone in 1808 first called attention to them, but the significance of the relation between the two texts, or rather between the institutions that the texts serve. For it is important to grasp that we are dealing not with the reflections of isolated individuals musing on current events but with expressions whose context is corporate and institutional.

William Strachey was a shareholder and secretary of the Virginia Company's colony at Jamestown; his letter on the events of 1609–10 was unpublished until 1625, not for want of interest but because the Virginia Company was engaged in a vigorous propaganda and financial campaign on behalf of the colony, and the company's leaders found Strachey's report too disturbing to allow it into print. Shakespeare too was a shareholder in a joint-stock company, the King's Men, as well as its principal playwright and sometime actor; *The Tempest* also remained unpublished for years, again presumably not for want of interest but because the theatre company resisted losing control of its playbook. Neither joint-stock company was a direct agent of the crown: despite the legal fiction that they were retainers of the monarch, the King's Men could not have survived through royal patronage alone, and they were not in the same position of either dependence or privilege as other household servants; the crown had deliberately withdrawn from the direction of the Virginia Company. Royal protection and support, of course, remained essential in both cases, but the crown would not assume responsibility, nor could either company count on royal financial support in times of need. Committed for their survival to attracting investment capital and turning a profit, both companies depended on their ability to market stories that would excite, interest, and attract supporters. Both Strachey and Shakespeare were involved in unusually direct and intricate ways in every aspect of their companies' operations: Strachey as shareholder, adventurer, and eventually secretary; Shakespeare as shareholder, actor, and playwright. Because of these multiple positions, both men probably identified intensely with the interests of their respective companies.

I want to propose that the relation between the play and its alleged source is a relation between joint-stock companies.[28] I do not mean that there was a direct, contractual connection.[29] As we have already seen with Latimer, the transfer of cultural practices and powers depends not upon contracts but upon networks of resemblance. In the case of Strachey and Shakespeare, there *are*, in point of fact, certain intriguing institutional affiliations: as Charles Mills Gayley observed many years ago, a remark- able number of social and professional connections link Shakespeare and the stockholders and directors of the Virginia Company; moreover, Strachey in 1605 wrote a prefatory sonnet commending Jonson's *Sejanus* and in 1606 is listed as a shareholder in an acting company known as the Children of the Queen's Revels, the company that had taken over the Blackfriars Theatre from Richard Burbage.[30] Still, I should emphasize that these affiliations do not amount to a direct transfer of properties; we are dealing with a system of mimetic rather than contractual exchange. The conjunction of Strachey's unpublished letter and Shakespeare's play signals an institutional circulation of culturally significant narratives. And as we shall see, this circulation has as its central concern the public management of anxiety.

Strachey tells the story of a state of emergency and a crisis of authority. The 'unmerciful tempest' that almost sank Sir Thomas Gates's ship, the *Sea Venture*, provoked an immediate collapse of the distinction between those who labour and those who rule, a distinction, we should recall, that is at the economic and ideological centre of Elizabethan and Jacobean society: 'Then men might be seen to labour, I may well say, for life, and the better sort, even our Governour, and Admiral themselves, not refusing their turn. . . . And it is most true, such as in all their life times had never done hours work before (their minds now helping their bodies) were able twice forty eight hours together to toil with the best' (in Purchas, 19: 9–11). 'The best' – the violence of the storm has turned Strachey's own language upside down: now it is the common seamen, ordinarily despised and feared by their social superiors, who are, as the Romans called their aristocrats, the *optimi viri*, the best of men.[31] Indeed the storm had quite literally a levelling force: while the governor was 'both by his speech and authority heartening every man unto his labour', a great wave 'struck him from the place where he sat, and groveled him, and all us about him on our faces, beating together with our breaths all thoughts from our bosoms, else then that we were now sinking' (10).

Even after the ship had run aground in the Burmudas and the one hundred fifty men, women, and children on board had been saved, the crisis of authority was not resolved; indeed it only intensified then, not because of a levelling excess of anxiety but because of its almost complete absence in the colonists. The alarm of the rulers makes itself felt in quirks of Strachey's style. He reports, for example, that many palmettos were cut down for their edible tops, but the report has a strange nervous tone, as the plants are comically turned into wealthy victims of a popular uprising: 'Many an ancient Burgher was therefore heaved at, and fell not for his place, but for his head: for our common people, whose bellies never had ears, made it no breach of Charity in their hot bloods and tall stomachs to murder thousands of them' (19).

The strain registered here in the tone stands for concerns that are partially suppressed in the published text, concerns that are voiced in a private letter written in December 1610 by Richard Martin, secretary of the Virginia Company in London, to Strachey, who was by then in Jamestown. Martin asks Strachey for a full confidential report on 'the nature & quality of the soil, & how it is like to serve you without help from hence, the manners of the people, how the Barbarians are content with your being there, but especially how our own people do brook their obedience, how they endure labour, whether willingly or upon constraint, how they live in the exercise of Religion, whether out of conscience or for fashion, And generally what ease you have in the government there, & what hope of success.'[32]

Here the deepest fears lie not with the human or natural resources of the New World but with the discipline of the English colonists and common seamen. And the principal questions – whether obedience is willing or forced, whether religious observance is sincere or feigned – suggest an interest in inner states, as if the shareholders in the Virginia Company believed that only with a set of powerful inward restraints could the colonists be kept from rebelling at the first sign of the slippage or relaxation of authority. The company had an official institutional interest in shaping and controlling the minds of its own people. But the Bermuda shipwreck revealed the difficulty of this task as well as its importance: set apart from the institutional and military safeguards established at Jamestown, Bermuda was an experimental space, a testing ground where the extent to which disciplinary anxiety had been internalized by the ordinary venturers could be measured.

The results were not encouraging. As Strachey and others remark, Bermuda was an extraordinarily pleasant surprise: the climate was healthful, the water was pure, there were no native inhabitants to contend with, and, equally important, there was no shortage of food. Tortoises – 'such a kind of meat, as a man can neither absolutely call Fish nor Flesh' $(24)^{33}$ – were found in great number, and the skies were dark with great flocks of birds:

> Our men found a pretty way to take them, which was by standing on the Rocks or Sands by the Sea side, and hollowing, laughing, and making the strangest out-cry that possibly they could: with the noise whereof the Birds would come flocking to that place, and settle upon the very arms and head of him that so cried, and still creep nearer and nearer, answering the noise themselves: by which our men would weigh them with their hands, and which weighed heaviest they took for the best and let the others alone.
>
> (Purchas, 19: 22–3)

Even to us, living for the most part in the confident expectation of full bellies, this sounds extraordinary enough; to seventeenth-century voyagers, whose ordinary condition was extreme want and who had dragged themselves from the violent sea onto an unknown shore with the likely prospect of starvation and death, such extravagant abundance must have seemed the fantastic realization of old folk dreams of a land where the houses were roofed with pies and the pigs ran about with little knives conveniently stuck in their precooked sides. In this Land of Cockaigne setting, far removed not only from England but from the hardships of Jamestown, the authority of Sir Thomas Gates and his lieutenants was anything but secure. For the perception that Bermuda was a providential deliverance contained within it a subversive corollary: why leave? why press on to a hungry garrison situated in a pestiferous swamp and in grave tension with the surrounding Algonquian tribesmen?[34]

According to Strachey, Gates was initially concerned less about his own immediate authority than about the possible consequences of his absence in Virginia. The *Sea Venture* had come to grief in the tempest, but Gates thought (correctly, as it happened) that the other two vessels might have reached their destination, and this thought brought not only consolation but anxiety, which focused, in characteristic Renaissance fashion, on the ambitions of the younger generation. Fearful about 'what innovation and tumult might happily [haply] arise, among the younger and ambitious spirits of the new companies to arrive in Virginia' (26) in his absence, Gates wished to construct new ships as quickly as possible to continue on to Jamestown, but the sailors and the colonists alike began to grumble at this plan. In Virginia, they reasoned, 'nothing but wretchedness and labour must be expected, with many wants and a churlish entreaty'; in Bermuda, all things 'at ease and pleasure might be enjoyed' (29) without hardship or threatening. There is, at least as Strachey reports it, virtually no internalization of the ideology of colonialism; the voyagers appear to think of themselves as forced to endure a temporary exile from home. As long as 'they were (for the time) to lose the fruition both of their friends and Country, as good, and better it were for them, to repose and seat them where they should have the least outward wants the while' (29). And to this dangerous appeal – the appeal, in Strachey's words, of 'liberty, and fulness of sensuality' (35) – was added a still more dangerous force: religious dissent.

Arguments against leaving Bermuda began to be voiced not only among the 'idle, untoward, and wretched number of the many' (29) but among the educated few. One of these, Stephen Hopkins, 'alleged substantial arguments, both civil and divine (the Scripture falsely quoted) that it was no breach of honesty, conscience, nor Religion, to decline from the obedience of the Governour, or refuse to go any further, led by his authority (except it so pleased themselves) since the authority ceased when the wrack was committed, and with it, they were all then freed from the government of any man' (30–31). Hopkins evidently accepted the governor's authority as a contractual obligation that continued only so long as the enterprise remained on course. Once there was a swerve from the official itinerary, that authority, not granted a general or universal character, lapsed, and the obedience of the subject gave way to the will and pleasure of each man.[35] We cannot know, of course, if Hopkins said anything so radical, but this is how his 'substantial arguments, both civil and divine', sounded to those in command. In Strachey's account, at least, the shipwreck had led to a profound questioning of authority that seems to anticipate the challenge posed by mid-seventeenth-century radicals like Winstanley. What are the boundaries of authority? What is the basis of its claim to be obeyed? How much loyalty does an individual owe to a corporation?

When the seditious words were reported to Gates, the governor convened a martial court and sentenced Hopkins to death, but the condemned man was so tearfully repentant that he received a pardon. This moving scene – the saving public display of anxiety – evidently did not settle the question of authority, however, for shortly after, yet another mutiny arose, this time led by a gentleman named Henry Paine. When Paine was warned that he risked execution for 'insolency', he replied, Strachey reports, 'with a settled and bitter violence, and in such unreverent terms, as I should offend the modest ear too much to express it in his own phrase; but its contents were, how that the Governour had no authority of that quality, to justify upon any one (how mean soever in the colony) an action of that nature, and therefore let the Governour (said he) kiss, &c.' (34). When these words, 'with the omitted additions', were reported, the governor, 'who had now the eyes of the whole Colony fixed upon him', condemned Paine 'to be instantly hanged; and the ladder being ready, after he had made many confessions, he earnestly desired, being a Gentleman, that he might be shot to death, and towards the evening he had his desire, the Sun and his life setting together' (34). 'He had his desire' – Strachey's sarcasm is also perhaps the representation of what those in authority regarded as an intolerable nonchalance, a refusal to perform those rituals of tearful repentance that apparently saved Hopkins's life. In effect Paine is killed to set an example, condemned to die for cursing authority, for a linguistic crime, for violating discursive decorum, for inadequate anxiety in the presence of power.

In his narrative, Strachey represents the norms Paine has challenged by means of his '&c.' – the noble lady to whom he is writing, like Mr. Kurtz's intended, must be sheltered from the awful truth, here from the precise terms of the fatal irreverent challenge to authority. The suppression of the offending word enacts in miniature the reimposition of salutary anxiety by a governor 'so solicitous and careful, whose both example ... and authority, could lay shame, and command upon our people' (28). The governor is full of care – therefore resistant to the lure of the island – and he manages, even in the midst of a paradisal plenty, to impose this care upon others. When the governor himself writes to a fellow officer explaining why all of the colonists must be compelled to leave the island, he invokes not England's imperial destiny or Christianity's advancement but the Virginia Company's investment: 'The meanest in the whole Fleet stood the Company in no less than twenty pounds, for his own personal Transportation, and things necessary to accompany him' (36). On the strength of his compelling motive, new ships were built, and in an impressive feat of navigation, the whole company finally reached Jamestown.

Upon their arrival Gates and his people found the garrison in desperate condition – starving, confused, terrorized by hostile and treacherous Indians, and utterly demoralized. In Gates's view, the problem was almost entirely one of discipline, and he addressed it by imposing a set of 'orders and instructions' upon the colony that transformed the 'government' of Jamestown 'into an absolute command'. The orders were published in 1612 by Strachey as the *Laws Divine, Moral, and Martial*, an exceptionally draconian code by which whipping, mutilation, and the death penalty might be imposed for a wide range of offences, including blasphemy, insubordination, even simple criticism of the Virginia Company and its officers. These orders, the first martial law code in America, suspended the traditional legal sanctions that governed the lives of Englishmen, customary codes based on mutual constraints and obligations, and instituted in their stead the grim and self-consciously innovative logic of a state of emergency. The company's claim upon the colonists had become total. The group that had been shipwrecked in Bermuda passed from dreams of absolute freedom to the imposition of absolute control.

Such then were the narrative materials that passed from Strachey to Shakespeare, from the Virginia Company to the King's Men: a violent tempest, a providential shipwreck on a strange island, a crisis in authority provoked by both danger and excess, a fear of lower-class disorder and upper-class ambition, a triumphant affirmation of absolute control linked to the manipulation of anxiety and to a departure from the island. But the swerve away from these materials in *The Tempest* is as apparent as their presence: the island is not in America but in the Mediterranean; it is not uninhabited – Ariel and Caliban (and, for that matter, Sycorax) were present before the arrival of Prospero and Miranda; none of the figures are in any sense colonists; the departure is for home rather than a colony and entails not an unequivocal heightening of authority but a partial diminution, signalled in Prospero's abjuration of magic.

> I'll break my staff,
> Bury it certain fadoms in the earth,
> And deeper than did ever plummet sound
> I'll drown my book.
>
> (V.i.54–7)[36]

If the direction of Strachey's narrative is toward the promulgation of the martial law codes, the direction of *The Tempest* is toward forgiveness. And if that forgiveness is itself the manifestation of supreme power, the emblem of that power remains marriage rather than punishment.

The changes I have sketched are signs of the process whereby the Bermuda narrative is made negotiable, turned into a currency that may be transferred from one institutional context to another. The changes do not constitute a coherent critique of the colonial discourse, but they function as an unmooring of its elements so as to confer upon them the currency's liquidity. Detached from their context in Strachey's letter, these elements may be transformed and recombined with materials drawn from other writers about the New World who differ sharply from Strachey in their interests and motives – Montaigne, Sylvester Jourdain, James Rosier, Robert Eden, Peter Martyr – and then integrated in a dramatic text that draws on a wide range of discourse, including pastoral and epic poetry, the lore of magic and witchcraft, literary romance, and a remarkable number of Shakespeare's own earlier plays.

The ideological effects of the transfer to *The Tempest* are ambiguous. On the one hand, the play seems to act out a fantasy of mind control, to celebrate absolute patriarchal rule, to push to an extreme the dream of order, epic achievement, and ideological justification implicit in Strachey's text. The lower-class resistance Strachey chronicles becomes in Shakespeare the drunken rebellion of Stephano and Trinculo, the butler and jester who, suddenly finding themselves freed from their masters, are drawn to a poor man's fantasy of mastery: 'the King and all our company else being drown'd, we will inherit here' (II.ii.174–5). Similarly, the upper-class resistance of Henry Paine is transformed into the murderous treachery of Sebastian, in whom the shipwreck arouses dreams of an escape from subordination to his older brother, the king of Naples, just as Antonio had escaped subordination to his older brother Prospero:

SEBASTIAN: I remember
                    You did supplant your brother Prospero.
ANTONIO: True.
                    And look how well my garments sit upon me,
                    Much feater than before. My brother's servants
                    Were then my fellows, now they are my men.

                                                        (II.i.270–74)

By invoking fratricidal rivalry here Shakespeare is not only linking the Strachey materials to his own long-standing theatrical preoccupations but also supplementing the contractual authority of a governor like Sir Thomas Gates with the familial and hence culturally sanctified authority of the eldest son. To rise up against such a figure, as Claudius had against old Hamlet or Edmund against Edgar, is an assault not only on a political structure but on the moral and natural order of things: it is an act that has, as Claudius says, 'the primal eldest curse upon't'. The assault is magically thwarted by Ariel, the indispensable agent of Prospero's 'art'; hence that art, potentially a force of disorder, spiritual violence, and darkness, is confirmed as the agent of legitimacy. Through his mastery of the occult, Prospero withholds food from his enemies, spies upon them, listens to their secret conversations, monitors their movements, blocks their actions, keeps track of their dealings with the island's native inhabitant, torments and disciplines his servants, defeats conspiracies against his life. A crisis of authority – deposition from power, exile, impotence – gives way through the power of his art to a full restoration. From this perspective Prospero's magic is the romance equivalent of martial law.

Yet *The Tempest* seems to raise troubling questions about this authority. The great storm with which the play opens has some of the levelling force of the storm that struck the *Sea Venture*. To be sure, unlike Strachey's gentlemen, Shakespeare's nobles refuse the boatswain's exasperated demand that they share the labour, 'Work you then,' but their snarling refusal – 'Hang, cur! hang, you whoreson, insolent noisemaker!' (I.i.42–4) – far from securing their class superiority, represents them as morally beneath the level of the common seamen.[37] Likewise, Shakespeare's king, Alonso, is not 'grovelled' by a wave, but – perhaps worse – he is peremptorily ordered below by the harried boatswain: 'What cares these roarers for the name of king? To cabin! silence! trouble us not' (I.i.16–18). And if we learn eventually that these roarers are in fact produced *by* a king – in his name and through his command of a magical language – this knowledge does not altogether cancel our perception of the storm's indifference to the ruler's authority and the idle aristocrat's pride of place.

The perception would perhaps be overwhelmed by the display of Prospero's power were it not for the questions that are raised about this very power. A Renaissance audience might have found the locus of these questions in the ambiguous status of magic, an ambiguity deliberately heightened by the careful parallels drawn between Prospero and the witch Sycorax and by the attribution to Prospero of claims made by Ovid's witch Medea. But for a modern audience, at least, the questions centre on the figure of Caliban, whose claim to the legitimate possession of the island – 'This island's mine by Sycorax my mother' (I.ii.331) – is never really answered, or rather is answered by Prospero only with hatred, torture, and enslavement.[38] Though he treats Caliban as less than human, Prospero finally expresses, in a famously enigmatic phrase, a sense of connection with his servant-monster, standing anxious and powerless before him: 'this thing of darkness I / Acknowledge mine' (V.i.275–6). He may intend these words only as a declaration of ownership, but it is difficult not to hear in them some deeper recognition of affinity, some half-conscious acknowledgement of guilt. At the play's end the princely magician appears anxious and powerless before the audience to beg for indulgence and freedom.

As the epilogue is spoken, Prospero's magical power and princely authority – figured in the linked abilities to raise winds and to pardon offenders – pass, in a startling display of the circulation of social energy, from the performer onstage to the crowd of spectators. In the play's closing moments the marginal, vulnerable actor, more than half-visible beneath the borrowed robes of an assumed dignity, seems to acknowledge that the imaginary forces with which he has played reside ultimately not in himself or in the playwright but in the multitude. The audience is the source of his anxiety, and it holds his release quite literally in its hands: without the crowd's applause his 'ending is despair' (Epilogue, 15). This admission of dependence includes a glance at the multitude's own vulnerability:

> As you from crimes would pardon'd be,
> Let your indulgence set me free.

> (Epilogue, 19–20)

But it nonetheless implicates the prince as well as the player in the experience of anxiety and the need for pardon.

Furthermore, even if we may argue that such disturbing or even subversive reflections are contained within the thematic structure of the play, a structure that seems to support the kind of authority served by Strachey, we must acknowledge that the propagandists for colonization found little to admire in the theatre. That is, the most disturbing effects of the play may have been located not in what may be perceived in the text by a subtle interpreter – implied criticisms of colonialism or subversive doubts about its structures of authority – but in the phenomenon of theatrical representation itself. In 1593 Sir Thomas Smith reminded each captain in Virginia that his task was 'to lay the foundation of a good and ... an eternal colony for your posterity, not a May game or stage play'.[39] Festive, evanescent, given over to images of excess, stage plays function here as the symbolic opposite to the lasting colony. So too in a sermon preached in London in 1610 to a group of colonists about to set out for Virginia, William Crashaw declared that the enemies of the godly colony were the devil, the pope, and the players – the latter angry 'because we resolve to suffer no Idle persons in Virginia'.[40] Similarly, at the end of the martial law text, Strachey records an exceptionally long prayer that he claims was 'duly said Morning and Evening upon the Court of Guard, either by the Captain of the watch himself, or by some one of his principal officers'. If Strachey is right, twice a day the colonists would have heard, among other uplifting sentiments, the following: 'Whereas we have by undertaking this plantation undergone the reproofs of the base world, insomuch as many of our own brethren laugh us to scorn, O Lord we pray thee fortify us against this temptation: let *Sanballat*, & *Tobias*, Papists & players, & such other *Ammonites* & *Horonites* the scum & dregs of the earth, let them mock such as help to build up the walls of Jerusalem, and they that be filthy, let them be filthy still.'[41] Even if the content of a play seemed acceptable, the mode of entertainment itself was the enemy of the colonial plantation.

What then is the relation between the theatre and the surrounding institutions? Shakespeare's play offers us a model of unresolved and unresolvable doubleness: the island in *The Tempest* seems to be an image of the place of pure fantasy, set apart from surrounding discourses; and it seems to be an image of the place of power, the place in which all individual discourses are organized by the half-invisible ruler. By extension art is a well-demarcated, marginal, private sphere, the realm of insight, pleasure, and isolation; and art is a capacious, central, public sphere, the realm of proper political order made possible through mind control, coercion, discipline, anxiety, and pardon. The aesthetic space – or, more accurately, the commercial space of the theatrical joint-stock company – is constituted by the simultaneous appropriation of and swerving from the discourse of power.

And this doubleness in effect produces two different accounts of the nature of mimetic economy. In one account, aesthetic representation is unlike all other exchanges because it takes nothing; art is pure plenitude. Everywhere else there is scarcity: wretches cling to 'an acre of barren ground, long heath, brown furze, any thing' (I.i.66–7), and one person's gain is another's loss. In works of art, by contrast, things can be imitated, staged, reproduced without any loss or expense; indeed what is borrowed seems enhanced by the borrowing, for nothing is used up, nothing fades. The magic of art resides in the freedom of the imagination and hence in liberation from the constraints of the body. What is produced elsewhere only by intense labour is produced in art by a magical command whose power Shakespeare figures in Ariel's response to Prospero's call:

> All hail, great master, grave sir, hail! I come
> To answer thy best pleasure; be't to fly,
> To swim, to dive into the fire, to ride
> On the curl'd clouds. To thy strong bidding, task
> Ariel, and all his quality.
>
> (I.ii.189–93)

This account of art as pure plenitude is perhaps most perfectly imaged in Prospero's wedding masque, with its goddesses and nymphs and dancing reapers, its majestic vision of

> Barns and garners never empty;
> Vines with clust'ring bunches growing,
> Plants with goodly burthen bowing.
>
> (IV.i.111–13)

But the prayer at the end of the martial law code reminds us that there is another version of mimetic economy, one in which aesthetic exchanges, like all other exchanges, always involve loss, even if it is cunningly hidden; in which aesthetic value, like all other value, actively depends upon want, craving, and absence; in which art itself – fantasy ridden and empty – is the very soul of scarcity. This version too finds its expression in *The Tempest* in the high cost Prospero has paid for his absorption in his secret studies, in Ariel's grumblings about his 'pains' and 'toil', and in the sudden vanishing – 'to a strange, hollow, and confused noise' – of the masque that had figured forth plenitude and in Prospero's richly anxious meditation on the 'baseless fabric' of his own glorious vision.

It is this doubleness that Shakespeare's joint-stock company bequeathed to its cultural heirs. And the principal beneficiary in the end was not the theatre but a different institution, the institution of literature. Shakespeare served posthumously as a principal shareholder in this institution as well – not as a man of the theatre but as the author of the book. During Shakespeare's lifetime, the King's Men showed no interest in and may have actually resisted the publication of a one-volume collection of their famous playwright's work; the circulation of such a book was not in the interests of their company. But other collective enterprises, including the educational system in which this study is implicated, have focused more on the text than on the playhouse.

For if Shakespeare himself imagined Prospero's island as the great Globe Theatre, succeeding generations found that island more compactly and portably figured in the bound volume. The passage from the stage to the book signals a larger shift from the joint-stock company, with its primary interest in protecting the common property, to the modern corporation, with its primary interest in the expansion and profitable exploitation of a network of relations. Unlike the Globe, which is tied to a particular place and time and community, unlike even the travelling theatre company, with its constraints of personnel and stage properties and playing space, the book is supremely portable. It may be readily detached from its immediate geographical and cultural origins, its original producers and consumers, and endlessly reproduced, circulated, exchanged, exported to other times and places.[42]

The plays, of course, continue to live in the theatre, but Shakespeare's achievement and the cult of artistic genius erected around the achievement have become increasingly identified with his collected works. Those works have been widely acknowledged as the central literary achievement of English culture. As such they served – and continue to serve – as a fetish of Western civilization, a fetish Caliban curiously anticipates when he counsels Stephano and Trinculo to cut Prospero's throat:[43]

> Remember
> First to possess his books; for without them
> He's but a sot, as I am; nor hath not
> One spirit to command: they all do hate him
> As rootedly as I. Burn but his books.

(III.ii.91–5)

I want to close with a story that provides an oddly ironic perspective on Caliban's desire and exemplifies the continued doubleness of Shakespeare in our culture: at once the embodiment of civilized recreation, freed from the anxiety of rule, and the instrument of empire. The story is told by H.M. Stanley – the journalist and African explorer of 'Doctor Livingstone, I presume?' fame – in his account of his journeyings through what he calls

'the dark continent'. In May 1877 he was at a place called Mowa in central
Africa. I will let him tell the story in his own words:

On the third day of our stay at Mowa, feeling quite comfortable amongst
the people, on account of their friendly bearing, I began to write down
in my note-book the terms for articles in order to improve my already
copious vocabulary of native words. I had proceeded only a few minutes
when I observed a strange commotion amongst the people who had been
flocking about me, and presently they ran away. In a short time we heard
war-cries ringing loudly and shrilly over the table-land. Two hours
afterwards, a long line of warriors, armed with muskets, were seen
descending the table-land and advancing towards our camp. There may
have been between five hundred and six hundred of them. We, on the
other hand, had made but few preparations except such as would justify
us replying to them in the event of the actual commencement of
hostilities. But I had made many firm friends amongst them, and I firmly
believed that I would be able to avert an open rupture.

When they had assembled at about a hundred yards in front of our
camp, Safeni [the chief of another tribe with whom Stanley had become
friendly] and I walked up towards them, and sat down midway. Some
half-dozen of the Mowa people came near, and the shauri began.

'What is the matter, my friends?' I asked. 'Why do you come with
guns in your hands in such numbers, as though you were coming to
fight? Fight! Fight us, your friends! Tut! this is some great mistake,
surely.'

'Mundelé,' replied one of them, ... 'our people saw you yesterday
make marks on some tara-tara' (paper). 'This is very bad. Our country
will waste, our goats will die, our bananas will rot, and our women will
dry up. What have we done to you, that you should wish to kill us? We
have sold you food, and we have brought you wine, each day. Your
people are allowed to wander where they please, without trouble. Why
is the Mundelé so wicked? We have gathered together to fight you if you
do not burn that tara-tara now before our eyes. If you burn it we go away,
and shall be friends as heretofore.'

I told them to rest there, and left Safeni in their hands as a pledge that
I should return. My tent was not fifty yards from the spot, but while going
towards it my brain was busy in devising some plan to foil this
superstitious madness. My note-book contained a vast number of
valuable notes; plans of falls, creeks, villages, sketches of localities,
ethnological and philological details, sufficient to fill two octavo volumes
– everything was of general interest to the public. I could not sacrifice it
to the childish caprice of savages. As I was rummaging my book box, I
came across a volume of Shakespeare (Chandos edition), much worn and
well thumbed, and which was of the same size as my field-book; its cover
was similar also, and it might be passed for the note-book provided that
no one remembered its appearance too well. I took it to them.

'Is this the tara-tara, friends, that you wish burnt?'

'Yes, yes, that is it!'

'Well, take it, and burn it or keep it.'

'M-m. No, no, no. We will not touch it. It is fetish. You must burn it.'

'I! Well, let it be so. I will do anything to please my good friends of Mowa.'

We walked to the nearest fire. I breathed a regretful farewell to my genial companion, which during many weary hours of night had assisted to relieve my mind when oppressed by almost intolerable woes, and then gravely consigned the innocent Shakespeare to the flames, heaping the brush-fuel over it with ceremonious care.

'Ah-h-h,' breathed the poor deluded natives, sighing their relief. 'The Mundelé is good – is very good. He loves his Mowa friends. There is no trouble now, Mundelé. The Mowa people are not bad.' And something approaching to a cheer was shouted among them, which terminated the episode of the Burning of Shakespeare.[44]

Stanley's precious notebook, with its sketches and ethnographic and philologic details, survived then and proved invaluable in charting and organizing the Belgian Congo, perhaps the most vicious of all of Europe's African colonies. As Stanley had claimed, everything was indeed of general interest to the public. After Stanley's death, the notebooks passed into the possession of heirs and then for many years were presumed lost. But they were rediscovered at the time of the Congo independence celebrations and have recently been edited. Their publication revealed something odd: while the notebook entry for his stay at Mowa records that the natives were angry at his writing – 'They say I made strong medicine to kill their country' – Stanley makes no mention of the burning of Shakespeare.[45] Perhaps, to heighten that general interest with which he was so concerned, he made up the story. He could have achieved his narrative effect with only two books: Shakespeare and the Bible. And had he professed to burn the latter to save his notebook, his readers would no doubt have been scandalized.

For our purposes, it doesn't matter very much if the story 'really' happened. What matters is the role Shakespeare plays in it, a role at once central and expendable – and, in some obscure way, not just expendable but exchangeable for what really matters: the writing that more directly serves power. For if at moments we can convince ourselves that Shakespeare *is* the discourse of power, we should remind ourselves that there are usually other discourses – here the notes and vocabulary and maps – that are instrumentally far more important. Yet if we try then to convince ourselves that Shakespeare is marginal and untainted by power, we have Stanley's story to remind us that without Shakespeare we wouldn't have the notes. Of course, this is just an accident – the accident of the books' resemblance – but then why was Stanley carrying the book in the first place?

For Stanley, Shakespeare's theatre had become a book, and the book in turn had become a genial companion, a talisman of civility, a source not of salutary anxiety but of comfort in adversity. The anxiety in his account – and it is not salutary – is among the natives, and it is relieved only when, as Caliban had hoped, the book is destroyed. But the destruction of one book only saves another, more practical, more deadly. And when he returned to London or New York, Stanley could always buy another copy (Chandos edition) of his genial companion.

Notes

All quotations from Shakespeare are taken from *The Riverside Shakespeare*, ed. G. Blakemore Evans (Boston: Houghton Mifflin, 1974) and will be identified in parentheses in the text.

1. 'First Sermon on the Lord's Prayer', in *The Works of Hugh Latimer*, 2 vols., ed. George Elwes Corrie, Parker Society (Cambridge: Cambridge University Press, 1844), 1:335. Though her mother was a near relation of Catherine of Aragon, the duchess of Suffolk was a staunch Protestant who went into exile during the reign of Mary Tudor.

Latimer's rhetorical occasion for relating this story is an odd one: he is commenting on the appropriateness of addressing God as 'our father', since God 'hath a fatherly and loving affection towards us, far passing the love of bodily parents to their children'. Latimer then cites a passage from Isaiah in which the prophet asks rhetorically, in speaking of God's love, 'Can a wife forget the child of her womb, and the son whom she hath borne?' Isaiah uses the image of a wife, Latimer remarks, 'because women most commonly are more affected towards their children than men be.' He then recalls with horror that under the devil's influence some women have in fact killed their own children, but he warns his listeners not to believe every story of this kind that they hear. And he proceeds to support this warning with the story of the Cambridge woman.

2. Alternatively, we might say that Latimer occupies a peculiarly intermediate position, anticipating that occupied by the players: at once free and constrained, the strutting master of the scene and the social inferior, the charismatic object of intense cathexis and the embodiment of dependence.

3. The closest parallel, I suppose, would be nocturnal emissions, about which there is a substantial literature in the Middle Ages and early modern period, but I am not sure a story about them would have been suitable for the duchess of Suffolk.

4. The gap is, at this point, a very small one, and on her release from prison the woman may well have been sent back to her husband. Latimer does not bother to say, presumably because the woman's fate was irrelevant to his homiletic point.

5. Though the justification for a transfer (as opposed to a simple elimination) is left vague, perhaps to spare the sensibility of the duchess of Suffolk, Latimer may believe that for some time after childbirth the woman's body is tainted – hence 'a green woman', as in green or tainted meat – and that in the interest of public health she should not be permitted contact, in particular sexual contact, with others. Or perhaps he simply believes that a woman still weakened from the ordeal of childbirth – hence a different meaning for 'green woman', as in a green or fresh wound – should be spared the normal demands on her energies.

6. See similarly Spenser's account of Duessa (*Faerie Queene* 1.8.46–48). There are many medical as well as literary and theological reflections on the innate filthiness of women.

7. The sermon is probably not a source for *Measure for Measure*, though it is intriguing

that another, more famous, sermon by Latimer – the first of the 'Sermons on the Card' – includes an emblematic story that bears a certain resemblance to Shakespeare's play. The king in Latimer's fable accepts into his favor 'a mean man', 'not because this person hath of himself deserved any such favour, but that the king casteth this favour unto him of his own mere motion and fantasy'. The man thus favoured is appointed 'the chief captain and defender of his town of Calais', but he treacherously violates his trust (*The Works of Hugh Latimer* 1:4–5).

8. Although one can readily imagine a detached response to a Shakespearean comedy, such a response would signal the failure of the play to please or a refusal of the pleasure the play was offering.

9. This is, however, only a *working* distinction, to mark an unstable, shifting relation between anxiety and pleasure. Anxiety and pleasure are not the same, but they are not simple opposites. Anxiety in the presence of real bodies put at real risk is a source of pleasure for at least some of the spectators, whereas in the theatre pleasure in imaginary situations is not entirely unmixed with (and does not entirely absorb and transform) anxiety. Even if we discount the rhetorical exaggerations of that anxiety in a literary criticism that often speaks of the excruciating pain and difficulty of spectatorship (or reading), we must acknowledge that Shakespeare often arouses considerable anxiety. Still, we must also acknowledge that for the collective body of spectators the ratio of anxiety to pleasure in the theatre was likely to have differed from that outside its walls.

10. Theatrical anxiety must not only give pleasure in the theatre but generate a longing for the theatre in those who have left its precincts. If large numbers of potential spectators feel they can get what they need in other places, they will not take the trouble to return. The point is obvious but still worth remarking, since we are likely to forget, first, that Elizabethan and Jacobean public theatres had extremely large capacities (as high as two thousand spectators) and hence were expected to draw substantial crowds and, second, that it was by no means simple to attend most of the theatres. A trip to the Globe took a good part of the day and involved considerable expense, including transportation by boat and refreshments. The theatre had to contrive to make potential spectators think, and think frequently, 'I wish I were at the theatre.' To do so, it could advertise through playbills and processions, but it could also count on deep associations: that is, certain anxieties would remind one of the theatre where those same anxieties were turned to the service of pleasure.

11. The very point of theatrical anxiety may be that it is not 'real' – that is, we are not threatened, there are no consequences in the real world to fortune or station or life, and so forth. But this formulation is at best only a half-truth, since at the level of feelings it is not always so easy to distinguish between the anxiety generated by a literary experience and the anxiety generated by events in one's own life.

12. He does, however, in some sense tell the story for his hearers' pleasure as well as instruction, and I think it is important to resist making too sharp a distinction between the purely theatrical uses of anxiety and the uses elsewhere in the culture. The distinction is practical and relative: no less important for that, but not to be construed as a theoretical necessity.

13. His strategy may also derive from a late-medieval clerical preoccupation with the distinction between *attrition* and *contrition*. The former was a change in behaviour caused by the buffets of fortune and the hope of escaping punishment through a prudent repentance; the latter was a more authentic repentance rooted not in calculation but in grief. Latimer may have felt that only when the woman was at the point of death could she experience a genuine contrition. I discuss below an instance of this distinction in *Measure for Measure*.

14. It is worth reflecting on the implications of this casual remark: 'the people' appear to believe that there is an inverse relation between the severity of the punishment and the heinousness of the crime.

15. For an account of the scene, see Catherine Drinker Bowen, *The Lion and the Throne: The Life and Times of Sir Edward Coke* (Boston: Little, Brown and Company, 1956), pp. 220–22.

16. For the text of James's letter, see *Letters of King James VI and I*, ed. G.P.V. Akrigg (Berkeley: University of California Press, 1984), pp. 218–19.

17. James himself was one of the most notoriously anxious monarchs in British history,

and with good reason. In the event, his son, as well as his mother and father, met a violent end.

18. Dudley Carleton's letter, dated 11 December 1603, is reprinted in Thomas Birch, *The Court and Times of James the First*, 2 vols. (London: Henry Colburn, 1849), 1:27–32. Carleton suggests that Sir Walter Raleigh, who had also been convicted in the Bye Plot, was the particular object of the king's techniques of anxiety arousal. Raleigh was to be executed on the following Monday and was watching the scene on the scaffold from a window in his cell. 'Raleigh, you must think,' writes Carleton, 'had hammers working in his head, to beat out the meaning of this stratagem' (31). In a comparable last-minute reprieve, James suspended Raleigh's execution as well; Raleigh was kept prisoner (and was considered to be legally dead) for thirteen years until, in the wake of the Guiana fiasco, he was executed (technically on the original charge from 1603) in 1618.

19. Their popularity as spectacle suggests that the fear was to some degree pleasurable to the onlookers, whether, as Hobbes argued, because they delighted in not being themselves the victims or, as official spokesmen claimed, because the horror was produced by a higher order whose interests it served. In either case, the experience, it was assumed, would make the viewers more obedient subjects.

20. Quoted in my *Renaissance Self-Fashioning: From More to Shakespeare* (Chicago: University of Chicago Press, 1980), p. 103.

21. Durandus of St Pourçain, quoted in Thomas N. Tentler, *Sin and Confession on the Eve of the Reformation* (Princeton: Princeton University Press, 1977), p. 251. Tentler observes that this psychologizing of the distinction is not characteristic of the medieval *summae* for confessors; the crucial distinction rather was between sorrow that was imperfect and sorrow that had been formed by grace and hence was perfect. In either case the limitation – and perhaps the cunning – of the distinction is that it is virtually impossible to establish with any confidence.

22. Recall Carleton's description of the expression on the faces of the Bye Plot conspirators as they were assembled together on the scaffold.

23. On the significance of pardon as a strategy in Renaissance monarchies, see Natalie Zemon Davis, *Fiction in the Archives* (Stanford: Stanford University Press, forthcoming). Davis's wonderful book, which she graciously allowed me to read in manuscript, shows that the system of pardons in France generated a remarkable range of narratives. Though the English legal system differed in important ways from the French, pardon played a significant, if more circumscribed, role. Shakespeare seems to have deliberately appropriated for *The Tempest* the powerful social energy of princely pardons.

24. In this regard Prospero resembles less a radical reformer like Latimer than a monarch like Queen Elizabeth: a ruler who abjured the complete inquisitorial control of the inner life and settled when necessary for the outward signs of obedience.

For a brilliant discussion of Prospero's relations with Antonio, see the introduction to the Oxford Shakespeare edition of *The Tempest*, ed. Stephen Orgel (Oxford: Oxford University Press, 1987). Throughout this chapter, I have profited from Orgel's introduction, which he kindly showed me in advance of its publication.

25. I am trying to resist here the proposition that Latimer's story is the actual practice that is then represented in works of art, and hence that in it we encounter the basis in reality of theatrical fictions. Even if we assume that the events in Cambridge occurred exactly as Latimer related them – and this is a large assumption based on a reckless act of faith – those events seem saturated with narrative conventions. It is not only that Latimer lives his life as if it were material for the stories he will tell in his sermons but that the actions he reports are comprehensible only if already fashioned into a story.

26. On Strachey's career, see S.G. Culliford, *William Strachey, 1572–1621* (Charlottesville: University Press of Virginia, 1965). See also Charles Richard Sanders, 'William Strachey, the Virginia Colony, and Shakespeare', *Virginia Magazine* 57 (1949): 115–32. Sanders notes that 'many of the eighteenth and nineteenth century Stracheys became servants of the East India Company' (118).

27. William Strachey, in Samuel Purchas, *Hakluytus Posthumus or Purchas His Pilgrimes*, 20 vols. (Glasgow: James Maclehose and Sons, 1905–7), 19:5–72. It seems worth remarking the odd coincidence between this circumstance and Latimer's presenting his

sermon also to a noble lady. Men in this period often seem to shape their experiences in the world to present them as instruction or entertainment to powerfully placed ladies. The great Shakespearean exploration of this social theme is *Othello*.

28. On joint-stock companies in the early modern period, see William Robert Scott, *The Constitution and Finance of English, Scottish, and Irish Joint-Stock Companies to 1720*, 3 vols (Cambridge: Cambridge University Press, 1912). On the theatre and the marketplace, see the excellent book by Jean-Christophe Agnew, *Worlds Apart: The Market and the Theatre in Anglo-American Thought, 1550–1750* (Cambridge: Cambridge University Press, 1986).

29. Indeed the demand for such connections, a demand almost always frustrated in the early modern period, has strengthened the case for the formalist isolation of art.

30. Charles Mills Gayley, *Shakespeare and the Founders of Liberty in America* (New York: Macmillan, 1917); William Strachey, *The Historie of Travell into Virginia Britania* (1612), ed. Louis B. Wright and Virginia Freund, Hakluyt Society 2d ser., no. 103 (London, 1953), p. xix.

31. Detestation of the sailors is a common theme in the travel literature of the period. One of the strongest elements of an elitist utopia in *The Tempest* is the fantasy that the sailors will in effect be put to sleep for the duration of the stay on the island, to be awakened only to labour on the return voyage.

32. Quoted in the introduction to *The Historie of Travell into Virginia Britania*, p. xxv.

33. I quote these lines because they may have caught Shakespeare's attention: 'What have we here?' asks Trinculo, catching sight of Caliban, 'a man or a fish? dead or alive? A fish, he smells like a fish' (II.ii.24–26). Prospero in exasperation calls Caliban a tortoise (I.ii.316).

34. The promotional literature written on behalf of the Virginia Company prior to the voyage of 1609 makes it clear that there was already widespread talk in England about the hardships of the English colonists. No one on the *Sea Venture* is likely to have harboured any illusions about conditions at Jamestown.

35. The office of governor was created by the royal charter of 1609. The governor replaced the council president as the colony's chief executive. He was granted the right to 'correct and punishe, pardon, governe, and rule all such the subjects of us ... as shall from time to time adventure themselves ... thither', and he was empowered to impose martial law in cases of mutiny or rebellion (quoted in *The Three Charters of the Virginia Company of London, with Seven Related Documents, 1606–1621*, ed. S.F. Bemiss, Jamestown 350th Anniversary Historical Booklet 4 [Williamsburg, Va., 1957], p. 52). See Warren M. Billings, 'The Transfer of English Law to Virginia, 1606–1650', in *The Westward Enterprise: English Activities in Ireland, the Atlantic, and America, 1480–1650*, ed. K.R. Andrews, N.P. Canny, and P.E.H. Hair (Liverpool: Liverpool University Press, 1978), pp. 214ff.

36. Leaving the island is not in itself, as is sometimes claimed, an abjuration of colonialism: as we have seen in the case of Bermuda, the enforced departure from the island signals the resumption of the colonial enterprise. On the other hand, insofar as *The Tempest* conflates the Bermuda and Virginia materials, the departure for Italy – and by implication England – would necessitate abandoning the absolute rule that had been established under martial law.

37. The noblemen's pride is related to the gentlemanly refusal to work that the leaders of the Virginia Company bitterly complained about. The English gentlemen in Jamestown, it was said, preferred to die rather than lift a finger to save themselves. So too when the boatswain urges Antonio and Sebastian to get out of the way or to work, Antonio answers, 'We are less afraid to be drown'd than thou art' (I.i.44–5).

38. For acute observations on the parallels with Sycorax, see Stephen Orgel, 'Prospero's Wife', *Representations* 8 (1985): 1–13; among the many essays on Caliban is one of my own: 'Learning to Curse: Aspects of Linguistic Colonialism in the Sixteenth Century', in *First Images of America: The Impact of the New World on the Old*, 2 vols., ed. Fredi Chiappelli (Berkeley: University of California Press, 1976), 2:561–80.

39. Quoted in Nicholas Canny, 'The Permissive Frontier: The Problem of Social Control in English Settlements in Ireland and Virginia, 1550–1650', in *The Westward Enterprise*, p. 36.

40. William Crashaw, *A sermon preached in London before the right honorable the Lord Lawarre, Lord Governour and Captaine Generall of Virginia ... at the said Lord Generall his leave taking of England ... and departure for Virginea, Febr. 21, 1609* (London, 1610), pp. Hlv–Hlr. The British Library has a copy of Strachey's *Lawes Diuine, Morall and Martiall* with a manuscript inscription by the author to Crashaw; see Sanders, 'William Strachey, the Virginia Colony, and Shakespeare', p. 121.

41. William Strachey, *For the Colony in Virginea Britannia. Lawes Diuine, Morall and Martiall, &c.* (London: Walter Burre, 1612), in Peter Force, *Tracts and Other Papers, Relating Principally to the Origin, Settlement, and Progress of the Colonies in North America, from the Discovery to the Year 1776*, 4 vols. (Washington, D.C., 1836–46), 3:67.

42. In our century the market for Shakespeare as book has come to focus increasingly upon adolescents in colleges and universities who are assigned expensive texts furnished with elaborate critical introductions and editorial apparatus. On the ideological implications of Shakespeare in the curriculum, see Alan Sinfield, 'Give an account of Shakespeare and Education, showing why you think they are effective and what you have appreciated about them. Support your comments with precise references', in *Political Shakespeare: New Essays in Cultural Materialism*, ed. Jonathan Dollimore and Alan Sinfield (Manchester: Manchester University Press, 1985), pp. 134–57.

43. But if Shakespeare's works have become a fetish, they are defined for their possessors not by their magical power to command but by their freedom from the anxieties of rule. They are the emblems of cultivation, civility, recreation, but they are not conceived of as direct agents in the work of empire.

44. Henry M. Stanley, *Through the Dark Continent*, 2 vols. (New York: Harper and Brothers, 1878), 2:384–6. I owe this story to Walter Michaels, who found it quoted by William James in a footnote. James's interest was aroused by what he saw as primitive literalism. The natives' oral culture makes it impossible for them to understand writing. They cannot distinguish between books that are reproducible and books that are unique, or for that matter between fiction and field notes, and because of this inability they cannot identify what was at least the immediate threat to their culture. In making the book a fetish they fail to make the necessary distinction between fantasy and truth, a distinction whose origins reside in texts like *The Tempest*, that is, in texts that thematize a difference between the island of art and the mainland of reality.

It is difficult to gauge how much of this analysis is only James's own fantasy. The natives may not actually have been incapable of making such a distinction. It is interesting, in this regard, that they are said to be carrying muskets, so there must already have been a history of involvement with Arabs or Europeans, a history that Stanley, making much of his role as explorer, represses. It is noteworthy too that as Stanley warms to his story, his natives increasingly speak in the racist idiom familiar from movies like *King Kong*: 'M-m. No, no, no.' And it is also possible, as I have already suggested, to see in Stanley the actual fetishism of the book: the attribution of power and value and companionship to the dead letter. In Stanley's reverie Shakespeare becomes a friend who must be sacrificed (as Stanley seems prepared to sacrifice Safeni) to protect the colonial project. Shakespeare is thus indispensable in two ways – as a consolation in the long painful trials of empire and as a deceptive token of exchange.

45. *The Exploration Diaries of H.M. Stanley*, ed. Richard Stanley and Alan Neame (New York: Vanguard Press, 1961), p. 187. Many of the journal entries that Stanley professes to transcribe in *Through the Dark Continent* are in fact invented: 'The so-called "extracts from my diary" in *Through the Dark Continent*,' the editors remark, 'are hardly more than a device for varying the typeface, for they are quite as deliberately composed as the rest of the narrative' (xvi). I should add that the day after the burning of his 'genial companion,' Stanley lost his close friend and associate Frank Pocock, who drowned when his canoe overturned. There is an odd sense of a relation between the loss of these two friends, as if Stanley viewed the burning of the one and the drowning of the other as linked sacrifices for the cause of empire.

7

Charivari and the Comedy of Abjection in *Othello*

Michael D. Bristol

If certain history plays can be read as rites of 'uncrowning' then *Othello* might be read as a rite of 'unmarrying'. The specific organizing principle operative here is the social custom, common throughout early modern Europe, of charivari.[1] The abusive language, the noisy clamour under Brabantio's window, and the menace of violence in the opening scene of the play link the improvisations of Iago with the codes of a carnivalesque disturbance or charivari organized in protest over the marriage of the play's central characters. Charivari does not figure as an isolated episode here, however, nor has it been completed when the initial onstage commotion ends.[2] Despite the sympathy that Othello and Desdemona seem intended to arouse in the audience, the play as a whole is organized around the abjection and violent punishment of its central figures.

Charivari was a practice of noisy festive abuse in which a community enacted its specific objection to inappropriate marriages and more generally exercised a widespread surveillance of sexuality. As Natalie Davis has pointed out,[3] this 'community' actually consists of young men, typically the unmarried ones, who represent a social principle of male solidarity that is in some respects deeply hostile to precisely that form of institutionally sanctioned sexuality whose standards they are empowered to oversee.[4]

As a violent burlesque of marriage, charivari represents the heterosexual couple in grotesquely parodic form. The bride, frequently depicted by a man dressed as a woman, will typically be represented as hyperfeminine. The groom, against whom the larger share of social animosity is often directed, is invariably represented as a type of clown or bumpkin. In addition, the staging of a charivari requires a master of ceremonies, a popular festive ringleader whose task is the unmaking of a transgressive marriage.[5] Even in its standard form, a full-blown charivari would be a disturbing spectacle to witness. The charivari that forms the comical substructure of *Othello* is even more powerfully troubling, because here the role of the clownish bridegroom is conflated with a derisory and abusive image of 'The Moor'.

The following analysis sketches out an interpretation of *Othello* as a carnivalesque text.[6] Carnival is operative as something considerably more than a novel decor for the *mise-en-scène* or an alternative thematics for interpretation. The play's structure is interpreted schematically as a carnivalesque derangement of marriage as a social institution and as an illustration of the contradictory role of heterosexual desire within that institution. The grotesque character of this popular festive scenario is heightened by its deployment of the stereotypical figure of an African, parodically represented by an actor in blackface. Heterosexual desire is staged here as an absurdly mutual attraction between a beautiful woman and a funny monster.

At the time of the play's earliest performances, the supplementary character of Othello's blackness would be apparent in the white actor's use of blackface to represent the conventionalized form of 'The Moor'. In the initial context of its reception, it seems unlikely that the play's appeal to invidious stereotypes would have troubled the conscience of anyone in the audience. Since what we now call racial prejudice did not fall outside prevailing social norms in Shakespeare's society, no one in the early audience would have felt sympathy for Othello simply on grounds that he was the victim of a racist society.[7] It is far more probable that 'The Moor' would have been seen as comically monstrous. Under these conditions the aspects of charivari and of the comical abjection of the protagonists would have been clear to an audience for whom a racist sensibility was entirely normal.[8]

At the end of the sixteenth century racism was not yet organized as a large-scale system of oppressive social and economic arrangements, but it certainly existed in the form of a distinctive and widely shared *affekt-complex*. Racism in this early, prototypical, form entails a specific physical repugnance for the skin colour and other typical features of black Africans. This sensibility was not yet generalized into an abstract or pseudoscientific doctrine of racial inferiority, and for this reason it would have been relatively difficult to conceive of a principled objection to this 'com-monsensical' attitude. The physical aversion of the English toward the racial other was rationalized through an elaborate mythology, supported in part by scriptural authority and reinforced by a body of popular narrative.[9] Within this context the image of the racial other is immediately available as a way of encoding deformity or the monstrous.

For Shakespeare and for his audience the sensibilities of racial difference are for all practical purposes abstract and virtually disembodied, since the mythology of African racial inferiority is not yet a fully implemented social practice within the social landscape of early modern

Europe. Even at this early stage, however, it has already occurred to some people that the racial other is providentially foreordained for the role of the slave, an idea that is fully achieved in the eighteenth- and nineteenth-century institution of plantation slavery and in such successor institutions as segregation and apartheid. The large-scale forms of institutional racism that continue to be a chronic and intractable problem in modern societies are, of course, already latent within the abstract racial mythologies of the sixteenth century, since these mythologies enter into the construction of the social and sexual imagery both of the dominant and of the popular culture. In more recent contexts of reception the farcical and carnivalesque potentiality of the play is usually not allowed to manifest itself openly. To foreground the elements of charivari and comic abjection would disclose in threatening and unacceptable ways the text's ominous relationship to the historical formation of racism as a massive social fact in contemporary Europe, and in the successor cultures of North and South America as well as in parts of the African homeland itself. Against this background the text of *Othello* has to be construed as a highly significant document in the historical constitution both of racist sensibility and of racist political ideology.

As a seriocomic or carnivalesque masquerade, the play makes visible the normative horizons against which sexual partners must be selected and the latent social violence that marriage attempts to prevent, often unsuccessfully, from becoming manifest. To stage this action as the carnivalesque thrashing of the play's central characters is, of course, a risky choice for a director to make, since it can easily transform the complex equilibrium of the play from tragedy to *opera buffa*. Although the play is grouped with the tragedies in the First Folio and has always been viewed as properly belonging to this genre, commentators have recognized for a long time the precarious balance of this play at the very boundaries of farce.[10] *Othello* is a text that evidently lends itself very well to parody, burlesque, and caricature, and this is due in part to the racial otherness of its protagonist.[11]

The relationship of marriage is established through forms of collective representation, ceremonial and public enactments that articulate the private ethos of conjugal existence and mark out the communal responsibilities of the couple to implement and sustain socially approved 'relations of reproduction'. In the early modern period the ceremonial forms of marriage are accompanied (and opposed) by parodic doubling of the wedding feast in the forms of charivari.[12] This parodic doubling is organized by a carnivalesque wardrobe corresponding to a triad of dramatic agents – the clown (who represents the bridegroom), the transvestite (who represents the bride), and the 'scourge of marriage', often assigned a suit of black (who represents the community of unattached males or 'young men').[13] Iago of course is neither unattached nor young, but part of his success with his various dupes is his ability to present himself as 'one of the boys'. Iago's misogyny is expressed as the married man's *ressentiment* against marriage, against wives in general, and against his own wife in particular. But this *ressentiment* is only one form of the more diffuse and pervasive misogyny typically expressed in the charivari. And of course Iago's more sinister function is his ability to encourage a kind of complicity within the audience. In a performance he makes his perspective the perspective of the text and thus solicits from the audience a participatory endorsement of the action.

The three primary 'characters' in charivari each has a normative function in the allocation of marriage partners and in the regulation of sexual behaviour. These three figures parody the three persons of the wedding ceremony – bride, groom, and priest. The ensemble performs a travesty of the wedding ceremony itself. The ringleader or master of ceremonies may in some instances assist the partners in outwitting parental opposition, but this figure may also function as a nemesis of erotic desire itself and attempt to destroy the intended bond. In the actual practice of charivari, the married couple themselves are forced to submit to public ridicule and sometimes to violent punishment.[14] In its milder forms, a charivari allows the husband and wife to be represented by parodic doubles who are then symbolically thrashed by the ringleader and his followers.

This triad of social agents is common to many of Shakespeare's tragedies of erotic life, and it even appears in the comedies. Hamlet stages 'The Murder of Gonzago' partly as a public rebuke to the unseemly marriage of Claudius and Gertrude (Davis, 'Reasons of Misrule' p. 75). This is later escalated to a fantasy of the general abolition of the institution of monogamy, 'I say we will have no moe marriage' (III.i.148). Hamlet's situation here expresses the powerful ambivalence of the unattached male toward marriage as the institutional format in which heterosexual desire and its satisfaction are legitimated. His objection to the aberrant and offensive union of mother and uncle is predicated on the idealization of marriage and in this case on the specific marriage of mother and father. This idealization is, however, accompanied by the fantasy of a general dissolution of the institution of monogamy back into a dispensation of erotic promiscuity and the free circulation of sexual partners. A similar agenda, motivated by a similar ambivalence, is pursued by Don John in *Much Ado about Nothing*, and by Iachimo in *Cymbeline*.

The argument I hope to sketch out here requires that readers or viewers of *Othello* efface their response to the existence of Othello, Desdemona and Iago as individual subjects endowed with personalities and with some mode of autonomous interiorized life. The reason for such selective or wilful ignorance of some of the most compelling features of this text is to make the determinate theatrical surfaces visible. To the extent that the surface coding of this play is openly manifested the analysis presented here will do violence to the existence of the characters in depth. I believe that the withdrawal of empathy and of identification from the play's main characters is difficult, not least because the experience of individual subjectivity as we have come to know it *is* objectively operative in the text. It has been suggested, in fact, that the pathos of individual subjectivity was actually invented by Shakespeare, or that this experience appears for the first time in the history of Western representation in that great socio-cultural laboratory known as Elizabethan drama.[15]

Whether this view is accurate or not, however, there is the more immediate difficulty that we desire, as readers and viewers, to reflect on and to identify with the complex pathos of individual subjectivity as it is represented in Shakespeare's oeuvre. This is especially so, perhaps, for professional readers and viewers, who are likely to have strong interests in the experience of the speaking/writing subject and in the problematic of autonomy and expressive unity. The constellation of interests and goal-values most characteristic of the institutional processing of literary texts has given rise to an extremely rich critical discourse on the question of the subject; it is precisely the power and the vitality of this discourse that makes the withdrawal of empathy from the characters so difficult. But when we acknowledge the characters not only as Othello, Desdemona and Iago, but also as components in a carnivalesque 'wardrobe' that is inscribed within this text, then this wardrobe assigns them the roles of clown, transvestite, and 'scourge of marriage' in a charivari.

The clown is a type of public figure who embodies the 'right to be other', as M.M. Bakhtin would have it (*Dialogic Imagination*, pp. 158–67), since the clown always and everywhere rejects the categories made available in routine institutional life. The clown is therefore both criminal and monster, although such alien and malevolent aspects are more often than not disguised. Etymologically 'clown' is related to 'colonus' – a farmer or settler, someone not from Rome but from the agricultural hinterland. As a rustic or hayseed the clown's relationship to social reality is best expressed through such contemporary idioms as 'He's out of it!', 'He doesn't know where it's at!', or simply 'Mars!' In the drama of the early modern period a clown is often by convention a kind of country bumpkin, but he is also a kind of 'professional outsider' of extremely flexible social provenance. Bakhtin has stressed the emancipatory capacity of the clown function, arguing that the clown mask embodies the 'right to be other' or *refus d'identité*. However, there is a pathos of clowning as well, and the clown mask may represent everything that is socially and sexually maladroit, credulous, easily victimized. And just as there is a certain satisfaction in observing an assertive clown get the better of his superiors, so is there also satisfaction in seeing an inept clown abused and stripped of his dignity.

This abuse or 'thrashing' of the doltish outsider provides the audience with a comedy of abjection, a social genre in which the experience of exclusion and impotence can be displaced onto an even more helpless caste within society.

To think of Othello as a kind of blackface clown is perhaps distasteful, even though the role must have been written not for a black actor, but with the idea of black makeup or a false-face of some kind. Othello is a Moor, but only in quotation marks, and his blackness is not even skin deep but rather a transitory and superficial theatrical integument. Othello's Moorish origins are the mark of his exclusion; as a cultural stranger he is, of course, 'out of it' in the most compelling and literal sense. As a foreigner he is unable to grasp and to make effective use of other Venetian codes of social and sexual conduct. He is thus a grotesque embodiment of the bridegroom – an exotic, monstrous, and funny substitute who transgresses the norms associated with the idea of a husband.

To link Othello to the theatrical function of a clown is not necessarily to be committed to an interpretation of his character as a fool. Othello's folly, like Othello's nobility and personal grandeur, is a specific interpretation of the character's motivation and of his competence to actualize those motives. The argument here, however, is that the role of Othello is already formatted in terms of the abject-clown function and that any interpretation of the character's 'nature' therefore has to be achieved within that format. The eloquence of Othello's language and the magnanimity of his character may in fact intensify the grotesque element. His poetic self-articulation is not so much the *expression* of a self-possessed subject but is instead a form of discursive indecorum that strains against the social meanings objectified in Othello's counter-festive *persona*. Stephen Greenblatt identifies the joke here as one of the 'master plots of comedy,' in which a beautiful young woman outwits an 'old and outlandish' husband.[16] Greenblatt reminds us here that Othello is functionally equivalent to the gull or butt of an abusive comic action, but he passes over the most salient feature of Othello's outlandishness, which is actualized in the blackface makeup essential to the depiction of this character. Greenblatt's discretion is no doubt a political judgement rather than an expression of a delicacy of taste. To present Othello in blackface, as opposed to presenting him just as a black man, would confront the audience with a comic spectacle of abjection rather than with the grand opera of misdirected passion. Such a comedy of abjection has not found much welcome in the history of the play's reception.

The original audience of this play in Jacobean England may have had relatively little inhibition in its expression of invidious racial sentiments, and so might have seen the derisory implications of the situation more easily. During the nineteenth century, when institutional racism was naturalized by recourse to a 'scientific' discourse on racial difference, the problem of Othello's outlandishness and the unsympathetic laughter it might evoke was 'solved' by making him a Caucasoid Moor, instead of a 'veritable Negro' (Newman, p. 144). Without such a fine discrimination, a performance of *Othello* would have been not so much tragic as simply unbearable, part farce and part lynch-mob. In the present social climate, when racism, though still very widespread, has been officially anathematized, the possibility of a blackface Othello would still be an embarrassment and a scandal, though presumably for a different set of reasons. Either way, the element of burlesque inscribed in this text is clearly too destabilizing to escape repression.

If Othello can be recognized as an abject clown in a charivari, then the scenario of such a charivari would require a transvestite to play the part of the wife. In the context of popular culture in the early modern period, female disguise and female impersonation were common to charivari and to a variety of other festive observances.[17] This practice was, among other things, the expression of a widespread 'fear' of women as both the embodiment of and the provocation to social transgression. Within the pervasive misogyny of the early modern period, women and their desires seemed to project the threat of a radical social undifferentiation.[18] The young men and boys who appeared in female dress at the time of Carnival seem to have been engaged in 'putting women in their place' through an exaggerated pantomime of everything feminine. And yet this very practice required the emphatic foregrounding of the artifice required for any stable coding of gender difference. Was this festive transvestism legitimated by means of a general misrecognition of the social constitution of gender? Or did the participants understand at some level that the association of social badness with women was nothing more than a patriarchal social fiction that could only be sustained in and through continuous ritual affirmation?

Female impersonation is, of course, one of the distinctive and extremely salient features of Elizabethan and Jacobean dramaturgy, and yet surprisingly little is known of how this mode of representation actually worked.[19] The practice of using boy actors to play the parts of women derives from the more diffuse social practice of female impersonation in the popular festive milieu. Were the boy actors in Shakespeare's company engaging in a conventional form of ridicule of the feminine? Or were they engaged in a general parody of the artifice of gender coding itself? A transvestite presents the category of woman in quotation marks, and reveals that both 'man' and 'woman' are socially produced categories. In the drama of Shakespeare and his contemporaries, gender is at times an extremely mobile and shifting phenomenon without any solid anchor in sexual identity. To a considerable degree gender is a 'flag of convenience' prompted by contingent social circumstances, and at times gender identity is negotiated with considerable grace and dexterity. The convention of the actor 'boying' the woman's part is thus doubly parodic, a campy put-down of femininity and, at another level, a way to theorize the social misrecognition on which all gender allocations depend.

Desdemona's 'femininity' is bracketed by the theatrical 'boying' of his/her part. This renders her/his sexuality as a kind of sustained gestural equivocation, and this corresponds to the exaggerated and equivocal rhetorical aspect of Desdemona's self-presentation. As she puts it, 'I saw Othello's visage in his mind' (I.iii.252); in other words, her initial attraction to him was not provoked by his physical appearance. The play thus stipulates that Desdemona herself accepts the social prohibition against miscegenation as the normative horizon within which she must act. On the face of it she cannot be physically attracted to Othello, and critics have usually celebrated this as the sign of her ability to transcend the limited horizons of her acculturation. These interpretations accept the premise of Othello as physically undesirable and therefore insinuate that Desdemona's faith is predicted on her blindness to the highly visible 'monstrosity' of her 'husband'. In other words, her love is a misrecognition of her husband's manifestly undesirable qualities. Or is it a misrecognition of her own socially prohibited desire? Stanley Cavell interprets her lines as meaning that she saw his appearance in the way that he saw it, that she is able to enter into and to share Othello's self-acceptance and self-possession.[20] In this view Desdemona is a kind of idealization of the social category of 'wife', who can adopt the husband's own narrative fiction of self as her own imaginary object. Desdemona is thus both a fantasy of a sexually desirable woman and a fantasy of absolute sexual compliance. This figure of unconditional erotic submission is the obverse of the rebellious woman, or shrew, but, as the play shows us, this is also a socially prohibited *métier* for a woman. In fact, as Greenblatt has shown in his very influential essay, the idea that Desdemona might feel an ardent sexual desire for him makes Othello perceive Iago's insinuations of infidelity as plausible and even probable (pp. 237–52). The masculine imagination whose fantasy is projected in the figure of Desdemona cannot recognize itself as the object of another's desire.

Like all of Shakespeare's woman characters, Desdemona is an impossible sexual object, a female artifact created by a male imagination and objectified in a boy actor's body. This is, in its own way, just as artificial and as grotesque a theatrical manifestation as the blackface Othello who stands in for the category of the husband. What is distinctive about Desdemona is the way she embodies the category of an 'ideal wife' in its full contradictoriness. She has been described as chaste or even as still a virgin and also as sexually aggressive, even though very little unambiguous textual support for either of these readings actually exists.[21]

Her elopement, with a Moor no less, signals more unequivocally than a properly arranged marriage ever could that the biblical injunction to leave mother and father has been fulfilled. It is probably even harder to accept the idea of Desdemona as part of a comedy of abjection than it is to accept Othello in such a context. It is, however, only in such a theatrical context that the hyperbolic and exacerbated misrecognition on which marriage is founded can be theorized.

At the level of surface representation, then, the play enacts a marriage between two complementary symbols of the erotic grotesque. This is a marriage between what is conventionally viewed as ipso facto hideous and repellent with what is most beautiful and desirable. The incongruity of this match is objectified in the theatrical hyper-embodiment of the primary categories of man and woman or husband and wife. It is not known to what extent Elizabethan and Jacobean theatre practice deliberately foregrounded its own artifice. However, the symbolic practice of grotesque hyper-embodiment was well known in popular festive forms such as charivari. The theatrical coding of gender in the early modern period is still contaminated by the residue of these forms of social representation.

The marriage of grotesque opposites is no more a private affair or erotic dyad than a real marriage. Marriage in the early modern period, among many important social classes, was primarily a dynastic or economic alliance negotiated by a third party who represents the complex of social sanctions in which the heterosexual couple is inscribed.[22] The elopement of Desdemona and Othello, as well as their reliance on Cassio as a broker or clandestine go-between, already signals their intention deliberately to evade and thwart the will of family interests. To the extent that readers or viewers are conditioned by the normative horizons that interpret heterosexual love as mutual sexual initiative and the transcendence of all social obstacles, this elopement will be read as a romantic confirmation of the spiritual and disinterested character of their love.[23] However, it can also be construed as a flagrant sexual and social blunder. Private heterosexual felicity of the kind sought by Othello and Desdemona attracts the evil eye of erotic nemesis.[24]

The figure of erotic nemesis and the necessary third party to this union is Othello's faithful lieutenant, Iago. It is Iago's task to show both his captain and his audience just how defenceless the heterosexual couple is against the resources of sexual surveillance. The romantic lovers, represented here through a series of grotesque distortions, do not enjoy an erotic autonomy, though such erotic autonomy is a misrecognition of the socially inscribed character of 'private' sexuality. His abusive and derisory characterizations of the couple, together with his debasement of their sexuality, are a type of social commentary on the nature of erotic romance. The notion of mutual and autonomous self-selection of partners is impugned as a kind of mutual delusion that can only appear under the sign of monstrosity. In other words, the romantic couple can only 'know' that their union is based on mutual love *and on nothing else* when they have 'transcended' or violated the social codes and prohibitions that determine the allocation of sexual partners.

Iago is a Bakhtinian 'agelast', that is, one who does not laugh. He is, of course, very witty, but his aim is always to provoke a degrading laughter at the follies of others rather than to enjoy the social experience of laughter *with* others. He is a de-mythologizer whose function is to reduce all expressivity to the minimalism of the quid pro quo. The process represented here is the reduction of quality to quantity, a radical undifferentiation of persons predicated on a strictly mechanistic, universalized calculus of desire. Characters identified with this persona appear throughout Shakespeare's oeuvre, usually in the guise of a nemesis of hypocrisy and dissimulation. Hamlet's 'I know not "seems"' (I.ii.76) and Don John's 'it must not be denied but I am a plain-dealing villain' (*Much Ado about Nothing* I.i.31) are important variants of a social/cognitive process that proclaims itself to be a critique of equivocation and the will to deception. It is ironic, of course, that these claims of honesty and plain dealing are so often made in the interests of malicious dissimulation. What appears to be consistent, however, in all the variants of this character-type, is the disavowal of erotic attachment and the contemptuous manipulation of the erotic imagination.

The supposedly 'unmotivated' malice enacted by this figure is puzzling, I believe, only when read individualistically. Is Iago envious of the pleasure Othello enjoys with Desdemona, or is he jealous of Othello's supposed sexual enjoyment of Emilia? Of course, both of these ideas are purely conjectural hypotheses that have no apparent bearing on Iago's actions. In any case, Iago shows no sustained commitment to either of these ideas, as numerous commentators have pointed out. Nevertheless, there is an important clue to understanding Iago as a social agent in these transitory ruminations. Iago seems to understand that the complex of envy and jealousy is not an aberration within the socially distributed erotic economy, but is rather the fundamental precondition of desire itself. Erotic desire is not founded in a qualitative economy or in a rational market, but rather in a mimetic and histrionic dispensation that Iago projects as the envy-jealousy system.[25] In this system men are the social agents, and women the objects of exchange. Iago's actions are thus socially motivated by a diffuse and pervasive misogyny that slides between fantasies of the complete abjection of all women and fantasies of an exclusively masculine world.

Iago's success in achieving these fantasies is made manifest in the unbearably hideous tableau of the play's final scene. If the play as a whole is to be read as a ritual of unmarrying, then this ending is the monstrous equivalent of a sexual consummation. What makes the play unendurable would be the suspicion that this climax expresses all too accurately an element present in the structure of every marriage. This is an exemplary action in which the ideal of companionate marriage as a socially sanctioned erotic union is dissolved back into the chronic violence of the envy-jealousy system. Iago theorizes erotic desire – and thus marriage – primarily by a technique of emptying out Othello's character, so that nothing is left at the end except the pathetic theatrical integument, the madly deluded and murderous blackface clown. Desdemona, the perfect wife, remains perfectly submissive to the end. And Iago, with his theoretical or pedagogical tasks completed, accepts in silence his allocation to the function of sacrificial victim and is sent off to face unnamed 'brave punishments'.

Finita la commedia. What does it mean to accept the *mise-en-scène* of this play? And what does it mean to *know* that we wish it could be otherwise? To the extent that we want to see a man and a woman defying social conventions in order to fulfil mutual erotic initiatives, the play will appear as a thwarted comedy, and our response will be dominated by its pathos. But the play also shows us what such mutual erotic initiatives look like from the outside, as a comedy of abjection or charivari. The best commentators on this play have recognized the degree to which it prompts a desire to prevent the impending debacle and the sense in which it is itself a kind of theatrical punishment of the observers.[26] This helpless and agonized refusal of the *mise-en-scène* should suggest something about the corrosive effect on socially inscribed rituals of a radical or 'cruel' theatricality.

The idea of theatrical cruelty is linked to the radical aesthetics of Antonin Artaud. However, the English term 'cruelty' fails to capture an important inflection that runs through all of Artaud's discussion of theatre. The concept is derived from words that mean 'raw' or 'unprocessed'. In French *'cruaute'* expresses with even greater candour this relationship with *'le cru'* and its opposition to *'le cuit'*. Cruelty here has the sense of something uncooked, or something prior to the process of a conventional social transformation or adoption into the category of the meaningful.[27] *Othello*, perhaps more than any other Shakespeare play, raises fundamental questions about the institutional position and the aesthetic character of Shakespearean dramaturgy. Is Shakespeare raw – or is he cooked? Is it possible that our present institutional protocol for interpreting his work is a way of 'cooking' the 'raw' material to make it more palatable, more fit for consumption?

The history of the reception of *Othello* is the history of attempts to articulate ideologically correct, that is, palatable, interpretations. By screening off the comedy of abjection it is possible to engage more affirmatively with the play's romantic *liebestod*. Within these strategies, critics may find an abundance of meanings for the tragic dimension of the play. In this orientation the semantic fullness of the text is suggested as a kind of aesthetic compensation for the cruelty of its final scenes. Rosalie Colie, for example, summarizes her interpretation with an account of the play's edifying power.

> In criticizing the artificiality he at the same time exploits in his play, Shakespeare manages in *Othello* to reassess and to reanimate the moral system and the psychological truths at the core of the literary love-tradition, to reveal its problematics and to reaffirm in a fresh and momentous context the beauty of its impossible ideals.[28]

The fullness of the play, of course, is what makes it possible for viewers and readers to participate, however unwillingly, in the charivari, or ritual victimization of the imaginary heterosexual couple represented here. Such consensual participation is morally disquieting in the way it appears to solicit at least passive consent to violence against women and against outsiders, but at least we are not howling with unsympathetic laughter at their suffering and humiliation.

Colie's description of the play's semantic fullness is based in part on her concept of 'un-metaphoring' – that is, the literalization of a metaphorical relationship or conventional figuration. This is a moderate version of the notion of theatrical cruelty or the unmaking of convention that does not radically threaten existing social norms. In other words, the fate of Desdemona and Othello is a cautionary fable about what happens if a system of conventional figurations of desire is taken literally. But the more powerful 'un-metaphoring' of this play is related not to its fullness as a tragedy, but to its emptiness as a comedy of abjection. The violent interposing of the charivari here would make visible the *political* choice between aestheticized ritual affirmation and a genuine refusal of the sexual *mise-en-scène* in which this text is inscribed.

Othello occupies a problematic situation at the boundary between ritually sanctioned reality and theatrically consensual fiction. Does the play simply depict an inverted ritual of courtship and marriage, or does its performance before an audience that accepts its status as a fiction also invite complicity in a social ritual of comic abjection, humiliation, and victimization? What does it mean, to borrow a usage from the French, to 'assist' at a performance of this text? At a time when large-scale social consequences of racist sensibilities had not yet become visible, it may well have been easy to accept the formal codes of charivari as the expression of legitimate social norms. In later contexts of reception it is not so easy to accept *Othello* in the form of a derisory ritual of racial and sexual persecution, because the social experience of racial difference has become such a massive scandal.

The history of both the interpretation and the performance of *Othello* has been characterized by a search for consoling and anaesthetic explanations that would make its depictions of humiliation and suffering more tolerable. On the other hand, some observers, like Horace Howard Furness, have been absolutely inconsolable and have even refused to countenance the play.[29] The need for consolation is of course prompted by the sympathy and even the admiration readers and spectators feel for the heterosexual couple who occupy the centre of the drama. The argument I have tried to develop here is not intended to suggest that the characters do not deserve our sympathy. Nevertheless, *Othello* is a text of racial *and* sexual persecution. If the suffering represented in this drama is to be made intelligible for us, then it may no longer be possible to beautify the text. It may be more valuable to allow its structures of abjection and violence to become visible.

Notes

1. See Carol Thomas Neely, *Broken Nuptials in Shakespeare's Plays* (New Haven: Yale UP, 1985). On charivari, see Jacques Le Goff and Jean-Claude Schmitt, eds, *Le charivari: Actes de la table ronde organisée à Paris (25–27 avril 1977) par l'Ecole des Hautes Etudes en Sciences Sociales et le Centre National de la Recherche Scientifique* (Paris: Mouton, 1977); E.P.Thompson, 'Rough Music: Le Charivari Anglais', *Annales: Economies, sociétes, civilizations* 27 (1972): 285–312; and David Underdown, *Revel, Riot, and Rebellion: Popular Politics and Culture in England, 1603–1660* (Oxford: Clarendon, 1985), pp. 99–103.

2. François Laroque, 'An Archaeology of the Dramatic Text: *Othello* and Popular Traditions', *Cahiers Elisabéthains* 32 (1987): 13–35. See also T.G.A. Nelson and Charles Haines, 'Othello's Unconsummated Marriage', *Essays in Criticism* 33 (1983): 1–18.

3. Natalie Zemon Davis, 'The Reasons of Misrule: Youth Groups and Charivaris in Sixteenth-Century France', *Past and Present* 50 (1971): 49–75.

4. On the topic of 'male solidarity' see Eve Kosofsky Sedgwick, *Between Men: English Literature and Male Homosocial Desire* (New York: Columbia UP, 1985).

5. Michael Neill, 'Unproper Beds: Race, Adultery, and the Hideous in Othello', *Shakespeare Quarterly* 40 (1989): 383–412.

6. M.M. Bakhtin, *Rabelais and His World*, trans. Hélène Iswolsky (Cambridge: MIT Press, 1968), pp. 145–96 and passim; see also his *The Dialogic Imagination*, trans. Caryl Emerson and Michael Holquist (Austin: Univ. of Texas Press, 1981), pp. 167–224 and Claude Gaignebet, *Le Carneval: Essais de mythologie populaire* (Paris: Payot, 1974).

7. G.K. Hunter, 'Elizabethans and Foreigners', *Shakespeare Survey* 17 (1964): 37–52; and 'Othello and Colour Prejudice', *Proceedings of the British Academy* 53 (1967): 139–63. See also Eldred D. Jones, *Othello's Countrymen: The African in English Renaissance Drama* (Oxford: Oxford UP, 1965); and Martin Orkin, 'Othello and the "Plain Face" of Racism', *Shakespeare Quarterly* 38 (1987): 166–88.

8. Karen Newman, '"And Wash the Ethiop White": Femininity and the Monstrous in *Othello*', *Shakespeare Reproduced: The Text in History and Ideology*, ed. Jean E. Howard and Marion F. O'Connor (New York: Methuen, 1987), pp. 143–62.

9. Winthrop D. Jordan, *White over Black: American Attitudes toward the Negro,*

1550–1812 (Chapel Hill: Univ. of North Carolina, 1968); Eliot H. Tokson, *The Popular Image of the Black Man in English Drama, 1550–1688* (Boston: Hall, 1982).

10. Thomas Rymer, *A Short View of Tragedy. Shakespeare: The Critical Heritage*, ed. Brian Vickers, 6 vols (London: Routledge, 1974–81) 2: 27. See also Susan Snyder, *The Comic Matrix of Shakespeare's Tragedies* (Princeton: Princeton UP, 1979), pp. 70–74.

11. Lawrence Levine, *Highbrow/Lowbrow: The Emergence of Cultural Hierarchy in America* (Cambridge: Harvard UP, 1988), pp. 14–20; Neill, 'Unproper Beds', pp. 391–3.

12. See Violet Alford, 'Rough Music or Charivari', *Folklore* 70 (1959): 505–18; Nicole Belmont, 'Fonction de la dérision et symbolisme du bruit dans le charivari', in Le Goff and Schmitt, pp. 15–21; Natalie Zemon Davis, 'Charivari, honneur et communauté à Lyon et à Génève au XVIIᵉ siècle', in Le Goff and Schmitt, pp. 207–20; Martine Grinberg, 'Charivaris au Moyen Age et à la Renaissance. Condamnation des remariages ou rites d'inversion du temps?' in Le Goff and Schmitt, pp. 141–7 and Michael D. Bristol, 'Wedding Feast and Charivari' in his *Carnival and Theater: Plebian Culture and the Structure of Authority in Renaissance England* (New York: Methuen, 1985), pp. 162–78.

13. For the importance of youth groups and of unmarried men, see Davis, 'The Reasons of Misrule'.

14. Martin Ingram, 'Le charivari dans l'Angleterre du XVIᵉ et du XVIIᵉ siecle. Aperçu historique' in Le Goff and Schmitt, pp. 251–64; Robert Muchembled, 'Des conduites de bruit au spectacle des processions. Mutations mentales et déclin des fêtes populaires dans le Nord de la France (XVᵉ–XVIᵉ siecle)' in Le Goff and Schmitt, pp. 229–36.

15. Catherine Belsey, *The Subject of Tragedy: Identity and Difference in Renaissance Drama* (London: Methuen, 1985); Bertolt Brecht, *The Messingkauf Dialogues*, trans. John Willett (London: Methuen, 1985).

16. Stephen Greenblatt, *Renaissance Self-Fashioning: From More to Shakespeare* (Chicago: Univ. of Chicago Press, 1980), p. 234.

17. Natalie Zemon Davis, 'Women on Top: Symbolic Sexual Inversion and Political Disorder in Early Modern Europe', *The Reversible World: Symbolic Inversion in Art and Society*, ed. Barbara A. Babcock (Ithaca: Cornell UP, 1978), pp. 147–90.

18. Linda Woodbridge, *Women and the English Renaissance: Literature and the Nature of Womankind, 1540–1620* (Urbana: Univ. of Illinois Press, 1984).

19. Phyllis Rackin, 'Androgyny, Mimesis, and the Marriage of the Boy Heroine on the English Renaissance Stage', *PMLA* 102 (1987): 29–41.

20. Stanley Cavell, *Disowning Knowledge in Six Plays of Shakespeare* (Cambridge: Cambridge UP, 1987), pp. 129ff.

21. Arguments for a chaste or virginal Desdemona are found in Nelson and Haines as well as in Pierre Janton, 'Othello's Weak Function', *Cahiers Elisabéthains* 34 (1988): 79–82. The idea of a sexually aggressive Desdemona is to be found in Greenblatt, pp. 237ff and in Stephen Booth, 'The Best Othello I Ever Saw', *Shakespeare Quarterly* 40 (1989): 332–6.

22. On the 'triangular' character of erotic desire see René Girard, *Deceit, Desire, and the Novel: Self and Other in Literary Structure*, trans. Yvonne Freccero (Baltimore: Johns Hopkins UP, 1965).

23. Niklas Luhmann, *Love as Passion: The Codification of Intimacy*, trans. Jeremy Gaines and Doris L. Jones (Cambridge: Harvard UP, 1986).

24. Paul Dumouchel and Jean-Pierre Dupuy, *L'Enfer des choses: René Girard et la logique de l'economie* (Paris: Seuil, 1979); see also Tobin Siebers, *The Mirror of Medusa* (Berkeley: Univ. of California Press, 1983).

25. Jean-Christophe Agnew, *Worlds Apart: The Market and Theater in Anglo-American Thought, 1550–1750* (Cambridge: Cambridge UP, 1986), pp. 6–7 and passim.

26. In addition to Cavell and Greenblatt see, for example, Kenneth Burke, 'Othello: An Essay to Illustrate a Method', *Hudson Review* 4 (1951): 165–203; Carol Thomas Neely, 'Women and Men in Othello: "What should such a fool / Do with so good a Woman?"' *The Woman's Part: Feminist Criticism of Shakespeare*, ed. Carolyn Ruth Swift Lenz, Gayle Greene and Carol Thomas Neely (Urbana: Univ. of Illinois Press, 1980), pp. 211–39; Patricia Parker, 'Shakespeare and Rhetoric: "Dilation" and "Delation" in Othello', *Shakespeare and the Question of Theory*, ed. Patricia Parker and Geoffrey Hartman (London: Methuen, 1985),

pp. 54–74; Edward A. Snow, 'Sexual Anxiety and the Male Order of Things in *Othello*', *English Literary Renaissance* 10 (1980): 384–412; Peter Stallybrass, 'Patriarchal Territories: The Body Enclosed', *Rewriting the Renaissance: The Discourses of Sexual Difference in Early Modern Europe*, ed. Margaret W. Ferguson, Maureen Guilligan and Nancy J. Vickers (Chicago: Univ. of Chicago Press, 1986), pp. 123–42.

27. Antonin Artaud, *The Theater and Its Double*, trans. Mary Caroline Richards (New York: Grove, 1958), pp. 42 and passim.

28. Rosalie Colie, *Shakespeare's Living Art* (Princeton: Princeton UP, 1974), p. 167. For other recuperative readings within quite different normative horizons see, for example, Newman; C.L. Parker and Richard P. Wheeler, *The Whole Journey: Shakespeare's Power of Development* (Berkeley: Univ. of California Press, 1986), pp. 272–81; Robert Heilman, *Magic in the Web: Action and Language in Othello* (Lexington: Univ. of Kentucky Press, 1956); Norman Holland, *The Shakespearean Imagination: A Critical Introduction* (Bloomington: Univ. of Indiana Press, 1964), pp. 197–216; and Arthur C. Kirsch, *Shakespeare and the Experience of Love* (Cambridge: Cambridge UP, 1981), pp. 10–39.

29. Horace Howard Furness, *Letters*, ed. Horace Howard Furness Jayne, 2 vols (Boston; Houghton, 1922). Furness found the play horrible, and wishes Shakespeare had never written it (2: pp. 149, 156). See also Cavell, pp. 98ff.

8

Proof and Consequences: Inwardness and Its Exposure in the English Renaissance

Katharine Eisaman Maus

I have that within which passes show,
These but the trappings and the suits of woe.

(Hamlet, I.ii.85–6)

Hamlet's distinction between external appearances and the inner, invisible truth of his grief could hardly have surprised a Jacobean audience. He applies to his own condition a truism endlessly rehearsed in Renaissance sermons, advice literature, coney-catching pamphlets, doctrinal debates, anti-theatrical writings, published reports of foreign and domestic turmoil, treatises on the passions and on the soul. Nor is he original in insisting that others cannot have immediate access to his thoughts and passions. 'Everyone may discover his fellow's natural inclinations', claims Thomas Wright in *The Passions of the Mind*, 'not by philosophical demonstration, but only by natural conjectures and probabilities':

> For that we cannot enter into a man's heart, and view the passions or inclinations which there reside and lie hidden; therefore, as philosophers by effects find out causes, by proprieties essences, by rivers fountains, by boughs and flowers the core and roots; even so we must trace out passions and inclinations by some effects and external operations.[1]

In *Basilikon Doron*, James I recommends a careful orchestration of the virtuous king's visible gestures and action on the grounds that 'they interpret the inward disposition of the mind, to the eyes of them that cannot see farther within him, and therefore must only judge of him by the outward appearance'.[2]

Although English Renaissance conceptions of subjectivity have attracted a good deal of productive attention recently, some of the most stimulating discussions are profoundly uncomfortable with Hamlet's contrast between an 'inner' self of superior authenticity and a public self, 'trappings and suits' of derivative or secondary status. A few critics claim that the psychological category of the inward or private hardly existed at all in Renaissance England. Francis Barker, for instance, argues that Hamlet's sense of inwardness is 'anachronistic', a premature manifestation of what he calls 'bourgeois subjectivity'. Only in the later seventeenth century, according to Barker, does bourgeois subjectivity come into its own, 'redolent with the metaphysics of interiority'.[3] Catherine Belsey likewise complains about those who approach Renaissance plays in search of the 'imaginary interiority' of the characters, an interiority that in her view is the imposition of the modern reader rather than a feature of the Renaissance text.[4] Another group of critics, including Jonathan Goldberg, Patricia Fumerton, Ann Rosalind Jones and Peter Stallybrass, acknowledges that the rhetoric of inwardness and privacy is highly developed in the English Renaissance but maintains that these terms inevitably refer to outward, public, and political factors. Goldberg argues that 'the individual derived a sense of self largely from external matrices'; Jones and Stallybrass that 'the supposedly "private" sphere ... can be imagined only through its similarities and dissimilarities to the public world'; Fumerton that Renaissance writers and artists 'can only achieve the inner *through* the outer, the private *through* the public, the sincere self through self-display'.[5]

The motives for this privileging of public over private are twofold. All these critics, despite differences in the details of their approaches, work from philosophical positions that reject as illusory the possibility of a subjectivity prior to or exempt from social determination. That is, they are making a claim not only about English Renaissance subjectivity but about subjectivity *tout court*. At the same time, they want to resist what they see as a specious generalization of modern bourgeois assumptions about 'the self' to a historically distant culture. Perhaps the historicist argument makes the philosophical argument seem more plausible; for if our intuitions about subjectivity are demonstrably absent in other cultures or periods, then those intuitions are unlikely to represent transcendental truths or transhistorical 'brute facts' about human nature. But the philosophical argument does not need to be made in historicist terms – and in fact, in some of its most influential formulations it is not so made – nor does the historicist project require this particular philosophical agenda.[6]

The difference is worth keeping in mind, because philosophical claims about the necessarily social constitution of *any* subjectivity, Renaissance or modern, sometimes seem to get confused with historicist claims about a specifically early modern form of subjectivity. Some critics apparently minimize or underestimate the significance of conceptions of psychological interiority for the English Renaissance because they imagine that admitting such significance would necessitate embracing a naive essentialism about 'human nature'. This is not the case. Surely nineteenth- and twentieth-century convictions about subjectivity are indeed culturally specific phenomena, and we risk misconstruing the Renaissance *mentality* if our criticism fails to take into account the immense cultural changes of the last four centuries. But adjusting our analytical categories is a more complicated endeavour than it might seem, since the modern 'idea of the subject' is not *an* idea.[7] It is, rather, a loose and varied collection of assumptions, intuitions, and practices that do not all logically entail one another and need not appear together at the same cultural moment. A well-developed rhetoric of interiority, for instance, may exist in a society that never imagines that such interiority might constitute a source of political rights. The intuition that sexual and family relations are 'private' may, but need not, coincide with strong feelings about the 'unity of the subject', or with convictions about the freedom, self-determination, or uniqueness of individuals.

Moreover, the fact that notions of subjectivity are socially constituted neither limits the extent of, nor determines the nature of, the power such notions can possess once they are culturally available. The pressures on thought and behaviour exerted by commonly held conceptions of sub-jectivity are interesting in their own right, regardless of whether it is possible to show that at some level the assumptions upon which they are based are inadequate or misleading. In other words, the effects of a particular set of beliefs are not simply reducible to its causes.

This essay examines some of the important epistemological problems that arise from English Renaissance assumptions about psychological interiority, not in order to reject but rather to refine and advance a historically self-conscious discussion of subjectivity in the early modern period. Instead of dismantling the Renaissance distinction between public and private – asking 'Is the distinction consistent or plausible?' – I shall attempt to analyse some of the ways the distinction *matters* – asking 'How does the existence of such categories help shape thought and behaviour?' I shall concentrate not, however, upon those places and genres in which the idea of privacy would seem, as it were, to find a natural habitat – the sonnet, the miniature painting, the bedroom, the privy chamber – but rather upon two emphatically public institutions, the courtroom and the theatre,[8] which were haunted by an anxiety about their limitations. For what makes Hamlet's claim startling is not its content but its context: What does it mean when one of the components of a dramatic spectacle denies the validity of 'show'? I shall argue that some of the affinities between English legal and theatrical rituals arise from a conviction that because Hamlet is right – because there *is* that within which passes show – the theatre, like the courtroom, must often deal in realities profoundly resistant to what would seem to be the exigencies of the form. My examination of actual trial practice in Tudor and Stuart England, and the philosophical assumptions upon which it is based, will provide a background for a discussion of the quasi-judicial discovery of inwardness in Shakespeare's *Othello*.

At his trial on a trumped-up treason charge in 1603, Sir Walter Ralegh complained that the prosecutors had 'not proved any one thing against me by direct Proofs, but all by circumstances'. Justice Warburton responded:

> I marvel, Sir Walter, that you being of such experience and wit, should stand on this point; for so many horse-stealers may escape, if they may not be condemned without witnesses. If one should rush into the king's Privy-Chamber, whilst he is alone, and kill the king ... and this man be met coming with his sword drawn all bloody; shall he not be condemned to death?[9]

Warburton's explication of English legal custom is correct. On the Continent, an elaborate set of rules strictly prescribed the kinds and amount of evidence necessary for conviction. Two eyewitnesses, or a confession – which could be obtained under torture – were ordinarily required for conviction. In England, by contrast, evidentiary rules remained loose, almost chaotic. Under most circumstances torture was impermissible, but, as John Langbein has pointed out, this apparent humanity was made possible by the fact that circumstantial evidence was all that was required for conviction. English courts made no rules about the admissibility of evidence, no qualitative distinction among kinds of proof, until well into the seventeenth century.[10] The power to convince the jury was all that mattered.

Less than a year after Ralegh's trial, the King's Men performed *Othello* for the first time. A debate about evidence occurs virtually in the centre of the play. To Othello's demands for 'ocular proof' of Desdemona's infidelity, Iago maintains that Othello must content himself with 'imputation and strong circumstances' – that is, the kind of inferential proof upon which English courts often relied. Othello's eventual acceptance of this argument, of course, leads directly to his downfall. Why should Shakespeare figure the pivotal moment of the tragedy in these terms? What is the relevance of evidentiary concerns to the marital difficulties of a Moor and a Venetian? Why should a play about a disastrous sexual jealousy begin, as Robert Heilman noted long ago, 'where some plays end, with a formal legal hearing that clears things up'; why should it 'advance by a series of scenes analogous to trials or court actions'?[11]

The answer lies in the similarity between some of the most fundamental issues of tragic subjectivity, as this play conceives them, and those raised by the procedures for criminal prosecution in Elizabethan and Jacobean England, procedures in many respects unique in Renaissance Europe.

Recently, literary critics who have written on English Renaissance crime and punishment have often followed Michel Foucault's lead, concentrating upon the scene of public execution.[12] But with the notable exception of some executions for treason and heresy, English executions tended to be relatively unspectacular affairs. Hanging by the neck until dead was the uniform method of capital punishment for most felonies under common law; the difference from the more ferocious and more delicately calibrated forms of execution on the Continent attracted considerable comment from contemporaries.[13] On the other hand, while the Continental trial was conducted in secret and much of the testimony was presented in writing, in England the trial was a public and oral event, sometimes drawing large crowds, and detailed accounts of important or sensational trials were printed shortly after they had occurred. Moreover, the English jury system, unique in Europe, made local laypeople not only onlookers but participants in the revelatory process. While France, Italy, and Germany put decisions about guilt or innocence into the hands of judges, in England the task of the bench was supposed to be restricted to 'finding law', that is to determining the applicable statutes and precedents. It was up to the English jury to 'find fact', that is, to determine what had really occurred and to deliver a verdict.[14] If an English defendant was convicted by process of common law, his or her punishment was not, as it was on the Continent, what Foucault calls 'the public support of a procedure that had hitherto remained in the shade'.[15] Public punishment in England was the final episode in a more protracted public spectacle. The effect of the English system, then, was to displace the focus of public attention from the processes of punishment to the processes of gathering and interpreting evidence. Many criminal trials – probably the vast majority – were perfunctory or uninteresting, just as they are today. But given the right situation, the English public trial could and did become an arena in which urgent questions of interpretation – questions with implications for a wide variety of social and intellectual practices – had to be addressed in practical terms before a large and curious audience.

What was the jury's 'finding of fact' supposed to involve? Cases of witchcraft and treason are particularly instructive, both because prosecutions for these two offences rose sharply in the English Renaissance, and because they are crimes with which *Othello* is explicitly concerned.[16] In both kinds of cases the problem of assessing guilt was bound up with problems of discovering an inward truth. Elizabethan and Jacobean statutes leave it unclear whether witchcraft is essentially a mental, inward crime – consisting in the secret allegiance to evil powers – or whether it is prosecuted because, like murder or theft, it ruins the lives and properties of others.[17] Contemporary commentators call this the problem of 'pact or act'; generally they argue that the pact constitutes the crime and that the

social harms that result constitute the evidence for the crime. English juries
were notoriously reluctant to convict in the absence of material damages,
but strictly speaking the blasted livestock, the wasted children, the
possessed neighbours, the milk that refused to become butter were merely
the effects or symptoms of witchcraft and not its essence. Reginald Scot
points out some of the problems of prosecuting a crime defined in this way
in his sceptical treatise *The Discovery of Witchcraft*. Scrutiny of motives,
Scot claims, is simply inappropriate for criminal prosecution:

> By which reason everyone should be executed, that wisheth evil to his
> neighbor. . . . But if the will should be punished by man, according to the
> offense against God, we should be driven by thousands at once to the
> slaughterhouse or butchery.[18]

The problem is easy for Scot, however, only because he does not believe
in witchcraft. Those who do, and who insist that the biblical injunction
against witches must be enforced, find themselves in an awkward dilemma.
On one hand they realize that witchcraft can only be discovered by the
effects it wreaks in the world – effects that, admittedly, can stem from a
variety of causes. 'The true marks of a witch, or mental characters, are not
easy to be discerned', writes John Gaule, insisting that because of the
unusually high possibility of error in such cases, the evidence for
conviction ought to be absolutely compelling. At the same time, the crime
is by nature secret and the forces it employs invisible. The witch does not
need to be present at the scene of the crime (so alibis cannot avail her) nor,
since she does not employ ordinary weapons, are investigators likely to
find unmistakable physical signs of her involvement. So Gaule later
concedes:

> Neither is it requisite that so palpable evidence for conviction should here
> come in, as in more sensible matters. It is enough if there be but so much
> circumstantial proof or evidence, as the substance, matter, and nature of
> such an abstruse mystery of iniquity will well admit.[19]

The standards of proof, in other words, should be both more stringent and
more lenient than they are in other cases. 'Circumstantial proof' seemed by
its nature dubious, likely to amount to no more than a collection of
fortuities. But in witchcraft cases it was normally all that was available.

It is easy to see how this problem arises. Even if juries tended to regard
seriously only those cases of alleged witchcraft in which harm had befallen
persons or property, they still needed to convince themselves that the
defendant had indeed produced the catastrophe in question by some occult
means. Their task, therefore, was essentially an inductive one. They had to

trace the observable evidence back to its supposed origin in the witch's inscrutable inward perversity.

The crime of treason presents related conceptual and practical problems. According to medieval statute, treason is the crime of 'compassing or imagining the death of the king', and this language persists through all the many Tudor and Stuart extensions and reformulations of the law. The legal commentator Fernando Pulton explains:

> [The law of treason] doth not only restrain all persons from laying violent hands upon the person of the King, but also by prevention it doth inhibit them so much as to compass, or imagine, or to devise and think in their hearts to cut off by violent or untimely death, the life of the King.

Treason, then, is a crime that occurs in the imagination, before and even in the absence of any manifestly treasonous activity. But how is the jury to know what a man has devised or thought in his heart? Pulton continues:

> Seeing compassing and imagination is a secret thing hidden in the breast of man, and cannot be known but by an open fact or deed, it is requisite to have some thing or means to notify the same to others before it can be discovered and punished.[20]

For treason as for witchcraft, then, the 'overt act' is the symptom of the crime not the crime itself, and trials throughout the sixteenth and early seventeenth century feature arguments over what counts as proof, as what Pulton would call 'notification', that treasonous imaginings have occurred. At his trial Henry Neville, one of Essex's friends, protested that he had not taken part in Essex's insurrection itself but merely participated in one of the conferences planning the rebellion: this, he maintained, 'was no more treason than the child in the mother's belly is a child'. In his view, treason still in the planning stages, because hidden and undeveloped, was therefore not yet a crime at all. But the judges replied that 'the compassing of the King's destruction ... implied in that consultation, was treason, in the very thought and cogitation'.[21] For them treason consisted in 'thought and cogitation', and the consultation was an 'overt act', the public manifestation that makes such thoughts liable to prosecution. Much more difficult was the earlier case of Thomas More, who refused to take the Oath of Supremacy and declined as well to specify his reasons. His silence seemed to present to observers a smooth and impenetrable surface; indeed, More reminded the court, silence was ordinarily construed under common law to signify consent.[22] Where was the 'overt act' that manifested his inward disaffection to the world? In order to obtain a conviction, the prosecutors had finally to resort to a dubious report of a conversation in which More was supposed to have denied Henry's authority in ecclesiastical matters. Shortly thereafter, a new statute classed refusal and silence themselves as 'overt acts' – as the circumstantial proof of what Pulton calls the 'secret thing hidden in the breast of man'.

Proceedings against witches and traitors threw into high relief the question of what relation holds between the overt and the covert, the visible effect and the invisible cause. Of course, the prosecution of other crimes could also entail questions of intention; as when a jury had to decide whether a homicide counted as accidental manslaughter or wilful murder. But treason and witchcraft, conceived as crimes that occur in the mind alone prior to any outward manifestation, pose in an especially acute form a kind of sceptical dilemma that was hardly new to the English Renaissance but that nonetheless acquired a special practical urgency in the upheavals associated with the Reformation and Counter-Reformation. Sixteenth- and seventeenth-century Catholics and Protestants, Anglicans and sectarians, as they endlessly debate the role of ceremony, ritual, and other 'outward respects' in the act of worship, argue not whether the distinction exists between what Augustine calls *homo interior* and *homo exterior* but what ought to be the significance of that distinction.[23] The record of religious persecution in England and on the Continent is full of heretics who preferred death in torment to conforming outwardly to a doctrine at variance with their inner convictions. But the difference between 'inward disposition' and the visible but less real 'outward appearance' could create opportunities, too, for religious minorities. Raphael Holinshed reports that when one Friar Forrest was apprehended in 1537 and accused of secretly rejecting Henry VIII's authority over the English church, he was asked why he had taken the Oath of Supremacy. 'He answered that he took his oath with his outward man, but his inward man never consenteth thereto'.[24] On the other end of the religious spectrum the Family of Love, a radical Protestant sect, taught that, provided the heart was right, the true believer might engage in any religious practice prescribed by the authorities without compromising his or her standing with God. And there were secular uses for, and dangers from, the difference between invisible private thoughts and visible public actions. Even Martin Cognet, the author of the *Politic Discourses Upon Truth and Lying*, who makes the lie the basis of all sin, concedes that 'if a man would ... discover to every man the secret of his mind, he should be counted but a dizzard'.[25] The notion that all social life is contingent upon realities not fully perceived or reliably revealed contributes powerfully to what Lacey Baldwin Smith has characterized as 'the paranoid mode' of English Renaissance political life: the pervasive suspicion of other people's motives and the conviction that conspiracy was everywhere.[26]

Coping with the inwardness of other people, therefore, requires certain interpretative tools. Social life demands the constant practice of induction, or what the physician John Cotta calls 'artificial conjecture':[27] reasoning from the superficial to the deep, from the effect to the cause, from seeming to being. But the inductive process is always liable to error. At times we may, as Thomas Wright says, trace out the roots by the evidence of the boughs and flowers, but, as William Vaughan reminds us, some thoughts and passions are 'concealed in a man's heart, as like unto a tree, which in outward appearance seemeth to be most beautiful, and is full of fair blossoms, but inwardly is rotten, worm-eaten, and withered'.[28] Hamlet knows that the forms, moods, and shapes of grief could as well be a calculated pretence as the symptoms of a genuine inner state.

Even when there was no intention to mislead, the effect of truthfulness could be difficult to convey to a wary audience. At his execution in 1609 Robert Logan, one of the earl of Gowrie's co-conspirators, professed his repentance to the spectators around the scaffold, but evidently believed that they were unconvinced. So 'he for the greater assurance of that his constant and true deposition, promised (by the assistance of God) to give them an open and evident token':

> Which he accomplished thereafter; for before his last breath, when he had hung a pretty space; he lifted up his hands a good height, and clapped them together aloud three several times, to the great wonder and admiration of all the beholders.[29]

Of course, even this surprising demonstration has no logical force; it would still be possible to assume that Logan had kept something in reserve, that he was still a performer at the last gasp. Immediately before he was hanged, castrated, disembowelled, and quartered in 1581, the Jesuit Edmund Campion insisted upon his innocence of treason in a graceful and moving speech. 'The outward protestations of this man', fumed Anthony Munday, 'urged some there present to tears, not entering into conceit of his inward hypocrisy'.[30] The possibility of some unexposed residue, some secret motive, could never be wholly discounted even when the gesture of self-revelation seemed most generous and complete.

The problems of interpreting persons under these vexed circumstances are closely analogous to problems of interpretation in other areas. Sixteenth- and seventeenth-century sermons and devotional literature rely heavily on 'arguments by design', reasoning inferentially from God's works to His invisible essence, from everyday events to His mysterious providence. Biblical interpreters similarly conceive of the literal text as a husk or veil that simultaneously conceals and indicates the contours of the truth at the sacred core. The traditional task of exegesis, as Frank Kermode

writes, 'is to penetrate the surface and reveal a secret sense; to show what
is concealed in what is proclaimed'.[31] At the same time, the perils of using
merely external manifestations as interpretative guides are dramatically
pointed up by Christ's career on Earth, as well as by the content of much
of his teaching. Renaissance religious culture nurtures in a wide variety of
ways habits of mind that encourage conceiving of human inwardness as
simultaneously privileged and elusive, an absent presence 'interpreted' to
observers by ambiguous signs and tokens.[32] Faith itself, in other words,
can encourage a kind of mistrust.

The 'problem of other minds' as it engages English Renaissance
thinkers and writers thus often presents itself as a question not so much of
whether those minds exist as of how to know what they are thinking.[33] The
short treatise *Sceptic, or Speculation*, attributed to Walter Ralegh, argues
against the authority of sense perceptions on the grounds that each
individual, necessarily limited to the evidence of his own senses, cannot
know whether the perceptions of others correlate with his own, nor to what
extent anyone's perceptions give an accurate idea of 'outward objects'.
Different people manifestly vary in their tastes and interests, and the
perceptions of beasts are likely to differ from human perceptions even
more radically:

> If a man rub his eye, the figure of that which he beholdeth seemeth long,
> or narrow; is it not then likely, that those creatures which have a long and
> slanting pupil of the eye, as goats, foxes, cats etc., do convey the fashion
> of that which they behold under another form to the imagination, than
> those that have round pupils do.[34]

The progress of this argument is interesting. Ralegh destabilizes a
commonsense notion of direct access to things-in-themselves by insisting
that the internal working of other minds, what he calls their 'inward
discourse', is remote and inaccessible.

> I may tell what the outward object seemeth to me; but what it seemeth
> to other creatures, or whether it be indeed that which it seemeth to me,
> or any other of them, I know not.[35]

But this perspectivism seems to strengthen, not weaken, the impulse to
investigate those minds. Ralegh's treatise is remarkable not for its
solipsism but for its attempt to reconstruct the 'inward discourse' of the
beast and the alien; he tries to duplicate in himself the different conditions
of animal perception, rubbing his eye into the shape of a cat's eye in order
to see as a cat sees. At the same time, the sceptical principles that generate

this attempt doom his empathy to remain inevitably unsatisfying and incomplete.

So the interpretation of other people is fraught with problems. But set against all this epistemological ambiguity – indeed, provoked by that ambiguity – is the desire for a reliable means for achieving certainty. Moreover, the implicitly or explicitly theistic context in which the problem of human inwardness is posed as a problem in the first place provides at the same time a standard of what would constitute such certainty. Inwardness in the English Renaissance is almost always formulated in terms of a double spectatorship. When Thomas Wright declares that 'hearts ... be inscrutable, and only open unto God',[36] he is typical in defining inscrutability as a relative and not an absolute phenomenon. The difference between the inner and the outer man is a function of the difference between the limited, fallible human observer and the unlimited divine observer, 'unto whom all hearts be open, all desires known, and from whom no secrets are hid'.[37] The work of interpretation is thus imagined as a process by which limited human spectatorship might approach divine omniscience.

When such investigation was effectively pursued, in a successfully conducted criminal trial, what did the jury expect to discover? John Cotta writes in *The Trial of Witchcraft*:

> Many offenses ... there are, neither manifest to sense, nor evident to reason, against which only likelihood and presumptions do arise in judgment: whereby notwithstanding, through narrow search and strict examination, circumspect and curious view of every circumstance ... unto the depth and bottom by subtle disquisition fathomed, the learned, prudent, and discerning judge doth oft detect and bring to light many hidden, intestine, and secret mischiefs.[38]

In trials for witchcraft, the accused was stripped and her whole body shaved in an attempt to find a 'witch's mark', a hidden nipple in her 'secret parts' at which she was supposed to suckle her familiar. This abnormality at a liminal area where inwardness and outwardness met seemed to provide a satisfactory basis for inferring horrible motives and desires further within.

The jury's process of discovery in other cases, too, was usually represented as an unveiling of something that nonetheless remained invisible, beyond sight. This visible invisibility is called the 'prodigious', the 'unnatural', the 'unspeakable', the 'monstrous'. ('How much more than too too monstrous shall all Christian hearts judge the horror of this treason?' asks the earl of Northumberland, rhetorically, at the trial of one of the Gunpowder Conspirators.)[39] Thus, as we have already seen, Judge

Warburton rationalizes the looseness of English evidentiary law, when Ralegh challenges it, in terms of a story about monstrous inwardness, an unnatural crime in the Privy Chamber. The language of monstrosity is characteristically vague, equally applicable to murder, theft, treason, witchcraft, sodomy, or whatever, so that an accusation of one particular crime tends to slide easily into an accusation of generalized criminality. And the monstrous is a slippery category in other respects as well. It is something the speaker or beholder desperately wants to differentiate himself from, define himself against. But the discovery of monstrosity is put into the hands of a jury of peers, chosen by their apparent resemblance to the defendant. They discover what seems absolutely alien, but they are equipped for this discovery by their similarity to what they investigate.[40]

In order to discover monstrosity the jury examines tokens, traces of a truth imagined as concealed inside the defendant. The purpose of the judicial inquiry – the evidence-gathering stage always, and the punishment stage sometimes – is to make that truth publicly available. Edward Coke, presiding at the trial of the Gunpowder Conspirators, describes to the prisoners the rationale behind the form of execution that awaits them: the traitor's 'bowels and inlay'd parts [are] taken out and burnt, who inwardly had conceived and harboured in his heart such horrible treason'.[41] The traitor comes to the scaffold quite literally to spill his guts, to have the heart plucked out of his mystery. The corporeal way inwardness is sometimes conceived in the English Renaissance has perhaps misled critics who think of the body as something displayed, something 'wholly present' to observation.[42] But only the surface of the body, strictly speaking, is really visible, and even that is normally 'cloaked', a favourite Renaissance word for hypocrisy. In sixteenth- and early seventeenth-century England its interior is still mysterious in a way perhaps hard to recapture in an age of medical sophistication, and in a way quite precisely analogous to the mysteriousness of human motives and desires.

England's idiosyncratic lack of articulated evidentiary standards and forms, in what was in many respects a highly formal judicial system, seems to reflect the notion that the jury's process of decision-making, however difficult it sometimes became, essentially involved interpretative skills so fundamental to everyday social existence that codified rules and specialized legal expertise were hardly requisite. Nonetheless, the social judgements the jurors were imagined as practising constantly in their own lives, and which equipped them for their role in the trial, were notoriously subject to error. The connection between outward, public symptom and inward, private cause was universally acknowledged to be tenuous and falsifiable. Under such circumstances, although a flexible attitude toward evidence may in fact have more often produced just verdicts than a strict and formal procedure, it could not provide the same basis for theoretical confidence that a more systematic approach could: it did not allow prosecutors, judges, or juries to content themselves in the knowledge that the formalities, at least, were being observed.

How might the jury's performance be made more reliable in the life-and-death matter of common-law felony prosecutions? The prisoner in the dock, asked how he or she would plead, had to answer, 'I put myself upon God and my country'. The formula both announces and obscures the difference between divine and human vision, the difference so crucial to Renaissance conceptions of inwardness. Are God and the 'country' invoked separately because they are not imagined as working together? Or were they rather supposed to collaborate? Edmund Campion, on trial for treason in 1581, told the jurors that his trial ought to be a 'mirror' of 'the dreadful Day of Judgment'.[43] More than two decades later, Sir John Croke similarly describes the trial of Henry Garnet in the language of Revelations:

> This person and prisoner here at the bar, this place, and this present occasion and action, do prove that true, which the author of all truth hath told us; that ... there is nothing hid that shall not be made manifest, there is nothing secret that shall not be revealed and come in public.[44]

The jury trial is supposed to bring human vision in line with divine vision – like God, the jury is supposed to see into the heart of the accused and discern the truth there. But how is it to perform this feat? Justices and defendants alike frequently express the hope that God would 'instruct' the jurors so that they would reach the correct verdict. But the jury trial is itself a replacement for the medieval trial by ordeal, which had been discredited by God's apparent reluctance to interfere with human juridical procedures. No one could be sanguine about an automatic correlation between God's verdict and the jury's.

In fact, the best the jury can do is to approach certainty in an asymptotic curve, evaluating the available tokens, traces, and effects of a guilt that cannot be perceived directly. Interestingly, under such circumstances the *sincerity* of the jury's decision – the fact that it reaches a 'verdict according to conscience' – becomes crucially significant. It is as if the invisible inwardness of the defendant were rendered accessible, or at least as accessible as it could ever become, by the jurors' resort to their own inwardness, as they look within their hearts and find a verdict there. The same word, *conviction*, stands both for the jurors' state of mind and for the imputation of a set of actions to the accused. The procedure tellingly resembles Ralegh's in *Sceptic, or Speculation*: he claims that the animal's mind is unknowable from our perspective, but at the same time tries to reproduce its 'inward discourse' by rubbing his own eye to make his perceptions more closely approximate the goat's or the fox's. The potential dangers in this procedure are recognized by those who, like John Cotta, exhort the jury scrupulously to maintain 'a true difference between that which our imagination doth represent to us, from within the brain, and that which we see without by the outward sense'.[45] The trial both exacerbates a sense of the inconclusive character of circumstantial evidence, and by its pressure toward a verdict, forces a certain representation of the hermeneutic difficulties involved in obtaining 'conviction'.

The English trial, then, is a ritual of discovery that attempts to perform the highly desirable but technically impossible feat of rendering publicly available a truth conceived of as initially – and perhaps inescapably – inward, secret, and invisible to mortal sight. In this sense the trial is a paradigm of all social relations that seem to rely upon a more or less highly developed capacity for accurate surmise. It exploits abilities that are supposed to be widely dispersed among the populace, as other skills of governance are certainly not imagined to be during this period. On the other hand, these 'easy', normal, everyday skills are almost impossible to codify, or to employ with any absolute certainty of success. Inference, empathetic projection, the careful weighing of probability, an openness to divine guidance: all are supposed to help the jury reach a verdict, but nothing can provide a sure means of escaping the limitations set upon even the most scrupulous human observation.

Othello, set in Venice and Cyprus, does not stage in any literal way the procedures of English justice. But the plot replicates the difficulties with which the English criminal courtroom often had to deal. Iago's temptation of Othello, as I have already mentioned, centres upon a discussion of what would constitute adequate proof of Iago's suggestion that Desdemona is unchaste. Although Othello initially insists upon 'ocular proof' – the strongest kind of evidence in both English and in Continental courts – he almost immediately modifies his demand:

> Make me to see't; or at the least so prove it
> That the probation bear no hinge nor loop
> To hang a doubt on.

> (III.iii.369–71)

With this revision he allows Iago to begin eroding his original evidentiary scruples, extending the category of acceptable proof to include mere 'imputation, and strong circumstances'.

Iago exploits Othello's irresolution in an interesting way. 'In Venice they do let God see the pranks / They dare not show their husbands', he tells Othello. 'It is impossible you should see this' (III.iii.206–7, 407). He pretends that the practical difficulty of surprising an illicit couple in bed represents a real epistemological limitation. Thus he encourages Othello to imagine adultery as an essentially invisible crime, in the same category with treason or witchcraft, fully displayed only before the omniscient eye of God. In this scheme, Othello's apparently unexceptionable demand for ocular proof comes to represent an impossible aspiration to the absolute knowledge of another person.

OTHELLO: By heaven, I'll know thy thought!
IAGO: You cannot, if my heart were in your hand.

(III.iii.166–7)

Iago tantalizes Othello by reminding him of the limitations of his 'mortal eyes' and then, by pretending to satisfy his longing, encourages him to imagine them as overcome. Othello lives out the epistemological dilemma of the English juryman to whom everything is supposed to be manifest but who is nonetheless forced to depend upon clues and surmises, who must treat as clearly visible that which is inevitably beyond sight. He supposes he is pursuing the kind of insight he attributes to his mother's friend, the Egyptian charmer who 'could almost read / The thoughts of people' (III.iv.57–8). But what he actually relies upon is circumstantial evidence – Iago's flag and sign of love; Desdemona's 'token', a handkerchief misleadingly mislaid. Either Othello must accept a degree of uncertainty in his relation to Desdemona, or he must repress his awareness of his own limitations as an observer.

Why does he choose the latter course? An alien in a place where the natives cultivate a sophisticated awareness of the difference between spurious surface and inward truth, Othello represents himself as incapable even of innocent hypocrisy. 'My parts, my title, and my perfect soul / Shall manifest me rightly', he declares when he hears of Brabantio's opposition to his marriage (I.ii.31–2); he assumes that the soul is as visible as parts and title to anyone who cares to look. Even late in the play, after he has killed Desdemona, Othello imagines the supremely precious object as a world made 'of one entire and perfect chrysolite' – that is, flawlessly perspicuous. Othello is thus, as Stephen Greenblatt notes, deeply attracted to the notion of confession, to a discourse of absolutely sincere revelation to religious or legal authorities.[46] But whereas confession is ordinarily an admission of guilt, for Othello it constitutes a theatrical display of innocence. He has, he claims, nothing to hide. In a play in which, as Patricia Parker demonstrates, problems of narrative unfolding are fore-grounded, Othello insists that he is always already unfolded. He does not so much tell his story to the Venetian court as he recounts having told it to Desdemona – and that telling is itself a repetition of a narrative previously offered to Brabantio, who now (ironically enough) accuses him of secret practices. This energetic guilelessness is perhaps compensatory, involving as it does a denial or avoidance of potential discrepancies between surface and interior: a counterstrategy to the Venetian racism that, in its more benign but still humiliating form, imagines Othello as a white man unaccountably lodged inside a black body.

Since Othello initially either lacks or repudiates Hamlet's sense of that within which passes show, it may seem curious that he proves so susceptible to Iago, the character who articulates most fully and cynically the difference between 'compliment extern' and 'the native act and figure of the heart'. Othello capitulates to Iago's slanders because they seem to allow him to preserve one version of his fantasy of perfect transparency: the fantasy that others are absolutely transparent to him. He grants that Desdemona's innocent looks may conceal a corrupt inward truth, but they do not successfully conceal anything from *him*: he imagines her deceptive surface penetrated by his omniscient gaze.

Between them Othello and Iago develop a way of comprehending Desdemona that corresponds closely with the judicial models provided in such abundance throughout the play: an inquiry that defines inwardness as guilty secrecy. Once Desdemona becomes a 'cause' to be investigated, what is discovered, almost inevitably, is monstrosity. For just as it did in actual legal proceedings, an intuition of invisible monstrosity provokes most of the legal proceedings in the play: the inquiry into what Brabantio claims is Othello's foul and secret sorcery; Othello's investigation into what he describes as the 'monstrous' behaviour of the revellers and which Cassio attributes to 'the invisible spirit of wine'; and finally, the discovery of the 'monstrous act' of murder when Desdemona cries out behind the closed curtains of the marriage bed. In this environment Iago functions as a sort of poet of monstrosity, lovingly dwelling on the gross issue, the monstrous birth, the unnatural thought, the palace into which foul things intrude.

When Othello comes under the spell of Iago's rhetoric of monstrosity he unknowingly makes serious compromises.

> It was my hint to speak – such was the process:
> And of the cannibals that each other eat,
> The Anthropophagi, and men whose heads
> Do grow beneath their shoulders.

> (I.iii.141–4)

Othello's courtship of Desdemona suggests that monstrosity has a positive valence – the allure of the marvellous or the exceptional. Desdemona loves him not because he is a wealthy curled darling of her nation but because he and his story are 'passing strange'. Othello's acceptance of conventional notions of criminal monstrosity becomes part of the complicated self-hatred that fuels both his jealousy and his final suicidal gesture. For his white colleagues define miscegenation in the same terms they use for adultery, as a monstrous union potentially productive of 'gross issue'.

> Foh! one may smell in such a will most rank,
> Foul disproportion, thoughts unnatural!

(III.iii.237–8)

Iago exploits the slipperiness of the language of monstrosity to especially perverse effect in this passage, entrapping Othello in a bizarre logic that makes Desdemona's 'unnatural' devotion to her black husband evidence for her 'monstrous' infidelities.

Desdemona, protesting that she has not offended Othello 'either in discourse of thought or actual deed' (IV.ii.185), invokes the standard of guilt applied to thought crimes like treason or witchcraft in order to deny the validity of the charge. Complexities in the way her virtue is defined, however, leave her vulnerable. For a discrepancy between surface and interior is one of the hallmarks of female modesty: Iago himself praises the woman who 'could think and ne'er disclose her mind' (II.i.157). The judicial imagination is likely to construe this reserve or hiddenness as duplicity. Moreover, although Desdemona protests that the difference between interior and exterior is not significant in her relationship to Othello, she is unable to bring her invisible conscience into court, and equally unable to force her judge to acknowledge the cogency of the unseen. For Othello imagines he can see everything, that there is no difference between the way one knows oneself and the way one knows other people. But chastity is as invisible as Iago claims infidelity to be – Desdemona's 'honour is an essence that's not seen' (III.iv.16). Stanley Cavell has therefore argued brilliantly that the mere fact that Desdemona possesses a 'discourse of thought' to which her husband is not privy terrifies Othello.[47] Cavell diagnoses the hero's sceptical problem as an inability to empathize, to grant to Desdemona the privileges of subjectivity he grants to himself. I would argue, on the contrary, that Othello suffers from a kind of empathetic excess, fatally accepting a European outlook when it is least in his interests, inappropriately applying to Desdemona the conditions by which he defines himself. This is indeed a form of scepticism, but it is the kind that we have seen Ralegh practising, in which the inaccessibility of the other produces not solipsism but a dubious attempt to reconstruct an alien point of view from the inside.

For loving not wisely but too well means making the beloved comprehensible as a version of oneself: fair warrior, captain's captain, general's general. Othello realizes himself in a narrative mode, in confession or storytelling – even in his last moments, as T.S. Eliot complains, he is imagining his career as it will be retold in the letters of the Venetian ambassadors.[48] Desdemona's susceptibility to Othello's story, on the other hand, is the consequence of her own relative inexperience. The apparent eventlessness of Desdemona's life, confined within her father's household, makes her as exotic to a man like Othello as he is to her. What kind of narrative can be constructed for the female subject, the greedy ear that devours up discourse? Othello's image suggests a sort of narrative black (or white) hole; as woman and as listener Desdemona is both perfect counterpart and absolute negation, a possibility both intensely desirable and intensely alarming to the phallic narrator. He does not know how to imagine Desdemona apart from her history, but, in the world of the play, for a beautiful young woman to have a history can mean only one thing. Insofar as she is a person she must have something to narrate, but if she has something to narrate she is no longer innocent.

'O curse of marriage, / That we can call these delicate creatures ours / And not their appetites!' (III.iii.272–4). Othello laments his wife's separateness, even while puzzling over the sense in which she is his own. Unaware of, or unwilling to acknowledge, the difference between one's knowledge of oneself and one's knowledge of other people, he is easily led by Iago to confuse the third-person narration he constructs for and imputes to Desdemona with a first-person narration imagined as self-evidently authentic. Thus as the play proceeds he becomes unable to distinguish between what is proper to him and what to Desdemona. 'Nature would not invest herself in such shadowing passion without some instruction', he tells himself (III.iv.38–40), confusing the possible origins of passion, projecting onto Desdemona his own fears and anxieties. In a striking and characteristic passage Othello tells Desdemona, immediately before he smothers her, not to plead innocence, because she cannot 'choke the strong conception / That I do groan withal' (V.ii.60–61). By this point in the play he has entirely reversed their roles in the tragic drama: the fertile young woman lying in what will become her deathbed becomes a strangler, the strangler a fertile woman crying out in labour. Discovering, he thinks, Desdemona's monstrosity, he wishes it upon, creates it for, himself: as Emilia says, jealous souls

> are not ever jealous for the cause,
> But jealous for they're jealous. It is a monster
> Begot upon itself, born on itself.

> (III.iv.157–9)

Like the jury that looks within itself to discover the polluted conscience of the criminal, a pollution otherwise inaccessible, Othello looks within himself and finds a corruption he attributes to Desdemona. He is wrong, of course, but wrong in a way that the interpretative process, so defined, seems to invite, because the activities of evidence gathering and of interpreting others are intimately tied up with a process of projection. 'By heaven, thou echo'st me / As if there were some monster in thy thought / Too hideous to be shown!' (III.iii.110–12). Othello's monster *is* an echo, a reverberation of the self ascribed to the other.

The insidiousness of the quasijudicial inquisitory procedures Othello employs lies in their seductive resemblance to the ordinary processes of romantic love. Desdemona's first thought, when Othello tells her the story of his life, is that 'she wished / That heaven had made her such a man' (I.iii.161–2). To marry Othello, in other words, is the next best thing to being him. 'I saw Othello's visage in his mind', Desdemona declares triumphantly to the Venetian senators (I.iii.214), imagining that the relation between lovers looks beyond the obvious in order to discover the hidden, erasing the boundary between public and private, outward and inward, the way one sees and the way one is seen. It does not occur to her to submit Othello's story to the sceptical criteria Iago invokes when he characterizes the traveller's tale of marvels as 'fantastical lies'. Collaborating in Othello's fantasy that his autobiographical narration is self-evidently true, Desdemona imaginatively leaps the gap between self-knowledge and the normally more limited and conditional knowledge of another.

Iago and Othello likewise erase such boundaries, or imagine themselves erasing them, by reading themselves into others. To Iago, the idea of crime is easy; his cynicism a villain's self-knowledge. Othello's own anxieties produce his suspicion of Desdemona. Evidence is in the eye of the beholder. This sounds like a familiar perspectivism, akin to what Ralegh offers in *Sceptic, or Speculation*. What the perceiver sees is determined by himself, not by what is 'out there'. But Ralegh's treatise allows a luxury of deferred judgement that Shakespeare's play, like the criminal trial, does not finally permit. This is not a tragedy that sidesteps moral absolutes. When Othello discerns that Iago has a horrible conceit shut up in his brain, he is quite correct, in a way he does not yet understand. The problem is not just that people create their own monsters but also that the monsters are out there and hard to find: the authorized means for detecting them are both deeply, inescapably unreliable and, at the same time, impossible to abandon.

The fundamental doubts cast on evidentiary procedure in *Othello* put its spectators in an uncomfortable position. We see more than Othello sees because we hear Iago's soliloquies, see Emilia give him the napkin, but not because we occupy a different order of perceptual reality. Ben Jonson's *Volpone* provides an instructive comparison as another play full of trial scenes in which the protagonists ruthlessly exploit the difference between insides and outsides, and in which possession or witchcraft becomes an important issue for the court. *Volpone*'s Venice is full of rich interiors carefully protected from the public view, and its characters are constructed on the same pattern as their houses, a shell around a secret, valuable core.

'Show 'hem a will. Open that chest', Volpone tells Mosca at the beginning of the last act. Indeed the universal preoccupation of most of the characters throughout the play is a 'will' hidden within a 'chest': the concealed intention of a supposed invalid, whose slight and ambiguous utterances and gestures require interpretation by a servant posing as skilled diviner. But throughout the play, the privacy the characters suffer and enjoy with respect to one another contrasts markedly with their total exposure on the public stage. In the trial scenes, we watch the mystified characters struggle to learn what we know already. The difference between spectators and characters is like the difference between divine omniscience and the circumstantial knowledge available to human beings – in the terms of the English Renaissance court, it is the difference between God and the 'country', the limited, fallible human jury. The plot of *Volpone* indeed suggests that a reliance upon the external and the visible is dangerous. But by exempting the author and his audience from epistemological limitations that it seems to represent as universal, Jonson vindicates the public medium of the theatre even as he seems to subvert it.[49] *Volpone* reassures its spectators of the validity of the theatrical mode by putting privacy on display.

In *Othello*, by contrast, the hidden realm remains incompletely revealed in the theatre. The inquiries in the play involve a series of events unseen by us: a courtship and a wedding that occur before the play begins; the mysterious movements of a Turkish fleet; an offstage quarrel between Cassio and Roderigo; Desdemona's non-existent affair with Cassio. Throughout the first two acts we are constantly asked to imagine Othello and Desdemona in the sexual act, an act that takes place offstage if, indeed, it ever takes place at all. Although favoured with Iago's confidence, the audience never gets a satisfactory account of his motives: while Volpone's final act of will is an act of revelation, an 'uncasing', Iago makes a defiant vow of silence. Like Othello, we must depend upon circumstantial evidence when we might have expected all to be revealed.

In *Othello* the capacity, or incapacity, to know another is as pertinent to the relation between spectator and character as it is between character and character. Even while the play encourages an intense identification with the suffering characters, the nature of their suffering suggests that such identification is highly problematic in its motives and often in its consequences. The same mechanisms that seem to break down the boundaries between self and other simultaneously insist that those boundaries can never really be eliminated. Perhaps this is why *Othello* has struck a number of critics as a play in which 'aesthetic distance' is unusually difficult to maintain. The impulse to interrupt, to tell Othello that he is wrong about Desdemona, seems so overpowering because there is a minimal epistemological boundary between characters and audience.

Recent critics like Barker and Belsey, who have claimed that the Renaissance lacked a conception of inwardness or privacy, have pointed to the dominance of the theatrical mode in this period to support their point, connecting it with a faith in the ultimate validity of what is displayed. But *Othello* and plays like it suggest that the theatre is as epistemologically problematic as social life itself. Truth exceeds public methods of representation, whether that truth be Cordelia's love, Desdemona's fidelity, or Hamlet's 'that within which passes show'. What can be seen on the stage is only part of the truth, an evidence of things not seen, or not entirely seen. The English Renaissance theatre, and the Shakespearean theatre perhaps most self-consciously, struggles like the English Renaissance courtroom with the limitations and potential falsifications involved in the process of making visible an invisible truth.

Notes

I have presented versions of this paper at the Modern Language Association, Renaissance Society of America, and Shakespeare Association of America annual conferences; and as a lecture at the University of Wisconsin, the University of Virginia, the University of Western Ontario, Cornell University, Ohio State University, Princeton University, the University of Florida, and the Massachusetts Institute of Technology. I am indebted to the audiences on these occasions for their many thoughtful comments. I would also like to thank Fred Everett Maus, James Turner, Richard Helgerson, and the editors of *Representations* for helpful specific suggestions.

1. Thomas Wright, *The Passions of the Mind in General* (1604), ed. Thomas O. Sloan (Urbana, Ill. 1971), pp. 104–5. For ease of reading, I have modernized spelling in the sixteenth- and seventeenth-century texts and titles quoted in this essay.

2. James I and VI, *The Basilikon Doron of King James VI*, ed. James Craigie (Edinburgh, 1944), p. 15.

3. Francis Barker, *The Tremulous Private Body* (New York, 1984), pp. 31, 58.

4. Catherine Belsey, *The Subject of Tragedy: Identity and Difference in Renaissance Drama* (New York, 1985), p. 48.

5. Jonathan Goldberg, *James I and the Politics of Literature* (Baltimore, 1983), p. 86; Ann Rosalind Jones and Peter Stallybrass, 'The Politics of *Astrophil and Stella*', *Studies in English Literature* 24 (1984): 54; Patricia Fumerton, '"Secret" Arts: Elizabethan Miniatures and Sonnets', *Representations* 15 (Summer 1986): 90.

6. Various forms of the philosophical argument are made in general terms by such writers as Freud, Marx, Foucault, Lacan, Derrida, and Wittgenstein; except in the case of Foucault, perhaps, their arguments do not stand or fall upon a particular reading of Renaissance culture. Anne Ferry makes the historicist argument apparently without sharing the philosophical agenda that motivates such critics as Barker or Belsey – although she, too, regards Renaissance conceptions of interiority as relatively undeveloped: 'Only some poets, and those almost exclusively in sonnets, seemed to have concerned themselves with what a modern writer would call the *inner life*'; *The 'Inward' Language: Sonnets of Wyatt, Sidney, Shakespeare, Donne* (Chicago, 1983), p. 14.

7. For helpful discussions of various conceptions of subjectivity, personal identity, individuality, and so on, and the complex ways such conceptions overlap and intersect, see the essays in John Perry, ed., *Personal Identity* (Berkeley, 1975), and Amelie Oksenberg Rorty, *The Identities of Persons* (Berkeley, 1976).

8. Since Aristotle, dramatic critics have drawn parallels between the public arts of the

courtroom and the public arts of the theatre. Moreover, the special fascination of English Renaissance drama with legal issues has long been recognized, and often attributed either to the legal background of many of the playwrights or to the fascination of their contemporaries with legal affairs. In *Poetic and Legal Fiction in the Aristotelian Tradition* (Princeton, N.J., 1986), Kathy Eden demonstrates, from a perspective quite different from my own, the significance of some of the connections between legal and poetic rhetoric in classical and Renaissance literature.

9. William Cobbett and Thomas Howell, eds, *Cobbett's Complete Collection of State Trials*, 33 vols. (London, 1809), 2:15.

10. For a discussion of the difference between the regular Continental use of judicial torture (that is, torture employed during the evidence-gathering stage) and its relatively infrequent use in England, see James Heath, *Torture and English Law* (Westport, Conn., 1982). In *Torture and the Law of Proof* (Chicago, 1977), John Langbein connects the Continental practice with strict evidentiary rules; if one could convict only those criminals who confessed, one had a very strong motive to compel that confession. He shows how both the relative infrequency of torture in England, and its abolition on the Continent in the eighteenth century, are directly linked not to the greater humaneness of prosecutors but to the acceptance of a looser evidentiary standard. Despite this looseness, both Langbein and John Bellamy, in *Criminal Law and Society in Late Medieval and Tudor England* (New York, 1984), argue that in the course of the sixteenth century English courts begin to pay more attention to the orderly gathering of evidence and its presentation in court. In *Probability and Certainty in Seventeenth-Century England* (Princeton, N.J., 1983), pp. 163–93, Barbara Shapiro describes the way the belated development of the English law of evidence in the seventeenth century reflects changes in the general intellectual climate during this period; the origins of the phenomena she describes can be traced in accounts of sixteenth-century criminal trials.

11. Robert Heilman, *The Magic in the Web: Action and Language in Othello* (Lexington, Ky., 1956), p. 129. Heilman relates *Othello*'s legal scenes and metaphors to ironies of justice (pp. 127–36, 152–68). Two sophisticated recent discussions of *Othello* have treated the issue of legality in terms of a rhetorical tradition inherited from Cicero and Quintilian. In '"Preposterous Conclusions": Eros, *Enargeia*, and the Composition of *Othello*', *Representations* 18 (Spring 1987): 129–57, Joel Altman discusses problems of probability in the play in terms of the figure of *hysteron proteron*. Patricia Parker, in 'Dilation and Delation in *Othello*', in Parker and Geoffrey Hartman, eds, *Shakespeare and the Question of Theory* (New York, 1985), pp. 54–74, analyses the significance of narrative unfolding in response to accusatory interrogation. Both these essays have informed my own.

12. See, e.g., Jonathan Goldberg, *James I and the Politics of Literature*, pp. 2–6; Francis Barker, *Tremulous Private Body*, pp.13–25, 62–5; Leonard Tennenhouse, *Power on Display: The Politics of Shakespeare's Genres* (New York, 1986), pp. 13–14, 115–46; Steven Mullaney, 'Lying Like Truth: Representation and Treason in Renaissance England', *ELH* 47 (1980): 32–3. Michel Foucault himself mentions the anomalies of the English system in *Discipline and Punish: The Birth of the Prison*, trans. Alan Sheridan (New York, 1977), p. 35.

13. Thomas Smith praised the relative humaneness of English common law in *De Republica Anglorum* (1583), ed. Mary Dewar (Cambridge, 1982), pp. 117–18, but the uniformity of punishment, and the illegality of torture under most circumstances, distressed commentators who thought it made insufficient distinction among crimes of varying degrees of heinousness. See, e.g., the prefatory letter in W.W., *A True and Just Record, of the Information, Examination, and Confession of All the Witches, Taken at St. Oses in the County of Essex* (London, 1582). For a useful overview of the important procedural differences in English and Continental criminal prosecution, see John Langbein, *Prosecuting Crime in the Renaissance: England, Germany, France* (Cambridge, 1974). J.S. Cockburn's *A History of English Assizes, 1558–1714* (Cambridge, 1972); and John Bellamy's *Criminal Law and Society in Late Medieval and Tudor England* (New York, 1984), give a more circumstantial account of the ordinary processes of English criminal justice in the sixteenth and seventeenth centuries. Thomas Andrew Green provides a helpful account of the development of the jury trial in *Verdict According to Conscience: Perspectives on the English Criminal Trial Jury, 1200–1800* (Chicago, 1985).

14. Green, *Verdict According to Conscience*, provides not only a helpful discussion of the significance of the distinction between finding fact and finding law in the English criminal trial, but an illuminating account of the way the distinction is reimagined in the course of the sixteenth and seventeenth centuries.

15. Foucault, *Discipline and Punish*, p. 43.

16. Neither of these crimes was new to the English Renaissance, but both were prosecuted with a zeal unknown in previous ages, and in both cases the definition of the crime was significantly expanded. For an account of the sudden upsurge in witchcraft prosecution in the sixteenth and early seventeenth century, see Keith Thomas, *Religion and the Decline of Magic* (New York, 1971), pp. 435–583; and Alan Macfarlane, *Witchcraft in Tudor and Stuart England* (New York, 1970), esp. pp. 200–207. For the prosecution of treason in the sixteenth century, see John Bellamy, *The Tudor Law of Treason: An Introduction* (Toronto, 1979).

17. Thomas, *Religion and the Decline of Magic*, pp. 435–68, plausibly ascribes the ambiguity of English conceptions of witchcraft to their double origin in indigenous popular belief, which emphasized *maleficium*, and an intellectual tradition that emphasized allegiance to the devil. (Contemporaries do not, however, make a clear distinction between the two positions.)

18. Reginald Scot, *The Discovery of Witchcraft* (1584), ed. Brinsley Nicholson (Totowa, N.J., 1973), p. ix.

19. John Gaule, *Select Cases of Conscience Touching Witches and Witchcraft* (London, 1646), pp. 91, 194.

20. Fernando Pulton, *De Pace Regis et Regnis, viz. a Treatise Declaring Which be the Great and General Offences of the Realm* (London, 1610), p. 108. In *The Third Part of the Institute of the Laws of England* ... (London, 1644), the important Jacobean jurist Edward Coke reviews the question of evidence in treason cases in similar terms, stressing that an insistence upon an 'overt act' protects the defendant.

21. Francis Bacon, *A Declaration of the Practices and Treasons Attempted and Committed by Robert, Late Earl of Essex, and His Complices* (London, 1601), K2r.

22. For an account of More's defence strategy, see G.R. Elton, *Policy and Police: The Enforcement of the Reformation in the Age of Thomas Cromwell* (Cambridge, 1972).

23. For a representative tract in which both Protestant and Catholic positions use Augustine's formulations to draw different conclusions, see, e.g., *A True Report of the Private Colloquy between M. Smith, alias Norrice, and M. Walker* (London, 1624). The topic of this dialogue is the relationship between the 'outward and extrinsical' and the 'inward or secret'. A different version of the distinction between the outward and the inward man descends from an Aristotelian distinction between appearances and internal or essential forms. Walter Ralegh is drawing upon the Aristotelian tradition, for instance, rather than the Augustinian one, when he opens his *History of the World* (London, 1614) by asserting that 'it is not the visible fashion and shape of plants and of reasonable creatures that makes the difference of working in the one and of condition in the other, but the form internal' (A1v). A similar distinction is important in the ontology and ethics of stoicism, which was enthusiastically revived in the Renaissance.

24. Raphael Holinshed et al., *Holinshed's Chronicles of England, Scotland, and Ireland*, 3 vols. (1587; reprint ed., London, 1808), 3:803.

25. Martin Cognet, [Matthieu Coignet], *Politic Discourses upon Truth and Lying*, trans. Sir Edward Hoby (London, 1586), p. 13.

26. In *Treason in Tudor England: Politics and Paranoia* (Princeton, N.J., 1986), Lacey Baldwin Smith argues that Tudor childrearing practices among the middle and upper classes rendered members of the ruling elite susceptible to paranoia: 'The central feature of the paranoid cognitive response to life is not simply suspicion. ... It is the conviction that things are never as they appear to be – a greater and generally more sinister reality exists behind the scenes – and the corollary that what is standing hidden in the wings, prompting, manipulating, but always avoiding exposure to the footlights, is the presence of evil' (36). The theatrical analogies that seem to come naturally to Smith in this description are, as I shall suggest later in the essay, hardly coincidental.

27. John Cotta, *The Trial of Witchcraft, Shewing the True and Right Method of Their Detection* (London, 1616).

28. William Vaughan, *The Golden-Grove, Moralized in Three Books* (London, 1600), L4r.

29. Cobbett and Howell, *State Trials*, 2:720.

30. Anthony Munday, *A Discovery of Edmund Campion and His Confederates ...* (London, 1582), G1v.

31. Frank Kermode, *The Genesis of Secrecy: On the Interpretation of Narrative* (Cambridge, 1979), p. x.

32. Perhaps the theistic assumptions and model for human inwardness in the Renaissance are one reason why, as Stephen Greenblatt has noted in 'Invisible Bullets: Renaissance Authority and Its Subversion', *Glyph* 8 (1981): 40–61, atheism seems to have proven an impossible conceptual position for the strenuous sixteenth-century self-fashioners of whom he writes.

33. Though he concentrates on French rather than English texts, and on scepticism about the phenomenal world rather than about other minds, Richard Popkin, in his *History of Scepticism from Erasmus to Descartes*, revised edn (New York, 1964), provides a helpful overview of the development of philosophical scepticism in the sixteenth century and its connection to doctrinal problems posed by the Reformation and Counter-Reformation.

34. Walter Ralegh, *Sceptic, or Speculation* (London, 1651), p. 4. Ralegh adapts his arguments from the first book of *Outlines of Pyrrhonism*, a late-classical work by Sextus Empiricus. In *Renaissance Self-Fashioning: From More to Shakespeare* (Chicago, 1980), pp. 224–5, Stephen Greenblatt describes the power relations that he sees as implicit in the act of empathy, an act not merely of generosity but of penetration and occupation. This analysis is helpful in understanding Ralegh's variety of scepticism, and also bears upon my discussion below of the jury's investigative practice.

35. Ralegh, *Sceptic, or Speculation*, p. 20.

36. Wright, *Passions of the Mind*, p. 27.

37. *The Prayer Book of Queen Elizabeth, 1559* (London, 1914), p. 92.

38. Cotta, *Trial of Witchcraft*, p. 18.

39. *Cobbett's State Trials*, 2:254.

40. In 'The Cultural Politics of Perversion: Augustine, Shakespeare, Freud, Foucault', *Genders* 8 (1990): pp. 1–16, Jonathan Dollimore describes how the orthodox Christian – originally Augustinian – insistence that evil is merely a privation of good, rather than a real principle in itself, complicates the relationship between normality and perversion, the natural and the unnatural, by including the latter within the former even while insisting upon their crucial disparities. The uncanny, parodic quality of evil so construed helps explain the complicated relationship of differentiation and identification in both the English jury trial and in *Othello*.

41. *Cobbett's State Trials*, 2:184. The rationale, like the punishment itself, is traditional; see John Bellamy, *The Law of Treason: England in the Later Middle Ages* (Cambridge, 1970), pp. 39, 47, 52.

42. Barker, *Tremulous Private Body*, p. 74; see also his comments on 'the spectacular visible body', pp. 23–6. In *Renaissance Fictions of Anatomy* (Amherst, Mass., 1985), Devon Hodges helpfully explores sixteenth- and early seventeenth-century conceptions of the dissected body.

43. *Cobbett's State Trials*, 1:1070.

44. Ibid., 2:217.

45. Cotta, *Trial of Witchcraft*, p. 83.

46. Greenblatt, *Renaissance Self-Fashioning*, pp. 220–54.

47. Stanley Cavell, *The Claim of Reason: Wittgenstein, Skepticism, Morality, and Tragedy* (Oxford, 1979), p. 491ff.

48. T.S. Eliot, 'Shakespeare and the Stoicism of Seneca', *Elizabethan Essays* (New York, 1964).

49. I mean here to be contrasting two plays, not two dramatists; the privileging of the audience is by no means the rule in Jonson's works. The controversial finale of *Epicene*, for instance, demonstrates to the audience that they too have succumbed to the wiles of one of the characters. For a more extended analysis of the position of the spectator in Renaissance drama in general and *Othello* in particular, see Katharine Eisaman Maus, 'Horns of Dilemma: Jealousy, Gender, and Spectatorship in English Renaissance Drama', *ELH* 54 (1987): 595–83.

9

Othello's African American Progeny

James R. Andreas

Derrida writes, 'There's no racism without a language'.[1] I take this to mean that racism – and all the violence historically associated with it – is generated by language. Racial difference is not genetically 'real', nor is it grounded in real experience but is a product of verbal conditioning.[2] Racism cannot long survive without the verbal and symbolic apparatus that generates and sustains it: the names, the jokes, the plays, the speeches, the casual exchanges, the novels. In short, racism is a cultural virus that is verbally transmitted and its antidote must therefore be verbally administered as well. *Othello* – along with the many African American texts it has inspired – provides a running record of Western civilization's attempt to confront what Paul Robeson called 'the problem of my own people'. *Othello*, he said, 'is a tragedy of racial conflict, a tragedy of honour, rather than jealousy'.[3]

As such, the play has traumatized African American literature, and indeed Western culture at large, for most of its existence. The racist's nightmare of biracial sexual relationships between white women and black males, which Gunnar Myrdal claimed suffered 'the full fury of anti-amalgamation sanctions',[4] is the paradigm for three great revisions – 'three rewritings' – of the myth: *Native Son* by Richard Wright, *Invisible Man* by Ralph Ellison, and *Dutchman*, by Amiri Baraka.[5] Briefly, Wright restages and reinterprets the problematic relationship of Othello and Desdemona; Ellison represents it comically; and Baraka reverses or inverts it. We might note in passing that many literary works have been written that deal with unwanted sexual attentions of white males sometimes violently imposed on African American females; among these works are many slave narratives, including *Incidents in the Life of a Slave Girl*, as well as a number of celebrated novels such as *Uncle Tom's Cabin, Puddn'head Wilson, Quicksand, Oxherding Tale, Beloved,* and *Absalom, Absalom!*[6] James Kinney claims that interracial sexual relations flourished in colonial and antebellum America and that the violent response to miscegenation

181

began only in the 1830s, 'when the economics of slavery led to [the] systematic justification [of slavery] based on innate irreconcilable "racial differences"'.[7] In any case, the vast number of nineteenth- and twentieth-century works that feature the fate of mulattoes in American culture provides graphic evidence that miscegenation has long been on the minds of African and European American authors alike. What we get in Shakespeare's play and the African American works under investigation here is, of course, the typical patriarchal perspective on the cultural trauma of miscegenation in the West. Another article representing women's perspectives on this trauma needs to be written.

Robeson's statement that *Othello* 'is a tragedy of racial conflict', would probably have seemed self-evident to Shakespeare and his contemporaries, both in terms of the social background and the performance and interpretation of the play.[8] A score of historical studies in the last thirty years has unearthed evidence proving that the response to Africans and Moors in the seventeenth century, before the advent of institutional slavery, was complicated and problematic.[9] Sylvan Barnet has shown in his masterful essay on the performance history of the play that 'the Elizabethans thought of Moors as black' (p. 274). Barnet and Errol Hill, in his *Shakespeare in Sable*, have demonstrated conclusively that Othello's part was played in blackface, corkface actually, well into the nineteenth century, because blacks were thought of as inappropriate for or incapable of playing the role.[10] A single quotation from Coleridge indicates what the problem was by the time of the romantics:

> Can we suppose [Shakespeare] so utterly ignorant as to make a barbarous *negro* plead royal birth? ... [N]egroes [were] then known but as slaves.... No doubt Desdemona saw Othello's visage in his [Othello's] mind; yet, as we are constituted, and most surely as an English audience was disposed in the beginning of the seventeenth century, it would be something monstrous to conceive this beautiful Venetian girl falling in love with a veritable negro. It would argue a disproportionateness, a want of balance in Desdemona, which Shakespeare does not appear to have in the least contemplated.
>
> (Quoted in Barnet, pp. 273–4)

Thus, by the nineteenth century, when the barbarities of 'the peculiar institution' of slavery had peaked in the Western world, audiences could no longer tolerate nor would directors depict the 'monstrous' sexual relationship of black males and white females on stage.[11] To get the picture, audiences no longer needed Iago lashing up racist sentiments in the credulous Roderigo and Brabantio with incendiary remarks such as 'Even now, ... an old black ram / Is tupping your white ewe'; '[Y]ou'll have your

daughter cover'd with a Barbary horse'; and 'Your daughter and the Moor
are now ... making the beast with two backs' (I.i.88–9, 110–11, 115–17).[12]
Such explosive preconceptions were ingrained in the psyches of playgoers
well before arriving at the theatre. Accordingly, Othello paled and such
lines were often cut in production; the Moor was played 'in tawny'
throughout the nineteenth and well into the twentieth century, as evidenced
by the films of Olivier and Jonathan Miller. In regard to the relatively
recent BBC version of the play, Jonathan Miller defended his choice of
Anthony Hopkins in blackface for the Moor because, he said, 'I do not see
the play as being about colour but as being about jealousy. ... When a black
actor does the part, it offsets the play, puts it out of balance. It makes it a
play about blackness, which it is not'.[13] Now that we are recovering the
black *Othello*, such sentiments seem a bit awkward, if not downright
ludicrous. Anyone who has seen Miller's *Othello* or a live production in
which the hero is played in blackface knows the murder scene may well
evoke laughter in the audience.

From the earliest moments in *Othello*, the language is imbued with
traditional racist sentiment and prejudice that erupt into predictable
violence by the play's end, when 'Chaos is come again' (III.iii.92).
Collective violence – read riot – is, in fact, the outcome of all the literary
vehicles of the myth under investigation here, even the comic *Invisible
Man*. The catalyst for and efficient cause of such violence in the play is
Iago, perhaps the most important of all Shakespeare's notorious stage
directors, with the possible exception of Hamlet. Both Iago and Hamlet are
tricksters, variations, as has often been noted, on the role of the traditional
fool. Iago's humour takes a *peculiar* turn, however. He is the racist
trickster; his is the scenario that eventually defines and corners Othello
exclusively in his colour, a scenario like the 'blueprints' for behaviour the
hero of *Invisible Man* must live with. Is Iago without motive, as he is
traditionally conceived to be? In terms of the racial themes in the play,
hardly! He tells us repeatedly that Othello has slept with his wife, Emilia,
and whether this is the case or not is irrelevant; as a racist, he believes what
he imagines and brilliantly formulates his preconceptions verbally to
himself and to others under his influence.

Iago fuels his nefarious plots to undermine the relationship between
Othello and Desdemona by playing the bigot's game; he preys upon the
vulnerability of all the players to sneaking suspicions about the behaviour
of the racial alien, in the long run convincing even Othello himself that he
is inferior. 'Rude ... in speech, and little blessed with the soft phrase of
peace', Othello declares himself while suing for Brabantio's daughter in
marriage, although he woos and wins Desdemona with his spellbinding
stories (I.iii.81–2). As an alien, Othello doubts his capacities for speech and
for peace. 'Haply, for I am black, / And have not those soft parts of

conversation / That chamberers have' (III.iii.264–5), he says. Brabantio, for one, is simply aghast that Desdemona has chosen 'to marry one'. Would his daughter 't'incur a general mock, / Run from her guardage to the sooty bosom / Of such a thing as thou – to fear, not to delight' (I.ii.69–71)? The disturbed father feels certain that Othello has influenced his daughter's foul choice with powerful drugs (I.ii.73–5). Centuries later, the police will assume Bigger Thomas has plied Mary Dalton with liquor before murdering her in *Native Son*, and Sybil is depicted as drunk when she is 'raped by Santa Claus' in *Invisible Man* (p. 511). Iago can even use blatant racist arguments on Othello, who does not seem to blink an eye:

> Ay, there's the point; as (to be bold with you)
> Not to affect many proposéd matches
> Of her own clime, complexion, and degree,
> Whereto we see in all things nature tends –
> Foh, one may smell in such, a will most rank,
> Foul disproportions, thoughts unnatural.
>
> (III.iii.228–33)

Does not Iago suggest throughout – even directly to Othello – that Desdemona is not to be trusted because she has already committed the unpardonable sin against her 'kind': the sexual choice of an alien? Even Othello accepts the argument, as is indicated by his admission that Desdemona's name and virtue have been blackened and fouled by her relationship with him: 'Her name, that was as fresh / As Dian's visage, is now begrim'd and black / As mine own face' (III.iii.386–7). This is a play about reputation, real and attributed, and the jealousy and passion that such 'reputation' can evoke. Racism is predicated on 'repute', that is, on 'evil' imputed to a cultural group so conditioned by the dominant culture that the 'evil' often materializes in real behaviour. Shakespeare, in fact, cleverly interweaves the themes of the destructive effects exerted by the emotions of sexual jealousy and racial bigotry in the play, both of which inflame the imagination with illusions about the 'other', alienate the parties involved artificially, and lead to violent ends based on often unfounded presuppositions or prejudices about the behaviour of the 'other'.

A number of motifs in the murder scene of the play will be echoed and revised in the African American scenarios to follow. When sexual consummation between the black male and white female is to occur in this 'master trope' of white racism, we get murder instead. The murder is always *witnessed* in the works investigated, often, significantly, by a white woman who is presumably forewarned of the consequences of her actions – Emilia in the play and Mrs Dalton in *Native Son*. Also, the murdered victims are portrayed as human beings of flesh and blood, not passive victims. During the scene just prior to the murder, when Desdemona asks

Emilia about fidelity and admits an attraction for Lodovico, we question
the credibility of the fragile purity that is usually attributed to Desdemona.[14] Like the white women who follow in the African American novel,
for example, Mary Dalton and the anonymous 'sister' in the brotherhood,
Desdemona is a woman with real desires and considerable courage. The
murderers in these works often remark that they feel like actors in a play
or figures in a dream. Othello carries a candle into the bedroom and
comments that he feels like a character in a dream. In *Dutchman*, Lula, as
we shall see, repeatedly calls the conversation she is having with Clay, her
future victim, a 'script'.

No matter how hard critics since Bradley have tried to saddle Othello
with the full burden of the guilt for his passionate crime and to view Iago
as 'motiveless', the play itself seems to incriminate Western society at
large for its predisposition to the periodic, ritual slaughter of marginal and
aboriginal groups and all whites – especially women – who consort with
them. Trevor Nunn's controversial production at the Young Vic in London
(fall 1989) unleashed the social and political possibilities of this play that
have lain dormant in the text for centuries, with the exception of the
powerful portrayals of Othello by Paul Robeson in the thirties and forties.
Nunn's production featured American Civil War decor and uniforms to
underscore the racial implications of the text, and Willard White, a black
operatic baritone debuted as a huge, barrel-chested Othello. Iago, played
brilliantly by Ian McKellan, entertained as he conspired with an audience
of white males – Roderigo, Cassio, and Brabantio – as willing partners in
his plot to murder lovers soiled in the blood feud between races. McKellan
as Iago assumed he had many willing collaborators in the audience,
because Iago projects and exacerbates the deepest Western fears of the
'other', of the alien free to prowl and pollute the streets of Venice. During
his many soliloquies – for Iago is the most perniciously private character
in all the canon – McKellan closed the shutters on the set, pulled up a chair,
leaned toward the audience and told them what they had been conditioned
to know and fear implicitly all their lives: a 'liver lips' has been given
professional preferment over him and has desired and taken his wife right
from under his very nose. What's more, this 'black ram', this 'Barbary
horse' is about to 'tup' the most eligible maid in Venice and produce the
'monstrous offspring' of miscegenation. Ian McKellan's Iago, like the
Native American mischief-maker *Iagoo*, was played as the sprite of malice,
in this case, of racial hatred. McKellan's purpose was to arrange and
realize our basest fears on stage: the ritual slaughter of a couple
transgressing racial and sexual codes. The invisible theme of racism and
the murder it provokes were rendered visible for all to see in this gruesome
production. The scenario of European colonial history with its periodic
racial assassination, rape, and riot was here dramatized; this was a history

that was beginning to peak during Shakespeare's time.

In *Exorcising Blackness: Historical and Literary Lynching and Burning Rituals*, Trudier Harris has given us a book on the subject of this gruesome scenario in its most virulent form, which developed after the American Civil War during Reconstruction. The 'primal crime' in a racist society, the coupling of black male and white female – either real or, most often, imagined and impugned – justifies and drives the ritual retaliation of the mutilation, castration and lynching of black male victims in the presence of white women and children, often on Sunday afternoons and accompanied by 'carnival'. Harris writes:

> I have defined ritual initially as a ceremony, one which by countless repetitions has made it traditional among a given group of people or within a given community. Such repetitions are homage to certain beliefs that are vital to the community. . . . To violate the inviolable, as any Black would who touched a white woman . . . is taboo. It upsets the white world view or conception of the universe. Therefore, in order to exorcise the evil and restore the topsy-turvy world to its rightful position, the violator must be symbolically punished.[15]

The horror of these events is graphically documented in the newspapers and monthlies of the times – *Harper's*, *The Atlantic Monthly* – and only then becomes the material fictionalized in the novels. Charles Herbert Stember calls 'intimacy between a Negro male and a white female' the 'master taboo' of white racism dating back for centuries.[16]

The 'primal scene' of the white racist, the 'black ram . . . tupping your white ewe', is recreated and revised by African American writers some 350 years after *Othello* in *Native Son*, *Invisible Man*, and *Dutchman*. Bigger Thomas is America's black 'native son', raised in the sordid conditions of ghetto life on Chicago's southside. Bigger, his name screaming the rhyme with 'nigger', is the all-but-inevitable product of the racist nightmare he will be made to play out in the novel. Perhaps drawing on the ultimate recognition and understanding of the racist process Othello experiences just before his suicide, Richard Wright takes Bigger through a long educational ordeal under the tutelage of Max, his lawyer. However, the primal scene and crime – the sexual relationship between black male and white female and its reputedly inevitable consequence, the brutal murder of the white female – is re-enacted with gruesome precision as the pivotal moment in the novel. Othello is momentarily accepted by Venetian society as an equal and, through the machinations of Iago, is reduced to acting the part of the alien 'Turk' or 'African' by the play's end. Bigger, however, is destined to act the 'young Turk' immediately, replicating the violent image of the 'African' he watches on the silver screen in films like *Trader Horn* every Saturday afternoon. As Wright explains in his introduction to the novel, 'How Bigger was Born', his hero 'is a product of a dislocated society; he is a dispossessed and disinherited man', and his violence is predictable and inevitable.[17] However, risking 'premature closure', Wright proceeds beyond the murder early in the novel to show that this violence, however misguided on Bigger's part, has spawned in his hero a new understanding of his life and destiny by the novel's end. After his conviction and reconciliation with Jan, the fiancé of the woman he has murdered, Bigger becomes what every Venetian wants to believe Othello is at the beginning of the play: aware, self-reflective, and bold.

> Having been thrown by an accidental murder into a position where he had sensed a possible order and meaning in his relations with the people about him; having accepted the moral guilt and responsibility for that murder because it had made him feel free for the first time in his life, [Bigger realizes] ... a new pride and a new humility would have to be born in him, a humility springing from a new identification with some part of the world in which he lived. (pp. 255–6)

Bigger is from the modern 'Cyprus' – the slums of south Chicago; the Daltons, of course, are 'Venetians' – from the suburbs. The ideological rivalry between the Turk and the Christian has been displaced by the confrontation between the Communists and capitalists in the novel. Moreover, Mary's father, Mr Dalton, as a wealthy slum landlord, is, like Brabantio, a true 'Senator', that is, Iago quips, 'a villain' (I.i.18–19). Mary Dalton, like Desdemona, is thrilled by what she imagines to be the primitive power of Bigger's race. To be sure, Mary is more aggressive in her pursuit of Bigger as an exotic than Desdemona is in her relationship with Othello, ostensibly because she, under the influence of Jan, is sympathetic with his political plight. '[T]his rich girl walked over everything, put herself in the way, and, what was strange beyond understanding, talked and acted so simply and directly she confounded him' (p. 56). Mary asks her boyfriend, 'Say, Jan, do you know many Negroes? I want to meet some.... They have so much emotion! What a people! If we could ever get them going.... And their songs – the spirituals! Aren't they marvelous?' (p. 76). The white heroine in each of our 'stories' becomes increasingly aggressive in pursuing her black lover, violently so, as we shall see, in *Dutchman*.

The sexuality of Desdemona has always been a moot question. As I suggested earlier, critics have debated just how aggressive and even promiscuous she is in her obvious interest in and pursuit of Othello.[18] There is no doubt that Mary Dalton, stimulated perhaps by all her drinking that evening, has sex on her mind just prior to the death scene in the novel, although Wright makes it clear that very little sexual contact occurs and that there certainly is no rape, no sexual consummation whatsoever, in spite of the lurid 'reports' in the Chicago newspapers. Mary sidles up to Bigger in the car drunk, garters showing, her scent arousing him, her breath, like Desdemona's in the death scene, on his face:

> She was resting on the small of her back and her dress was pulled up so far that he could see where her stockings ended on her thighs.... He helped her and his hands felt the softness of her body as she stepped to the ground. Her dark eyes looked at him feverishly from deep sockets. Her hair was in his face, filling him with its scent. (pp. 80–81)

Most significantly, in all versions of the primal scene of biracial contact and murder, witnesses to the murder are involved, either directly, as in the case of *Othello*, or implied, as in the case of *Native Son*. Emilia in the former and Mrs Dalton in the latter both intrude on the ritual murder, which in each of the works begins as a sexual encounter. In both cases white females who are blind to their own husband's evil witness the murder. My point here, and perhaps this is the point of the biracial myth I am trying to identify, is that sexual encounters between the races are not private moments as they would be in normal relationships. They represent a public shattering of the racist taboo and as such demand an audience whose predisposition toward the event alters its outcome in violent, ritualistic ways. Once that audience appears, the deed can run its gruesome course.

In both *Othello* and *Native Son*, the females are passive when they are murdered, in every sense sacrificial victims to what might be interpreted psychologically as the demands of the *mythos* – the script being enacted through their characters and witnessed by the onstage audience. It is significant that Iago is always played as an eavesdropper, whose access to private moments allows him to reinterpret events in a manner that will inevitably precipitate the racial violence at the play's climax. In the Nunn production, McKellan's Iago returns just before curtain to glare at the lovers finally united in bed – dead. Both Mary in *Native Son* and, as we shall see, Sybil in *Invisible Man*, are drugged in a sense and are thus not cognizant of their participation in this ritual event. Desdemona is nearly asleep when Othello strangles her. There are other similarities in the structures of *Othello* and *Native Son* that we might mention in passing. The novel has a Cassio figure in Jan and a Bianca in Bessie, and both works conclude with a judgement scene and the final appearance of the heroes, Othello and Bigger, who are given speeches underscoring the dignity and pathos of their respective characters.

Ralph Ellison sums up the problem under investigation here succinctly and comically in *Invisible Man*:

Why did they have to mix their women into everything? Between us and
everything we wanted to change in the world they placed a woman:
socially, politically, economically. Why, goddamit, why did they insist
upon confusing the class struggle with the ass struggle, debasing both us
and them – all human motives?[19]

The hero confronts a series of white women in *Invisible Man*, beginning
with the stripper who is brought in by the elders to teach little black boys
a lesson in attraction and repulsion; they are encouraged to desire sexually
what they cannot have – a white woman. The stripper is as frightened as
the boys, and when she performs, both parties are watched by the elders
who represent the omnipresent audience cueing and skewing the interpretation of these illicit, public sexual events. There are other brief
encounters between the hero and white women, one on the subway where
he is pressed by the crowd up against a blond in a scene that may have
sparked the imagination of Baraka, who stages his fatal biracial ritual on
the subway in *Dutchman*. White women represent one of the perpetual
challenges the hero faces throughout the novel along with his speeches, the
accumulation of the bric-a-brac of his 'heritage' in the briefcase he is
perpetually trying to discard, and his run-ins with various political parties.

Ellison is perfectly aware that his hero is acting in a performance
scripted with racist assumptions, and the result in the novel is usually
farcical. Before his affair with the appropriately anonymous white wife of
a 'brother', the hero wishes he were Paul Robeson:

> If only I were a foot taller and a hundred pounds heavier, I could simply
> stand before them with a sign across my chest, stating I KNOW ALL
> ABOUT THEM, and they'd be as awed as though I were the original
> boogey man – somehow reformed and domesticated. I'd no more have
> to speak than Paul Robeson had to act; they'd simply thrill at the sight
> of me. (p. 399)

'They', of course, are the audience intruding on the couple in each of the
instances examined here. When the hero first meets this woman, she
'glowed as though acting a symbolic role of life and feminine fertility'
(p. 399). The white woman here has become more solicitous than Mary
Dalton and conspicuously more aggressive than Desdemona. She is almost
a willing pawn in the white racist's game. She appears by 'the uncoiled fire
hose' (p. 400), and the phallic jokes abound in this chapter, just as they do
in *Othello*, where Cassio quips to Iago 'That he [Othello] may bless this
bay with his tall ship, / Make love's quick pants in Desdemona's arms'
(II.i.79–80) and Othello himself remarks, after he has killed his own wife
on the night he is to have consummated his marriage, 'Behold, I have a

weapon; / A better never did itself sustain / Upon a soldier's thigh' (V.ii.259–61).

The woman's conversation is full of erotic overtones of which she, as opposed to her predecessors, seems perfectly aware. She is attracted to the hero by the same attributes Desdemona discovers in Othello: both are drawn to the primitive 'vitality', exoticism, and strength of the African. Of the hero's ideology, she wishes to embrace '[a]ll of it, ... to embrace the whole of it' (p. 402). Like Desdemona, she thrills to hear the hero speak: '[S]omehow you convey the great throbbing vitality of the movement' (p. 402). His speech is so 'primitive, ... *forceful*, powerful.... [It] has so much naked power that it goes straight through me' (p. 403).

The hero sees the 'ivory' arms of the woman in her huge 'white bed' (p. 407), just as Othello had characterized Desdemona's skin as 'whiter ... than snow, / And smooth as monumental alabaster' (V.ii.4–5). But the hero, unlike Othello, watches himself and his sexual actions replicated infinitely in the bedroom's multiple mirrors, 'caught in a guilty stance, my face taut, tie dangling; and behind the bed another mirror which now like a surge of the sea tossed our images back and forth, back and forth, furiously multiplying the time and the place and the circumstance' (p. 406). Moreover, the hero thinks he might have seen the husband of the woman at the door momentarily. He also conjectures that he might just be dreaming. Here we have the omnipresent witness to the act again as well as the suggestion that the terrible ritual of sexual contact between the races is a collective dream or nightmare. As ritual scenario, biracial sexual contact can be infinitely duplicated, reflected in the repetition of the infamous act. What has changed in Ellison's novel for the most part is the genre; Ellison replays the mating ritual of blacks and whites comically. The hero is a little man, a clown in a farce that Robeson would not dignify, and like all clowns, he is self-reflective. He sees what the audience demands even before he performs his role.

Farce gives way to high comedy in the hero's escapade with Sybil at the end of the novel. By this time the hero is perfectly aware that he is playing a role, although Sybil, his white victim, is still in the dark. She, like Mary Dalton, is intoxicated throughout the encounter, but she wants to be 'raped'. However, the hero has learned to manipulate the illusions of racism to his own advantage from one Rinehart, a hustler-turned-preacher on the streets of Harlem. In short, he has become his own Iago and continues to monitor himself in the mirror of others' expectations for him. Sybil, consistent with the preconceptions she has about her race and sex in the biracial context, claims to be a 'nymphomaniac' (p. 508). What other motive could she have in seeking out the sexual favours of a 'black buck'? '"Threaten to kill me, if I don't give in. You know, talk rough to me, beautiful,"' she pleads (p. 508). 'What would Rinehart do about *this*', the hero ponders, 'and knowing', he is 'determined not to let her provoke [him] to violence' (p. 506).

Unlike Othello, his literary progenitor, Ellison's hero will not be manipulated sexually and racially. He speculates on the motives behind the ridiculous spectacle that he and Sybil are cornered into performing to corroborate preconceptions about sexual relationships between the races: 'Who's taking revenge on whom? But why be surprised, when that's what they [white women] hear all their lives.... With all the warnings against it, some are bound to want to try it out for themselves. The conquerors conquered' (p. 509). The hero's reaction is pity for Sybil: 'She had me on the ropes; I felt punch drunk, I couldn't deliver and I couldn't be angry either. I thought of lecturing her on the respect due one's bedmate in our society' (p. 509). He realizes she thinks he is an 'entertainer', and he accepts the role temporarily. The hero, however, assumes control of the script, the blueprint, as Ellison calls it, for the spectacle. There will be no sex, no rape, no violence, no murder. He gets Sybil drunk, promising her that he 'rapes real good' when he's drunk, and scribbles across her belly with lipstick, 'Sybil, you were raped by Santa Claus. Surprise!' (p. 511). The hero has anticipated the outcome of the tragedy he is expected to play out; he recontextualizes the encounter as comedy, and hearts and lives are spared in the process. Like the other roles the hero attempts, manipulates, and sets aside for further refinement, the 'part' of Othello is played only momentarily, and its 'erasure' allows the hero the opportunity to spare Sybil the mutual humiliation and injury of 'raping' her. But of course, the function of comedy is to repeat in a finer tone, to recontextualize tragic situations, and to reverse tragic outcomes through reconciliation and clarification. The variation Ellison achieves in his representation of the racist *mythos* is a function of generic – read verbal – manipulation.

Dutchman may well represent the ultimate African American revision of *Othello*. Amiri Baraka alludes to Shakespeare frequently in his works, particularly in *The Slave*, the companion piece to *Dutchman*. The myth of the ritual murder of innocent white virgins is, in *Dutchman*, fully deconstructed or inverted to reflect more accurately the relationship between the races that has existed throughout Western history. Lula – the white woman – has become the aggressor in a war overtly declared and waged between the races, and Clay is her black victim. Baraka is suggesting that the true victim in the biracial sexual struggle is the black *male*, and he is the partner who is ritually sacrificed in *Dutchman*. The setting of the play is the subway, which is 'heaped in modern myth' (p. 3). Clay, a poet who would be 'the black Baudelaire', watches Lula enter the car and take the seat next to him in an ironic recreation of the very action that launched the civil rights movement just ten years before the first production of the play – integration of the city transit system.

Clay, 'without a trace of self-consciousness', naively 'hopes that his memory of this brief encounter will be pleasant' (p. 4). The young black man, putty or 'clay' in the hands of the white vamp, will be made to react to a taunting series of white stereotypes about black male behaviour, and Lula will cue the 'lines' (p. 16) he is 'supposed' (p. 10) to say. Clay does realize early on that the 'struggle' here is indeed over 'abstract asses' (p. 7) and that nothing sexual will come of this relationship. As we have seen in previous versions of the biracial sexual encounter, the act is rarely consummated. Nevertheless, Lula immediately accuses Clay, saying, 'You think I want to pick you up, get you to take me somewhere and screw me, huh?' (p. 8).

Unlike any of her predecessors, Lula knows what she is doing throughout the play – lying. 'I lie a lot. It helps me control the world' (p. 9). She tells Clay she is an actress, and he nicknames her Tallulah Bankhead. Both 'players' agree they know what is 'supposed to happen' between them (p. 10). Only Lula really does, however. Lula thinks Clay is a 'well-known type' (p. 12) and proceeds to 'dictate' the script, the 'chronicle' as Clay calls it, of their predictable melodrama (p. 24). Lula cues Clay throughout the play with taunts such as, 'It's your turn, and let those be your lines' (p. 16). She warns him, 'Don't get smart with me, Buster, I know you like the palm of my hand' (p. 17). Lula suggests a series of stereotypes for Clay to emulate. She notices he is wearing a three-button suit, even though his grandfather had been a slave. Lula claims he does not know who he is, taunting him by saying, 'I bet you never once thought you were a black nigger' (p. 19). Clay hopes the two of them can pretend to be 'free of [their] own history', but Lula knows better (p. 21). She has another more predictable and more violent outcome in mind. They are about to 'groove', as she announces at the end of scene 1 – and they are indeed in the 'groove' of the biracial ritual (p. 21).

At the beginning of scene 2, the players are rehearsing their 'codes of lust' (p. 23). Lula will 'make a map' of Clay's 'manhood' (p. 26). She tries to pretend they are in *Romeo and Juliet* (p. 26). He will call her room 'black', when they arrive there later, 'like Juliet's tomb'. But the play is not *Romeo and Juliet*, it is *Othello* revised. Lula will be no victim of jealousy and racial misunderstanding, much less a suicide-for-love at the end of the play. She is the murderer this time. The black male is the victim as he so often is in the very real historical lynchings of the nineteenth and early twentieth century.

Clay wants 'the whole story', and he will get it; Lula will keep 'turning pages' to arrive at the ritual climax of the story (p. 28). As the scenario unfolds, Lula realizes there is a problem here: Clay, like Othello, Bigger, and Ellison's hero, is 'an escaped nigger' (p. 29). As such, he must be exposed; she threatens him in front of an audience of middle-class businessmen that assembles in the car between scenes. These businessmen represent the ever-important witnesses to the biracial murder who will, in Baraka's version, become accomplices, and the jury judging the deed as well. Lula continues her verbal abuse: she calls Clay a 'black son of a bitch', an 'Uncle Thomas Woolly-Head', and an 'Uncle Tom Big Lip' because he will not do the belly-rub with her (pp. 32–3). 'You're afraid of white people. And your father was', she taunts (p. 33). What follows is Clay's impassioned plea to let him live, to let him be, to let him make choices about his life, even the choice to be middle class if that is what he wants (p. 33).

Finally angered, Clay explains why blacks should kill, but usually show restraint. Like his predecessors, Clay is ready to strangle the symbolic white female. 'Such a tiny ugly throat. I could squeeze it flat, and watch you turn blue, on a humble. For dull kicks. And all these weak-faced ofays squatting around here, staring over their papers at me. Murder them too. Even if they expected it' (p. 33). The moment of truth has arrived; the audience has been primed; but, Clay, just as Ellison's hero, refuses to play the role. Othello and Bigger have wised up in *Invisible Man* and *Dutchman*. Ellison and Baraka have revised, actually inverted, the paradigm of the biracial sexual encounter. Clay then proceeds to tell us what he and black artists do instead of killing hateful whites – they create music and poetry: 'And the only thing that would cure the neurosis would be your murder. Simple as that. I mean if I murdered you, then other white people would begin to understand me. You understand? . . . If Bessie Smith had killed some white people she wouldn't have needed that music. She could have talked very straight and plain about the world. No metaphors' (p. 35). In short, the '[c]razy niggers [are] turning their backs on sanity. When all it needs is that simple act. Murder. Just murder! Would make us all sane' (p. 35). But he 'wearies' and counters his own argument. 'Ahhh. Shit. But who needs it? I'd rather be a fool. Insane. Safe with my words, and no deaths, and clean, hard thoughts, urging me to new conquests. My people's madness' (p. 35).

At this point, Baraka tells us that Lula's 'voice takes on a different, more businesslike quality'. She concludes, 'I've heard enough' (p. 36) and stabs Clay with an impunity that might well have anticipated that of Bernard Goetz. The businessmen on the car then 'come and drag Clay's body down the aisle' (p. 34). In *Othello* and *Native Son*, the citizens of Venice and Chicago are violently outraged about the murders of Desdemona and Mary Dalton, but the murder of Clay in *Dutchman* is virtually ignored. Lula's next young victim then enters the car and the ritual begins again, but not before an old black conductor tips his hat to Lula and shuffles down the aisle exiting the train, a survivor in the struggle, like Ellison's 'moon-mad' war veterans in *Invisible Man* (p. 132).

Baraka knows precisely what he is up to here, and in *The Slave*, a companion play usually reprinted with *Dutchman*, he tells us all about it. In this play, Easely, a white professor, argues politics with Walker Vessels, a former black theatre student, and Grace, Easely's wife, listens in. Grace announces that 'Mr Vessels is playing the mad scene from *Native Son*', when Walker mentions having played a 'second-rate Othello' in college: 'Grace there was Desdemona ... and you [Easely] were Iago ... [*Laughs*] or at least between classes you were Iago.... If a white man is Iago when you see him ... uhh ... chances are he's eviler when you don't'. Grace, like Lula, tells Vessels to shut up, but, like Clay in *Dutchman*, Vessels refuses (pp. 57–8).

Black writers have revised the biracial sexual myth that represents the primal impediment to the freedom and equal treatment of black people as human beings. Sexual parity is the ultimate expression of racial equality. If language inscribes racial difference and dissension and then ascribes or even prescribes behaviour based on that inscription, perhaps it may also *de-scribe* such behaviour, or at least rewrite the story as it exists in the Western mind. Obviously such a hope informs the rereading and representation of the crucial myth of biracial relationship discussed here.

The philologist Leo Spitzer offers us some help. The problem of 'race', the great problem of our century according to W.E.B. DuBois, might indeed hinge on the misunderstanding of a single word: the word 'race' itself. In his inimitable fashion Spitzer, as linguistic sleuth, traces the word 'race' through its German, French, Italian and English uses and abuses to the Latin root *ratio*. The concept of race, and perhaps the attitudes associated with racism, are all locked up in this term *ratio*, perhaps most artfully wielded by Thomas Aquinas in his *Summa*: 'God, in willing himself, wills all the things which are in himself; but all things in a certain manner preexist in him by their types (*rationes*)'.[20] Spitzer explains, 'Thus *rationes* is a rendering of *ideai* and can shift to the meaning "types" [which becomes "races"] precisely because all the different *rationes* of things are integrated in the creator of things' (p. 148). *Rationes* or 'races' may be conceived, then, as figments of the collective mind derived from what are presumed to be God's categories of human existence. Spitzer concludes, 'What a significant comment this affords on the modern "racial" beliefs!' (p. 152).

If 'race' is a platonic concept, existing in genres and not in genes, existing in subjective human judgements rather than in the 'nature of things' and if it is historically conditioned instead of 'predetermined', then this notion, this 'idea', can be changed, can be modified, can be adapted to new circumstances and experience. Through language, which gave us the notion of 'race' in the first place, we can model a new reality, a reality that reverses outcomes posited as necessities in the racist mentality.

Through the clever manipulation of the language of traditional character and circumstance, the writers under investigation here, Shakespeare included, have helped us perceive new solutions to a problem that remains catastrophically troublesome in the modern world, the problem of racial violence.

Notes

1. Jacques Derrida, 'Racism's Last Word', in Henry Louis Gates, Jr., ed., *'Race,' Writing, and Difference* (Chicago: Univ. of Chicago Press, 1985), pp. 329–38. Derrida continues, 'The point is not that acts of racial violence are only words, but rather that they have to have a word. [Racism] institutes, declares, writes, inscribes, prescribes' (p. 331).

2. Tzvetan Todorov writes, '[W]hereas racism is a well-attested social phenomenon, "race" itself does not exist! Or, to put it more clearly: there are a great number of physical differences among human groups, but these differences cannot be superimposed; we obtain completely divergent subdivisions of the human species according to whether we base our description of the "races" on an analysis of their epidermis or their blood types, their genetic heritages or their bone structures. For contemporary biology, the concept of "race" is therefore useless' ('"Race", Writing and Culture', in Gates, *'Race,' Writing, and Difference*, pp. 370–71).

3. Quoted in Sylvan Barnet, 'Othello on Stage and Screen', *Othello*, ed. Alvin Kernan (New York: Signet, 1986), p. 280. For an honest history of Robeson's reactions to his roles in the two great productions of *Othello* in which he starred (London, 1930, and New York, 1943) and the pronounced racial implications of and reactions to these productions, see Martin Duberman's biography of Robeson, *Paul Robeson* (New York: Knopf, 1989), pp. 134, 263. Some items of interest: Peggy Ashcroft, who played Desdemona in the London production, found her entire experience in *Othello* (1930) 'an education in racism', particularly the public reaction to the kissing scenes between Desdemona and Othello (pp. 134–5); significant passages from the play were cut by the director, Nellie Van Volkenburg, who Ashcroft decided was a 'racist' because of her treatment of Robeson. The murder scene was staged with the bed tucked inconspicuously away in a corner of the room, and the light was so dimmed to the point of 'inscrutability' that Ralph Richardson, who played Iago, kept a flashlight up his sleeve to negotiate the stage after his departure (p. 136). The attempt to take the production to the United States was virtually sabotaged, and when it was produced there in 1943, it provoked broad racial protest, especially in the southern states (p. 265).

4. Gunnar Myrdal writes, 'The illicit relations freely allowed or only frowned upon are, however, restricted to those between white men and Negro women. A white woman's relation with a Negro man is met by the full fury of anti-amalgamation sanctions' – *An American Dilemma* (New York: Harper, 1944), p. 56.

5. The original edition of Baraka's play *Dutchman* used in this essay was published under his original name, Leroi Jones (New York: Morrow, 1964).

6. I am in debt here to an anonymous reader for *South Atlantic Review* who provided this list of novels dealing with our theme and who suggested especially that Charles Johnson's *Oxherding Tale* offers 'first a kind of mock acknowledgement of the myth of the supersexual black male, and then [completely dismantles] the tradition ... of its origins, fears, prejudices, and taboos'.

7. James Kinney, *Amalgamation! Race, Sex, and Rhetoric in the Nineteenth-Century American Novel* (Westport, Conn.: Greenwood, 1985), p. xii. Kinney goes on to discuss some sixty novels of the nineteenth and early twentieth centuries with the theme of miscegenation, novels by luminaries in the canon including James Fenimore Cooper, William Gilmore Simms, George Washington Cable and W.E.B. DuBois.

8. The re-evaluation of *Othello* in its historical context is well underway at this point.

I am much indebted to Emily Bartels's 'Making More of the Moor: Aaron, Othello, and Renaissance Refashionings of Race', *Shakespeare Quarterly* 41 (1990): 433–54. Bartels's article as well as my own are products of a seminar on 'Shakespeare's Aliens' convened at the 1988 meeting of the Shakespeare Association of America by Edward Berry. On the matter of race, see Phyllis Braxton's article, 'Othello: The Moor and the Metaphor', in *South Atlantic Review* 55.3 (1990): 1–17, which argues that Othello's colour outweighs in significance the element of race' (p. 1). According to Braxton, Shakespeare leaves the matter of Othello's ethnic identification deliberately ambiguous but ominous, because 'the Other is always mysterious and without clear definition. Once defined, he is no longer the Other' (p. 9).

9. See for instance Anthony Barthelemy, *Black Face, Maligned Race: The Representation of Blacks in English Drama from Shakespeare to Southerne* (Baton Rouge: Louisiana State UP, 1987); Phyllis Braxton, 'Othello'; Paul Brown, '"This thing of darkness I acknowledge mine": *The Tempest* and the Discourse of Colonialism', *Political Shakespeare: New Essays in Cultural Materialism*, ed. Jonathan Dollimore and Alan Sinfield (Ithaca, NY: Cornell UP, 1985), pp. 48–71; David Dabydeen, ed., *The Black Presence in English Literature* (Manchester: Manchester UP, 1985); Jack D'Amico, *The Moor in English Renaissance Drama* (Tampa: UP of South Florida, 1991); Peter Hulme, *Colonial Encounters: Europe and the Native Caribbean, 1492–1797* (London: Methuen, 1986); G.K. Hunter, 'Othello and Color Prejudice', *Dramatic Identities and Cultural Tradition: Studies in Shakespeare and His Contemporaries*, ed. G.K. Hunter (New York: Barnes, 1978), pp. 31–59; Eldred D. Jones, *The Elizabethan Image of Africa* (Charlottesville: UP of Virginia, 1971) and *Othello's Countrymen: The African in English Renaissance Drama* (London: Oxford UP, 1965); Winthrop D. Jordan, *White Over Black: American Attitudes Toward the Negro, 1550–1812* (New York: Norton, 1968); Ania Loomba, *Gender, Race, Renaissance Drama* (Manchester: Manchester UP, 1989); Christopher Miller, *Blank Darkness: Africanist Discourse in French* (Chicago: Univ. of Chicago Press, 1985); Mary Louise Pratt, 'Scratches on the Face of the Country: Or, What Mr Barrow Saw in the Land of the Bushmen', *Critical Inquiry* 12 (1985): 119–43; Edward W. Said, *Orientalism* (London: Routledge, 1978); Eliot H. Tokson, *The Popular Image of the Black Man in English Drama, 1550–1688* (Boston: Hall, 1982).

10. Errol Hill, *Shakespeare in Sable: A History of Black Shakespearean Actors* (Amherst: UP of Massachusetts, 1984). Black actors, too, have been strongly attracted to the role because, as Hill suggests, the play offers 'an opportunity vividly to convey to audiences the message that racism is the green-eyed monster that destroys not just its victim but also its perpetrator and innocent bystanders who fall into its clutches' (p. 41).

11. For other indignant, clearly racist reviews of nineteenth-century performances of the play, see Ruth Cowhig, 'Blacks in English Renaissance Drama' in Dabydeen, *The Black Presence* (pp. 14–20).

12. All quotations from the plays are taken from *The Riverside Shakespeare*, ed. G. Blakemore Evans (Boston: Houghton, 1974).

13. Quoted in Barnet, 'Othello', p. 284. Miller's sentiment typifies critical comment about all of Shakespeare's plays dealing with the problem of 'complexion' – *Titus Andronicus, The Merchant of Venice* and *Othello*. For instance, both Frank Kermode and Alvin Kernan ignore racial themes altogether in their respective introductions to *Othello* in *The Riverside Shakespeare* and the 1987 Signet edition of the play. Kermode does use interesting language to discuss other issues arising in the text, however: 'The whiteness of Desdemona blackened, we see the white and tranquil mind of Othello darkened by atavistic shock and disgust.... He has behaved like a Turk (used throughout the play as an enemy of civility and grace, a type of cunning and disorder). He has become that person of different "clime, complexion, and degree" whom it was wanton of Desdemona to marry' (*The Riverside Shakespeare*, p. 1201). Braxton claims Miller was trying to 'minimize the differences between Othello and Desdemona' by using Anthony Hopkins in the role ('Othello', pp. 2–3 and 14).

14. See, however, Wayne Holmes's article, 'Othello: Is't Possible?', *Upstart Crow* 1 (1978): 1–23. Holmes goes so far as to suggest 'that Desdemona and Cassio, some time prior to Desdemona and Othello's marriage, had an affair' (p. 1).

15. Trudier Harris, *Exorcising Blackness: Historical and Literary Lynching and Burning Rituals* (Bloomington: Indiana UP, 1984), pp. 11–12. Harris speculates, 'Almost all of the deaths [by ritual lynchings] have as their causes the improper interactions of black males and white females. But what happened in depictions after 1968? Are black writers now beginning to suggest that black males and white females can interact with each other without some fatal violence occurring?' (p. xii). In another passage she writes, 'Historically, in their ritualistic lynchings of black people, white Americans were carrying out rites of exorcism in which they seemed determined to eradicate the black "beast" from their midst, except when he existed in the most servile, accommodationist, and helpful of positions' (p. xiii).

16. Charles Herbert Stember, *Sexual Racism: The Emotional Barrier to an Integrated Society* (New York: Elsevier, 1976), p. 10.

17. Richard Wright, *Native Son* (New York: Harper, 1940), p. xx.

18. Howard Felperin, for one, is so incensed by Holmes's suggestion (cited in note 14 above) that Desdemona might be more 'experienced' than we usually suppose her, that he charitably leaves the author of the article 'unnamed for reasons by now apparent' ('The Deconstruction of Presence in *The Winter's Tale*', *Shakespeare and the Question of Theory*, ed. Patricia Parker and Geoffrey Hartman (New York: Methuen, 1985), p. 3).

19. Ralph Ellison, *Invisible Man* (New York: Vantage-Random House, 1972), p. 408.

20. Quoted in Leo Spitzer, 'Ratio Race', *Essays in Historical Semantics* (New York: Russell, 1948), p. 147.

10

Representation and Performance:
The Uses of Authority in
Shakespeare's Theatre

Robert Weimann

The twentieth century has witnessed a crumbling not just of diverse types
of authority but of the social and intellectual foundations on which the very
idea of authority is built. This 'crisis of authority' needs to be viewed in
historical perspective. Ever since the Protestant Reformation, attempts
have been made to internalize authority, 'to shift the basis of its verification
from external and public modes to internal and private ones'.[1] This
controversial shifting of credentials is connected to a comparable change
in the representational forms and functions of authorizing discourse. The
increasingly uncertain premises of representation, especially its ambivalence as a mode of linguistic and cultural organization, appear to have
much to do with the 'present confusion' of authority.[2] Since many voices
have been raised against representation, there is little need to document the
intellectual disaffection it has produced, except to recall what, in our
context, is the most characteristic charge of all: namely, that the much
deplored power of representation to order and to command language and
to impose on it 'the imperious unity of Discourse'[3] forces on us an
incompatible link between language and humankind.

The issue of authority and representation in early modern discourse
requires an awareness of the historicity of our own perspectives. As we set
out to redefine the relations between language and history, between
signification and socialization, it would be reckless to assume that these
relations can be discussed innocently today. Rather, we should think in two
directions, for the representations of Shakespeare's day appear to an
astonishing extent to interrogate not only the institutionalized authority of
office, law, and penalty but the internalized authority of 'epistemic' or
'moral' credentials.[4] At the same time that our present experience may
provide fresh insight into Renaissance uses of authority and representation,
these reconstructions of the past may lead us to a deeper understanding of
our own problems.

Analogies between then and now carry perils; the establishment of similitude invites at best self-projection, at worst self-congratulation. To avoid these dangers, one might note that – in contrast to our own discursive practice – the Reformation and late-Renaissance crises in authority challenge as well as broaden representational discourse. How can we account for this pattern, which – strangely enough, for us – appears to privilege culturally potent links between the crisis of authority and a vulnerable expansion of representational forms and functions?

The ever more precarious contemporary appropriation of authority is symptomatic of an altogether different crisis that is partly connected with a vast and – in its consequences – unforeseeable inflation and differentiation in the uses of signs. The process of inflation jeopardizes traditional legitimations of humanistic education, which associate the individual's assimilation of the broadest range of signs, messages, and information with the highest stature of the educated subject. At the same time, the process of differentiation creates increasingly divisive barriers among the spheres of culture, science, economics, and politics and among their respective discourses. As sociologists like Daniel Bell and Jürgen Habermas show,[5] these trends have affected the cultural discourse of modernism by undermining whatever socially representative gestures of protest and consensus the avant garde continued to uphold; and as poststructuralist critics might add, the processes of inflation and differentiation challenge the logocentric authority of the subject in the project of modernity. The divisions of discourses, accompanied by the subject's diminishing potency as a source of internalized authority, undercut the universalizing applications of representation mapped out at the beginning of the modern period by Luther, Erasmus, Rabelais, Shakespeare, and Cervantes.

In our time, such division of representational activities imposes on the uses of language a particular need for legitimation. The ever-growing self-sufficiency and differentiation of the various discourses – what Habermas calls their *Ausdifferenzierung* – make it increasingly difficult for any one of them to feel authorized to represent the others, even to represent part of the referents of the others. Representation has become questionable when the rhetoric of synecdoche, the representational figure par excellence, is automatically suspected of false totalizations. If the *Ausdifferenzierung* of discourses can no longer be coped with by 'thick description', by the representational plenitude of interdisciplinary historiography, to what extent must the part–whole relation finally be dispensed with?

These brief comments must suffice to historicize the locus of this critical project. To raise the question of authority in representation is to become mindful of the distance between contemporary and Renaissance discourses. In the most sweeping terms, Renaissance culture is both premodern (in its medieval and communal traditions) and modern (in its political economy of gain through the provision of pleasure). Recognition of the areas of (dis)continuity between past and present significations facilitates a response to the recent upheavals against the traditional territorial boundaries of Shakespeare criticism. With the customary divisions between history and text already in disarray, the time has come to replace these binary concepts with practical counterproposals.

The Elizabethan theatre provided a unique space for subtle, flexible relations between social institution and theatrical language. The actors' use of signs in dramatic representations did not prevent the act of signification itself from being in-formed by the circumstances of the performance. In other words, relations between the representation of fictional roles and the actors' existence in their own identities as entertainers before a live audience continued to be fruitful. This was so even after the work of the clown, as extempore entertainer par excellence, was presumably curtailed in the wake of Will Kempe's departure from the Lord Chamberlain's Men. In fact, these relations continued to thrive on the mingle-mangle conditions of an institution that held sway in the city's 'Liberties' or beyond its jurisdiction, as Nicholas Woodroffe, lord mayor of London, complained in 1580.[6] The place of this unruly stage was, in a geographical sense, secure enough to defy the authority of the city and, in a cultural sense, broad enough to complement the representation of the signs of authority with a self-authorization of signs and significations through which the needs and perspectives of the theatre asserted themselves. The concomitant drama-turgy had to confront a divided space for performance that, in one direction, exceeded the boundaries of representation. Hence, to define the complex range of playing, we need to approach the arts of performance in terms of a non-classical concept of mimesis that allows for wide and open frontiers of representation, comprehending its achievements as well as its limits.

Such a postulate would acknowledge what recent critics of performance have achieved but would not conceal a surprising paradox in their method and approach. For while they have certainly brought criticism closer to the theatre they have rarely brought the theatre closer to the concepts of criticism. The theatre – although it can, of course, be textualized – cannot quite be reduced to the status of a text; a residue remains that refuses to be contained by the textual representation of dramatic fiction. At the bottom of this residue is the act of performance itself, at least insofar as it involves an irreducible investment of the non-representable energy, labour, needs, and exhaustion of the actors' minds and bodies.

In this connection the new performance criticism, for all its fruitfulness, has paid little or no attention to the frontiers of representation and the horizon beyond dramatic fiction. But I suggest that we need to confront both the gaps and the links between representation and existence in the theatre. In particular, it seems important to explore the relation (which I do not hesitate to call central) between the representation of fictive meaning and the actual circumstances of performing practice. To look beyond the representational function of the dramatic text, critics have to view representation and performance as far from continuous, let alone identical. They must recognize that tension and discontinuity are involved when the textualized fiction of dramatic dialogue is simultaneously exposed to, and realized by, the order of performance. In its substance, the order of performance is one not of fiction but of existence. Between dramatic representation and theatrical performance there is no doubt plenty of concurrence and complementarity, but there is also an irreducible element of incongruity, which has to do with, more than anything else, the anthropological order of the theatre. This artful medium of fictional representations is, quite undeniably, a site of real work and profit, an existential location of human effort and chaos, a source of postscriptural memory, forgetfulness and desire. In Shakespeare's theatre, these diverse purposes of playing need especially to be taken into account: dramatic fictions themselves were authorized and performed in what must be recognized as a divided theatrical space. The rich cultural semiotics of this diversity existed because there were particularly vital and consequential gaps as well as links between actors and roles, between the performing agents and the performed agenda of representation itself. Perhaps it is no exaggeration to say that in the Elizabethan theatre these gaps could more effectively be closed and these links more consequentially broken than in any other theatre culture before or since. In these historical circumstances, the act of performance itself could assimilate the crucial but precarious site on which the awareness of social occasion and the uses of significations came together in a particularly compelling fashion.

Shakespearean Versions of Authority

The word *authority* occurs no fewer than sixty times in Shakespeare's work. His resort to authority in representation is too diverse to be usefully reduced to a single paradigm, but to make an initial foray into the subject, aimed at larger theoretical and historical issues, we may begin by examining two key scenes where authority is deeply implicated in strategies of dramatic representation that are characteristic of his most mature writing.

The first text is from *Troilus and Cressida*, the second from *King Lear*. When Troilus, accompanied by Ulysses, spies on Cressida's encounter with Diomedes in the Grecian camp, the dramatic constellation is vastly different from what it is when Lear in his madness engages blinded

Gloucester on the heath. Yet in both scenes theatrical language, achieving an unusual density of signification, involves representation in its most contradictory and potentially paradoxical mode. The representation of authority here implies a new, unheard-of author-ity in representation. On the strength of this self-fashioned author-ity, the Shakespearean theatre radically challenges the Renaissance discourse of similitude, decorum, and catharsis, substituting for the unifying purposes of humanist poetics the representation of difference. But when I say 'difference', I am adapting the poststructuralist concept not only to the linguistic discontinuity between signs and meanings but to the rupture between authority and power.

Troilus, in his great moment of crisis, embraces both these dimensions:

> This she? – No, this is Diomed's Cressida.
> If beauty have a soul, this is not she;
> If souls guide vows, if vows be sanctimonies,
> If sanctimony be the gods' delight,
> If there be rule in unity itself,
> This is not she. O madness of discourse,
> That cause sets up with and against itself!
> Bifold authority! where reason can revolt
> Without perdition, and loss assume all reason
> Without revolt. This is, and is not, Cressid.
> Within my soul there doth conduce a fight
> Of this strange nature, that a thing inseparate
> Divides more wider than the sky and earth;
> And yet the spacious breadth of this division
> Admits no orifex for a point as subtle
> As Ariachne's broken woof to enter.
> Instance, O instance! strong as Pluto's gates:
> Cressid is mine, tied with the bonds of heaven.
> Instance, O instance! strong as heaven itself:
> The bonds of heaven are slipp'd, dissolv'd, and loos'd;
> And with another knot, five-finger tied,
> The fractions of her faith, orts of her love,
> The fragments, scraps, the bits, and greasy relics
> Of her o'er-eaten faith are given to Diomed.
>
> (V.ii.136–59)[7]

The crisis in authority here takes the form of a division between godlike reason and sensory perception, and it places discourse in a maddeningly contradictory position between the 'bonds of heaven' and the 'fragments, scraps, the bits, and greasy relics' of sensuous as well as sensual experience. Authority consequently surrenders its orthodox connotations of unquestioned validity. As in *King Lear*, it is reassessed against the frontiers of '[r]eason in madness' (IV.vi.176). For Troilus, 'madness of discourse' serves as a vehicle of discontinuity, upsetting the language of representation through a bewildering separation of visible signs from transcendental meanings. A deep gulf divides the authority of cosmological order from the discourse of individual experience ('th'attest of eyes and ears' [V.ii.121]). But, astonishingly, this discontinuity serves both as a site of philosophical and moral scepticism and as a divided space on the platform stage. Within this split in thought and in theatrical space authority is renegotiated. Having shed its innocent claim on validity, it emerges into the modern world of early seventeenth-century England as conflictual.

The link between divisions in thought and divisions on the stage implies neither homology nor continuity. In this indeterminate relation, divided constellations of authority in discourse constitute, and are in turn constituted by, a highly heterogeneous theatrical space. The interrogation of authority seems to thrive on the ununified space of the Elizabethan stage, a space marked by the simultaneous availability, even the interplay, of localized and neutral areas. Far from being a merely technical phenomenon, the differentiation is rooted in the multiple cultural functions of performance on the Elizabethan and pre-Elizabethan stage.

In the scene from *Troilus and Cressida*, such differentiated uses of theatrical space appear quite deliberate. Diomedes's lascivious courtship is set in a self-contained locus marked as Calchas's tent in the Grecian camp. Like other sites on the Elizabethan stage, the tent, whether stage property or imaginative projection, is a fairly verisimilar specified locality, but for the audience this locality interacts with less specified space on the platform stage. Two further uses of theatrical space contrast with the representation of Diomedes's courtship and mediate it to the audience with less self-enclosed representations: (1) Troilus and Ulysses's hiding place and (2) Thersites's position as commentator and sardonic chorus. Although these two sites differ radically in their relation to the drama in front of the tent, they have at least one thing in common: though concealed from the localized characters, both are open to the spectators, who witness Troilus's watchful anguish and Thersites's blunt sarcasm. While the figures in hiding may be said to inhabit an intermediate space between the upstage tent and Thersites's position near the audience (perhaps 'hiding' in front of one of the pillars), Thersites may best be envisioned on a neutral site in the tradition of the audience-related *platea*, the space on the platform stage most easily neutralized.[8] Here Thersites could discharge his distancing function of irreverent commentator in a language that pointedly deflates the iambic structure and rhetorical pathos of Troilus's verse: 'Will a swagger himself out on's own eyes?' (V.ii.135).

In such a moral, spatial, and discursive constellation, the representation of authority projects what Troilus calls 'the spacious breadth of this division'. Since 'bifold authority' disrupts not simply the unity of reason and experience but also the connection between transcendental meanings and naturalized signs, the moment of division affects the theatrical process itself. It is therefore possible that Troilus's language rehearses a divided stagecraft: 'This is, and is not, Cressid'. The painfully felt contrast between the expectation of reason and the shock of experience may involve awareness of the difference between theatrical fiction and the reality of gender and institution: the imaginary product of representation (the role and female identity of Cressida) is and is not continuous with the actual theatrical process (the work and body of the boy actor who plays the part). At one remove both from the *platea* inhabited by Thersites and from the *locus* of verisimilitude, Troilus is perfectly equipped to stimulate the audience to view simultaneously the represented and the representer. As the spectators face the depth of the division of authority, they are not allowed to swagger themselves out of their own eyes: the fiction of dramatic representation appears coextensive with the divisive uses of theatrical space and the bifold poles of performance.

Compared with these complex dimensions of authority in *Troilus and Cressida*, the 'great image of authority' in *King Lear* seems to inhabit a more nearly homogeneous type of theatrical space. Even so, the sensory premises of the epistemology of representation enter self-reflexively into the picture. The madness in Lear's language, much more than the 'madness of discourse' in *Troilus and Cressida*, is made to 'invert th'attest of eyes and ears'. While Troilus challenges the bewildering work of his own organs of perception, Lear appears to take his cue from blinded Gloucester, from the violent destruction of light. The cruel inversion serves as an appropriate figure of readjustment through which, 'handy-dandy', the upside-down relation of justice and thief can be perceived. For Lear to 'see with no eyes' and to tell Gloucester to '[l]ook with thine ears' constitutes an inverted link between the perception and the representation of 'the great image of authority':

LEAR. ... Your eyes are in a heavy case, your purse in a light; yet you see how this world goes.

GLO. I see it feelingly.

LEAR. What, art mad? A man may see how this world goes with no eyes. Look with thine ears. See how yond justice rails upon yond simple thief. Hark, in thine ear: change places and, handy-dandy, which is the justice, which is the thief? Thou hast seen a farmer's dog bark at a beggar?

GLO. Ay, sir.

LEAR. And the creature run from the cur? There thou mightst behold the great image of authority: a dog's obey'd in office.
Thou rascal beadle, hold thy bloody hand.
Why dost thou lash that whore? Strip thy own back;
Thou hotly lusts to use her in that kind

For which thou whip'st her. The usurer hangs the cozener.
Through tatter'd clothes small vices do appear;
Robes and furr'd gowns hide all. Plate sin with gold,
And the strong lance of justice hurtless breaks;
Arm it in rags, a pigmy's straw does pierce it.
None does offend, none – I say none; I'll able 'em.
Take that of me, my friend, who have the power
To seal th'accuser's lips. Get thee glass eyes,
And, like a scurvy politician, seem
To see the things thou dost not. Now, now, now, now!
Pull off my boots. Harder, harder – so.

EDG.　　O, matter and impertinency mix'd! Reason in madness!

(IV.vi.147–76)[9]

In *Troilus and Cressida*, the unorthodox definition of authority is couched in language concerned with perception as a mode of representation. In *King Lear*, madness unhinges the difference in the perceptions of the individual senses themselves. In this instance, probably unique in early seventeenth-century discourse, authority is defined as a version of brute force that copes with the division of society in the name of the law.

If madness foregrounds what Susan Wells calls the 'indeterminate register' of representation, in this particular passage it also fortifies the 'typical register', that is, the referential power of the text.[10] For in depicting the beggar, Shakespeare's tragic language intercepts the English social history of his day: the beggar who 'runs from the cur' may be read not only as an autonomous symbol but as an image of contemporary vagrancy. Paradoxically, this starkly referential dimension in the tragic theme of 'true need' (II.iv.272) is achieved not through a realistic mode of representation but through the theatrical conventions of madness and disguise as indeterminate vehicles of unsanctioned significations. Again, the density of signs and sensory perceptions goes hand in hand with unstable representations and provides a theatrical code that can disrupt certain Elizabethan meanings of justice and authority.

Even more important, this topsy-turvying treatment of authority is accompanied by a theatrical strategy that allows for a significant differentiation in the structure of both dramatic language and histrionic performance. The passage falls into three parts. First, the dramatic dialogue culminates in Lear's questions, 'Thou hast seen a farmer's dog bark at a beggar? ... And the creature run from the cur?' This exchange in prose, which includes Gloucester's answer, leads, second, to a monologue-like statement, elevated in iambic metre, rhetoric, and imagery. Supported by the convention of Lear's visionary madness, the stylized language of 'Thou rascal beadle, hold thy bloody hand. / Why dost thou lash that whore? Strip thy own back' is not an address, question, or answer to anyone on stage.

But, third, after the representation of dialogue as an image of verbal exchange has collapsed, Lear's utterance leads back to renewed dialogue in the completely unstylized, unrhetorical, and unmetrical 'Now, now, now, now!' This almost naturalistic gesture culminates in 'Pull off my boots. Harder, harder – so'. The prose sentence, actually a remarkably profound piece of stage direction, sets forth in physical terms an extreme violation of neoclassical decorum, thus turning the king's *sermo humilis* into performative language and action. Even more important, it is Lear's response to the images of authority that, like '[r]obes and furr'd gown', now stand revealed as false symbols, signs of status and authority that have been stripped of their legitimation. Abandoning his precious leather boots, Lear sheds the signs of his own royal authority as mere 'lendings'.

The platform stage leaves considerable space for authorizing linguistic and, at the same time, social differences. It is impossible to appreciate the sheer scope of Lear's language without recourse to this highly disjunctive stage that could localize the tragic scene in dialogue but could just as easily neutralize it in some unlocalized theatrical space. Lear's language freely adapts and modifies the move of theatrical action from locality to a *platea*-like neutral 'place' and back to locality.

In short, the dramatically rendered crisis of authority in the text of both plays interlocks with comparable strategies of theatrical performance. The three-tiered theatrical setting in *Troilus and Cressida* is incorporated into the immense spatial, moral and verbal scope of Lear's speech and action. The Elizabethan theatre, inhabiting the 'virtually ungoverned areas' in the 'Liberties' of London, projected its own 'incontinent rule' onto the spatial form and verbal dimension of the platform stage.[11] So it happened that the dominant political, religious, and juridical discourses of authority were interrogated on this stage as nowhere else in late sixteenth- and early seventeenth-century England. As both scenes suggest, in this half-unlicensed place the mimesis of madness and blindness could be used to shed assumptions of identity and rank and to challenge the dominant discourses articulating (or silencing) contemporary practices of courtship, vagrancy, class and power. When in *King Lear* and in *Troilus and Cressida* the drama of perception is played out ('As if those organs had deceptious functions' [*Tro.* V.ii.123]), authority as a divisive force in discourse is interrogated in a way that discloses the vulnerability of representation itself. What, finally, is at stake when 'matter and impertinency' are 'mix'd' is the representational function of discourse, a function that enters into crisis when unitary authority is questioned.

Representation, Embodiment and Theatrical Space

As my reading of these scenes suggests, the semiotic dimensions of representation are to be viewed in conjunction with its social register, or what elsewhere I have called representativity. Many years ago, anticipating the exploration of such links, Kenneth Burke considered it 'no mere accident of language that we use the same word for sensory, artistic, and political representation'.[12] As Frank Lentricchia, rereading Burke, has noted, 'the term "representation" becomes a sign of the convergence of the political and the aesthetic, and of the complicity of the aesthetic with political power'.[13] Catherine Gallagher has taken a comparable position in her studies of the 'relationship between political and literary representation' in Victorian fiction – for instance, in Disraeli's writings, which characterize the connection as 'isomorphic'.[14] Similarly, and perhaps surprisingly, Jacques Derrida's reading of Heidegger underlines the links between the semiotics and the politics of representation:

> How is man, having become a representative in the sense of *Vorstellend* (i.e., an agent of conceptions and ideas), also and at the same time a representative in the sense of *Repräsentant*, in other words, not only someone who has representations, who represents himself, but also someone who himself represents something or someone?

In answering this question, Derrida suggests that 'we can reconstitute the chain of consequences that sends us back from representation as idea to representation as delegation, perhaps political'.[15]

The Elizabethan theatre – as written text and as cultural institution – occupies a site of intense interaction and contradiction between the linguistic and the social components of representation and, even more important, provides a heterogeneous space for tensions between these two dimensions. But the theatre does not simply command a space with differing registers of representation, in the sense that agents, representing themselves, also represent something and someone else. The two registers are deeply involved in historical and cultural relations.

From a historicizing perspective, certain spatial constellations of the Elizabethan platform stage – here defined at the interaction of *locus* and *platea* – have social and linguistic correlatives. As the discussions of *Troilus and Cressida* and *King Lear* suggest, the stage's dual capacity could be projected between an imagined *locus* of verisimilitude and the *platea* materiality of 'this unworthy scaffold' as a nonfictional site of institutionalized entertainment. Associated with the specifying capacities of an enacted role, the *locus* tended to privilege the authority of what and who was represented. But the *platea*-like dimension of the platform stage

– the bustling space of theatrical 'sound and fury' that as neutral matter was literally 'signifying nothing' and representing little – privileged the authority not of what was represented (in historiographical and novelistic narrative) but of what was representing and who was performing.

The locus-centred authority of the represented was usually defined in accordance with a certain amount of verisimilitude, decorum, aloofness from the audience, and representational closure. For instance, in Shakespeare the throne is the representational locus of privileged royalty, the bed a locus of patriarchal power and female sacrifice, and the tomb a topos of family dignity and piety. The playwright demonstrates language's vast potential for mirroring chastity, honour, and warlike resolution and draws on a full repertoire of signs to denote the household and the innate strength of parental authority. The representational structure and effect of such loci were to a large extent already inscribed in Tudor historiography and in Shakespeare's fictional narrative sources; the signs were part of a dominant ideology and were widely used as figurations of the current relations of power.

If, however, the locus-centred authority of what was represented could be confirmed, it could also be profoundly challenged. The challenge was usually geared to whatever *platea* dimension Shakespeare's stage retained or revitalized. In *Hamlet* the language of privilege and the mirror of representation, faithfully held up to a previously inscribed idea of virtue or vice 'showing her own feature', could be deflected from their customary locus of decorum by an impertinent or 'antic disposition' of dramaturgy (I.v.172). When the *platea*-like space was used in this manner, 'Th'expectancy and rose of the fair state, / The glass of fashion and the mould of form', together with 'that noble and most sovereign reason', could be '[b]lasted with ecstasy' under the mantle of assumed madness (III.i.154–62), a highly indecorous convention of audience-related acting and speaking. The glass of fashion and courtly virtue, far from showing 'her own' already given image, could be distorted by a set of socially, spatially, and verbally encoded theatrical forms.

Among these forms, the figures of wordplay and impertinency loom large, as does the ordinary and sometimes deflating language of the proverb. Even more important, the conventions of disguise and clowning, together with memories of misrule and topsy-turvydom, all helped potentially to undermine whatever respect the represented loci of authority invoked for the Elizabethan audience. Usually such comedy could involve a sub-version of the performed fictions. The social occasion inside the public theatre remained, as did the materiality of things on the scaffold stage, the unmistakable body of a well-known actor, and the awareness of the dramatic language itself. The play metaphor reveals the actor, the person who is performing: moving between these two types of identity (and authority), the actor must have resembled the 'poor player' (V.v.24) in *Macbeth* or the performer in the title role, who in his own way would be overwhelmed by the 'borrowed robes' of kingship and other irreducible materials of theatrical signification.

In emphasizing the multiple and heterogeneous functions of Shakespeare's platform stage, I am not primarily concerned with technique as a (perfectly legitimate) element of dramaturgy. The variegated uses of both representational and nonrepresentational types of mimesis, I suggest, are entangled in the social, cultural, and discursive divisions and proliferations of sixteenth-century English history. The heterogeneous effects of theatrical language, for instance, should be correlated to the largely unsanctioned diffusion of signifying activities, in particular to the post-Reformation explosion of ideological 'discord'; to the growth in debate, translation, and interpretation; and to the continuous spread of literacy, made possible by the increased circulation of printed vernacular texts. Under these conditions, sixteenth-century English society witnessed the beginnings of a new mode of discourse that – suspending, exhausting, and finally breaking with the order of similitude – culminated in the disparate set of relations between language and existence that the Shakespearean theatre exemplifies.

If, then, historical activity is to be situated in the representational process itself, such activity must be traced in the gaps and links between what was represented and what was representing or, to shift the emphasis somewhat, between the forms of fiction and the force of performance. On the Elizabethan stage, these gaps could be closed when the actor's available signs functioned as part of the signified fiction of his role. In contrast to such closure, which occurred at moments of dramatic illusion and verisimilitude, the recourse to rupture – for example, when links between role and actor were suspended – was equally significant. Whichever the gesture, historical activity can be discerned in the differing purposes of playing.

This distinction, schematic as it may be, is not simply theoretical. The constellation of representational activities in Shakespeare's theatre marks a profound and complex division of social interests and cultural attitudes. This division derives historically from the existence of an institution whose cultural identity was primarily established by the social experience and the political economy of those who ran the playhouse and worked in it, those whose minds and bodies provided the means of signification. But while such performing agents of representation, together with most of the agents of reception, were (as Jean Howard noted in a seminar discussion[16]) drawn from 'unsanctioned groups' in society, the performed figures of representation almost invariably were not. In the tragedies and histories the serious dramatis personae almost always stem from the nobility and gentry, and even the leading figures in the comedies are portrayed as patricians rather than as plebeians. So, in contrast to much of the modern theatre, the representing agents and the represented objects of drama were not of the same social order. There were tensions and gaps in experience between roles and actors, between dramatic signifieds and signifying minds and bodies. While in the great scenes of dramatic illusion representation could close gaps and naturalize norms and choices, it also had to cope with 'the spacious breadth of this division'.

To take advantage of the disparity between the agents and the objects of representation and to confront the overwhelming authority of what was already represented in contemporary discourse, the Elizabethan theatre foregrounded the sense of theatricality – the performing work of actors' minds and bodies. But Shakespeare's metadramatic strategies were no purely self-sufficient endeavours of art. As I have argued elsewhere ('Bifold Authority'), at about the turn of the century the uses of 'this unworthy scaffold' were renegotiated through an awareness of the requirements and the limits of 'the swelling scene' (*HV* pro.4). For the recently established Globe to 'digest / Th'abuse of distance, force a play' (*HV* II.chorus.31–2), a new alertness to the limits of the platform stage vis-à-vis the needs (and vulnerabilities) of historiographic representations was necessary. Especially after William Kempe's departure,[17] the achieved sense of theatricality depended on conventions of *platea*-oriented speech and action adapted to an even broader, less determinate spatial and typical register of representation.

Text, History and Theatre

Where transitions such as those between dramatic fiction and theatrical institution, text and history, are especially swift, no literary concept of the text can satisfy. Instead, it is imperative to start from a concept of text that effectively recognizes the gulf between culture and language, history and discourse, especially in a theatre where the interaction between script and performance appears to have been intensely reciprocal. For Shakespeare, as we know, writing and acting were intimately linked. His use of the arts of language must have been powerfully stimulated by his theatrical experience and vice versa. There is no better education for a dramatist than to assist at the points of intersection of the spoken (the performed) and the written word, particularly when the bond between the two was produced by the needs of common players aspiring to national excellence.

Hence, it is not too much to say that language in the Elizabethan theatre was radically affected by the institution's social and cultural functions, so much so that it is dangerous to assume, as many critics still do, the priority of the written script over the performed play, especially when the performance is described as a realization of the script. Even though the dramatic text precedes the performance text and in several important ways constrains the production through the prefiguration of action, character and setting, the written text by itself is radically incomplete. What is more, the dramatic text, and more markedly the Shakespearean text, is 'conditioned by its performability ..., is determined by its very need for stage contextualization'.[18]

If, then, we regard the text as performed as well as written, language in Shakespearean drama cannot be divorced from its cultural functions and theatrical manifestations.[19] Once this relation is conceived as reciprocal, Shakespeare's language can no longer be subsumed under a purely linguistic concept of textuality. The plays were written for and performed in a theatre that, though deeply indebted to the humanist poetics of inscribed language, remained close to a culture of voices and performatives, close to a civilization in which the signs of visible status, the signs of the alphabet, and the sounds of speech ('th'attest of eyes and ears') could coincide or collide, in which blindness itself (and the unliterary spectator) could be told to 'look with thine ears'. This state of affairs embraced a larger context of cultural reproduction, public memory, and popular entertainment against which the important contributions of neoclassical poetics and rhetoric fall into place. The larger context was worlds apart from a 'writing that breaks with the *phonè* [that] is the representer in its pure state'.[20] Although audience response in an Elizabethan theatre involved an intimate knowledge of the arts of writing, an awareness of script, it was also rooted in a culture not entirely literate. This transition from declining orality to emerging literacy, rather than benefiting institutionalized locations of writing, such as learned humanism and jurisprudence, must have immensely stimulated the cultural functions of an inscribed performative in the popular Renaissance theatre.

Representation on the Shakespearean stage thus occupied a vulnerable space where the authorization of discourse was radically tangential to the function of cultural activities and social occasions. The fiction of theatrical signs, suspended in the performative act of oral or visual communication, could produce a form of audience involvement in which the spectator, much like the *platea*-situated actor, related to both the represented and the representing. Neoclassical forms of representation and dramatic fiction were disrupted when, for instance, clowns would 'themselves laugh, to set on some quantity of barren spectators to laugh too' (*Ham.* III.ii.40–41).[21] It is not, then, by playing fictional roles but by embodying their own clownish selves that these comic actors 'themselves laugh', unauthorized by the textual representations. Hence, the spectator can laugh with the clowning actor rather than merely at the comic role. When the symbolic (representational) functions of laughter find themselves side by side with its postritual or existential (nonrepresentational) functions, the result is an extraordinary ensemble of signs and bodies, signification and socialization.

These considerations remind us of representation's limits and of the need to apply a larger concept of mimesis to Shakespeare's theatre. If laughter or the comic effects of disguise may constitute a nonrepresentational (and only partially textualized) situation, so too may the existential (nonfictional) uses of public memory and emotion. Such uses inform a pretextualized constellation or even, at the endings of several Shakespearean plays, a postscriptural future to which the Elizabethan theatre generously responds. At the play's closure, the representation is allowed to collapse and the text is made to refer beyond itself, as when 'the story' is offered to (not to say urged upon) the audience as something to be completed or to be (re)told in such a way that it 'must / Take the ear strangely' (*Temp.* V.i.312). The image of a memorable action ('of whose memory / Hereafter more' [*Tim.* V.i.80–81]) lives on through its collective reproduction. In more than one sense, the public impact and the cultural potential of the Shakespearean drama were inseparable from the text's incompleteness. The oral form and its visual concomitants themselves involved distinct rites of memory, which could collide with, or be fortified by, the 'rights of memory', those unforgotten claims that Fortinbras, saluting Hamlet's 'passage', invokes in close conjunction with 'the rite of war' (V.ii.380–91). Over and beyond the textual version, it was possible '[t]o *hear* the rest untold' (*Per.* V.iii.85) and 'to have more *talk* of these sad things' (*Rom.* V.iii.306; emphasis mine) after the play had ended. The text in the theatre, both projecting and responding to potent figurations of public memory, is an agent of that memory itself: 'Yet he shall have a noble memory. / Assist' (*Cor.* V.vi.154–5). These concluding words of *Coriolanus* link the performance and the audience's appropriation of the fiction: at the crucial moment of closure, the inscribed stage direction authorizes both the performing 'three o' th' chiefest soldiers' to 'bear from hence his body' (ll. 149, 143) and the audience, by remembering him, to ensure the play's future in the nonfictional world beyond the gates of the theatre.

This points to the larger cultural context in which the most effective of Shakespeare's epilogues operate. Although, as Rosalind says at the end of *As You Like It*, 'a good play needs no epilogue' (epi.5), the epilogue effects a transition between the represented world of the playful fiction and the representing world of the Elizabethan playhouse. The actor, speaking still within the role of Rosalind, marks this transition at the beginning of the epilogue: 'It is not the fashion to see the lady the epilogue'. But as he proceeds, he gradually distances the assimilated fiction, making his own cultural and sexual em-bodi-ment supersede whatever representation overlapped with the public dissolution of the play's illusion. He associates himself one last time with the represented 'lady', only to end up pledging, 'If I were a woman, I would kiss as many of you as had beards that pleas'd me' (16). The transition is from textual representation to theatrical reality, from the assumed identity of the role of 'the lady' to the reality of the body of the boy actor, who congenially establishes his true nonrepresentational identity by saying, 'If I were a woman'.

Similarly, at the end of *The Tempest*, Prospero dislodges the boundary between the represented fiction in the text of the play and the representing agent in the real world of the playhouse. Having abjured 'this rough magic' from within the role of the enlightened magician, having broken his 'staff', drowned his 'book' (V.i.50–57), the imaginary figure of representation called Prospero collapses. But here again, as this textual figuration is being released into the actual body of the actor, there hovers over the play's ending a precarious poise between fictional representation and true em-bodi-ment. This balance informs the delicate interplay between the 'bare island' in the text of *The Tempest* and the unworthy scaffold on which the actor is left behind, somewhat wary, lest his true 'project fails, / Which *was* to please' (epi.12–13; emphasis mine). Almost unnoticeably the 'charms' in the text of the fiction turn into past tense once they are referred to the achieved cultural 'project' of dramatic entertainment. Whatever authority the representation of Prospero may have enjoyed in the text is now abdicated to that nonrepresentational realm in which the true pleasure of the audience serves as final arbiter of the fate of the drama in performance: 'But release me from my bands / With the help of your good hands' (epi.9–10). The renegotiation of authority is realized through the interplay between represented theatrical signs and their representing function, between the imaginative language of the text and the play's social history in the theatre.

Authority Represented versus Author-ity Representing

The interplay between text and theatre suggests that authority in the Shakespearean drama can be and, in fact, must be read beyond the limits of textuality and even of representation. The text, as we have noted, can be made to refer beyond itself, to the nondramatic, nonfictional reality of the socio-cultural process inside and outside the theatre. The issue of authority in the theatre is most radically interrogated at the end (and through the ends) of dramatic representation. The differential meaning is situated at the intersection between the actual location of the theatre and the fictional setting, a point that is symptomatic of the difference between two types of discourse and appropriation: in Shakespeare's theatre, the difference is negotiated between the presence of the actor and the 'absent' representation of his role, between the materiality of theatrical communication and the fictionality of textual configurations.

When the subtly balanced movement from fictional text to cultural reality is arrested at the end of a Shakespearean play, the drama cancels its representational dimension by projecting itself into a nonfictional social occasion. The dramatic representation, in acknowledging its finiteness, confronts the precariousness of its 'little brief authority' (*MM*. II.ii.117). If we read Prospero's strength as the capacity to authorize and adequately to perform his part, then his theatrical authority is situated beyond the boundaries of representation. Once the character's 'charms are all o'erthrown' (epi.1), the actor's 'strength' is to be found outside, no longer inside, the representational fiction of the text. The 'I' (in 'what strength I have's mine own' [epi.2]) is that of the representer, not the represented. The actor steps forward only after, in his role, he has abjured his 'so potent art', broken his 'staff', drowned his 'book' (V.i.50–57), thereby relinquishing the images of authority associated with his representation. What remains after these signs of authority are all 'o'erthrown' is the actor's competence in the delivery of language and gesture. As opposed to the signs of authority, this competence, the authority of his performance, must be endorsed according to the rules of theatrical entertainment. No longer enhanced by the great images of power and powerful magic, this type of strength or performative authority is 'most faint' indeed (epi.3). It needs to be acknowledged by success in the playhouse. In other words, the authority of the actor, once it is signifying nothing, is not that of the text but that of performance itself.

At this juncture the appearance of any opposition between text and history is suspended. The epilogue projects itself into a post-textual future that is anticipated by the concluding gestures through which actors 'abjure' their fictional roles only to assert their social status as cultural entertainers. The uses of authority, based on a bifold pattern of legitimation, here reveal themselves most clearly: they are vitally connected with this theatre's (dis)continuity between the representation of authority and the author-ity of its own representations.

When the representational images of magic, sovereignty, order, and magnanimity are all discarded, the language that counts is that of the theatre in its institutionalization of what Prospero calls the 'project ... to please'. Like this project, its legitimation must be traced both within and without the theatrical process of representation. Even more important, the uses of authority in these two instances are not the same; between them, there is a potentially (dis)continuous operation of credentials.

Bifold authority, viewed in its performative implications, has to do with the divided functions of discourse within and without representation. At work in this broader context is the 'principle of multi-consciousness'[22] or 'double-eyedness'[23] that, as we noticed, allows Troilus to say *from a distance*, 'This is, and is not, Cressid'. Similarly, it might be said, 'this is, and is not, Macbeth', especially when this character likens life to 'a poor player', so that the actor who speaks (or at least performs) the dramatist's language, like Macbeth himself, 'is the poor player whose mediations block any smooth passage to what is being represented and ... [who] foregrounds the irreducible materials of signification in signifying nothing'.[24] Such bifold authority in representation results when a figure in the text is and is not a character, because this same individual simultaneously is and is not the voice and body of the actor impersonating an artificial person through his own embodiment. In this dramaturgic sense, bifold authority obtains when authority is perceived as the representation of royalty, the playing of power, yet continues to be associated with the institutionalized 'project ... to please', that is, with the pleasure-giving thrill of representing royally, of playing powerfully.

There was no tidy sociology of class conflict in Elizabethan and early Jacobean England, but the basic modes of legitimating social and cultural experience were more heterogeneous than they were in subsequent theatre history. This heterogeneity has to do with the structure of a highly transitional culture that had room for traditional uses of authority, as in the aristocratic display of ceremony or the feudal show of status symbols. In the class-ridden world of Shakespeare's England, a good many signs were fixed, their meanings preordained. We need only recall that in dress the type of fabric (from russet to velvet), the wearing of furs, the choice of colours were all subsumed under an elaborate system of status signs. Some of these were literally signs of authority, visible in the public exhibitions and carefully classified rituals of church and state that externalized social norms and values as emblems of given relations of power.

In view of these social and semiotic fixtures, the new forces of capitalism, the emerging relations of economic and cultural exchange, the volatile and increasingly placeless institution of the market must have constituted countervailing energies that, as Jean-Christophe Agnew has shown, profoundly involved the theatre. This is not the place to explore the depth of 'the social and political crisis of representation that agricultural and commercial capitalism introduced into England's semifeudal society';[25] but it is in the midst of these relations of change and crisis that the theatre found itself in an unprecedented position of contingency to negotiate and experiment with both fixture and rupture in representation.

Finally, to historicize the cultural space of signification in the social context of semiotics itself, we must situate the central distinction of Renaissance representational strategies – the distinction between the signs of authority (a dramatic image of power represented) and the authority of signifying activities (the competence of the theatre as a socio-cultural agency of pleasure and communication) – in the specific circumstances of contemporary discursive practices. It therefore behoves us to approach the issue of authority through the changing history of the authorization, distribution, and appropriation of discursive activities in the sixteenth century. To move from authority in representation to the conditions of authorship and performance, from the history of these conditions to the rules of authorization, is to explore the social and topographical space in which writing, reading, and playing were legitimated. In the early Tudor period this space was far from fixed; in the course of the sixteenth century, it expanded radically and, in its diversification, was profoundly affected by a ground swell of social, cultural and technological change. As the social functions of discourse began to multiply, the issue of authority was thrust ever more deeply into the world of ideological debate. Thus the difference between authority represented and author-ity representing must be relocated in the rapidly expanding cultural history of communication. In other words, it is necessary to explore the divergent uses of authority as they have been affected by the conditions, the expanding media, and the multiplying aims of discursive practice itself.[26]

Notes

1. R. Baine Harris, ed., *Authority: A Philosophical Analysis* (University: Univ. of Alabama Press, 1975), p. 1.

2. Hannah Arendt, 'What is Authority?' *Between Past and Present* (New York: Penguin, 1987), p. 95.

3. Michel Foucault, *The Order of Things: An Archaeology of the Human Sciences* (New York: Random, 1973), p. 386.

4. For the distinction between 'epistemic' and 'moral' credentials, see E.M. Adams, 'The Philosophical Grounds of the Present Crisis of Authority', in Harris, *Authority*.

5. Daniel Bell, *The Cultural Contradictions of Capitalism* (New York: Basic, 1976); Jürgen Habermas, *The Philosophical Discourse of Modernity: Twelve Lectures*, trans. Frederick Lawrence (Cambridge: MIT Press, 1987).

6. Steven Mullaney, *The Place of the Stage: License, Play, and Power in Renaissance England* (Chicago: Univ. of Chicago Press, 1988), p. 49.

7. *Troilus and Cressida*, ed. Kenneth Palmer (London: Methuen, 1982). Unless otherwise noted, Shakespeare's text is quoted from *The Complete Works*, ed. Peter Alexander (London: Collins, 1951).

8. For this difference in the use of theatrical space, see my definition below (pp. 207–10), which further develops my suggestion in *Shakespeare and the Popular Tradition in the Theater: Studies in the Social Dimension of Dramatic Form and Function*, ed. Robert Schwartz (Baltimore: Johns Hopkins UP, 1987), esp. pp. 73–85. For a more recent approach to *locus* and *platea* conventions, see my 'Bifold Authority in Shakespeare's Theatre', *Shakespeare Quarterly* 39 (1988): 401–17.

9. Here I use the otherwise dated *King Lear* in Peter Alexander's edition, because with the exception of 'change places and' (line 154) – not in the Folio – and occasional spellings, the texts in the Quarto and the Folio are virtually the same (even though the Folio has 'great vices' (line 164)).

10. Susan Wells, *The Dialectics of Representation* (Baltimore: Johns Hopkins UP, 1985), pp. 19, 36.

11. Mullaney, *The Place of the Stage*, pp. 21, 49.

12. Kenneth Burke, *The Philosophy of Literary Form: Studies in Symbolic Action* (Berkeley: Univ. of California Press, 1973), p. 26.

13. Frank Lentricchia, *Criticism and Social Change* (Chicago: Univ. of Chicago Press, 1985), p. 155.

14. Catherine Gallagher, *The Industrial Reformation of English Fiction: Social Discourse and Narrative Form, 1832–1867* (Chicago: Univ. of Chicago Press, 1985), p. 217.

15. Jacques Derrida, 'Sending: On Representation', *Social Research* 49 (1982), p. 316. For a more extended discussion of the theory and the sociology of representation, see my 'Text, Author-Function, and Appropriation in Modern Narrative: Toward a Sociology of Representation', *Critical Inquiry* 14 (1988) 431–47.

16. See Jean E. Howard and Mario F. O'Connor, eds, *Shakespeare Reproduced: The Text in History and Ideology* (London: Methuen, 1987).

17. David Wiles, *Shakespeare's Clown: Actor and Text in the Elizabethan Playhouse* (Cambridge: Cambridge UP, 1987), pp. 35–40.

18. Keir Elam, *The Semiotics of Theatre and Drama* (London: Methuen, 1980), p. 209.

19. The recent emphasis on performance criticism provides a welcome corrective to the lingering preoccupation with the written text. See, for example, Richard Hornby, *Script into Performance: A Structuralist Approach* (New York: Paragon, 1987); Richard Schnechner, *Performance Theory*, rev. edn (London: Routledge, 1988); Harry Berger, Jr., *Imaginary Audition: Shakespeare on Stage and Page* (Berkeley: Univ. of California Press, 1989); Marvin Carlson, *Places of Performance: The Semiotics of Theatre Architecture* (Ithaca: Cornell UP, 1989); Marvin Thompson and Ruth Thompson, eds, *Shakespeare and the Sense of Performance: Essays in the Tradition of Performance Criticism in Honor of Bernard Beckerman* (London: Associated UP, 1989); W.B. Worthen, 'Deeper Meanings and Theatrical Technique: The Rhetoric of Performance Criticism', *Shakespeare Quarterly* 40 (1989): 441–55.

20. Jacques Derrida, *Of Grammatology*, trans. Gayatri Chakravorty Spivak (Baltimore: Johns Hopkins UP, 1976), p. 312.

21. William Shakespeare, *Hamlet*, ed. Harold Jenkins (London: Methuen, 1982).

22. S.L. Bethell, *Shakespeare and the Popular Dramatic Tradition* (London: King, 1944).

23. A.P. Rossiter, *Angel with Horns and Other Shakespeare Lectures*, ed. Graham Storey (London: Longmans, 1961), p. 52.

24. Malcolm Evans, *Signifying Nothing: Truth's True Contents in Shakespeare's Text* (Athens: Univ. of Georgia Press, 1986), p. 133.

25. Jean-Christophe Agnew, *Worlds Apart: The Market and the Theater in Anglo-American Thought, 1550–1750* (Cambridge: Cambridge UP, 1986), p. 60; see also Douglas Bruster, 'Horns of Plenty: Drama and the Market in the Age of Shakespeare', diss. Harvard University, 1990.

26. This text is part of the introduction to a book-length study of authority and representation in the Elizabethan theatre and is indebted to an earlier version in German, published under the title *Shakespeare und die Macht der Mimesis* (Berlin: Aufbau, 1988).

11

'What Ish My Nation?': Shakespeare and National Identities

Graham Holderness

Offhand I can't remember a day when it seemed so marvellous or mad to be English. Suddenly the chronic inconvenience of London's transport strike and the continuing horrors of the mining dispute were put into the merciful perspective of history.

It began in Westminster Abbey where I sat close to the Queen Mother and watched her fight back tears and surrender to smiles with a packed congregation as the funniest hours of her reign were celebrated in the familiar words and music of Sir Noel Coward.

And it ended here at Stratford, with a young, brave and poetic Henry bridging the centuries between by reminding us of the unlikely spirit which won Agincourt. Nothing much seemed so very different ...

What links the vision of young Mr Kenneth Branagh, making his Royal Shakespeare debut as a raw, stocky warrior, with Coward's latterday musings, is the patriotic poet which lurked beneath their different facades ...

To hear Mr Branagh wonder incredulously at the valour of his ragtag-and-bobtail troops was to hear echoes of Derek Jacobi reading the moving war diaries of Coward at the unveiling of his memorial stone.

And when Branagh squats among his men, blackened with the efforts of the war, and urges them once more into the breach – well, – we had heard that sentiment back in the Abbey when Penelope Keith set the sea of hankerchiefs dabbing at moist eyes ...

I won't press the coincidence. Suffice to say that neither the service at the Abbey nor Adrian Noble's spare, bare production at Stratford were mere tub-thumping exercises in mindless nationalism.

There was pain, irony, wit and humanity in both. As Ian McDairmid's conversational chorus informs us: Henry had a kingdom for a stage. Which of course was like Coward turning his stage into a kingdom. Both, in their way make a little thing like a transport shutdown seem irrelevant. All this from old masters and new blood! Between Harry's Harfleur spirit and Coward's London Pride, it did not, after all, seem

improbable that there are still good reasons to be in England now that
April's almost here.

Jack Tinker, *Daily Mail*, 29 March 1984[1]

The distinction here between 'patriotism' (of the handkerchief dabbing
type) and 'nationalism' (of the tub-thumping variety) is a reasonable
starting-point for the following explorations of British patriots and national
identities, as they appear mediated through the cultural reproduction of
Shakespearean drama, and in particular through Kenneth Branagh's widely
celebrated film adaptation of *Henry V*, itself based on the 1984 Royal
Shakespeare Company stage production eulogized in Jack Tinker's
review.[2] To have a forceful and vigorous ideology of nationalism, you have
to have a forceful and vigorous nation to enact and substantiate it. If the
'nation' in question happens, like Britain, to be an eclipsed world power
– no longer a great imperial aggressor, no longer a significant colonial
leader, no longer a dominant industrial or economic force – then what basis
remains for a particular, quantifiable 'national' consciousness? If the
political and economic character of the 'nation' owes more to its
participation in larger political and economic units – the EEC, NATO,
American foreign policy, the multinational capitalist economy, the International Monetary Fund – then what sense does it make to continue talking
about a specific, isolable 'national' identity?

All that seems left to the disappointed or reformed British nationalist is
an emotion of 'patriotism', which can evidently be distinguished from the
politics of nationalism, and is capable of surviving such losses and
transformations as the demise of Empire and the descent from world
eminence relatively undamaged and unscathed. Patriotism is associated
with 'poetry', with emotion, with the heart, with tears; 'nationalism' with
'mindless' aggression, with 'tub-thumping' jingoistic assertiveness. In a
review of the subsequent film version of *Henry V*, Tom Hutchinson in the
Mail on Sunday later proposed the same distinction: 'the film ... touches
the heart of emotion rather than the instinct for patriotism'.[3] But in the
earlier review of the stage production, patriotism is indissolubly linked
with the past. The plangency of patriotic feeling here derives from what
Tom Nairn calls 'the glamour of backwardness': a nostalgia, a craving,
unappeasable hunger for that which is irretrievably lost. Yet that loss may
be regarded also as neither complete nor inconsolable, since the utterances
of a 'patriotic poet' such as William Shakespeare (or Noel Coward) can
transcend the absence and negation of history, and suffuse the soul with –
not exactly a new fulfilment, but at least a new longing, a new mixing of
memory and desire. Militaristic violence, inseparable from the historical
actuality of nationalism, is strangely appeased in this flood of remembrance,[4] strangely pacified by 'the merciful perspective of history'. The

British patriot, now no longer a nationalist, looks back regretfully, with resigned sadness, to his 'finest hour' in 1940, or the 'unlikely' victory of his ancestors at Agincourt; but, as reawakened memories, these scenes of historical violence, recollected in tranquillity, acquire a power to comfort and console.

The patriotic emotion is anchored in the past. Inspired by the 'valour', 'gallantry' and 'courage' displayed by the manly deeds of a warrior race, and immortalized in the words of the 'old masters' (represented here by the in this context unfortunately named 'Shake-spear' and 'Coward'), patriotism paradoxically expresses itself in gestures of weakness, in a 'surrender' to tears. The binary polarization of gender implicit in this construction is evident in the femininity shared by those cast, respectively, as tear-jerker and tear-jerked (Penelope Keith and the Queen Mother); and the contradictory quality of the patriotic emotion itself manifested in the male observer's luxurious relishing of a weakness discovered in the contemplation of strength – like D.H. Lawrence, the writer here enjoys feeling his 'manhood cast / Down in the flood of remembrance' as he 'weeps like a child for the past'.[5]

The patriotic emotion is anchored in the past, and besieged, embattled in the present. The England that surrounds Jack Tinker gives him no cause for patriotic celebration: it is rather a scene of bitter social conflict and class-antagonism, an England of transport and coalfield strikes. The English patriot doesn't see his emotional conviction rooted in the actuality of the nation that surrounds him, which seems systematically to negate his ideal national image. The patriotic emotion searches past and future for a habitable space, nostalgically embracing the glamour of backwardness, and optimistically extrapolating a projected landscape of hope. Elsewhere in the review Tinker quotes some lines from Noel Coward's *Cavalcade*, which exactly encapsulate that contradictory emotion:

> Let's drink to the spirit of gallantry and courage that made a strange Heaven out of unbelievable Hell, and let's drink to the Hope, that one day this country of ours, which we love so much, will find dignity and greatness and peace again.

The authentic accent of what might anachronistically be described as a 'postmodern' patriotism can in fact be located in what we think of as the very heart of the traditional discourse of British nationalism: it is even there in that notorious speech attributed to John of Gaunt in Shakespeare's *Richard II*, which in turn provided subsequent ages with a basic vocabulary of patriotic rhetoric.

> This royal throne of kings, this sceptred isle
> This earth of majesty, this seat of Mars,

This other Eden, demi-paradise,
This fortress built by Nature for herself
Against infection and the hand of war,
This happy breed of men, this little world,
This precious stone set in a silver sea
Which serves it in the office of a wall
Or as a moat defensive to a house
Against the envy of less happier lands,
This blessed plot, this earth, this realm, this England ...

(Richard II, II.i.40–50)

It is natural to think of this fictionalized John of Gaunt as a great supporter of monarchical prerogative and royal power: certainly outside the play his famous patriotic speech has invariably been employed to endorse absolute authority, to support the autocratic will of many subsequent British kings and governments. Within the play of course this speech actually functions as a diatribe of criticism against the ruling monarch: Gaunt is not even depicting the England of the present, but expressing a nostalgic regret for an England which has long since vanished into the historical past. It is precisely because the England he sees before him – Richard's England – falls so far short of his idealized vision of what he believes England once was, that his poetic vision of national glory is so brightly and vividly imagined.

The realm of England is here defined largely in terms of its monarchy, its history distinguished by the quality of its kings: but the monarchs Gaunt idealizes are not like Richard. They are the warlike, crusading, feudal kings of the early Middle Ages: so Gaunt's speech is after all no panegyric of royal absolutism, but a lament for the passing of a feudal kingdom in which king and nobility were united by a natural balance of forces into a united 'happy breed of men'. Gaunt's speech is not merely an appeal for strong leadership in the king, and it is certainly not a defence of the Renaissance doctrine of divine right and absolute royal authority. On the contrary, he imagines royal authority as inseparable from the power of the nobility; the golden age he longs for and regrets is that of a feudalism held together by the authority of a strong king *and* by the power of a strong aristocracy. Gaunt's attack on Richard's style of government concentrates on the fact that Richard has replaced the feudal bonds of 'fealty' – the system of reciprocal obligations which bind lord and subject in a feudal polity – with economic contracts:

England, bound in with the triumphant sea ...
... is now bound in with shame,
With inky blots and rotten parchment bonds

(II.i.63–4)

Richard is now a mere 'landlord' of England, rather than a king; he has sought to dispense with the loyal co-operation of the nobility, and to rule with the assistance of an upstart bureaucracy of 'favourites'. Determined to shake off the influence of the barons, he has introduced radical economic policies to raise revenue without reliance on the great landholders. The unacceptability of Richard's kingship consists, in Gaunt's eyes, in his modernizing programme of de-feudalization, and his consequent slighting of the traditional aristocracy. It is ironic that so many subsequent appeals to English patriotism have been mounted on the basis of this elegant and barbaric statement of baronial self-interest, this celebration of a class that has scarcely earned the unqualified admiration of even the most conservative of thinkers. But as we shall see, this hypostatization of a sectional class-interest as the ideology of a 'nation' is a symptomatic element in the history of British patriotism.

When the patriotic rhetoric of this speech is imitated, Gaunt's investment in the glamour of backwardness is often incorporated along with the imperious vigour of his nationalistic vision. Some years ago the Department of the Environment produced a television advertisement as part of an anti-litter campaign. A succession of visual images depicted urban squalor, industrial detritus and general untidiness – a river sweating oil and tar; empty streets blowing with waste paper like tumbleweed in a Western ghost-town; a cat snarling in a filthy gutter outside the idly flapping doors of a pub. The images were accompanied by those famous and familiar Shakespearean lines, spoken in voice-over commentary. Lines we are accustomed to hear uttered with a hush of reverence and breathless adoration, and with a musical effect akin to the sound of the last post being played at sunset across some colonial parade-ground in the Far East, were here intoned harshly, with an accent of resentment, bitterness, and dissatisfaction. Gaunt's patriotic speech was made to operate as an aggrieved, harshly ironic commentary on the scenes of depressing untidiness. At some time, the voice implied, things have been different; Britain was once a proud (and tidy) nation; this royal throne of Kings has not always been so besmirched and soiled by – litter; there was a time when the seat of Mars was cleaned regularly, and when this other Eden was genuinely fit for human habitation.

A moment's consideration of the standards of civic hygiene prevalent in the 1590s would provoke some scepticism about this implicit claim. The advertisement however had little use for authentic historical difference, being concerned only to construct, through the language of Shakespeare, an ideal type of 'the English nation', against which image the shortcomings of the present might be measured. Its persuasive discourse was no simple reproof, admonishment, or rational appeal, but rather a paternalistic rebuke, a constituting of the untidy British subject as a violator of purity and innocence, guilty of profaning an idealized image of what the nation once was, and might be again. Think, intones the Shakespearean voice, think of the august and distinguished company of ancestral illuminati, ancient and modern, you are offending by your anti-social behaviour: those celebrated knights of the theatre like Sir Laurence Olivier and Sir John Gielgud, with whom such speeches are customarily associated: their great chivalric grandsires, that earlier generation of militaristic rather than histrionic knights, such as John of Gaunt; various kings and queens, ancient and modern, sometime rulers of 'this sceptred isle'; and above all their heir, the modern custodian of this precious stone, set in a silver sea – (Mrs) Thatcher, the national housekeeper Herself. Thus a text which was originally the expression of an inconsolable nostalgia for another time, is mobilized as an authoritative voice enjoining on us all an active commitment to the glamour of backwardness. The nostalgic lament for a vanished Elizabethan age takes us spiralling vertiginously down the intertextual labyrinths of quotation, with no terminus in sight, this side of Paradise, other than a fourth term of Tory government.

We began in Westminster Abbey, that focal point of traditional 'British' culture where the institutions of church, monarchy, and democratic constitution (in Philip Larkin's words) 'meet, blend and are robed as destinies'.[6] With imagined wing our swift scene now flies, via John of Gaunt's image of England as a 'precious stone set in a silver sea', to a margin, an edge, a border; to the south coast of Britain, and specifically to those white cliffs of Dover, over which, in Vera Lynn's wartime song, 'there will be bluebirds' – 'tomorrow, just you wait and see'. What more lyrical expression could there be of the patriotic hunger for an endlessly deferred fulfilment than that poignant expression of elegiac existentialism which, like John of Gaunt's speech, and Noel Coward's *Cavalcade*, attaches its emotion to the past and future as a way of confronting the absence and pain of the present? The iconic image that goes with the song is of course the famous white cliffs themselves, that long chalk escarpment which offers to the envy of less happier lands so characteristically 'English' a seascape.

'Wherefore to Dover?' my reader might well enquire, echoing the accumulating incredulities of Regan and Cornwall in *King Lear*: 'Wherefore to *Dover*?'. The seaport of Dover, those famous white cliffs, and more generally the stretch of coastline from Southampton to the Thames estuary, occupy a peculiar and privileged place in the iconography and mythology of British nationalism. My initial reference to Vera Lynn invokes the Second World War, and specifically the period 1940–44 when France was under German occupation, and Britain in constant fear of an invasion. That 'rump' of England then felt (not for the first time) the vulnerability of exposure to another land-mass, the threatening point of France that pokes aggressively towards southern Britain, intimately close in space (narrow enough to swim across) yet always mistrusted, perpetually perceived as alien, frequently feared. Of course in a war of aerial transport, long-range heavy bombers, guided missiles, that part of England was (though subject to shelling from the French coast) in many ways no more vulnerable than any other, its borders capable of being breached at any point. But it is those cliffs of the south coast that provide us with our most characteristic national image of vulnerability, exposure, openness to the peril of foreign invasion.

The mythological status of the white cliffs of Dover is far more ancient than 1940. In those legendary and mythological narratives that preceded the advent of modern historiography, Dover was actually what the anthropologist Malinowski called a 'spot of origins', a particular geographical location regarded by tradition as the source of a nation's genesis. Anthropologists have identified in the proliferation of such narratives a structural form which they term the 'myth of origin', a narrative which purports to explain the process of a nation's appearance in history. Medieval historians traced the ancestry of their various national populations and monarchies to the dispersal of the Trojan princes after the fall of Troy: Geoffrey of Monmouth claimed that the English were descended from Brutus, allegedly a descendant of Aeneas. In Holinshed there is a narrative describing the conquest of what was to become Britain by Brutus, whose companion Corineus succeeded in overthrowing the giant Gogmagog, the island's original inhabitant – 'by reason whereof the place was named long after, *The Fall or leape of Gogmagog*, but afterwards it was called *The Fall of Dover*'.[7] As John Turner has shown, such pseudo-historical narratives were retold in the Renaissance as morality fables, calculated to guide political conduct; but they were also retold as myths, designed to legitimize power: 'The black holes in time were to be occluded, the dangerous discontinuities of history papered over with myths that would confirm authority and marginalize the claims of political opposition'.[8] When James I in 1604 had himself proclaimed King of 'Great Britain', he was deliberately reintroducing an antiquarian geographical term in order to establish 'one single rule' over England and Scotland. The name itself was falsely derived from Brutus, and in 1605 James was celebrated in the Lord Mayor's show as the second Brutus who, in fulfilment of Merlin's ancient prophecy, would 'reunite what the original Brutus had put asunder'.[9]

The narratives of this 'mythical charter' enact a sequence of invasion, conquest, colonization and fragmenting. Dover is the point of entry, the aperture through which a new force of domination can enter the territory, settle it, and then – in a tragic political error – part it asunder. Reading through the political to the sexual, Britain is the female body, invaded by the colonizing male; the appropriate feminine resistance is overthrown, and the country planted with fertile seed. The inevitable result of this process is however not unity, but parturition, splitting, division; not the formation of a single unified whole, but the multiplying of centrifugal energies. The myth imagines national origin as a cyclical process of invasion, unification, plantation, and division.

Precisely because in this myth Dover is the source of national identity, it is also the weakest point of the territory's physical defences. What one male can do to a female body, what one conqueror can do to a territory, another male, another conqueror, can repeat; and in every repetition the action is (in an important sense) identical. The fundamentally unitary nature of conquest/intercourse cuts sharply across powerful taboos based on binary oppositions of difference (legitimate/illegitimate, married/ unmarried, pure/contaminated, good/evil); and thereby forms the basis of that male sexual jealousy which in turn butts on to xenophobic nationalism: that point where the linked elements of 'father' and 'fatherland' in the word 'patriotism' meet. Along the south coast England presents her white, chaste purity to the potential invader as a defensive repellent, but also as a temptation. 'Succeed where Napoleon failed' urges an advertisement for the local South-East England tourist industry, the words emblazoned across an aerial photograph of the familiar iconic escarpment: 'spend a day in White Cliffs country'. The point where the nation's identity begins is also the point where it could most easily be violated or re-conquered.[10]

A key scene of Shakespeare's *Henry V* (Act II, scene ii) is set on that coastline, historically at Southampton (though usefully, for my purposes, the Folio text of the play misprints Southampton as 'Dover'). Henry and his nobles have here reached the 'extreme verge' of their territorial confine, a point of no return. Everything has been staked on the success of the French adventure; at the end of the scene Henry affirms, rhetorically but accurately, that his authority as monarch depends on victory: 'No King of England, if not King of France'. At this margin of the kingdom, which has the perilous quality of all territorial borders, the riskiest, most dangerous aspect of the whole enterprise – more subversive than the uneven odds at Agincourt – is encountered: internal dissension, mutiny within the ranks, self-betrayal. The periphery of England, that no-man's-land between England and France, marked by the sharp dividing line of the white cliffs, sanctified by the legendary myth of origins, is the point chosen for the enactment of a particular ritual: the cleansing of the English body politic by a sacrificial execution.

In the play-text Exeter defines the treachery of the conspirators simply as a hired murder, a contract killing undertaken for a French purse. On discovery, however, one of them, the Earl of Cambridge, hints at an ulterior motive:

> For me, the gold of France did not seduce,
> Although I did admit it as a motive
> The sooner to effect what I intended.

(II.ii.151–3)

In fact of course the three men arraigned here historically represented the cause of the deposed Richard II; the Earl of Cambridge's ulterior motive was that of re-establishing the legitimate dynasty toppled by the Lancastrians' usurpation. Ultimately they succeeded in forming the Yorkist power in the Wars of the Roses, in murdering Henry's son and in putting three kings on the English throne. The narrowing-down of this complex constitutional problem to a simple focus on the question of political loyalty is a characteristic achievement of Henry's style of government, and of course a familiar mechanism of ideological coercion in times of war. Political dissent becomes treachery: internal difference is forced to collapse under the moral and ideological pressures of international conflict.[11]

Kenneth Branagh placed particular emphasis on his decision to reinstate sections of the play-text omitted from Laurence Olivier's film version, and in particular the whole of Act II, scene ii:

> I decided on including some significant scenes that Olivier's film, for obvious reasons, had left out: in particular, the conspirators' scene where Henry stage-manages a public cashiering of the bosom friends who have been revealed as traitors. The violence and extremism of Henry's behaviour and its effect on a volatile war cabinet were elements that the Olivier version was not likely to spotlight.[12]

The general line of comparison here is that Olivier's film treatment was severely constrained by its wartime context of production: as a patriotic celebration of Britain's military strength and resolve, sponsored by the Ministry of Information, indissolubly linked both psychologically and strategically with the projected (and of course successful) Allied invasion of occupied France, the film was unlikely to place any emphasis on internal treachery, or to foreground qualities in Henry's character and behaviour that might be read as unpleasantly 'violent' or 'extreme'.

Both film versions establish this scene by adapting the device of Shakespeare's Chorus. In the Olivier version, a painting of the white cliffs of Southampton/Dover frames an unmistakably theatrical set, the prow of a stage ship where Henry and his nobles receive the sacrament before embarking. The overtly theatrical quality of the scene relates it closely to the reconstructed Elizabethan stage on which all the earlier scenes have been played. In the Branagh version Derek Jacobi as Chorus appears on a cliff-top (white, of course) from which he delivers the prologue to Act II. The sequence of directions reads:[13]

> *The Chorus is standing on a grassy cliff edge, looking out to sea. He turns to look at the camera.*
>
> CHORUS
> The French, advised by good intelligence
> Of this most 'dreadful' preparation ...
>
> *He turns to look towards the cliff top and we cut closer to the traitors who have now appeared, passing through frame as their names are mentioned.*
>
> CHORUS
> One, Richard Earl of Cambridge ...
>
> *As he walks away along the cliff edge, wrapping his scarf around him against the cold sea air, beyond him we see the dramatic white cliffs of the English coastline.*

Once the dramatic action is resumed, the Chorus disappears (though in the original theatrical production he frequently remained on stage), and the 'traitor scene' is established firmly in a naturalistic 'hostelry' (p. 36). The action is also played naturalistically, with a consistent emphasis on individual emotion. The key issue here is personal rather than political; the key emphasis falls on the shocking treachery of Henry's friends, particularly his 'bed-fellow' the Earl of Cambridge. At one point Henry throws Cambridge over a table with an almost sexual intensity, violently enacting the pain of personal betrayal (s.d. p. 40, illustration p. 41). The conspirators confess only their guilt: Cambridge's lines about an alternative motive are cut.

The main interest of the scene as presented here consists in a dramatization of the psychological stresses and strains of such a critical situation, as experienced in Henry's character. The dominant device of close-up is used here, as throughout the film, to register the psychological costs of authority. Branagh's intention may have been to foreground the violence and extremism of Henry's behaviour: but the naturalistic medium ensures that the nature of the spectator's engagement with the action is one of individual identification. Branagh's use, in the above quotation, of theatrical metaphors – 'stage-manages', 'spotlight' – actually draws attention to the *anti-theatrical* medium of filmic naturalism, in which very little space is left for the spectator to reflect on the nature of the dramatic medium itself. No one could gather from this scene, any more than from Olivier's version of the same scene, that there is implicit in the dramatic text a subtext related to the critical question of legitimacy. Branagh has conspired with the character of Henry himself to obliterate the play's momentary exposure of a stress-point in the unity of the commonwealth. In this way the possibility of political dissent can be completely occluded, both within and through the text, since all political opposition is converted on this ideological terrain to civil treachery and personal betrayal.

The key difference between the two film versions seems to me to reside in their respective adaptations of Shakespeare's Chorus. I have argued elsewhere[14] that Olivier's adaptation of the Chorus, and his initial setting of the production-text within a reconstructed Elizabethan theatre, put into circulation some of the 'radical and subversive potentiality of Shakespeare's play ... to foreground the artificiality of its dramatic devices'. Branagh's adaptation of the Chorus is equally inventive and in many ways effective. The device of beginning with the Chorus in an empty film studio, and opening set doors on to the dramatic action, is an ingenious updating of Olivier's mock Globe theatre. Though the Chorus is sometimes shown to be involved in the action (e.g. at the siege of Harfleur), he more characteristically appears as an alienation-effect, emerging surprisingly from behind a tree after the execution of Bardolph, or appearing to block out the final scene of diplomatic reconciliation in the French court, where he delivers that sharply undercutting prophecy which calls into question Henry's political achievement. But the radical departure from Olivier's use of this device rests in the fact that although the Chorus becomes involved in the action, the action never strays on to the territory of the Chorus. At one point in the original Royal Shakespeare Company stage production, Henry and the Chorus, in a brilliant *coup de théâtre*, almost bumped into one another, miming a surprised double-take of near-recognition: with a shock of delight we saw the fictional world of the dramatic action suddenly enter the fictionalizing activity of the Chorus. But in the film the naturalism of the action itself is never compromised in this way, despite the self-reflexive interventions of the intrusive choric witness.

It is abundantly clear, despite its radical features, in what relation Olivier's film stood to the nationalistic ideology of its time. But where does the Branagh film stand in relation to contemporary patriotic and nationalist ideologies? The original (1984) stage production, directed by Adrian Noble, and in which Branagh played the king, became known as the 'post-Falklands' *Henry V.* That suggests of course a prevailing mood of revulsion against war, against imperialistic shows of strength, against militaristic patriotism. The film can easily be read in line with this view: it was 'made for a generation with the Indo-China war and the Falklands behind it and is wary of calls to arms', according to Philip French.[15] Branagh has 'stripped the veneer of jingoism from the play and shown war in its true horror';[16] the film 'emphasises the horror and futility of battle'.[17]

But the term 'post-Falklands' may not be quite as simple as that. 'Post' (as in 'postmodernism') does not always translate easily as 'anti' or 'counter': and it could well be that along with the obvious political advantages accruing to the power victorious in a military conflict ('no Prime Minister of Britain, if not Empress of South Georgia'), the Falklands war bequeathed to British culture a decidedly ambiguous interest in war, not entirely unconnected with the characteristic emotions of patriotism. Certainly many of the post-Falklands cultural productions, such as Charles Wood's play *Tumbledown*,[18] betray a fascination with the experience of combat, with soldierly camaraderie, with the anguish of extreme suffering, with the psychological stresses of military leadership. Branagh's approach to the character of *Henry V*[19] was certainly to some degree founded on exactly such a fascination with the moral and emotional complexities made available in the theatre of war. His notorious consultation of Prince Charles,[20] by way of research into the isolation of office and the loneliness of command, indicates a readiness to refer directly and to attend sympathetically to the contemporary experience of monarchical power. In the stage production he played the character of Henry so as to disclose those emotional complexities, to reveal weakness as well as strength, self-suppression as well as self-aggrandisement, personal loss as well as national victory. In that production the Brechtian device of the Chorus was able to offer a counterpoise to this open though ambivalent admiration for the heroic individual: in the relatively naturalistic medium of the film, and of course under Branagh's own direction, there is no such system of checks and balances to subvert the invitation to empathic identification with the psychology of power.

Again, if we compare the very different social roles of Olivier and Branagh, we would expect very different perspectives on the play to emerge. The one was almost a natural product of the English *ancien régime*, his manly shoulders practically designed for the touch of the regal sword; the other aggressively constructs his own social persona as the tough and ambitious boy from working-class Belfast, determined to make it in the competitive market-place of the British theatre, as impatient with traditional institutions and fossilized establishments as the young shock-troops of the Thatcherite Stock Exchange. Now it is quite evident that Branagh's studious and systematic campaign of self-publicity, a strategy he obviously considers necessary to the fulfilment of his artistic ambitions, engages with the naturalistic medium of the film to provoke a structural parallelism between actor and hero.[21] This theme runs through all the reviews of the film. In deciding to make it, Branagh 'took on much the same odds as Henry did at Agincourt';[22] he 'has marshalled his forces as well as Henry led his army'.[23] 'Clearly he has some sort of affinity with the part of King Henry, but it doesn't seem an actorly affinity. Branagh too talks like a winner, and *Henry V* offers him better than any other play in the repertoire what might be called a yuppy dynamic, a mythology of success and self-definition rather than struggle'.[24]

A structural parallel is also perceived between the 'band of brothers' with whose help Henry achieves such extraordinary success, and the team of actors assembled by Branagh to make the film. Here in the reviews we encounter a series of metaphors which oddly and unselfconsciously link theatrical and militaristic vocabularies. 'Before shooting started, Branagh, like Henry, addressed his troops, his happy few, saying he wanted to make it a "company picture"'.[25] 'There is already something of the spirit of Henry's happy few in the cast and crew behind the camera ... every member of this film unit would go to the wall for Kenneth Branagh'.[26] 'The actors ... beamed like the happy few, ready to cry God for Kenneth'.[27]

Even odder is a tendency, quite in the spirit of that great tradition of public school patriotism which identified hand grenades with cricket balls, to express the relationship between theatre and heroic combat in metaphors of sport. Branagh himself dubbed his team 'the English all-stars', and several critics quipped along the same hearty and sporting lines: 'Branagh has fielded the first XV'.[28] 'This is how Englishmen play their football, so it seems a perfectly natural style in which to wage their wars'.[29] 'The English take Harfleur with the help of one horse and the first XI'.[30] Alexander Walker described Branagh as resembling 'a rugby forward who collects a bloody nose on the battlefield'.[31] We don't have to search for long among these testaments of reception to observe the repressed spirit of patriotic emotion returning in these attenuated forms.

Lastly there is the crucial relationship between this film as a cultural product and the kind of cultural pattern being forged by Branagh in his entrepreneurial interventions into the theatrical economy. He stands for a reaction against the established national institutions of theatre, such as the Royal Shakespeare Company, and for the development of a privatized theatrical economy, with organizations like his own Renaissance Theatre Company supported by private and corporate sponsorship. Those who also approve of such developments are filled with passions of admiration when they contemplate Branagh's audacity, energy, ambition, nerve, determination, etc., etc., right through the whole vocabulary of self-help and entrepreneurial capitalism. 'Branagh's blitzkrieg left the profession breathless at his nerve, his energy and his disregard for the obstacles'.[32] 'The cream of our classical talent and an army of extras, horses and stunt-men ... was in itself a saga of nail-biting crises surmounted by his calm certainty of what he wants to do, and unshakeable confidence in being able to do it'.[33] Emma Thompson, who is married to Branagh and who plays

Katharine in the film, embraces the same free-market vocabulary of risk and initiative, linked with the heroic language of war: 'These are the warrior years. These are the times to take the risks and do the big things we might not have the courage or energy for later on'.[34] Some critics offered a clearer-sighted analysis, whether prompted by enthusiasm or reservation: Richard Corliss in *The Times* called Branagh 'an icon of Thatcherite initiative', and Adam Mars-Jones in *The Independent* proposed an exact model for the cultural dialectics involved: 'The real chemistry is not between actor and part, but between the idea of the star as entrepreneur and the idea of the king as a self-made man'.[35] Clearly the myth enacted in this film is capable of signifying at this level, perhaps even more readily than at the level of national culture and politics.

I still of course haven't answered the question posed in my title: 'What ish my nation?', as the Irishman Macmorris belligerently inquires of the Welshman Fluellen in *Henry V* (III.ii.125). The answer will lie, I think, in a recognition that the emotion of patriotism and the politics of nationalism always involve, in any given historical situation, attachment to a particular sectional group, or class, or 'team', or army, which can be seen as bearing or leading the national destiny. At the same time in every historical situation there is a larger, more pluralistic and multiple, more complex and contradictory national collective which any sectarian nationalistic ideology must ignore, deny, or suppress. The most natural context for this operation to be successfully conducted is that of war: and we have seen in the dramatization of Henry V's policy how it can be done. We also know from our own experience of the Falklands war that it is possible for a government voted into power by 40 per cent of the population, and an army voted into power by nobody, to become self-appointed bearers of the entire nation's moral consciousness.

Raphael Samuel suggests that in contemporary Britain patriotic and nationalist feeling has sought and found a new home in the concept of the individual.[36]

Orwell wrote in 1940 that the 'privateness' of English life was one of the secrets of its strength ... his account anticipates some major themes in post-war British life, in particular the break-up, or erosion, of corporate loyalties, and the increasingly home-centred character of British social life. Patriotism, on the face of it, is one of the victims of those developments. Yet it may be that, denied expression in the public sphere, it is finding subliminal support in the semiotics of everyday life.

Individualism also has more solid material supports. The spread of home ownership, the sale of council houses, and the inflation of house prices has renewed the importance of family wealth and given a whole new terrain to Lockean notions of private property. The revival of small businesses – a feature of British as of other post-industrial societies – is multiplying the number of home-based or family-run concerns, while the dispersal of employment shows signs of reunifying work and home. Ideologically, public spirit is much less highly regarded than it was in the 1930s and 1940s. On both Left and Right of the political spectrum, self-expression is treated as the highest good, individual rights as sacrosanct, and the enlargement of personal freedom – or its protection – the ideal object of policy. Government, for its part, has built a whole platform out of freedom of choice, making, or attempting to make, health, insurance, pensions, and schooling matters of individual responsibility, and turning non-intervention into the highest of statesmanly tasks. As Margaret Thatcher put it in one of her best-remembered maxims: 'There is no society, only men and women and families.'

Branagh's film version of *Henry V* is very clearly a product of this new age of individualism, and it is in this respect that it differs so sharply from the play-text of the 1590s and the Olivier film of the 1940s. Denied a home in nationalist politics, the emotional resources of patriotism gravitate inexorably towards their true heartland in the individualism of the new entrepreneur, whose conquest of new economic and artistic worlds continually endorses the cultural and ideological power of the old.

Kenneth Branagh did not, however, become constituted as such an individual subject, this 'icon of Thatcherite initiative', without a complex process of cultural negotiation. The film also has another history, through which can be traced the possibilities of its being read otherwise. Branagh is himself, of course, as a product of working-class Protestant Belfast, a compatriot of Captain Macmorris, as well as a fellow-countryman of William Shakespeare, heir to the mantle of Lord Olivier, and a loyal subject of Prince Charles's mother. The question 'what ish my nation?' would at certain stages of his life, if now no longer, have been capable of provoking in him an existential anxiety parallel to the confused and exasperated anger voiced by Shakespeare's Captain Macmorris. When in 1970 his family, horrified by the growth of political violence in the province, moved permanently to England (where his father had already been working for some years) Branagh felt, according to the testimony of his 'autobiography', 'like a stranger ... in a very strange land'.[37] This initial condition of alienation was resolved only by the assumption of 'dual nationality' in a divided self: 'After a year or so I'd managed to become English at school and Irish at home' (p. 23). He lived, he acknowledges, a 'double life' (p. 24), perpetually conscious of a deep cultural difference masked by apparent assimilation and ethnic homogeneity.

Branagh's formative childhood experience was thus enacted on a highly significant marginal space of 'British' culture, close to another of those territorial borders on which the contradictions of a nationalist ideology

become acutely visible. Born a British citizen, within the borders of the
'United' Kingdom, Branagh inherited a particular Irish subculture, that of
a large working-class extended family on the edge of the Belfast docks. He
was also heir, however, to the questionable advantages of that 'British'
culture of self-improvement and meritocratic social mobility which took
him eventually to RADA, the RSC and Kensington Palace. These social
contradictions of divided culture and fragmented nationality can be read
immediately from the brash, ambitious, self-mocking, self-important,
painfully unstable discourse of Branagh's premature 'autobiography', a
project in itself designed to consolidate a coherent social identity out of a
fissured and contradictory social experience. They can also be read from
the film, which, despite its totalizing attempt to relocate the problems of
national identity and international conflict within the charismatic individual, occasionally uncovers and discloses surprising depths of cultural
anxiety.

This anxiety can be traced in a symptomatic moment of textual 'excess',
a point where the filmic narrative discloses an ideological 'stress-point' by
delivering an emotional affect which remains unexplained by the contingent dramatic circumstances. As the miraculous victory of Agincourt
becomes apparent, Captain Fluellen (played by Ian Holm) reminds Henry
of the heroic deeds of his ancestor Edward, 'the Black Prince of Wales'.
Fluellen offers a Celtic rereading of Anglo-Norman history, celebrating the
heroic deeds of Welsh men-at-arms at Crecy, and appropriating Edward
himself as an honorary Welshman. Branagh's screenplay interprets this
exchange as follows:[38]

FLUELLEN
... I do believe your Majesty takes no scorn to wear the leek upon Saint
Davy's day.

*The power of the Welshman's simple feeling is too much for the King who
speaks the following through tears which he cannot prevent. He is near
collapse.*

HENRY V
I wear it for a memorable honour;
For I am Welsh, you know, good countryman.

The King breaks down, and the two men hug each other.

Such cinematic surges of emotional intensity are of course ambiguous in
their effects, and can be read in many ways. Here there are readily available
psychological explanations: this is the bitter price of heroism and military
success; the post-orgasmic melancholy of the victor, satiated on violence;
or the human cost of successful rule. Branagh's Henry also sheds tears at

the hanging of Bardolph, the screenplay emphasizing the 'enormous cost' to the King of this necessary exercise of impartial justice (pp. 71–4). More generally, the film's capacity to reduce its participants and observers to tears is frequently cited as a measure of its authenticity: after the shooting of Agincourt, Branagh 'went home exhausted and somehow defeated, and for no good reason burst into tears';[39] and Prince Charles is reputed to have been similarly 'reduced to tears' at a special preview.[40] The demonstrative parading of open grief may at first sight appear subversive of the values of tough masculinity, the rigid suppression of emotion required for the serious business of warfare. But it should be clear from the sodden royal handkerchief with which we began, that these tears are closer to those rituals of mourning (such as the militaristic memorial service of 'Remembrance Day'), which are rather a liturgical collusion with the ideology of patriotic war than an emotional interrogation of its values.

The moment in the film of extreme emotional exchange between Fluellen and Henry is in fact quite different from these examples. Neither the film-text nor the screenplay can adequately explain its intensity, its excessive superabundance of significance. And that leaking out of embarrassingly public grief seems to me to locate a fault-line in the film's hegemony: for the sudden burst of reciprocal grief is linked by the dialogue with questions of national identity. As we observe the dramatization of an English king and a Welsh soldier plangently embracing in a symbolic ritual of national unity, we also catch a momentary glimpse of an Irishman and a Scot weeping over the historical devastations of British imperialism. Can we not then read through the film's imagery of post-Agincourt 'carnage and wreckage' (p. 113) the smoking ruins of that battlefield that is Ulster? And can we not catch in those verminous men and women 'pillaging the bodies of the dead' (p. 113) a fleeting glimpse of the young Kenneth Branagh, joining in the looting of a bombed-out Belfast supermarket?[41] The iconic image of the dead boy carried by Henry throughout this sequence, in turn carries in this respect richer and deeper psychological reverberations than I have space to explore.

One of the most interesting details of Branagh's *Henry V* does not appear in the film (and is not therefore in the published screenplay, which is a record of the final edited version, not the screenplay from which the film was developed). When shooting the scene where the Chorus strides the white cliffs of Southampton/Dover (filmed in fact at Beachy Head, which is of course midway between the two), Branagh tried to use the same location for another sequence:[42]

> We tried unsuccessfully to get another shot which I had felt at one stage could open the movie – a pan across the French coastline eventually taking in the white cliffs of England and ending on the contemplative face

of yours truly. The whole thing was accompanied by the hollow crown soliloquy from *Richard II*, which seemed to express something of the message of our *Henry V.* The shot did not work, and I decided to drop the Richard anyway. It simply didn't belong.

Who, in that strangely elliptical and impersonal phrase, is 'yours truly'? The actor or the role? English Harry or Irish Ken? The doubling of identities is paralleled by a corresponding spatial ambivalence: that camera-pan simultaneously offers a depiction of the point-of-view of King Henry, firmly established on his own territory, contemplatively surveying the enemy coast; and delivers an external view of the 'English' coast as it would be seen by an enemy, an invader – or an immigrant. Prompted by the echoing words of Richard II, a king ousted from his own territory by the usurper whose heir now literally occupies its commanding heights, and by the semiotic value latent in Branagh's 'dual identity', the spectator presented with this filmic moment would have had ample opportunity to appreciate the position of an internal *émigré*, whose status within the nation is in some way questionable; the paradox of belonging and alienation, the cultural anxiety of the internal *émigré* about to establish his own territorial rights by violently overthrowing another's.

What would this sequence, if included in the film, have signified; and what are the underlying reasons for its exclusion? The speech in question from *Richard II* (III.ii. 144–77) is a penetrating interrogation of the realities of power. The state is about to fall into the hands of Bolingbroke, Henry V's father, and Richard's imagination is released to a vivid realization of the difference between effective power and mere legitimacy. Richard has no property in the realm to bequeath to his heirs, only the experience of royal tragedy – 'sad stories of the deaths of kings'. The imagery of hollowness runs throughout the speech, taking in the hollow grave, the hollow crown, and the 'wall of flesh' encircling the mortal life, which seems impregnable as a castle, yet contains only a vulnerable, isolated life. If the king's body is mortal, then sovereignty is a mere pageant, a stage performance, and the real sovereign of the royal court is death, the 'antic' who parodies and mocks all seriousness. The awareness of royal tragedy expressed here is nothing less than the Divine Right of Kings inverted, hollowed out to disclose the true nature of power.[43]

In the projected additional scene of Branagh's film, Richard's challenging interrogation is placed exactly on the sharp white line of a territorial border. Located there, the insistent questioning of the speech goes beyond an expression of melancholy resignation at the emptiness of power (the kind of thing calculated to set Prince Charles clutching for the royal nose-rag), to an earnest meditation on the nature of the peripheral delineations by which such spaces of hollowness are bound and contained. If we read that border as simultaneously the south coast of England, and the border between Ulster and Eire, we can grasp simultaneously the paradox of definition and arbitrariness, of clear geographical division and constructed geopolitical disposition, which belongs to all territorial borders, especially those between an imperialist and a colonized nation. Travelling back to that mythical spot of origins, which is simultaneously a possible point of exit (Beachy Head is a favourite haunt of suicides), some of the fundamental questions of British national identity can at last be posed. Does a geographical boundary such as the English Channel prescribe mutual hostility and reciprocal violence between the neighbouring nations?

> the contending kingdoms
> Of France and England, whose very shores look pale
> With envy of each other's happiness,
> May cease their hatred
>
> (*Henry V*, V.ii.377–9)

The inclusion of that speech from *Richard II*, significantly poised on the edge of England, could have hollowed out an illuminating space between actor and character: a disclosure which could have expressed these cultural contradictions even more eloquently, if the film had found a means of including Shakespeare's reference to Essex, returning from Ireland, 'bringing Rebellion broached on his sword'. Meanwhile, as the film cameras whirred on the summit of Beachy Head, constructing a sequence destined to become a hollow absence in the film-text, far below and out to sea, other kinds of machinery were simultaneously hollowing out a link between 'the contending kingdoms', that 'Chunnel' which when completed will rob the white cliffs of much of their centuries-old symbolism. For once Britain is physically a part of Europe, the ideological stress on ancient national mythologies will be enormously intensified. The interesting combination, on the part of Britain's Tory government, of pro-European commitment and chauvinistic resistance to European union, testifies to the problems facing British national ideology. The government's insistence on the private funding of what is self-evidently a public construction project (leading to an endless series of financial crises), and the anxieties frequently expressed about what kinds of contamination may enter the realm once a major transport artery is plugged deep into its vitals (those who applaud the demolition of the Berlin Wall tend, when contemplating the Chunnel, towards extravagant fantasies of invasion by terrorists and rabid animals), indicate deep ideological ambivalences towards the destruction of a 'natural' boundary. Some residual reverence for the acculturated sanctity of the south coast even underlies reasonable conservationist anxieties about the fate of the white cliffs themselves;

focusing as they do in particular on a spot some distance from the site of the tunnel itself, but legitimated by its very name as a space of that England (of which, according to the words of another popular wartime song, there will always be one) to be conserved: Shakespeare Cliff, near Dover.

Notes

1. Reprinted in *London Theatre Record*, IV: 7 (1984), p. 270.

2. *Henry V*, directed by Kenneth Branagh, produced by Bruce Sharman (1989); based on a 1984 production of the Royal Shakespeare Company, directed by Adrian Noble. My description 'widely celebrated' can be measured in the press reviews quoted later in this paper; and see also the *Shakespeare on Film Newsletter*, 14:2, which cites in support of Robert F. Wilson's positive evaluation ('*Henry V*/Branagh's and Olivier's Choruses') a celebratory 'Chorus of critics' (pp. 1–2). Branagh received Academy Award nominations as best actor and best director.

3. Tom Hutchinson, *The Mail on Sunday*, 8 October 1989.

4. The phrase derives of course from D.H. Lawrence's poem 'Piano' (see note 5), but occurs in the stage directions of Branagh's *Henry V* screenplay: see K. Branagh, *Henry V by William Shakespeare: A Screen Adaptation* (London: Chatto & Windus, 1989), p. 32.

5. D.H. Lawrence, 'Piano', in K. Sagar, ed., *Selected Poems of D.H. Lawrence* (Harmondsworth: Penguin Books, 1972), p. 21.

6. Philip Larkin, 'Church Going', *The Less Deceived* (London: Faber & Faber, 1957).

7. Holinshed's *Chronicles*, I, p. 443.

8. J. Turner, '*King Lear*', in G. Holderness, N. Potter, and J. Turner, *Shakespeare: The Play of History* (London: Macmillan, 1988), p. 92. See also T. Hawkes, 'Lear's Map: A General Survey', *Deutsche Shakespeare-Gesellschaft West Jahrbuch* (1989), pp. 36–7.

9. Turner, in Holderness, Potter, and Turner (1988), p. 93.

10. Cf. Seamus Heaney's poem 'Act of Union', where a sexual relationship is linked metaphorically with the political connection of Britain and Ireland, colonizer and colonized: 'I grow older / Conceding your half-independent shore / Within whose borders now my legacy / Culminates inexorably'.

11. See K.P. Wentersdorf, 'The Conspiracy of Silence in *Henry V*', *Shakespeare Quarterly*, 27 (1976), and G. Holderness, '*Henry V*', in Holderness, Potter, and Turner (1988), pp. 70–72.

12. Branagh, *Henry V* (1989), p. 12.

13. Ibid., pp. 35–6.

14. See G. Holderness, 'Agincourt 1944: Readings in the Shakespeare Myth', *Literature and History*, 10:1 (1984), pp. 31–4; *Shakespeare's History* (Dublin: Gill & Macmillan, 1985), pp. 184–91; and Holderness, Potter, and Turner (1988), pp. 72–9.

15. P. French, in *The Observer*, 8 October 1989.

16. A. Mars-Jones, in *The Independent*, 5 October 1989.

17. C. Tookey, in *The Sunday Telegraph*, 8 October 1989.

18. Charles Wood, *Tumbledown* (Harmondsworth: Penguin Books, 1987).

19. Kenneth Branagh discusses his approach to the stage role of Henry V in Philip Brockbank, ed., *Players of Shakespeare* (Cambridge: Cambridge University Press, 1985), and in his own autobiography, *Beginning* (London: Chatto & Windus, 1989), pp. 137–9.

20. See Branagh, *Beginning*, pp. 141–4.

21. See Michael Quinn, 'Celebrity and the Semiotics of Acting', *New Theatre Quarterly*, VI:22 (1990).

22. P. Lewis, *Sunday Times*, 10 September 1989.

23. P. French, *Observer*, 8 October 1989.

24. A. Mars-Jones, *Independent*, 5 October 1989.

25. P. Lewis, *Sunday Telegraph*, 24–30 September 1989.

26. B. Bamigboye, *Daily Mail*, 18 November 1989.

27. P. Lewis, *Sunday Times*, 10 September 1989.

28. Ian Johnstone, *Sunday Times*, 8 October 1989.

29. A. Lane, *The Independent*, 30 September 1989.

30. A. Bilson, *Sunday Correspondent*, 8 October 1989.

31. A. Walker, in the *London Evening Standard*, 25 May 1989. Branagh himself ironically traced the roots of his career to a conjuncture of drama and sport: at school he was made captain of both rugby and football teams, 'I suspect for my innate sense of drama – I loved shouting theatrically butch encouragement to "my lads"' (Branagh, *Beginning*, p. 28).

32. P. Lewis, *Sunday Times*, 10 September 1989.

33. P. Lewis, *Sunday Telegraph*, 24–30 September 1989.

34. Quoted by P. Lewis, *Sunday Telegraph*, 24–30 September 1989.

35. R. Corliss, *The Times*, 13 November 1989, and A. Mars-Jones, *The Independent*, 5 October 1989.

36. Raphael Samuel, 'Introduction: Exciting to Be English', in Raphael Samuel, ed., *Patriotism: The Making and Unmaking of National Identity*, vol. 1, *History and Politics* (London: Routledge, 1989), pp. xli–xlii, xxxix–xl.

37. Branagh, *Beginning*, p. 22.

38. Branagh, *Henry V*, p. 111.

39. Quoted by P. Lewis, *Sunday Times*, 10 September 1989.

40. H. Davenport, *Daily Telegraph*, 5 October 1989.

41. See Branagh, *Beginning*, p. 20.

42. Ibid., p. 239.

43. See Holderness (1985), pp. 59–61.

12

Scolding Brides and Bridling Scolds:
Taming the Woman's Unruly Member

Lynda E. Boose

For feminist scholars, the irreplaceable value if not pleasure to be realized by an historicized confrontation with Shakespeare's *The Taming of the Shrew* lies in the unequivocality with which the play locates both women's abjected position in the social order of early modern England and the costs exacted for resistance. For romantic comedy to 'work' normatively in *Shrew*'s concluding scene and allow the audience the happy ending it demands, the cost is, simply put, the construction of a woman's speech that must unspeak its own resistance and reconstitute female subjectivity into the self-abnegating rhetoric of Kate's famous disquisition on obedience. The cost is Kate's self-deposition, where – in a performance not unlike Richard II's – she moves centrestage to dramatize her own similarly theatrical rendition of 'Mark, how I will undo myself'.

Apparently from the play's inception its sexual politics have inspired controversy. Within Shakespeare's own lifetime it elicited John Fletcher's sequel, *The Woman's Prize, or The Tamer Tam'd*, which features Petruchio marrying a second, untamable wife after his household tyranny has sent poor Kate to an early grave. As the title itself announces, Fletcher's play ends with Petruchio a reclaimed and newly lovable husband – 'a woman's prize' – and, needless to say, a prize who still has the last words of the drama. Yet Fletcher's response may in itself suggest the kind of discomfort that *Shrew* has characteristically provoked in men and why its many revisions since 1594 have repeatedly contrived ways of softening the edges, especially in the concluding scene, of the play's vision of male supremacy. Ironically enough, if *The Taming of the Shrew* presents a problem to male viewers, the problem lies in its representation of a male authority so successful that it nearly destabilizes the very discourse it so blatantly confirms. Witness George Bernard Shaw's distress:

> No man with any decency of feeling can sit it out in the company of a
> woman without being extremely ashamed of the lord-of-creation moral

implied in the wager and the speech put into the woman's own mouth.[1]

Yet the anxiety that provokes Shaw's reaction hardly compares with what the play's conclusion would, by that same logic, produce in women viewers. For Kate's final *pièce de non résistance* is constructed not as the speech of a discrete character speaking her role within the expressly marked-out boundaries of a play frame; it is a textual moment in which, in Althusserian terms, the play quite overtly 'interpellates', or hails, its women viewers into an imaginary relationship with the ideology of the discourse being played out onstage by their counterparts.[2] Having 'fetched hither' the emblematic pair of offstage wives who have declined to participate in this game of patriarchal legitimation, Kate shifts into an address targeted at some presumptive Everywoman. Within that address women viewers suddenly find themselves universal conscripts, trapped within the rhetorical co-options of a discourse that dissolves all difference between the 'I' and 'you' of Kate and her reluctant sisters. Kate vacates the space of subjectivity in

> I am ashamed that women are so simple
> To offer war where they should kneel for peace,
> Or seek for rule, supremacy and sway,
> When they are bound to serve, love and obey....
> Come, come, you froward and unable worms,
> My mind hath been as big as one of yours,
> My heart as great, my reason haply more,
> To bandy word for word and frown for frown.
> But now I see our lances are but straws,
> Our strength as weak, our weakness past compare,
> That seeming to be most which we indeed least are.
> Then vail your stomachs, for it is no boot,
> And place your hands below your husband's foot.
>
> $\qquad\qquad\qquad\qquad$ (V.ii.161–4, 169–77)[3]

In doing so, she rhetorically pushes everyone marked as 'woman' out of that space along with her. And it is perhaps precisely because women's relationships to this particular comedy are so ineluctably bound up in such a theatricalized appropriation of feminine choice that Shakespeare's play ultimately becomes a kind of primary text within which each woman reader of successive eras must renegotiate a (her) narrative.

Inevitably, it is from the site/sight of the subjected and thoroughly spectacularized woman that virtually all critiques of *The Taming of the Shrew* have felt compelled to begin. For when Kate literally prostrates herself in her final lines of the play and thus rearranges the sexual space onstage, she reconfigures the iconography of heterosexual relationship not merely for herself but for all of those 'froward and unable worms'

inscribed within her interpellating discourse. Not surprisingly, the dis-
comforts of such a position have produced an investment even greater in
female than in male viewers in reimagining an ending that will at once
liberate Kate from meaning what she says and simultaneously reconstruct
the social space into a vision of so-called 'mutuality' – an ending that will
satisfy the 'illusion of a potentially pleasureable, even subversive space for
Kate'.[4] Thus, the critical history of *Shrew* reflects a tradition in which such
revisionism has become a kind of orthodoxy. For albeit in response to a
play which itself depends upon the exaggerations of gender difference, the
desires of directors, players, audiences, and literary critics of both sexes
have been curiously appeased by a similar representation: whether for
reasons of wishing to save Kate from her abjection or Petruchio from the
embarrassment of having coerced it, almost everyone, it seems, wants this
play to emphasize 'Kate's and Petruchio's mutual sexual attraction,
affection, and satisfaction [and] deemphasize her coerced submission to
him'.[5] Ultimately, what is under covert recuperation and imagined as
tacitly at stake is the institution of heterosexual marriage.

To insist upon historicizing this play is to insist upon placing realities
from the historically literal alongside the reconstructive desires that have
been written onto and into the literary text. It is to insist upon invading
privileged literary fictions with the realities that defined the lives of
sixteenth-century 'shrews' – the real village Kates who underwrite
Shakespeare's character. Ultimately, it is to insist that a play called 'The
Taming of the Shrew' must be accountable for the history to which its title
alludes. However shrewish it may seem to assert an intertextuality that
binds the obscured records of a painful women's history into a comedy that
celebrates love and marriage, that history has paid for the right to speak
itself, whatever the resultant incongruities.

As dominant onstage as the ameliorative tradition of *Shrew* production
has been,[6] the impulse to rewrite the more oppressively patriarchal material
in this play serves the very ideologies about gender that it makes less
visible by making less offensive. To tamper with the literalness of Kate's
physical submission onstage deflects attention away from an equally literal
history in which both Kate and the staging of her body are embedded. As
it turns out, the play's most (in)famous theatrical moment owes far less to
Shakespeare's imagination than it does to a concrete analogue that Kate's
prostration seems to be staging. For whatever else may be going on in *The
Taming of the Shrew*'s finale, the scene dramatizes a now correctly ordered
version of the play's earlier negated, parodic marriage. It represents a
ritually corrected replay of both the offstage church ceremony that had
been turned into anti-ceremony by Petruchio's irreverent behaviour and the
bridal feast at which Kate was dis-placed and re-placed by the seemingly
virtuous Bianca, who, at the end of III.ii, was chosen to 'bride it' in her

wayward sister's stead. Finally, after Kate is allowed to return to Padua for Bianca's wedding, it is Kate who displaces Bianca as the virtuous and honoured bride. This displacement converts what was billed as Bianca's bridal feast into the missing communal celebration to honour the earlier marriage that Kate's staged submission here recuperates into communal norms. Neither the feast nor the postponed consummation may take place in this play until the hierarchical features of the marriage rite have thus been restoratively enacted.

The referential context for Kate's bodily prostration in V.ii is anchored by its placement inside a speech that incorporates verbatim the 'serve, love and obey' (1.164) of a bride's wedding vows. Not only do her words re-present those vows, however; her body reenacts them. For what transpires onstage turns out to be a virtual representation of the ceremony that women were required to perform in most pre-Reformation marriage services throughout Europe. In England this performance was in force as early as the mid fifteenth century and perhaps earlier; and it may well have continued in local practice even after Archbishop Cranmer had reformed the Book of Common Prayer in 1549 and excised just such ritual excesses.[7] Kate's prostration before her husband and the placing of her hand beneath his foot follow the ceremonial directions that accompany the Sarum (Salisbury) Manual, the York Manual, the Scottish Rathen Manual, and the French Martène (*Ordo IV*) for the response the bride was to produce when she received the wedding ring and her husband's all-important vow of endowment.

According to the Use of Sarum, after the bridegroom had given the vow, 'With this rynge I wedde the, and with this golde and siluer I honoure the, and with this gyft I dowe thee', the priest next 'asks the dower of the woman'. If 'land is given her in the dower', the bride 'prostrates herself at the feet of the bridegroom'. In one manuscript of the Sarum Rite, the bride is directed to 'kiss the right foot' of her spouse, which she is to do 'whether there is land in the doury or not'.[8] The York, Rathen, and Martène manuals, however, direct 'this courtesying to take place only when the bride has received land as her dower'. As Shakespeare's audience knows, Petruchio has indeed promised Baptista that he will settle on his wife an apparently substantial jointure of land. And while Kate offers to place her hands below her husband's foot rather than kiss it, the stage action seems clearly enough to allude to a ritual that probably had a number of national and local variants. Thus Giles Fletcher, Queen Elizabeth's ambassador to Russia, writes of a Russian wedding:

> the Bride commeth to the Bridegroome (standing at the end of the altar or table) and falleth downe at his feete, knocking her head upon his shooe, in token of her subjection and obedience. And the Bridegroom

again casteth the cappe of his gowne or upper garment over the Bride, in
token of his duetie to protect and cherish her.[9]

Within the multi-vocal ritual logic of Christian marriage discourse, the
moment in which the woman was raised up probably dramatized her
rebirth into a new identity, the only one in which she could legally
participate in property rights. Yet the representation of such a public
performance obviously exceeds the religious and social significances it
enacts. Giles Fletcher, for instance, reads the Russian ceremony through its
political meanings. In its political iconography the enactment confirms
hierarchy and male rule. And yet in its performance both in church and
onstage, the woman's prostration – which is dictated by the unvoiced
rubrics of the patriarchal script – is staged to seem as if it were an act of
spontaneous gratitude arising out of choice.

From the perspective of twentieth-century feminist resistance, it is
hardly possible to imagine this scene outside the context of feminine
shame. Yet is it necessarily ahistorical to presume the validity of such a
reading? Absent any surviving commentaries from sixteenth-century
women who performed these rituals, perhaps we can nonetheless indirectly
recover something about such women's reactions. In 1903 the Anglican
church historian J. Wickham Legg transcribed the French Roman Catholic
cleric J.B. Thiers's discussion of the ways that eighteenth-century French
women had come to restage this ceremony:

> the bride was accustomed to let the ring fall from her finger as soon as
> it was put on. Necessarily she would stoop to pick up the ring, or make
> some attempt at this, and so a reason would be given for her bending or
> courtesying at her husband's feet, and the appearance of worship paid to
> him would be got rid of.[10]

What seems at work in the women's behaviour is the same impulse that
motivates certain feminist *Shrew* criticism – the creation of explanatory
scenarios that will justify Kate's actions. Confronted by a ritual of self-
debasement, the women strive to construct another narrative that will
rationalize their stooping.

To locate the staging of *The Taming of the Shrew*'s final scene inside of
the pre-Reformation English marriage ceremony may provide the missing
historical analogue, but it hardly explains why Shakespeare chose to use
it. For the wedding ceremony that Shakespeare's text alludes to, while
almost certainly recognizable to an audience of the 1590s, was itself an
anachronistic form outlawed by the Act of Uniformity over forty years
earlier. Embedding the Kate and Petruchio marriage inside of a performance understood as prohibited inscribes the play's vision of male

dominance as anachronism; but the very act of inscription collocates the anachronistic paradigm with the romantically idealized one and thus also recuperates the vision into a golden-age lament for a world gone by – a world signified by a ceremony that publicly confirmed such shows of male dominance. On the other hand, through just that collocation, the play has situated the volatile social issue of the politics of marriage on top of the equally volatile contemporary political schism over the authority of liturgical form. By means of constructing so precarious and controversial a resolution, the play works ever so slightly to unsettle its own ending and mark the return to so extremely patriarchal a marriage as a formula inseparable from a perilously divisive politics.

Thus it seems appropriate to perceive both *Shrew* and the world that produced it as texts in which gender is foregrounded through the model of a layered social fabric, with crisis stacked upon social crisis. According to David Underdown, the sense of impending breakdown in the social order was never 'more widespread, or more intense, than in early modern England'; moreover, the breakdown was one that Underdown sees as having developed out of a 'period of strained gender relations' that 'lay at the heart of the "crisis of order".'[11] The particular impact of this crisis in gender speaks through records that document a sudden upsurge in witchcraft trials and other court accusations against women, the 'gendering' of various available forms of punishment, and the invention in these years of additional punishments specifically designated for women. As the forms of punishment and the assumptions about what officially constituted 'crime' became progressively polarized by gender, there emerged a corresponding significant increase in instances of crime defined as exclusively female: 'scolding', 'witchcraft', and 'whoring'. But what is striking is that the punishments meted out to women are much more frequently targeted at suppressing women's speech than they are at controlling their sexual transgressions. In terms of available court records that document the lives of the 'middling sort' in England's towns and larger villages, the chief social offences seem to have been 'scolding', 'brawling', and dominating one's husband. The veritable prototype of the female offender of this era seems to be, in fact, the woman marked out as a 'scold' or 'shrew'.

Sixteenth-century Scolds and Nineteenth-century Antiquarians

Much of what we can recover about the lives of sixteenth- and seventeenth-century English women and men we owe to the English antiquary societies that arose during the nineteenth century. Just past the midpoint of that century, on one side of the Atlantic Ocean one English-speaking nation moved inexorably towards a civil war over the proprietary ownership of slaves. On the other, more ancient and presumably more civilized, parent side of the ocean, in the calm of an autumn evening in 1858 at the home of a member of the Chester Archaeological Society in the County of Chester, Mr T.N. Brushfield, Medical Superintendent of the Cheshire Lunatic Asylum, presented a two-part paper, 'On Obsolete Punishments, With particular reference to those of Cheshire'.[12] His title betrays no sense that his real fascination throughout both parts of the paper is with devices that were used in bodily punishments meted out in sixteenth- and early seventeenth-century English villages and towns to women judged guilty of so egregiously violating the norms of community order and hierarchy as to have been labelled 'scolds' or 'shrews'. What becomes apparent from Brushfield's material is that being labelled a 'shrew' or 'scold' had very real consequences in the late sixteenth century – consequences much more immediate and extreme than the only one that overtly confronts Shakespeare's Kate, which is to play out the demeaning role of being a single woman in married culture and to have to 'dance barefoot on her [younger sister's] wedding day' and 'lead apes in hell' (II.i.33–4).

Among the 'obsolete punishments' of Brushfield's disquisition lie the real consequences. The instrument to which one part of his presentation is devoted is the 'cucking stool', a chair-like apparatus into which the offender was ordered strapped and then, to the jeers of the crowd, was dunked several times in water over her head – water that might be a local river but was equally likely to have been the local horsewash pond (Fig. 1). Although Brushfield is unaware of the point, gender-specific punishments for minor offences only became the rule in English towns and villages by the fifteenth century.[13] The cucking stool, which had apparently originated as a punishment for crimes most often linked with marketplace cheating on weights or measures, had been used until then as a punishment for men as well as women.

The cucking stool – which seems to have originated as a dung cart and in many places retained its association with excrement through such designs as the privy-stool model[14] (Fig. 2) – went by several different names and existed in a variety of models in several English counties. Often it seems to have been either mounted on a cart or affixed with wheels (Figs. 3, 4, and 5) in order that the occupant could be drawn through the streets and publicly displayed en route to her ducking. Indeed, in the first of the Padua scenes, the very real cultural consequences of being defined as a scold leak through the layers of fictive insulation. What the old pantaloon Gremio proposes – that instead of 'courting' Katherina a man should 'cart her rather' (I.i.55) – is a fate probably much like that which a Norfolk woman was ordered to undergo: 'to ryde on a cart, with a paper in her hand, and [be] tynkled with a bason, and so at one o'clock be led

Fig. 1: Brushfield, p. 203.

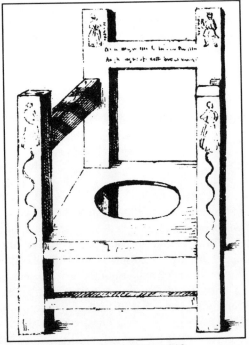

Fig. 2: Brushfield, p. 218.

Fig. 3: Brushfield, p. 233.

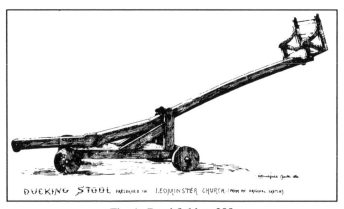

Fig. 4: Brushfield, p. 208.

Fig. 5: Brushfield, p. 233.

to the cokyng stool and ducked in the water'.[15] As folklorist John Webster Spargo makes clear, 'Punishing scolds was not ... the semihumorous hazing which it sometimes seems to be'.[16] According to a 1675 legal summary,

> A Scold in a legal sense is a troublesome and angry woman, who by her brawling and wrangling amongst her Neighbours, doth break the publick Peace, and beget, cherish and increase publick Discord. And for this she is to be presented and punished in a Leet, by being put in the Cucking or Ducking-stole, or Tumbrel, an Engine appointed for that purpose, which is in the fashion of a Chair; and herein she is to sit, and to be let down in the water over head and ears three or four times, so that no part of her be above the water, diving or ducking down, though against her will, as Ducks do under the water.[17]

Punishing scolds with the cucking stool and male brawlers with the pillory was apparently so orthodox a response to disorder that the practices are affirmed even in the Book of Homilies. In the words of Hugh Latimer in his homily 'Agaynst strife and contention':

> And, because this vice [of contention] is so much hurtful to the society of a commonwealth, in all well ordered cities these common brawlers and scolders be punished, with a notable kind of pain, as to be set on the cucking stool, pillory, or such like.... If we have forsaken the devil, let us use no more devilish tongues.[18]

As to exactly what kinds of brawling, wrangling, breaking of the public peace and begetting of public discord were considered disruptive enough to define a woman as a scold, most descriptive evidence from court records simply problematizes the definition further by expanding the term. In the mid sixteenth century at Halton, one Margaret Norland was ordered to the cucking stool for having 'made an attack upon Robert Carrington, and struck him with her hand contrary to the peace'; Alice Lesthwyte, widow, is likewise ordered cucked 'for entertaining other men's servants'; and the wives of three townsmen are similarly sentenced because they 'were common liars and scolds'.[19] Woven into various court records is the information that women called 'common chiders amonge their neighbours' or women haled in for the offence of 'Flyten or chiden'[20] might likewise belong to the category of 'common scold'. Above all, the scold seems to have been an assumed category of community life. But since this almost exclusively female category[21] was defined by an exclusively male constabulary, and since the number of charges for verbal disruption brought against males are by comparison negligible, one can speculate that a 'scold' was, in essence, any woman who verbally resisted or flouted authority publicly and stubbornly enough to challenge the underlying dictum of male rule. What is ultimately at stake in the determination to gender such criminal categories as 'scold' and 'brawler' is the reinforcement of hierarchy through the production of difference. And when the society's underlying model of 'the publick Peace' is inseparable from and constituted by the reinforcement of gender difference, then behaviour that is tolerated – even tacitly encouraged – for the gander can, for the goose, become perceived of as a serious offence.[22]

The records of cucking-stool punishments occasionally make a reader aware of the victim's fear, pain and jeopardy. Both this instrument and the scold's bridle, however, were devised primarily as shaming devices; both are implicated in the long history of women's socialization into shame and its culturally transmitted, narrowed allowances of female selfhood that linger on as omnipresent, internalized commandments long after the historical experiences from which they arose have passed from memory. And in this regard the ritual of female punishment seems fundamentally different from that of punishments devised for men. The cucking of scolds was turned into a carnival experience, one that literally placed the woman's body at the centre of a mocking parade. Whenever local practicalities made it possible, her experience seems to have involved being ridden or carted through town, often to the accompaniment of musical instruments of the distinctly 'Dionysian' variety,[23] making sounds such as those that imitated flatulence or made some degrading association with her body. By contrast, the male ritual of being pilloried in the town square, while a more protracted and in some respects physically harsher ritual of public exposure, did not spectacularize or carnivalize the male body so as to degrade it to nearly the same extent. Nor for that matter was the body of a male offender subjected to the same disequilibrium of being hoisted and immersed, a movement that spatializes the social categories of high-low/ male-female, or to the loss of self-possession that is literalized by depriving the scold of the ability to stand her ground. Furthermore, for a woman to be paraded through town in a cart carried the special disgrace of being made analogous to a capital offender, the only other criminal transported by cart to meet his/her punishment.

The punishments designated for scolds were part of an ideological framework through which a patriarchal culture reinscribed its authority by ritual enactment. Because scolds were seen as threats to male authority, their carnivalesque punishments of mocking enthronement partake of the inverted structure of 'world-upside-down' rites.[24] Especially given the restriction of both the crime and its punishment to women, however, such enactments also suggest a blunted form of community sacrifice, a scapegoating mechanism through which the public body expels recognition of its own violence by projecting it onto and inflicting it upon the private body of a marginal member of the community.[25] Thus both the figure of the 'scold' and the cucking stool belong to the purview of comedy in ways that the male brawler and his punishment at the pillory do not. The shrew is, according to M.C. Bradbrook, 'the oldest and indeed the only native comic role for women'.[26] And during this period, the 'scold' or 'shrew' flourished as the object of mockery in such literary forms as the drama and ballad. In Fletcher's shrew play, *The Woman's Prize, or The Tamer Tam'd*, outraged husbands mock their rebellious wives by imagining them as explorers of a new world who discover not a continent of riches but islands of obedience:

> We'l ship 'em out in Cuck-stooles, there they'l saile
> As brave *Columbus* did, till they discover
> The happy Islands of obedience.
>
> (II.i.57–9)[27]

Yet beneath these frequent belittlements of women's authority lurk the anxieties that must have prompted such displacements in the first place. Below, in the lines of a late sixteenth-century ballad that is representative of the genre, the parodic picture of a female monarch who had 'rid in state' and sat 'inthroned' suggests the kind of cultural hysteria that Underdown documents between 1560 and 1640.[28]

> She belonged to Billingsgate
> And often times had rid in state,
> And sate i' the bottome of a poole,
> Inthroned in a *cucking-stoole*.[29]

Beyond the obvious patriarchal capital, the creation of the social mechanism of shaming rituals for women is paradoxically even more effectively conservative for the way it sets up an equally powerful counter-site for the containment of men. For the abjection of what is already subordinate or marginal creates a social space where, by mere association, the dominant group may itself be controlled.[30] It is fear of that very association that makes Mr T.N. Brushfield react with an excessive and inappropriate overflow of sympathy when he reads about a group of thirteenth-century male bakers who cheated their customers at market and who were consequently sent to the cucking stool along with guilty female brewers. When he reads of men being made to endure a punishment he assumes must always have been used exclusively for women, Brushfield rallies his indignation against the 'excesses of mayors and others having authority' for having caused the 'greater degree of degradation' that the bakers 'must have felt ... by being exposed to the public gaze' in a punishment 'reserved for females'.[31] Characteristically, he passes over various descriptions of women's punishments unremarked. As a nineteenth-century Englishman, Brushfield simply assumes both the gendering of punishment and the abjection of the feminine and thus erroneously projects that model back on to the social space of thirteenth-century England.

During the sixteenth century, local authorities seem to have recognized how effectively male social behaviour could be controlled by kidnapping the popular traditions of gender inversion and using them to shame acts of male rebellion inside the abjected feminine space. As Natalie Davis has demonstrated, gender inversion in European folkloric tradition originates as a means by which the overthrow of social order could be ritually represented.[32] It had thus evolved as a subversion from below. By the late sixteenth century, however, the political symbolism of the cross-dressed, unruly woman seems to have been appropriated for new uses, this time from above. In reactions against enclosure that Underdown aptly defines as involving a complex 'combination of conservatism and rebelliousness',[33] peasants from especially the western wood-pasture regions of England dressed as women and, through riot, attempted to return the world to the status quo that enclosure had turned upside down. In Wiltshire the leaders of 'skimmington' peasant riots adopted the name of 'Lady Skimmington', a folk hero(ine) signifying unruliness, and led 'skimmingtons' (demonstrations) against 'Skimmington', an authority figure.[34] In another enclosure riot in Datchet, Buckinghamshire, near Windsor, in 1598, the men cross-dressed, likewise signifying their rebellion under the sign of the universal figure of disorder. When the Datchet rioters and later the 'Lady Skimmington' leaders from Braydon were caught, they were punished by being made to stand pilloried in women's clothing.[35] By signifying male rebellion against hierarchical privilege as a feminized act, the authorities located insurrection within the space where it could be most effectively controlled: in the inferiorized status of a 'womanish' male. The women convicted of the Datchet riot were, by contrast, sentenced to their usual punishment at the cucking stool, wearing their usual clothing. The site of shame for both sexes was, it seems, the same: the space of the feminine.

In *The Merry Wives of Windsor* (written perhaps in the same year as the Datchet riot) Falstaff's public humiliation is played out by featuring him cross-dressed at a fictional site closely associated with the place where the Datchet rioters were punished. In *The Taming of the Shrew* Kate is the archetypal scold whose crime against society is her refusal to accept the so-called natural order of patriarchal hierarchy. But since Kate cannot be socially controlled by gender inversions that would treat her like a man, she, like her sister scolds of the era and the rebellious women in Datchet, is instead treated to ritual humiliation inside the space of the feminine. In Shakespeare's play the shaming rites begin at the famous wedding. Kaja

Silverman's comments on clothing are helpful in understanding this scene. As Silverman rightly notes, it is historically inaccurate to equate spectacular display in the sixteenth century with the subjugation of women to the controlling male gaze. Until the eighteenth century, when 'the male subject retreated from the limelight, handing on his mantle to the female subject. . . . in so far as clothing was marked by gender, it defined visibility as a male rather than a female attribute'.[36] On the day of the bridal – traditionally named for the bride because she is the ritual figure being honoured on that day – Petruchio's actions make Kate the object not of honour but of ridicule. Usurping the bride's traditional delayed entry and robbing her by his outlandish attire of the visual centrality that custom invests in brides synecdochically in the bridal gown,[37] Petruchio spectacularizes himself in such a way as to humiliate the bride. Without ever falling into the abjected space of being 'womanish' himself, he deprives her of the reverence that she is on this one day due. To her father's distress at 'this shame of ours' (III.ii.7), Kate rightly insists that Petruchio's delayed arrival – which initiates a behaviour that he will later insist is 'all . . . in reverend care of her' (IV.i.175) – is really an instrument by which publicly to shame her:

> No shame but mine. . . .
> Hiding his bitter jests in blunt behaviour.
> And to be noted for a merry man,
> He'll woo a thousand, 'point the day of marriage,
> Make feast, invite friends, and proclaim the banns,
> Yet never means to wed where he hath wooed.
> Now must the world point at poor Katherine,
> And say, 'Lo, there is mad Petruchio's wife,
> If it would please him come and marry her!'
>
> (III.ii.8, 13–20)

Having cuffed the priest, quaffed the bridal Communion,[38] sworn in church 'by gogs-wouns', thrown the sops in the sexton's face, then grabbed 'the bride about the neck / And kissed her lips with such a clamorous smack / That at the parting all the church did echo' (ll. 167–9), Petruchio succeeds in converting the offstage wedding ceremony into such a disgrace that its guests depart the church 'for very shame'. He then follows up this performance by asserting his first head-of-household decision. In spite of custom, community, and even an unexpected entreaty from Kate herself, this 'jolly surly groom' refuses Kate her bridal dinner, defining his wife as his material possession and making the arbitrary, even anti-communal determinations of a husband's authority supreme:

> I will be master of what is mine own.
> She is my goods, my chattels; she is my house.

My household-stuff, my field, my barn,
My horse, my ox, my ass, my anything....

(ll. 218–21)

Because shame is already a gendered piece of cultural capital, Petruchio can transgress norms of social custom and instigate the production of shame without it ever redounding upon him. He politicly begins his reign, in fact, by doing so. By inverting the wedding rite in such a way that compels its redoing and simultaneously depriving Kate of her renown as the 'veriest shrew' in Padua, he seizes unquestioned control of the male space of authority. Of course, all the woman-shaming and overt male dominance here are dramatically arranged so as to make Kate's humiliation seem wildly comic and to festoon Petruchio's domination with an aura of romantic bravado bound up with the mock chivalry with which he 'saves' Kate by carrying her away from the guests in a ritual capture, shouting, 'Fear not, sweet wench, they shall not touch thee, Kate' (l. 227). But what is being staged so uproariously here is what we might call the benevolent version of the shaming of a scold. Kate is not being encouraged to enjoy even what pleasures may have attended the narrowly constructed space of womanhood. She is being shamed inside it. For, as Petruchio says in IV.i, she must be made, like a tamed falcon, to stoop to her lure – to come to know her keeper's call, and to come with gratitude and loving obedience into the social containment called wifehood. But she will do so only when she realizes that there are no other spaces for her to occupy, which is no doubt why Petruchio feels such urgency to shunt her away from the bridal feast and its space of honour in Padua and lead her off to the isolation defined by 'her' new home, the space over which Petruchio has total mastery. Petruchio's politic reign is to construct womanhood for Kate as a site of seeming contradiction, the juncture where she occupies the positions of both shamed object and chivalric ideal. But it is between and inside those contradictions that the dependencies of 'wifehood' can be constructed. When Kate realizes that there are no other socially available spaces, and when she furthermore realizes that Petruchio controls access to all sustenance, material possession, personal comfort, and spatial mobility, she will rationally choose to please him and encourage his generosity rather than, as he says, continue ever more crossing him in futile imitation of birds whose wings have been clipped – birds that are already enclosed but nonetheless continue to try to fly free: 'these kites' – or kates – 'That bate and beat and will not be obedient' (ll. 166–7). Ultimately, in her final speech, Kate does, literally, 'stoop' to her lure.

Kate is denied her bridal feast. Nonetheless, in the bridal feast that is absent the bride acts as a particularly apt metaphor for the entire play, for the space of the feminine is actually the space under constant avoidance throughout. Even Bianca, who has seemed to occupy the space with relish, bolts out of it in the surprise role reversal at the end of the play. But in a world where gender has been constructed as a binary opposition, someone is going to be pushed into that space. Inside the pressures of such a binary, if the wife refuses or escapes this occupation, the husband loses his manhood. And thus, as Kate is being 'gentled' and manipulated to enter the feminine enclosure of the sex-and-gender system, the audience is also being strategically manipulated to applaud her for embracing that fate and to resent Bianca for impelling poor adoring Lucentio into the site of non-manhood. Through Bianca's refusal to compete in the contest of wifely subordination, Lucentio is left positioned as the play's symbolically castrated husband whose purse was cut off by a wife's rebellion. Since someone must occupy the abjected space of a binary – and since doing so is so much more humiliating for men – better (we say) in the interest of protecting the heterosexual bond that women should accept their inferiorization. By dramatizing Kate's resignation as her joyous acceptance of a world to which we recognize no alternatives exist, Shakespeare reinscribes the comfortingly familiar order inside of a dialogue that challenges the social distributions of power but concludes in a formula that invites us to applaud the reinstatement of the status quo.

In the past fifteen years or so, historical scholarship has shifted away from its perennial concentration on the structures of authority and has begun to view history from the bottom up. What has emerged from approaching historical records in entirely new ways and proposing newly complex intersections of such data[39] is a picture of England that requires us to read the social text in terms of such phenomena as the widespread and quite dramatic rise in the years 1560–1640 in those crimes labelled as ones of 'interpersonal dispute', that is, ones involving sexual misconduct, scolding, slander, physical assault, defamation, and marital relations. Keith Wrightson and David Levine offer an instructive explanation of this phenomenon: the statistical increase during these years reflects less a 'real' increase in such crimes than a suddenly heightened official determination to regulate social behaviour through court prosecution.[40] This itself reflects the wider growth of a 'law and order consciousness', the increase of fundamental concern about social order that manifested itself in the growing severity of criminal statutes directed primarily against vagrants and female disorder. In other words, what had sprung into full operation was a social anxiety that came to locate the source of all disorder in society in its marginal and subordinate groups. And in the particular types of malfeasance that this society or any other seeks to proscribe and the specific groups it thereby implicitly seeks to stigmatize, one may read its ideology.[41]

For Tudor-Stuart England, in village and town, an obsessive energy was invested in exerting control over the unruly woman – the woman who was exercising either her sexuality or her tongue under her own control rather than under the rule of a man. As illogical as it may initially seem, the two crimes – being a scold and being a so-called whore – were frequently conflated. Accordingly, it was probably less a matter of local convenience than one of a felt congruity between offences that made the cucking stool the common instrument of punishment. And whether the term 'cucking stool' shares any actual etymological origins with 'cuckold' or not, the perceived equation between a scolding woman and a whore or 'quean' who cuckolded her husband probably accounts for the periodic use of 'coqueen' or 'cuckquean' for the cucking stool.[42] This particular collocation of female transgressions constructs women as creatures whose bodily margins and penetrable orifices provide culture with a locus for displaced anxieties about the vulnerability of the social community, the body politic. Thus Ferdinand, in saying that 'women like that part, which, like the lamprey, / Hath nev'r a bone in't. / ... I mean the tongue',[43] jealously betrays his own desire for rule over what he sees as the penetrable misrule of his Duchess-sister's body/state. In this discussion of the grotesque tropes that connect body and court, Peter Stallybrass comments on the frequency with which 'in the Jacobean theatre, genital differentiation tended to be subsumed within a problematically gendered orality'.[44] Within that subsumption the talkative woman is frequently imagined as synonymous with the sexually available woman, her open mouth the signifier for invited entrance elsewhere. Hence the dictum that associates 'silent' with 'chaste' and stigmatizes women's public speech as a behaviour fraught with cultural signs resonating with a distinctly sexual kind of shame.[45]

Given these connections between body and state, control of women's speech becomes a massively important project. By being imagined as a defence of all the important institutions upon which the community depends, such a project could, in the minds of the magistrates and other local authorities, probably rationalize even such extreme measures as the strange instrument known as the 'scold's bridle' or 'brank'. Tracing the use of the scold's bridle is problematic because, according to Brushfield,

> notwithstanding the existence at Chester of so many Scold's Bridles, no notice of their use is to be found in the Corporation [town or city] books, several of which have been specially examined with that object in view. That they were not unfrequently called into requisition in times past cannot be doubted: but the Magistrates were doubtless fully aware that the punishment was illegal, and hence preferred that no record should remain of their having themselves transgressed the law.[46]

Since the bridle was never legitimate, it does not appear, nor would its use have been likely to be entered, in the various leet court records with the same unself-conscious frequency that is reflected in the codified use of the cucking stool. Because records are so scarce, we have no precise idea of how widespread the use of the bridle really was. What we can know is that during the early modern era this device of containment was first invented – or, more accurately, adapted – as a punishment for the scolding woman. It is a device that today we would call an instrument of torture, despite the fact – as English legal history is proud to boast – that in England torture was never legal. Thus, whereas the instrument openly shows up in the Glasgow court records of 1574 as a punishment meted out to two quarrelling women, if the item shows up at all in official English transactions, it is usually through an innocuous entry such as the one in the 1658 Worcester Corporation Records, which show that four shillings were 'Paid for mending the bridle for bridleinge of scoulds, and two cords for the same'.[47]

In the absence of what historians would rank as reliable documents, very little has been said by twentieth-century historians about the scold's bridle.[48] There are those who attempt by this lack of evidence to footnote it as an isolated phenomenon that originated around 1620, mainly in the north of England and one part of Scotland. I myself have some increasingly documented doubts. And while problems of documentation have made it possible for historians largely to ignore the scold's bridle even within their new 'bottom-up' histories of topics such as social crime, I would argue that its use and notoriety were widespread enough for it to have been an agent in the historical production of women's silence. As such, the bridle is both a material indicator of gender relations in the culture that devised it and a signifier crucial for reconstructing the buried narrative of women's history. Records substantiate its use in at least five English counties as well as in several disparate areas of Scotland; furthermore, likely pictorial allusions turn up, for example, on an eighteenth-century sampler handed down in an Irish family originally from Belfast,[49] or in the frontispiece of the 1612 edition of Hooker's *Laws of Ecclesiastical Polity*, where a woman kneels, a skull placed close by, and receives the Bible in one upstretched hand while in the other she holds a bridle, signifying discipline.[50] As I will argue below, the instrument is probably also signified in a raft of late sixteenth-century 'bridling' metaphors that have been understood previously as merely figurative; the item itself may well have appeared onstage as a prop in Part II of *Tamburlaine the Great* and *Swetnam the Woman-hater Arraigned by Women*. Moreover, it almost certainly appears as the explicit reference in several widely read seventeenth-century Protestant treatises published in London.

In Mr T.N. Brushfield's Cheshire County alone he was able to discover thirteen of these 200–250-year-old artifacts still lying about the county plus an appallingly large number of references to their use. In fact some eighteen months after he had presented his initial count in 1858, Mr Brushfield, with a dogged empiricism we can now be grateful for, informed the Society that he had come across three more specimens. There are, furthermore, apparently a number of extant bridles in various other parts of England, besides those in Chester County that Brushfield drew and wrote about,[51] and each one very likely carries with it its own detailed, local history. Nonetheless, so little has been written about them that had the industrious T.N. Brushfield not set about to report so exhaustively on scolds' bridles and female torture, we would have known almost nothing about these instruments except for an improbable-sounding story or two. As it is, whenever the common metaphor of 'bridling a wife's tongue' turns up in the literature of this era, the evidence should make us uncomfortably aware of a practice lurking behind that phrase that an original audience could well have heard as literal.

Scolds' bridles are not directly mentioned as a means for taming the scold of Shakespeare's *Shrew* – and such a practice onstage would have been wholly antithetical to the play's desired romantic union as well as to the model of benevolent patriarchy that is insisted on here and elsewhere in Shakespeare.[52] What Shakespeare seems to have been doing in *Shrew* – in addition to shrewdly capitalizing on the popularity of the contemporary *'hic mulier'* debate by giving it romantic life onstage – is conscientiously modelling a series of humane but effective methods for behavioural modification. The methods employed determinedly exclude the more brutal patriarchal practices that were circulating within popular jokes, village rituals, and in such ballads as 'A Merry Jest of a Shrewde and Curste Wyfe, Lapped in Morrelles Skin, for Her Good Behavyour', in which the husband tames his wife by first beating her and then wrapping her in the salted skin of the dead horse, 'Morel'. In 1594 or thereabout Shakespeare effectively pushes these practices off his stage. And in many ways his 'shrew' takes over the cultural discourse from this point on, transforming the taming story from scenarios of physical brutality and reshaping the trope of the shrew/scold from an old, usually poor woman or a nagging wife into the newly romanticized vision of a beautiful, rich and spirited young woman. But the sheer fact that the excluded brutalities lie suppressed in the margins of the shrew material also means that they travel, as unseen partners, inside the more benevolent taming discourse that Shakespeare's play helps to mould. And, as Ann Thompson's synopsis of *Shrew*'s production history clearly demonstrates, such woman-battering, although not part of Shakespeare's script, repeatedly leaks back in from the margins and turns up in subsequent productions and adaptations (including, for instance, the Burton–Taylor film version, to which director Franco Zefferelli added a spanking scene):

In the late seventeenth century, John Lacey's *Sauny the Scott, or The Taming of the Shrew* (c. 1667), which supplanted Shakespeare's text on stage until it was replaced in 1754 by David Garrick's version called *Catherine and Petruchio*, inserts an additional scene in which the husband pretends to think that his wife's refusal to speak to him is due to toothache and sends for a surgeon to have her teeth drawn. This episode is repeated with relish in the eighteenth century in James Worsdale's adaptation, *A Cure for a Scold* (1735).[53]

What turns up as the means to control rebellious women imagined by the play's seventeenth- and eighteenth-century versions is, essentially, the same form of violence as that suppressed in Shakespeare's playscript but available in the surrounding culture: the maiming/disfiguring of the mouth.

The scold's bridle is a practice tangled up in the cultural discourse about shrews. And while it is not materially present in the narrative of Shakespeare's play, horse references or horse representations – which are, oddly enough, an almost standard component of English folklore about unruly women – pervade the play.[54] The underlying literary 'low culture' trope of unruly horse/unruly woman seems likely to have been the connection that led first to a metaphoric idea of bridling women's tongues and eventually to the literal social practice. Inside that connection, even the verbs 'reign' and 'rein' come together in a fortuitous pun that reinforces male dominance. And there would no doubt have been additional metaphoric reinforcement for bridling from the bawdier use of the horse/rider metaphor and its connotations of male dominance. In this trope, to 'mount' and 'ride' a woman works both literally and metaphorically to exert control over the imagined disorder presumed to result from the 'woman on top'. Furthermore, the horse and rider are not only the standard components of the shrew-taming folk stories but are likewise the key feature of 'riding skimmington', which, unlike the French charivari customs of which it is a version, was intended to satirize marriages in which the wife was reputed to have beaten her husband (or was, in any case, considered the dominant partner).[55]

In shrew-taming folktale plots in general, the taming of the unruly wife is frequently coincident with the wedding trip home on horseback.[56] The trip which is itself the traditional final stage to the 'bridal', is already the site of an unspoken pun on 'bridle' that gets foregrounded in Grumio's horse-heavy description of the journey home and the ruination of Kate's 'bridal' – 'how her horse fell, and she under her horse; ... how the horses ran away, how her bridle was burst' (IV.i.54, 59–60). By means of the syntactical elision of 'horse's', the phrase quite literally puts the bridle on Kate rather than her horse. What this suggests is that the scold's bridal/

horse bridle/scold's bridle associations were available for resonant recall through the interaction of linguistic structures with narrative ones. The scold's bridle that Shakespeare did not literally include in his play is ultimately a form of violence that lives in the same location as the many offstage horses that are crowded into its non-representational space. The bridle is an artifact that exists in *Shrew*'s offstage margins – along with the fist-in-the-face that Petruchio does not use and the rape he does not enact in the offstage bedroom we do not see. Evoked into narrative possibility when Petruchio shares his taming strategy with the audience –

> This is a way to kill a wife with kindness,
> And thus I'll *curb* her mad and headstrong humour.
> He that knows better how to tame a shrew,
> Now let him speak – 'tis charity to show
>
> (IV.i.179–82, my italics)

– the scold's bridle exists in this drama as a choice that has been deliberately excluded.

The antiquarians and few historians who have mentioned this instrument assign its initial appearance to the mid 1620s – a date that marks its first entry in a city record in northern England. There is, however, rather striking literary evidence to suggest that the scold's bridle not only existed some twenty to thirty years earlier but was apparently familiar to the playwrights and playgoers of London. The bridle turns up in Part II of Christopher Marlowe's *Tamburlaine the Great* (c. 1587) not as a metaphor but explicitly described as an extremely cruel instrument of torture that Tamburlaine devises for Orcanes and the three Egyptian kings who dare to protest when he kills his son, Calyphas, for being too womanish to fight. Demeaning their protest as dogs barking and scolds railing, Tamburlaine determines how he will punish their insolence:

> Well, bark, ye dogs! I'll bridle all your tongues
> And bind them close with bits of burnish'd steel
> Down to the channels of your hateful throats;
> And, with the pains my rigor shall inflict,
> I'll make ye roar. . . .[57]

The scold's bridle is, furthermore, the key referent to understanding the condign nature of the punishment that the women jurors of the 1620 *Swetnam the Woman-hater Arraigned by Women* devise for the pamphlet writer, Joseph Swetnam, who had publicly declared himself the chief enemy to their sex. The dramatists, most probably women, dared – at a unique moment in English theatre history – to produce and have put on the stage at the Red Bull theatre a bold, political retaliation against the author of the notoriously misogynist pamphlet, *The Arraignment of Lewde, idle,*

froward, and unconstant women. Having brought 'Misogynos' to trial,
they order him to wear a 'Mouzell', be paraded in public, and be shown

> In every Street i'the Citie, and be bound
> In certaine places to Post or stake,
> And bayted by all the honest women in the Parish.[58]

The above lines describe the standard humiliations involved in the bridling
of a scold. Probably because so little has to date been said about scolds'
bridles, Simon Shepherd gives a tentative and parenthetical interpretation
that '(presumably "Mouzell" alludes again to [Rachel] Speght's pamphlet)'.[59] Unwittingly, the gloss obscures the key point in the women
dramatists' triumph. Onstage, their play seeks poetic parity through
condemning Swetnam to endure precisely the kinds of humiliation that
women were sentenced to undergo based on nothing more than the kinds
of stereotyped accusations Swetnam's pamphlet reproduces.

Another pre-1620 allusion where the literal bridle seems once again the
likely referent occurs in the exchange Shakespeare earlier wrote for his
first 'shrew scene', the argument between Antipholus the Ephesian's angry
wife, Adriana, and her unmarried, dutiful, and patriarchally correct sister,
Luciana. Luciana's insistence that 'a man is master of his liberty' and
Adriana's feminist challenge, 'Why should their liberty than ours be
more?' provokes a dialogue that seems to turn around a veiled warning
about scolds' bridles from Luciana and the furious rejection of that
possibility from Adriana.

> LUC.   O, know he is the bridle of your will.
> ADR.   There's none but asses will be bridled so.
> LUC.   Why, headstrong liberty is lash'd with woe....
>
> (*The Comedy of Errors*, II.i.13–15)

Another likely scold's bridle allusion turns up inside the shrew discourse
in *Mundus Alter et Idem*, the strange voyage fantasy purportedly written by
the traveller 'Mercurius Brittanicus' but actually written by Joseph Hall
and published (in Latin) in 1605. The work – which Hall never publicly
acknowledged but which went through several printings and was even
'Englished' as *The Discovery of a New World* in an unauthorized 1609
translation by John Healey[60] – is accompanied by elaborate textual
apparati that include a series of Ortelius's maps, on top of which Hall has
remapped his satiric fantasy. In Hall's dystopia the narrator embarks on the
ship *Fantasia* and discovers the Antarctic continent, which is geographically the world upside down and therefore contains such travesties
of social organization as a land of women. This is named 'New Gynia,
which others incorrectly call Guinea, [but which] I correctly call Viraginia,
located where European geographers depict the Land of Parrots'.[61] The

geography of Viraginia includes Gynaecopolis, where Brittanicus is enslaved by its domineering women until he reveals 'the name of my country (which is justly esteemed throughout the world as the "Paradise of Women")'.[62] In the province of 'Amazonia, or Gynandria', the fear of a society based on gender inversion emerges into full-blown nightmare: men wear petticoats and remain at home 'strenuously spinning and weaving' while women wear the breeches, attend to military matters and farming, pluck out their husband's beards and sport long beards themselves, imperiously enslave their husbands, beat them daily, and 'while the men work, the women ... quarrel and scold'.[63] What constitutes treason in this fantasized space is for any woman to treat her husband gently or with the slightest forbearance. As punishment for such treason, Hall's misogynistic satire adds one more twist to the shame-based model of gendered punishment by invoking a scenario of transvestite disguise similar to that which Shakespeare exploits in the boy-actor/Rosalind/Ganymede complications of *As You Like It*: the guilty wife 'must exchange clothes with her husband and dressed like this, head shaved, be brought to the forum to stand there an entire day in the pillory, exposed to the reproach and derisive laughter of all onlookers ... [until she] finally returns home stained with mud, urine, and all sorts of abuse....'[64] Mercurius Brittanicus is able to escape only because, since he is dressed in 'man's attire and ... in the first phase of an adolescent beard',[65] he is assumed to be female and thus enjoys a woman's freedom of movement.

Hall's Amazon fantasy – in which men may not select their dress, eat their food, conduct any business, go anywhere, speak to anyone, or ever speak up against their wives' opinions – is, of course, only an exaggeration of the lessons Kate is compelled to learn in Petruchio's taming school. The parallels derive from the fact that underlying both Hall's satire and Shakespeare's play is the same compulsive model that underwrites their culture – the male fantasy of female dominance that is signified by the literary figure of the shrew/scold. Long before the Amazon fantasy emerges, the shrew story is implicit even in Mercurius Brittanicus's opening description of Viraginia's topographical features. In the region of Linguadocia (tongue), the society has ingeniously devised a means to control the 'enormous river' called 'Sialon' (saliva) that flows through the city of 'Labriana' (lips). The overflow from Labriana could 'scarcely ... be contained even in such a vast channel, and indeed, ... the Menturnea Valley [chin] – would be daily threatened by it had not the rather clever inhabitants carefully walled up the banks with bones'.[66] In the Healey translation the reference to scolds and the implied model of containing them is even clearer. In Healey almost all provinces and cities are associated with women/excess voicing/mouth through such names as 'Tattlingen', 'Scoldonna', 'Blubberick', 'Gigglottangir', 'Shrewes-bourg',

'Pratlingople', 'Gossipingoa', and 'Tales-borne'. To control the river 'Slauer' from bursting out and overflowing 'Lypswagg', the 'countrimen haue now deuised very strong rampires of bones and bend lether, to keepe it from breaking out any more, but when they list to let it out a little now & then for scouring of the channell'.[67]

Scolding is a verbal rebellion and controlling it was, in the instrument of the bridle, focused with condign exactitude on controlling a woman's tongue – the site of a nearly fetishized investment that fills the discourse of the era with a true 'lingua franca', some newly invented, some reprinted and repopularized in the late sixteenth to mid seventeenth century. Among this didactic 'tongue literature' there is a quite amazing play by Thomas Tomkis that went through five printings from 1607 to 1657 before its popularity expired. In this play, called *Lingua: Or The Combat of the Tongue, And the five Senses For Superiority*, a female allegorical figure – Lingua, dressed in purple and white – is finally brought to order by the figures of the five senses who force her into compelled servitude to 'Taste'.[68]

If – as I have speculated – the underlying idea for bridling a woman comes initially from a 'low-culture' material association between horse/ woman, it was an association being simultaneously coproduced on the 'high-culture' side within a religious discourse that helped to legitimate such a literalization. For in addition to a number of repopularized theological treatises in Latin that dedicate whole chapters to the sins of the tongue and emblem book pictures that show models of the good wife pictured as a woman who is literalizing the metaphoric by grasping her tongue between her fingers, the era is stamped by that peculiarly Protestant literature of self-purification in which the allegorical model of achieving interior discipline by a 'bridling of the will' appears as an almost incessant refrain. From the Protestant divines came a congeries of impassioned moral treatises that, as they linguistically test out their truths by treading the extreme verge between literal and metaphoric, frequently move close to eliding any boundary between interior and exterior application of self-discipline. Such suggestions occur in works like *The Poysonous Tongue*, a 1615 sermon by John Abernethy, Bishop of Cathnes, in which the personified tongue – 'one of the least members, most moueable, and least tyred' – is ultimately imagined as an inflamed and poisonous enemy, especially to the other bodily members, and therefore the member most worthy to be severely, graphically punished.[69]

Discourse about the tongue is complexly invested with an ambivalent signification that marks it always as a discourse about gender and power – one in which the implied threat to male possession/male authority perhaps resolves itself only in the era's repeated evocation of the Philomela myth (a narrative that Shakespeare himself draws upon in a major way for three different works) – where a resolution to such gender contestation is achieved by the silencing of the woman, enacted as a cutting out – or castration – of her tongue. It was a male discourse that George Gascoigne had already taken to perhaps the furthest limits of aggression in 1593. Reduced to a court hack by the censorship of his master work, *A Hundreth Sundrie Flowers* (which he had retitled *The Posies* and tried without success to slip past the censors), Gascoigne, in his last moralistic work, *The Steel Glas*, created a poetic persona who has been emasculated – hence depotentiated into the feminine – only to be raped and then have her tongue cut out by 'The Rayzor of Restraint'.[70]

A discourse that locates the tongue as the body's 'unruly member' situates female speech as a symbolic relocation of the male organ, an unlawful appropriation of phallic authority in which the symbolics of male castration are ominously coimplicit. If the chastity belt was an earlier design to prevent entrance into one aperture of the deceitfully open female body, the scold's bridle, preventing exit from another, might be imagined as a derivative inversion of that same obsession. Moreover, the very impetus to produce an instrument that actually bridled the tongue and bound it down into a woman's mouth suggests an even more complicated obsession about women's bodies/women's authority than does the chastity belt: in the obsession with the woman's tongue, the simple binary between presence and absence breaks down. Here, the obsession must directly acknowledge, even as it attempts to suppress, the presence in woman of the primary signifier of an authority presumed to be masculine. The tongue (at least in the governing assumptions about order) should always already have been possessed only by the male. Needless to say, theologians found ways of tracing these crimes of usurpation by the woman's unruly member back to the Garden, to speech, to Eve's seduction by the serpent, and thence to her seductive appropriation of Adam's rightful authority. Says the author of a sermon called *The Government of the Tongue*:

> Original sin came first out at the mouth by speaking, before it entred in by eating. The first use we find *Eve* to have made of her language, was to enter parly with the temter, and from that to become a temter to her husband. And immediately upon the fall, guilty *Adam* frames his tongue to a frivolous excuse, which was much less able to cover his sin than the fig-leaves were his nakedness.[71]

Through Eve's open mouth, then, sin and disorder entered the world. Through her verbal and sexual seduction of Adam – through her use of that other open female bodily threshold – sin then became the inescapable curse of humankind. All rebellion is a form of usurpation of one sort or another, and if Eve's sin – her 'first use of language' through employment of her tongue – is likewise imagined as the usurpation of the male phallic instrument and the male signifier of language, the images of woman speaking and woman's tongue become freighted with heavy psychic baggage. Perpetually guilty, perpetually disorderly, perpetually seductive, Eve and her descendants become *the* problem that society must control.

In relation to scolds' bridles and the ways that the violent self-discipline urged by these treatises seeks to legitimate a literal practice, Thomas Adams's 1616 sermon, 'The Taming of the Tongue', is of particular interest. With a title suggestively close to that of Shakespeare's play, it envisions a future of brimstone and scalding fire for the untamable tongue and warns that the tongue is so intransigent that 'Man hath no bridle, no cage of brasse, nor barres of yron to *tame* it.'[72] Likewise, in a sermon by Thomas Watson, we are told that

> The Tongue, though it be a little Member, yet it hath a World of Sin in it. The Tongue is an unruly Evil. We put *Bitts* in Horses mouths and rule them: but the Tongue is an unbridled Thing. It is hard to find a Curbing-bitt to rule the Tongue.[73]

Thus, when William Gearing dedicates his ominously titled treatise, *A Bridle for the Tongue: or, A Treatise of ten Sins of the Tongue* to Sir Orlando Bridgman, Chief Justice of the Court of Common Pleas, his use of the bridle goes too far beyond the metaphoric to be construed as such. If anything, it seems prescriptive. In the dedication Gearing points out that the 'Tongue hath no Rein by nature, but hangeth loose in the midst of the mouth', and then invokes the Third Psalm to proclaim that the Lord will 'strike' those who scold 'on the cheekbone (jawbone), and break out their teeth'. Speaking here in an already gendered discourse, Gearing appears to invoke scriptural authority as justification for legalizing the iron bridle as an instrument of official punishment.[74] In the process, his scriptural reference graphically suggests what could well have happened to the hapless women who were yanked through town, a lead rope attached to the metal bridle locked firmly around their heads, their tongues depressed by a two-to-three-inch metal piece called a 'gag'. Besides effecting the involuntary regurgitation that the term suggests, the gag could easily have slammed into their teeth with every pull, smashing their jawbones and breaking out their teeth, until finally the offending shrew would be tied up and made to stand in the town square, an object to be pissed on and further ridiculed at will.

There is one known account written by a woman who was bridled. We may infer from Dorothy Waugh's testimony that she experienced the bridling as a sexual violation. When her narrative reaches the moment of the gag being forced into her mouth, her embarrassment nearly over-

whelms description and her words stumble as they confront the impossibility of finding a language for the tongue to repeat its own assault.
Repeatedly, she brackets off references to the bridle with phrases like 'as
they called it', as if to undermine its reality. Physically violated, made to
stand bridled in the jail as an object of shame for citizens to pay twopence
to view, and released still imprisoned in the bridle to be whipped from town
to town in a manner that parallels the expulsion of a convicted whore,
Dorothy Waugh several times asserts 'they had not any thing to lay to my
Charge', as if the assertion of her innocence could frame her experience
within the discourse of legality and extricate it from the one of sexual
violation that it keeps slipping towards. Waugh's account of her *cruell
usage by the Mayor of* Carlile' occurs as the final piece of seven Quaker
testimonies that comprise *The Lambs Defence against Lyes. And A True
Testimony given concerning the Sufferings and Death of James Parnell*
(1656). Originally haled off to prison after she had been 'moved of the
Lord to goe into the market of *Carlile*, to speake against all deceit &
ungodly practices', Dorothy Waugh's implicit subversions of the local
authority and substitution of biblical quotations as a source of self-
authorization is clearly what impelled the mayor into so implacable an
antagonism. To the mayor's question from whence she came, Waugh
responded:

> I said out of *Egypt* where thou lodgest; But after these words, he was so
> violent & full of passion he scarce asked me any more Questions, but
> called to one of his followers to bring the bridle as he called it to put upon
> me, and was to be on three houres, and that which they called so was like
> a steele cap and my hatt being violently pluckt off which was pinned to
> my head whereby they tare my Clothes to put on their bridle as they
> called it, which was a stone weight of Iron by the relation of their own
> Generation, & three barrs of Iron to come over my face, and a peece of
> it was put in my mouth, which was so unreasonable big a thing for that
> place as cannot be well related, which was locked to my head, and so I
> stood their time with my hands bound behind me with the stone weight
> of Iron upon my head and the bitt in my mouth to keep me from speaking;
> And the Mayor said he would make me an Example.... Afterwards it was
> taken off and they kept me in prison for a little season, and after a while
> the Mayor came up againe and caused it to be put on againe, and sent me
> out of the Citty with it on, and gave me very vile and unsavoury words,
> which were not fit to proceed out of any mans mouth, and charged the
> Officer to whip me out of the Towne, from Constable to Constable to send
> me, till I came to my owne home, when as they had not anything to lay
> to my Charge.[75]

If we may be thankful about anything connected with the scold's bridle, it is that so many were found in a county whose antiquarian groups were especially diligent in recording and preserving the local heritage. Mr T.N. Brushfield meticulously preserved all records he uncovered, even to the extent of making detailed drawings of the bridles he found in Cheshire and neighbouring areas. But in doing so, he also unwittingly managed to preserve some of the ideas and attitudes that had originally forged these instruments. Thus his own discourse, as he describes these appalling artifacts and instances of their use, stands smugly disjunct from its subject and seems disconcertingly inappropriate in its own investments and responses. As he opens his introduction of the scold's bridle, for instance, he rhetorically establishes a legitimating lineage for his authority by deferring to – without ever considering the implications of the text he invokes – the work of one of England's earliest antiquarians. He thus begins: 'In commencing a description of the Brank or Scold's Bridle, I cannot do better than quote a passage from Dr Plot's *Natural History of Staffordshire*' (1686). He then proceeds, without the slightest dismay or query, to pass along the following description from Dr Plot:

> Lastly, we come to the *Arts* that respect *Mankind*, amongst which, as elsewhere, the civility of precedence must be allowed to the *women*, and that as well in punishments as favours. For the former whereof, they have such a peculiar *artifice* at *New Castle* (under Lyme) and *Walsall*, for correcting of *Scolds*; which it does, too, so effectually, and so very safely, that I look upon it as much to be preferred to the *Cucking Stoole*, which not only endangers the *health* of the *party*, but also gives the tongue liberty 'twixt every dipp; to neither of which is this at all lyable; it being such a *Bridle* for the *tongue*, as not only quite deprives them of speech, but brings shame for the transgression, and humility thereupon, before 'tis taken off ... which, being put upon the offender by order of the magistrate, and fastened with a *padlock* behind, she is lead round the towne by an *Officer* to her shame, nor is it taken off, till after the party begins to show all external signes imaginable of humiliation and amendment.[76]

To be released from the instrument that rendered them mute, the silenced shrews of Dr Plot's narrative were compelled to employ their bodies to plead the required degradation. Yet to imagine just what pantomimes of pain, guilt, obeisance to authority and self-abjection might have been entailed is almost as disturbing an exercise as is imagining the effects of the bridle itself.

Although Brushfield did unearth evidence that the scold's bridle had been used as late as the 1830s, it is clear that the use of such an instrument of torture at any time in England's history had managed to disappear beneath a convenient public amnesia until only a decade prior to his 1858 report. No longer used in public punishments, the bridles had been recycled behind the walls of state institutions; most turned up in places like women's workhouses, mental institutions, and other such establishments that, by the nineteenth century, had conveniently removed society's marginal people from public view. In the 1840s the scold's bridle seems to have caught the eye of the antiquarians, and Brushfield is therefore at pains to describe in detail the variety of bridles in the rich trove he has collected in Cheshire. Some, he tells us, are

> contrived with hinged joints, as to admit of being readily adapted to the head of the scold. It was generally supplied with several connecting staples, so as to suit heads of different sizes, and was secured by a padlock. Affixed to the inner portion of the hoop was a piece of metal, which, when the instrument was properly fitted, pressed the tongue down, and effectually branked or bridled it. The length of the mouthpiece or gag varied from $1\frac{1}{2}$ inch to 3 inches, – if more than $2\frac{1}{2}$ inches, the punishment would be much increased, – as, granting that the instrument was fitted moderately tight, it would not only arrest the action of the tongue, but also excite distressing symptoms of sickness, more especially if the wearer became at all unruly. The form of the gag was very diversified, the most simple being a mere flat piece of iron; in some the extremity was turned upwards, in others downwards; on many of the specimens both surfaces were covered with rasp-like elevations. The instrument was generally painted, and sometimes in variegated colours, in which case the gag was frequently red. . . . A staple usually existed at the back part of the instrument, to which was attached a short chain terminating in an iron ring; – any additional length required was supplied by a rope.
>
> Wearing this effectual curb on her tongue, the silenced scold was sometimes fastened to a post in some conspicuous portion of the town – generally the market-place. . . .[77]

One bridle (Fig. 6) that was formerly used in Manchester Market 'to control the energetic tongues of some of the female stall-keepers', as Brushfield puts it, was found in the mid nineteenth century still retaining its original coverings of alternating white and red cotton bands; its 'gag being large, with rasp-like surfaces; the leading-chain three feet long, and attached to the front part of the horizontal hoop'.[78] The spectacular red and white carnival festivity of the Manchester bridle would have no doubt been augmented not only by some appropriately carnivalesque parade and by the bridled woman comically resembling a horse in tournament trappings but likewise by the colourful if painful effects that almost any gag would have been likely to produce. Such effects are vividly illustrated in the account of a witness to a 1653 bridling, who saw:

Fig. 6: Brushfield, p. 269.

one Ann Bidlestone, drove through the streets, by an officer of the same
corporation [i.e., the city of Newcastle], holding a rope in his hand, the
other end fastened to an engine, called the branks, which is like a crown,
it being of iron which was musled, over the head and face, with a great
gap [*sic*], or tongue of iron, forced into her mouth, which forced the
blood out; and that is the punishment which the magistrates do inflict
upon chiding, and scoulding women.[79]

The same witness declared that he had 'often seen the like done to others'.

Brushfield – having described some six or seven variations of the bridle,
including one 'very handsome specimen' that was 'surmounted with a
decorated cross'[80] (Fig. 7) – leads up to his tour de force, the 'Stockport
Brank' (Fig. 8). This 'perfectly unique specimen.... by far the most
remarkable in this county', currently belongs, he tells us, to the corporate
authorities of Stockport, whom he thanks effusively for granting him the
honour of being the very first person privileged to sketch it:

> The extraordinary part of the instrument . . . is the *gag*, which commences
> flat at the hoop and terminates in a bulbous extremity, which is covered
> with *iron pins*, nine in number, there being three on the upper surface,
> three on the lower, and three pointing backwards; and it is scarcely
> possible to affix it in its destined position without wounding the tongue.

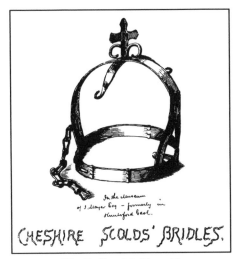

Fig. 7: Brushfield, p. 42.

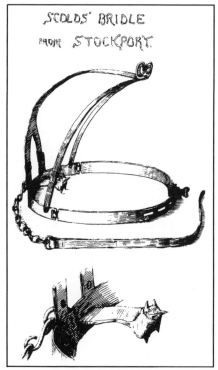

Fig. 8: Brushfield, p. 80.

> To make matters still worse, the chain (which yet remains attached, and
> ... measures two feet) is connected to the hoop at the fore part, as if to
> *pull* the wearer of the Bridle along on her unwilling tour of the streets;
> for it is very apparent that any motion of the gag must have lacerated the
> mouth very severely. Another specimen was formerly in the WORKHOUSE
> AT STOCKPORT, and was sold, a few years ago, as old iron![81]

As he recounts the unauthorized sale of this extraordinary item as scrap
iron, Brushfield rises to outrage. He then launches into an indignant
description of how this bridle – which was originally and legally the
property of Brushfield's own Chester – had been given away some thirty
years before by the Chester jailer. Of this abuse of property rights,
Brushfield insists that, while 'The liberality of the donor cannot perhaps be
questioned ... the right of transfer, on the part of that official, is altogether
another matter!' Therefore, 'An inventory of these curious relics, taken
once or twice a year under the authority of the city magistrates, would',
Brushfield exclaims, 'effectually curb these "fits of abstraction".'[82] And as
T.N. Brushfield's disquisition on scolds' bridles devolves to issues of male
ownership, legitimate transmission, and proprietary rights, as his language
slides into a recommendation for *curbing* dangerous signs of liberality, and
as he speaks forth his own authoritative proposals for instituting control
over rights to own these brutal instruments that carry with them a silenced
women's history, it may well seem to the stultified reader that 1858 is
really still 1598 as far as any progress in the complexly burdened history
of women's space within culture is concerned. Were we to shift the venue
from sex to race, the assumption would be accurate. For while Mr T.N.
Brushfield read his paper on 'obsolete punishments' and registered genteel
disapproval over his forefathers' use of such a barbaric control on the fair
sex of Chester County, on the other side of the Atlantic, England's cultural
heirs had carried this model of control one step further. By 1858 – as
readers of Toni Morrison's *Beloved* will recall – the scold's bridle had been
cycled over to the American South and the Caribbean, where in 1858 it was
being used to punish unruly slaves.[83]

   Among historians, 'scolds' or 'shrews' are commonly defined as a
particular category of offender, almost without exception female. In David
Underdown's descriptive scenario, 'women who were poor, social out-
casts, widows or otherwise lacking in the protection of a family, or
newcomers to their communities, were the most common offenders. Such
women were likely to vent their frustration against the nearest symbols of
authority.'[84] And, we might add, such women were also the most likely to
have the community's frustration vented against them. But the evidence
that T.N. Brushfield has left about the bridle suggests that this definition
of scolds – which is derived mainly from various legal records, most of

which are, in any case, documents of cucking-stool punishments – may be far too narrow.

From the rich evidence T.N. Brushfield compiled from a variety of archaeological journals, offbeat treatises, collective town memories, and information given him by senior citizens acting as quasi-official transmitters of oral history in towns and cities around Cheshire, we discover that the scold's bridle was apparently a symbol of mayoral office that passed from one city administration to the next, being delivered along with the mace and other recognized signs of officialdom into the keeping of the town jailer. The jailer's services, we learn,

> were not unfrequently called into requisition. In the old-fashioned, half-timbered houses in the Borough, there was generally fixed on one side of the large open fire-places, a hook; so that when a man's wife indulged her scolding propensities, the husband sent for the Town Jailer to bring the Bridle, and had her bridled and chained to the hook until she promised to behave herself better for the future.[85]

One member of Brushfield's antiquary group was a former mayor of the town of Congleton, where hooks on the side of fireplaces still existed. According to his account, so chilling was the memory of this method of controlling domestic disputes that husbands in nineteenth-century Congleton could still induce instant obedience from their wives just by saying, 'If you don't rest with your tongue, I'll send for the Bridle, and hook you up'. The local bookseller at Macclesfield reported to Brushfield that he had frequently seen the bridle produced at petty sessions of the court 'in terrorem, to stay the volubility of a woman's tongue; and that a threat by a magistrate to order its appliance, had always proved sufficient to abate the garrulity of the most determined scold'.[86] By 1858, although the signified object had disappeared from social practice, it still existed within the culture as a powerful signifier of what had become a silenced history of women's silencing.

For evidence like the above we probably owe T.N. Brushfield a debt of gratitude. He preserved material that suggests a whole secondary, shadowed subtext to the history of women and the law – a history outside the law and yet one that took place inside England's much touted rule of law; a history that had no juries, no court trials, no official sentences, and that left few telltale records of itself; yet a history that was nonetheless passed down, circulated, and tacitly authorized in town after town, inside county courthouses, city jails, mayoral offices, corporate holdings, and authenticated by an entire set of legitimating signifiers. In the town of Congleton, not only was a husband 'thy lord, thy king, thy governor / ... thy life, thy keeper, / Thy head, thy sovereign' (Shrew, V.ii.138,

146–7), he was also the law, and his tyrannies were supported by the existing legal institutions. And while such a grim history as that which is carried by the iron bridle may seem far indeed from Shakespeare's zesty comedy about the taming of shrews into conformable Kates, I would insist that it is not. For Kate the fictional shrew is but one of those women whose real history can all too easily be hidden behind and thus effectively erased by the romanticized version of her story that Shakespeare's play participates in creating.

Around 1640 the proverbial scold seems virtually to disappear from court documents. As Susan Amussen informs us, the 'formal mechanisms of control were rarely used after the Restoration'.[87]

> The prosecution of scolds was most common before 1640; while accusations on scolding, abusing neighbours, brawling in church and other forms of quarrelling usually make up between a tenth and a quarter of the offences in sample Act Books of the Archdeacons of Norwich and Norfolk before 1640, they do not appear in the samplebooks after 1660.[88]

Why did 'scolds' apparently disappear? Were they always just the projections of an order-obsessed culture, who disappeared when life became more orderly? Or is the difference real and the behaviour of women in the early modern era indeed different from the norms of a later one? Did they really brawl, curse, scold, riot and behave so abusively? Brushfield clearly assumes that they did, and thus is able to rationalize the otherwise disturbing fact that so many of these illegal instruments of torture turned up in good old Cheshire County, his own home space. As he says, 'if such a number of tongue-repressing Bridles were required', then they were so because the women must have been so disorderly as to have turned Cheshire into 'a riotous County indeed'. Benevolently, however, he then continues, forgiving England its disruptive foremothers and invoking the authority of the Bard himself to authorize his beatific vision of silent women:

> Suffice it, however, for us to say, – and I speak altogether on behalf of [all] the gentlemen, – that whatever it may have been in times gone by, yet it is certain that the gentleness and amiability of the ladies of the present generation make more than ample amends for the past; and Shakespeare, when he wrote those beautiful words,
>   'Her voice was ever soft, / Gentle and low; an excellent thing in woman,'
> unintentionally, of course, yet fully anticipated the attributes of our modern Cheshire ladies.[89]

And it well may be that in his work on scolds' bridles, T.N. Brushfield may unwittingly have described the silent process of how gender is historicized. He may have recorded the social process by which the women of one generation – perhaps as rowdy, brawling, voluble, and outspoken as men have always been authorized to be – were shamed, tamed, and reconstituted by instruments like cucking stools and scolds' bridles, into the meek and amiable, softspoken ladies he so admires in his own time.[90] Perhaps the gentle and pleasing Stepford Wives of mid-nineteenth-century Chester are precisely the products that such a searing socialization into gender would produce – and would continue to reproduce even long after the immediate agony of being bridled or of watching a daughter, mother or sister being paraded through the streets and forced to endure that experience had passed from personal and recorded memory. The history of silencing is a history of internalizing the literal, of erasing the signifier and interiorizing a signified. The iron bridle is a part of that history. Its appropriate epigraph is a couplet from Andrew Marvell's 'Last Instructions to a Painter'[91] – a couplet that could in fact have been written at exactly the moment that some curst and clamorous Kate in some English town was being bridled:

Prudent Antiquity, that knew by Shame
Better than Law, Domestic Crimes to tame.

Notes

1. *Saturday Review*, 6 November 1897, as quoted in editor Ann Thompson's introduction to the New Cambridge Shakespeare *The Taming of the Shrew* (Cambridge: Cambridge Univ. Press, 1984), p. 21. See Thompson's introduction for further instances of this reaction. All *Shrew* citations refer to this edition, and quotations from other Shakespeare plays refer to *The Riverside Shakespeare*, ed. G. Blakemore Evans (Boston: Houghton Mifflin, 1974): all references will appear in text.
2. Louis Althusser, 'Ideology and Ideological State Apparatuses' in *Lenin and Philosophy and Other Essays*, trans. Ben Brewster (London: New Left Books, 1971).
3. My discussion does not impinge upon the textual controversies surrounding the play. Nonetheless, an essay that has influenced my thinking about the text is Leah S. Marcus's as yet unpublished essay, 'The Shakespearean Editor as Shrew Tamer': see also Marcus's 'Levelling Shakespeare: Local Customs and Local Texts' in *Shakespeare Quarterly (SQ)* 42 (1991).
4. The phrase comes from Barbara Hodgdon's essay, forthcoming in *PMLA*, 'Katherina Bound, or Pla(k)ating the Stictures of Everyday Life', which offers an insightful assessment of the visual pleasures that performance of this play makes available to the female spectator.
5. Carol Thomas Neely, *Broken Nuptials in Shakespeare's Plays* (New Haven: Yale Univ. Press, 1985), p. 218. Other essays that specifically address the knotty problem of reading through gender that this play in particular poses include Shirley Nelson Garner, '*The Taming of the Shrew*: Inside or Outside of the Joke?' and Peter Berek, 'Text, Gender, and Genre in *The Taming of the Shrew*', both in *'Bad' Shakespeare: Revaluations of the Shakespeare Canon*, Maurice Charney, ed. (London and Toronto: Associated Univ. Presses,

1988), pp. 105–19 and 91–104; Joel Fineman, 'The Turn of the Shrew' in *Shakespeare and the Question of Theory*, Patricia Parker and Geoffrey Hartman, eds (London: Methuen, 1985), pp. 138–59, esp. pp. 141–4; Marianne L. Novy, 'Patriarchy and Play in *The Taming of the Shrew*', *English Literary Renaissance*, 9 (1979), 264–80; Kathleen McLuskie, 'Feminist Deconstruction: Shakespeare's *Taming of the Shrew*', *Red Letters*, 12 (1982), 15–22; Martha Andresen-Thom, 'Shrew-taming and Other Rituals of Aggression: Bating and Bonding on the Stage and in the Wild', *Women's Studies*, 9 (1982), 121–43; John Bean, 'Comic Structure and the Humanizing of Kate in *The Taming of the Shrew*', in *The Woman's Past: Feminist Criticism of Shakespeare*, Carolyn Ruth Swift Lenz, Gayle Greene, and Carol Thomas Neely, eds (Urbana: Univ. of Illinois Press, 1980), pp. 65–78; Jeanne Addison Roberts, 'Horses and Hermaphrodites: Metamorphoses in *The Taming of the Shrew*', *SQ*, 34 (1983), 159–71; Coppélia Kahn, '*The Taming of the Shrew*: Shakespeare's Mirror of Marriage,' *Modern Language Studies*, 5 (1975), 88–102; Robert B. Heilman, 'The *Taming Untamed*, or, The Return of the Shrew', *Modern Language Quarterly*, 27 (1966), 147–61; and Richard A. Burt, 'Charisma, Coercion, and Comic Form in *The Taming of the Shrew*', *Criticism*, 26 (1984), 295–311.

6. For accounts of this production history, see Ann Thompson, pp. 17–24. In his discussion of the inappropriate historicization at work in Jonathan Miller's attempt to imagine Petruchio as spokesman for the new Puritan ideals of companionate marriage, Graham Holderness demonstrates how the Miller BBC television production provides yet another instance of a theatrical attempt to save this play from its own ending (*The Taming of the Shrew* in the Shakespeare in Performance series [Manchester and New York: Manchester Univ. Press, 1989], pp. 21–5).

7. J. Wickham Legg, *Ecclesiological Essays* (London: de la More Press, 1903), p. 190.

8. George Elliott Howard, *A History of Matrimonial Institutions*, 2 vols. (London: T. Fisher Unwin, 1904), vol. 1, pp. 306–7. '*Tunc procidat sponsa ante pedes ejus, et deosculetur pedem ejus dextrum; tunc erigat eam sponsus*' (*Surtees Society Publications*, 63, 20 n.). See also J. Wickham Legg, pp. 189–90, and *The Rathen Manual: Catholic Church, Liturgy and Ritual*, ed. Duncan MacGregor (Aberdeen: Aberdeen Ecclesiological Society, 1905), p. 36. In comments on the wedding-ritual structure that underwrites the scene of Lear, Cordelia, and her suitors, I had earlier suggested the possibility of such a literal, ceremonial basis to the line 'I take up what's cast away' (I.i.253) that France speaks to Cordelia ('The Father and the Bride in Shakespeare,' *PMLA*, 97 [1982] 325–47, esp. pp. 333–4).

9. *Of the Russe Common Wealth*, chap. 24, fol. 101, as quoted in Legg, p. 190.

10. Legg, p. 190. See also J.B. Thiers, *Traité des Superstitions qui regardent les Sacrements*, 4th ed. (Avignon, 1777), book 10, chap. 11, p. 457. Although the 'falling at the feet of the husband' had been banished from the Anglican Rite for some 350 years by the time Legg wrote, his recognition of the women's resistance in the French text prompts him to decry 'innovators in their slack teaching on the subject of matrimony' and comment acerbically that 'the modern upholders of the rights of women would never endure this ceremony for one moment'. As stays against such 'modern ideas', he then invokes Augustine and Paul and digresses from his topic (marriage customs) to include Augustine's definition of a 'good *materfamilias*' as a woman who 'is not ashamed to call herself the servant (*ancilla*) of her husband' (pp. 190–91).

11. 'The Taming of the Scold: The Enforcement of Patriarchal Authority in Early Modern England' in *Order and Disorder in Early Modern England*, Anthony Fletcher and John Stevenson, eds (Cambridge: Cambridge Univ. Press, 1985), pp. 116–36, esp. pp. 116, 136.

12. *Chester Archaeological and Historic Society Journal*, 2 (1855–62), 31–48 and 203–34.

13. Underdown, p. 123.

14. In his otherwise quite useful book, *Juridical Folklore in England: Illustrated by the Cucking-stool* (Durham, N.C.: Duke Univ. Press, 1944), John Webster Spargo spends pages trying to deny the cucking stool-privy stool connection and invalidate, one by one, the etymological links in the numerous terms that support that connection. His argument is finally unpersuasive and seems ultimately to depend upon no more than his own determination not to believe that this could have been possible. It seems to me, however,

quite logical to believe that cucking-stool punishments would have included the additional humiliation of enthroning a woman on a privy stool before riding her through town and ducking her. The punishment was primarily a shaming ritual to begin with, and women's shame has a long history of connection to the body 'privates'.

On matters of the reliability of T.N. Brushfield's research, however, Spargo's comments – together with his widely accepted respectability as a folklorist – prove quite helpful. In Spargo's own work on cucking stools, he relied often upon Brushfield's research, calling his paper on punishment the 'best of all' and 'most comprehensive' (chap. 1, n. 15, and p. 11).

15. Brushfield, p. 219. Since the use of 'rough music' or noise-making instruments to call people out of house to watch the shaming of the scold is common to this punishment, I assume 'bason' refers to such an instrument. The paper that the Norfolk woman carries would most likely have had 'scold' written on it for her to display and thus participate in her own humiliation.

16. p. 122.

17. William Sheppard (or Shepherd). *A Grand Abridgment of the Common and Statute Law of England* (London, 1675), s.v. 'scold', as quoted in Spargo, p. 122.

18. Church of England, *Certain Sermons or Homilies* (London: Society for Promoting Christian Knowledge, 1908), p. 154.

19. Quoted from Brushfield, p. 217.

20. p. 222.

21. In 'Sex Roles and Crime in Late Elizabethan Hertfordshire', *Journal of Social History*, 8 (1975), 38–60, Carol Z. Wiener notes that she has found two cases of male scolds (one in 1584, another in 1598) in the St Albans archdeaconry court (p. 59, n. 64).

22. Lewis Coser has even suggested that violence cannot be considered entirely deviant for men, since within certain subcultures it begets respect ('Some Social Functions of Violence' in *Annals of the American Academy of Political and Social Science*, 364 (1966), 8–18); and Carol Z. Wiener, citing Coser, suggests that Elizabethan communities may have admired the violent behaviour of males, even when it was illegal (p. 59, n. 65). Such attitudes would logically produce different ways of seeing verbal disruptions and noisy challenges to authority.

23. L.J. Ross, 'Shakespeare's "Dull Clown" and Symbolic Music', *SQ*, 17 (1977), 107–28, discusses the distinction that was made between the use of 'Apollonian' and 'Dionysian' music for specific occasions. The charivari is, of course, another 'rough music' ritual.

24. On inversion see Natalie Zemon Davis, 'Women on Top' in *Society and Culture in Early Modern France* (Stanford, Calif.: Stanford Univ. Press, 1975), pp. 124–51; Peter Stallybrass and Allon White, *The Politics and Poetics of Transgression* (Ithaca, N.Y.: Cornell Univ. Press, 1986); Ian Donaldson, *The World Upside-Down: Comedy from Jonson to Fielding* (Oxford: Clarendon Press, 1970); and essays in *Popular Culture in Seventeenth-Century England*, Barry Reay, ed. (New York: St. Martin's Press, 1985), including Reay's introduction, pp. 1–30, Martin Ingram's 'Ridings, Rough Music and Mocking Rhymes in Early Modern England', pp. 166–97, and Peter Burke's 'Popular Culture in Seventeenth-Century London', pp. 31–58.

25. See especially René Girard, *Violence and the Sacred*, trans. Patrick Gregory (Baltimore: Johns Hopkins Univ. Press, 1977). But see also Patricia Klindienst Joplin's perceptive critique of Girard's failure to consider how issues of gender relate to the selection of a scapegoat figure on whom a society's own violence can be both enacted and blamed ('The Voice of the Shuttle is Ours', *Stanford Literature Review*, 1 (1984), 25–53).

26. 'Dramatic Rôle as Social Image: A Study of *The Taming of the Shrew*', *Shakespeare-Jahrbuch*, 94 (1958), 132–50, esp. p. 134.

27. *The Dramatic Works in the Beaumont and Fletcher Canon*, ed. Fredson Bowers, 7 vols. (Cambridge: Cambridge Univ. Press, 1979), vol.4, p. 43.

28. See 'The Taming of the Scold' (cited in n. 11, above).

29. Quoted from Brushfield, p. 226.

30. The totalizing power of Lady Macbeth's three-word injunction – 'Be a Man!' – whether spoken by a woman or another man and whether spoken in 1591 or 1991, is so powerfully controlling only because the threatened category it invokes – woman – has been

276   MATERIALIST SHAKESPEARE

culturally defined as the space of abjection. Conversely, note how powerless is the injunction to 'Be a Woman!'

31. p. 212.

32. See Davis, 'Women on Top'.

33. *Revel, Riot, and Rebellion: Popular Politics and Culture in England 1603–1660* (Oxford: Clarendon Press, 1985), p. 110.

34. See especially pages 106–12 in *Revel, Riot, and Rebellion* for a detailed discussion of 'skimmington' and of the complex political associations that were deployed through gender inversions in the popular politics preceding the Civil War. Also see Buchanan Sharp, *In Contempt of All Authority: Rural Artisans and Riot in the West of England, 1586–1660* (Berkeley: Univ. of California Press, 1980), pp. 100–108, 129.

35. *Revel, Riot, and Rebellion*, p. 111, n. 20.

36. 'Fragments of a Fashionable Discourse' in *Studies in Entertainment: Critical Approaches to Mass Culture*, Tania Modleski, ed. (Bloomington: Indiana Univ. Press, 1986), pp. 139–52, esp. p. 139.

37. The attention paid to Hero's dress in *Much Ado About Nothing*, III.iv, fits into this tradition.

38. As another indicator that *Shrew*'s wedding ceremonies evoke the pre-1549 rite, the offstage act of Communion to which the text alludes is, once again, an anachronism. Prior to the reform, the Sarum, Hereford, Exeter, Westminster, and Evesham books had all included a special bridal Communion of bread and wine. Legg even notes the connection: 'Shakespeare, no doubt describing an Elizabethan marriage in ... *Shrew*, speaks of the drink brought at the end of the ceremony and of the sops in it' (p. 196).

39. For an exemplum text on working with multiple documents coming from a variety of sources, including hitherto unused ones, see Alan Macfarlane, with Sarah Harrison, *The Justice and the Mare's Ale: Law and Disorder in Seventeenth-century England* (New York: Cambridge Univ. Press, 1981).

40. *Poverty and Piety in an English Village: Terling, 1525–1700* (New York: Academic Press, 1979). See also J.A. Sharpe, *Crime in Early Modern England 1550–1750* (London: Longman, 1984), p. 53; and 'Crime and Delinquency in an Essex Parish 1600–1640' in *Crime in England 1550–1800*, J.S. Cockburn, ed. (London: Methuen, 1977), pp. 90–109.

41. In the twentieth century the social offenders who had four centuries earlier been signified by whoring, witchcraft, scolding, and being masterless men and women have been replaced by those whose identity may be similarly inferred from the fetishized criminality the state currently attaches to abortion, AIDS, street drugs, and, most recently, subway panhandling (read homelessness).

42. Spargo devotes considerable time to examining this and other etymological questions: see esp. pp. 3–75. An exchange in Middleton's *The Family of Love* depends on the equation. In response to her husband's threat, 'I say you are a scold, and beware the cucking-stool', Mistress Glister snaps back, 'I say you are a ninnihammer, and beware the cuckoo' (*The Works of Thomas Middleton*, ed. A.H. Bullen, 8 vols (London: Nimmo, 1885), V.i.25–8). My thanks to Sarah Lyons for this reference.

43. John Webster, *The Duchess of Malfi*, ed. Elizabeth M. Brennan (New York: Norton, 1983), I.ii.255–56, 257.

44. 'Reading the Body: *The Revenger's Tragedy* and the Jacobean Theater of Consumption', *Renaissance Drama*, 18 (1987), 121–48, esp. p. 122. See also Frank Whigham, 'Reading Social Conflict in the Alimentary Tract: More on the Body in Renaissance Drama', *English Literary History*, 55 (1988), 333–50; and Patricia Parker, *Literary Fat Ladies: Rhetoric, Gender, Property* (London and New York: Methuen, 1987).

45. The stigma that joins these two signs is clearly a durable one, for even in the twentieth century, if a woman is known as 'loud mouthed' or is reputed to participate (especially in so-called 'mixed company') in the oral activities of joking, cursing, laughing, telling boisterous tales, drinking, and even eating – activities that are socially unstigmatized for males – she can still be signified negatively by meanings that derive from an entirely different register.

46. p. 46.

47. Brushfield, p. 35 n.

48. David Underdown's 'The Taming of a Scold' is a notable exception. Literary essays that have brought the scold's bridle into focus and have included depictions of it include Joan Hartwig's 'Horses and Women in *The Taming of the Shrew*', *Huntington Library Quarterly*, 45 (1982), 285–94; Valerie Wayne's 'Refashioning the Shrew', *Shakespeare Studies*, 17 (1985), 159–88; and Patricia Parker, who calls the scold's bridle 'a kind of chastity belt for the tongue' (*Literary Fat Ladies*, p. 27).

49. The sampler is an heirloom in the family of Michael Neill, who provided this information.

50. My knowledge of this bridle comes from Deborah Shuger. In the frontispiece the woman with the bridle is only one figure in a quite complex visualization of interior Protestant virtues, and it is impossible to know whether the bridle she holds intentionally depicts the instrument used on scolds or is purely an allegorical representation of interior discipline. But in a culture where the allegorical is simultaneously the literal and a bridle is being used to produce exterior discipline on unruly women, the problem of signification is such that one representation cannot, it seems to me, remain uncontaminated from association with the other.

51. I am particularly indebted to Susan Warren for her invaluable research in Cheshire County into this issue. Not only was she able to locate the whereabouts of several of these items, but she discovered from an overheard conversation between two women that the notion of a woman 'needing to be bridled' was apparently still alive in the local phrasing.

52. See especially Peter Erickson, *Patriarchal Structures in Shakespeare's Drama* (Berkeley: Univ. of California Press, 1985).

53. pp. 18–19.

54. See especially Joan Hartwig (cited in n. 48, above) and Jeanne Addison Roberts (cited in n. 5 above), as well as Linda Woodbridge, *Women and the English Renaissance: Literature and the Nature of Womankind, 1540–1620*, (Urbana: Univ. of Illinois Press, 1984).

55. Antiquarian folklorist C.R.B. Barrett notes the first recorded skimmington at Charing Cross in 1562. See Barrett '"Riding Skimmington" and "Riding the Stang"', *Journal of the British Archaeological Association*, 1 (1895), 58–68, esp. p. 63. Barrett discusses the way that a skimmington usually involved not the presentation of the erring couple themselves but the representation of them acted out by their next-door neighbours, other substitutes, or even effigies. Thomas Lupton's *Too Good to be True* (1580) includes a dialogue that comments acerbically upon the use of neighbours rather than principles.

As Martin Ingram (cited in n. 24, above) notes, 'the characteristic pretext' for such ridings 'was when a wife beat her husband or in some other noteworthy way proved that she wore the breeches' (p. 168). The skimmington derisions frequently incorporated the symbolics of cuckoldry – antlers, or animal horned heads, once again collapsing the two most pervasively fetishized signs of female disorder into a collocation by which female dominance means male cuckoldry.

56. See Thompson (cited in n. 1, above), p. 12.

57. *Tamburlaine the Great, Parts I and II*, ed. John D. Jump (Lincoln: Univ. of Nebraska Press, 1967), IV.i.180–84.

58. *Swetnam the Woman-hater: The Controversy and the Play*, ed. Coryl Crandall (Purdue, Ind.: Purdue Univ. Studies, 1969), V.ii.331–3. Given the impetus behind the writing of this play, it seems at least worth speculation that if women ever did dislodge the convention of boy actors during this period and appear onstage in women's roles themselves, this play would seem a prime location for such a possibility.

59. *Amazons and Warrior Women: Varieties of Feminism in Seventeenth-Century Drama* (New York: Harvester Press, 1981), p. 208.

60. Huntington Brown, ed. (Cambridge, Mass.: Harvard Univ. Press, 1937).

61. *Another World and Yet the Same: Bishop Joseph Hall's* Mundus Alter et Idem, trans. and ed. John Millar Wands (New Haven and London: Yale Univ. Press, 1981): see 'Book Two: Viraginia, or New Gynia', pp. 57–67, esp. p. 57.

62. p. 58.

63. p. 64.

64. p. 65.

65. p. 66.

66. p. 57.

67. Brown, pp. 64–5.

68. Catherine Belsey also refers to this play; see *The Subject of Tragedy: Identity and Difference in Renaissance Drama* (London and New York: Methuen, 1985), p. 181.

69. Other tongue treatises include an address by George Webbe, Bishop of Limerick, called *The Arraignement of an unruly Tongue. Wherein the Faults of an euill Tongue are opened, the Danger discouered, the Remedies prescribed, for the Taming of a Bad Tongue, the Right Ordering of the Tongue* ... (London, 1619); an offering by William Perkins in *A Direction for the Gouernment of the Tongue according to Gods Word* (Cambridge, 1593); a sermon by Thomas Adams on *The Taming of the Tongue* (London, 1616); a series of 'tongue' sermons by Jeremy Taylor (1653); and Edward Reyner's *Rules for the Government of the Tongue* (1656). The latter is accompanied by a prayer that the book shall prove 'effectuall to tame that unruly Member thy Tongue, and to make thee a good Linguist in the School of Christ'. Spargo provides further data on the publication of all these treatises (pp. 110–20).

70. In particular see Richard C. McCoy's essay, 'Gascoigne's *"Poëmata castrata"*: The Wages of Courtly Success', *Criticism*, 27 (1985), 29–55.

71. As quoted in Spargo, pp. 118–19, n. 28; Spargo notes that there has been considerable controversy over authorship.

72. Quoted here from Spargo, p. 115, n. 21, the sermon was first printed in Adams's *The Sacrifice of Thankfulness* (London, 1616).

73. 'On the Government of the Tongue' appears in *A Body of Practical Divinity* ... (London, 1692), pp. 986–94.

74. (London, 1663); Spargo concurs with my reading (p. 118, n. 26).

75. pp. 29–30. My thanks to Ann Blake for alerting me to the existence of this first-person account.

76. Quoted from Brushfield, p. 33.

77. p. 37.

78. p. 269. This information was forwarded to the Chester Archaeological Society some eighteen months after Brushfield had read his paper and is included by the secretary in the 4 April (1860?) minutes. In the body of the paper, he had earlier noted that bridles with their leading-chains attached to the nose-piece or front of the horizontal hoop – as is the chain on the Manchester bridle – were those designed to 'inflict the greatest lacerations to the wearer's tongue' (p. 37).

79. Brushfield, p. 37.

80. p. 44.

81. p. 45.

82. p. 45.

83. In Morrison, Paul D. carries with him the memory of having 'had a bit in [his] mouth. . . . about how offended the tongue is, held down by iron, how the need to spit is so deep you cry for it. [Sethe] already knew about it, had seen it time after time. . . . Men, boys, little girls, women. The wildness that shot up into the eye the moment the lips were yanked back. Days after it was taken out, goose fat was rubbed on the corners of the mouth but nothing to soothe the tongue or take the wildness out of the eye' (New York: Alfred A. Knopf, 1987, pp. 69, 71).

84. 'The Taming of the Scold' (cited in n. 11, above), p. 120. It was thought unseemly to duck or publicly punish women of higher status, primarily because in that class the status of the husband was invested in the wife, no doubt making officials reluctant to sentence such wives to punishments more harsh than a fine.

85. p. 42.

86. p. 42.

87. *An Ordered Society: Gender and Class in Early Modern England* (London: Basil Blackwell, 1988), p. 130.

88. p. 122.

89. p. 47. The Shakespeare lines Brushfield quotes are, of course, King Lear's words as he bends over the dead – and very silent – Cordelia.

90. Such a progress would complement the transformation Margaret George defines as 'From "Goodwife" to "Mistress": the transformation of the female in bourgeois culture', *Science and Society*, 37 (1973), 152–77.

91. I defer to David Underdown, who earlier used these lines as an epigraph to 'The Taming of the Scold'.

13

'Fashion It Thus': *Julius Caesar* and the Politics of Theatrical Representation

John Drakakis

In David Zucker's 1988 film of *The Naked Gun*, a hapless Los Angeles Chief of Police, Lieutenant Frank Drebin, is warned by his relatively pacifist Mayoress employer to curb his propensity for violence. Drebin, himself an exaggerated postmodernist collocation of easily recognizable film texts, counters with a policy statement of his own sufficient to rival any pronouncement of Clint Eastwood's Dirty Harry: 'Yes, well when I see five weirdos dressed in togas stabbing a guy in the middle of the park in full view of a hundred people, I shoot the bastards. That's my policy.' The response of his outraged employer is the embarrassed revelation that: 'That was a Shakespeare in the park production of *Julius Caesar* you moron. You killed five actors: good ones.' The choice of the assassination scene from *Julius Caesar* to illustrate the violence necessary to redress an alleged crime echoes parodically one of two familiar critical readings of this Shakespearian text. In Zucker's film the comic extolling of Caesarism through the wholly inept efficiency of a law enforcement officer unaware of his own representational status and also, at the same time, unable to distinguish other forms of representation, is reinforced by the reactionary nature of his task: the protection of a visiting English queen against the threat of assassination. The latter, ironically republican critical perspective is exemplified in Alex Cox's film *Walker* (1988) which utilizes a scene from *Julius Caesar* to explore, in the thinly veiled allegorical setting of nineteenth-century Nicaragua, the ironies and contradictions inherent in an imperialist project.[1]

The case of Lieutenant Drebin is not unlike that of Julius Caesar himself, who, according to Thomas Heywood, was so accomplished an 'actor' that on at least one occasion he was involuntarily taken in by the veracity of representation itself. In *An Apology for Actors* (1612), in an argument designed, astonishingly, to advance the cause of acting, Heywood relates the following incident:

Julius Caesar himselfe for his pleasure became an Actor, being in shape, state, voyce, judgement, and all other occurrents, exterior and interior excellent. Amongst many other parts acted by him in person, it is recorded of him, that with generall applause in his owne Theater he played *Hercules Furens*, and amongst many other arguments of his compleatenesse, excellence, and extraordinary care in his action, it is thus reported of him: Being in the depth of a passion, one of his seruants (as his part then fell out) presenting *Lychas*, who before had from *Deianeira* brought him the poysoned shirt, dipt in the bloud of the Centaure, *Nessus*: he in the middest of his torture and fury, finding this *Lychas* hid in a remote corner (appoynted him to creep into of purpose), although he was, as our Tragedians vse, but seemingly to kill him by some false imagined wound, yet was *Caesar* so extremely carryed away with the violence of his practised fury, and by the perfect shape of the madnesse of *Hercules*, to which he fashioned all his actiue spirits, that he slew him dead at his foot, & after swoong him *terq; quaterqu*; (as the Poet sayes) about his head.[2]

This incident is not recorded, unfortunately, in North's translation of *Plutarch's Lives*, and it has all the hallmarks of an apocryphal story. Indeed, apart from Caesar's allegedly acting in a Senecan play, at least some forty years before the birth of Seneca, it is likely that Heywood confused two stories from Philemon Holland's translation of Suetonius's *The Historie of Twelve Caesars* (1606), conflating episodes from the lives of Julius Caesar and Nero.[3] For Heywood Julius Caesar forsakes his status as a historical personage and becomes an actor himself, a focus for a range of narratives invested with sufficient authority to underwrite the activities of other 'actors'. In short, Caesar is adapted for a particular purpose, endowed with what Roland Barthes might call 'a type of social *usage*',[4] accorded the status of a 'myth' which is then used to legitimize an institution whose preoccupation is the business of representation itself. As a mythical entity, the figure of Caesar consisted of material that, as Barthes would say, had *already* been worked on so as to make it suitable for communication.[5]

Some twelve years before the appearance of Heywood's *An Apology for Actors*, and in the newly built Globe Theatre, on 21 September 1599, the Lord Chamberlain's Men mounted a production of *The Tragedie of Julius Caesar*. A Swiss visitor, Dr Thomas Platter, saw the performance, and recorded that 'at the end of the play they danced together admirably and exceedingly gracefully, according to their custom, two in each group dressed in men's and two in women's apparel'.[6] *Julius Caesar* is hardly a play to set the feet tapping, and if, indeed, this was the play that was written, as Dover Wilson conjectured, 'expressly for the opening' of the Globe[7] then the dance about which Dr Platter enthused may have had more to recommend it than mere 'custom'. Indeed, in the light of a persistent outpouring of anti-theatrical sentiments throughout this period, combined with what Jonas Barish identified as 'a deep suspicion toward theatricality as a form of behaviour in the world',[8] such as a gesture, in a newly opened theatre, may be interpreted as an act of flagrant political defiance.[9] This view receives some general reinforcement from Steven Mullaney's persuasive argument that the suburbs where the public theatres were situated constituted 'a geo-political domain that was crucial to the symbolic and material economy of the city ... traditionally reserved for cultural phenomena that could not be contained within the strict or proper bounds of the community'.[10] Moreover, the potential for resistance derived from this contextualization of the theatre is reinforced by his suggestion that dramatic performance may be defined as 'a performance *of* the threshold, by which the horizon of community was made visible, the limits of definition, containment and control made manifest'.[11] In other words, the liminal position of the theatre, which it shared with other forms of festivity, far from simply ventriloquizing the discourses of political domination, engaged in forms of representation through which other, potentially subversive voices could be heard.

A useful model for this complex process might be Volosinov's reformulation of the Freudian opposition between the 'conscious' and the 'unconscious', as a conflict between 'behavioural ideology', which, he argues, is, in certain respects, 'more sensitive, more responsive, more excitable and livelier' and 'an ideology that has undergone formulation and become "official"'.[12] In an attempt to recuperate the Freudian unconscious for a political account of the relationship between the individual and society, Volosinov insists that what is repressed or censored represents a *conscious* expression of 'behavioural ideology' in so far as it expresses 'the most steadfast and the governing factors of class consciousness'.[13] More recently, Antony Easthope has challenged the notion of a 'political unconscious' as it emerges in the work of Pierre Macherey and Fredric Jameson, on the grounds that while the notion of 'class' as a means of positioning the individual 'is involuntary and acts against the individual's will ... it is not *unconscious* or *repressed* in the psychoanalytic sense of these terms'.[14] For Volosinov, where forms of human behaviour which are not divorced from what he calls 'verbal ideological formulation', but which remain 'in contradiction with the official ideology', it is manifestly not the case that they 'must degenerate into indistinct inner speech and then die out', but rather that they 'might well engage in a struggle with the official ideology'.[15] It is the resultant maintenance of contact both with society and with communication that gives to certain forms of behavioural ideology their revolutionary potential. Volosinov grounds the motive for such a struggle on '*the economic being of the whole group*', but he goes on to suggest that such motives develop within 'a small social milieu' before being driven into 'the underground – not the psychological underground of repressed complexes, but the salutary political under- ground'.[16] This is not to suggest that the Elizabethan public theatre was a fully conscious proponent of 'revolutionary ideology', but it does go some way to ascribing intention of a sort within a very complex social formation, while at the same time designating this emergent institution as responsive, excitable, and lively. Indeed, when we consider the timing of perfor- mances, the constraints of official censorship, the social heterogeneity and consequent volatility of public theatre audiences,[17] along with the desire for respectability amongst practitioners, and the attempts to secure influential patronage, it becomes clear that the liminal status of a theatre such as the Globe effectively guaranteed its relative 'openness' to the production of contradictory cultural meanings. In addition, Volosinov goes on to suggest that where there is discontinuity between behavioural and official ideologies, then the result is a radical decentring of the individual human subject; he argues:

> Motives under these conditions begin to fail, to lose their verbal countenance, and little by little really do turn into a 'foreign body' in the psyche. Whole sets of organic manifestations come, in this way, to be excluded from the zone of verbalized behaviour and may become *asocial*. Thereby the sphere of the 'animalian' in man enlarges.[18]

We see some evidence of this decentring, and of the crisis of representation which results from it, in Shakespeare's second tetralogy, and especially in *Henry V*, a play very close temporally and thematically to *Julius Caesar*, where theatrical production itself is something for which a choric apology is required as the precondition of a larger revisionary justification for authority.[19] For Henry V, like his father before him, authority resides primarily in those ritual representations through which class interests and force are articulated: the 'idol ceremony' which is defined, somewhat defensively, in terms of a rhetorical question which discloses the operations of ideology: 'Art thou aught else but place, degree, and form, / Creating awe and fear in other men?' (*Henry V*, IV.i.243–4). As Jonathan Dollimore and Alan Sinfield have cogently argued, at this point the king 'claims to be an effect of the structure which he seemed to guarantee',[20] but he also manipulates those symbols from which he seeks some temporary disengagement in order to elicit sympathy for what we might call, with the benefit of hindsight, 'the management interest'. Of course, the figure of the king is what Derrida, in another context, identifies as a 'central presence',[21] responsible for the ordering, extending and multiplying of a range of signifiers. And it is precisely this presence, 'which has never been itself, has always already been exiled from itself into its own substitute',[22] which the decline and death of Richard II reinforces as what we might call an '*imaginary* signification'.[23] The difficulty for *Henry V* arises directly from the confrontation which takes place in the play between a central organizing signification charged with the task of reconstituting its authority, and the behavioural ideology which challenges, on the terrain of history itself, its efficacy as an instrument for restricting meaning. The relocation – which is also to some extent a dislocation – of this process in the setting of the beginnings of Imperial Rome, and the invocation of a narrative *differentially* constructed along the axis of an opposition between 'popular' and 'humanist' readings of the Caesarian myth, makes *The Tragedie of Julius Caesar* an exemplary text whose own 'ambivalence' is brought into constitutive alignment with the openness and instability of the theatre itself. Indeed, as I shall try to show, the play's concern is not with the *subject* of representation: that is, of rendering a hitherto inaccessible reality present whose ontological status is not in question; but rather with what Robert Weimann has identified as the 'difference within the act of representation' through which a struggle for 'material interests' is articulated.[24] Indeed, if the theatre deals in representations and metaphors it also has the capability to disclose the power that authority *invests* in them, sometimes in the very act of denying their efficacy.

As a number of commentators have shrewdly observed, *Julius Caesar* contains no king; that is, absent from the play is what Derrida calls 'a re-assuring certitude which is itself beyond the reach of play'.[25] Caesar's appropriation of the feast of Lupercal, historically and mythically a festival of origins, clearly has the effect of suppressing *difference*, although this ceremonial affirmation of presence is rendered ambivalent by the anti-theatrical puritanism of Flavius and Marullus who challenge this specific *use* of 'holiday'.[26] In his instruction to Marullus to 'Disrobe the images / If you do find them decked with ceremonies' (I.i.64–5), Flavius initiates a deconstruction of the very representations which are a constitutive element of Caesar's success. They are the signifying practices which position Caesar 'above the view of men' at the same time as they reinforce the social hierarchy by keeping 'us all in servile fearfulness' (I.i.74–5). The following scene firmly inscribes Caesar in the process of 'ceremony' both as a producer and an actor, of whom Antony can say: 'When Caesar says "Do this", it is perform'd' (I.ii.12), and who insists upon a complete performance: 'Set on, and leave no ceremony out' (I.ii.13). By contrast, Brutus admits, 'I am not gamesom' (I.ii.30), although this anti-festive expression is quickly belied by a tacit admission of consummate acting: 'If I have veiled my look, / I turn the trouble of my countenance / Merely upon myself' (I.ii.39–41); and similarly, the Cassius who eschews ritual but articulates his political desires through its language is later affirmed by Caesar as an enemy of theatrical performance: 'He loves no plays' (I.ii.204). But it is ironical that while one performance is taking place elsewhere, to which the audience is denied full access, Cassius proposes to Brutus a performance of another kind, deeply dependent upon the mechanics of representation. In an attempt to disclose his 'hidden worthiness' (I.ii.59), Cassius constructs a 'self' for Brutus which the latter identifies as both dangerous and alien, and it is one which involves the exposure of the means through which the allegedly tyrannical image of Caesar is sustained. Ironically, the demythologizing of Caesar, which involves divesting his name of political resonance, is itself dependent upon a representation: 'I, your glass, / Will modestly discover to yourself / That of yourself which you yet know not of' (I.ii.70–3). Here the 'self' is not that ontologically stable '*Center* of my circling thought' of Sir John Davies's *Nosce Teipsum*,[27] but a fabrication that can be persuaded that it is fully the subject of its own actions:

> Men at some time were masters of their fates.
> The fault, dear Brutus, is not in our stars,
> But in ourselves, that we are underlings.
>
> (I.ii.140–42)[28]

Indeed, it is characteristic of all the conspirators that they oppose 'truth' to a distinctly theatrical falsity, as evidenced in the opposition Casca sets up between Caesar the theatrical performer and himself as a 'true man': 'If the tag-rag people did not clap him and hiss him, according as he pleased and displeased them, as they use to do the players in the theatre, I am no true man' (I.ii.258–61). Also, it is not entirely inappropriate that Messala's eulogy over the body of Cassius at the end of the play should focus upon the ambivalence of representation itself: 'Why dost thou show to the apt thoughts of men / The things that are not?' (V.iii.67–8). Indeed, in the play as a whole, one man's truth is another man's theatre. If, as Ernest Schanzer speculated, 'perhaps there is no real Caesar, that he merely exists as a set of images in other men's minds and his own.',[29] then the same is doubly true of Brutus, a self fashioned in accordance with the demands of an ambivalent narrative which elicits, to use Schanzer's phrase, 'divided responses'.[30]

Cassius, the stage machiavel, whose metaphorical location in the play, despite protestations in principle to the contrary, is 'Pompey's Theatre' (I.iii.152) – significantly, also, the place where Caesar's own death will be staged in accordance with the generic demands of *de casibus* tragedy – initiates here a theatrical process which resonates through the remainder of the play. Casca, plucked by the sleeve, will, like a metropolitan drama critic, 'after his sour fashion, tell you / What hath proceeded worthy note

today' (I.ii.181–2). Cassius himself will script the representations of an
alternative theatre where language itself is an irreducibly material phenomenon, and where signifiers such as 'offence', 'virtue' and 'worthiness' will
depend for their meanings upon the alchemical process produced by an
appearance: 'that which would appear offence in us / His countenance, like
richest alchemy, / Will change to virtue and to worthiness' (I.iii.158–60).
As a subject of this discourse, where the stakes are political supremacy,
Brutus, to use Althusser's phrase, works by himself. Indeed, in a speech
which, in part, echoes Marlowe's Machevil,[31] he fabricates a narrative
which radically opposes personal obligation – the friendship and 'love'
through which imperial politics articulate their hierachical interests –
against a republican view which justifies human intervention in the social
order:

> But 'tis a common proof
> That lowliness is young ambition's ladder,
> Whereto the climber-upward turns his face;
> But when he once attains the upmost round,
> He then unto the ladder turns his back,
> Looks in the clouds, scorning the base degrees
> By which he did ascend. So Caesar may.
> Then lest he may, prevent. And since the quarrel
> Will bear no colour for the thing he is,
> Fashion it thus:

                                                          (II.i.21–30)

Brutus, like Cassius before him, conjures here a representation of a Caesar
that the play never allows us to observe as anything other than a wholly
fabricated identity, and as a consequence the action is pushed further into
that liminal realm already occupied by the theatre itself.

   Cassius and Casca's 'fashioning' of Brutus is an indispensable precondition for the success of the conspiracy, and Brutus's soliloquy at the
beginning of Act II moves the action deeper into that liminal area where
ideology and subjectivity intertwine. It is also the area where strategies for
the controlling and contesting of meaning are formulated. There is very
little in the play as a whole that does not generate alternative readings,
whether it be public display, ritual sacrifice, or psychic phenomenon, and
it is this hermeneutic instability, the consequence of the existence of two
radically opposed forms of authority in Rome, that returns the analysis of
motive and action to the space occupied by the theatre which can now
claim both to produce *and* to interrogate ideologies. The theatre itself
achieves this complex objective, to use Michael Holquist's formulation,
through bending language 'to represent by representing languages';[32] and
we can see precisely what is involved here in Brutus's response to

Cassius's suggestion that Antony and Caesar should 'fall together' (II.i.161). In this debate, as elsewhere in the play, critics of the most liberal of persuasions have sided with Cassius,[33] but it is Brutus more than Cassius who grasps the importance of mediating the conspiracy through existing rituals and institutions.[34] Here representation accumulates a level of irony which discloses it as misrepresentation:

> Let's be sacrificers, but not butchers, Caius.
> We all stand up against the spirit of Caesar,
> And in the spirit of men there is no blood.
> O, that we then could come by Caesar's spirit,
> And not dismember Caesar! But alas,
> Caesar must bleed for it.

> (II.i.166–71)

Clearly, liberation from alleged tyranny cannot be permitted to result in absolute freedom for all. If so, authority and power are not worth having. Resistant though the conspirators are to the Caesarian control of institutions and meanings, they formulate a strategy of temporary release and restraint which parallels the *ideological* usage of festivity, extending the potential for containment to the affective power of tragic form itself. These concerns are concentrated with remarkable economy in Brutus's appeal to his fellow conspirators: 'And let our hearts, as subtle masters do, / Stir up their servants to an act of rage, / And after seem to chide 'em' (II.i.175–7). From this point on the talk is of 'fashioning', of manufacturing, and hence of historicizing, truth, and, inevitably, of theatrical representation. The fully fashioned Brutus will now undertake to 'fashion' Caius Ligarius (II.i.219), an assertion that may well have received an added irony in the original performance where it is thought that the parts of Cassius and Caius Ligarius may have been doubled.[35] Such a suggestion would give added ironical point to Cassius's own speculation in his soliloquy at I.ii.314–15: 'If I were Brutus now, and he were Cassius, / He should not humour me.' Also Cassius's bid to revive Roman self-presence with his exhortation to the conspirators to 'Show yourselves true Romans' (II.i.222) is expanded by the one character whose 'countenance' is endowed with transformative power: 'Let not our looks put on our purposes; / But bear it as our Roman actors do, / With untired spirits and formal constancy' (II.i.224–6). Here theatrical representation is neither illusion nor self-delusion, rather it is the ground upon which the symbols of authority are contested. It is no accident that Thomas Beard could refer to the conspirators as those who 'were actors in this tragedy'[36] or that William Fulbecke could refer to Brutus as 'chiefe actor in Caesars tragedie'.[37]

If the conspirators are exhorted to sustain a 'formal constancy', then the Caesar which the first two acts of the play reveals is as consummate a

Roman actor as his adversaries. To recuperate the assassination as the *origin* of a theatrical tradition in which the tragic protagonist is the unwitting participant, as Cassius later does, is simultaneously to expose the discursive mechanisms, at the moment that it seeks to reinforce, the historical and material determinants, of political power: 'How many ages hence / Shall this our lofty scene be acted over / In states unborn and accents yet unknown!' (III.i.112–14). In an augmentation of the practice of scripting, Brutus urges his accomplices to: 'Let's all cry "Peace, freedom, and liberty"!' (III.i.111), but this is followed almost immediately by the entry of a 'servant' who produces, not the voice of a free subject, but that of his 'master' Antony which he proceeds to ventriloquize. In the following scene it is the plebeian voice, emanating from an onstage audience credited with a dutiful quiescence which the actual Globe audience was unlikely to have reflected, which, ironically, through a replication of conspiratorial locutions, confirms the continuity of the rhetoric and symbols of political power: 'Let him be Caesar', 'Caesar's better parts / Shall be crowned in Brutus' (III.ii.51–3). As in the later play *Coriolanus* the 'audience' is simultaneously empowered and disempowered, allotted a role from which it cannot escape. In the later play, where the Roman populace is given a more substantial critical voice, the *irony* of this position is laid open to question as the Citizens are obligated to support a patrician in whom they have little confidence:

> We have power in ourselves to do it, but it is a power that we have no power to do. For if he show us his wounds and tell us his deeds, we are to put our tongues into those wounds and speak for them; so if he tell us his noble deeds we must also tell him our noble acceptance of them. Ingratitude is monstrous, and for the multitude to be ingrateful were to make a monster of the multitude, of the which we, being members, should bring ourselves to be monstrous members.
>
> (*Coriolanus* II.iii.4–13)[38]

If this is so, then it is extremely doubtful whether such self-consciously theatrical allusions serve, as Anne Righter has argued, 'pre-eminently to glorify the stage'.[39] This representation of the workings of political power, irrespective of intention, discloses an unstable institution proceeding gingerly into a terrain fraught with considerable political danger. Cast in a subversive role, confronted with the demands of official censorship, but nevertheless seeking legitimation, the actual choice of dramatic material would have been crucial. In *Julius Caesar* the Chamberlain's Men could displace their own professional anxieties onto a narrative which, by virtue of its very ambivalence, offered a space for the exploration of the ideology which governs the exchange of representations which take place between society and theatre, centre and margins.

In a culture in which those who would oppose theatrical representation continued to insist upon the power that inheres in the theatrical image itself, *Julius Caesar* is not so much a celebration of theatre as an unmasking of the politics of representation per se. The play does not *express* meaning; rather, in its readings of Roman history it *produces* meanings. Moreover, in its shuttling between the generic requirements of *de casibus* tragedy, and the Senecan tragedy of revenge, historical possibilities are simultaneously disclosed and withdrawn, in such a way as to propose an alignment of enjoyment with danger and with resistance. In its vacillation between 'fate' and human agency as the origins of action, and hence of history itself, *Julius Caesar* enacts the precarious position of the Globe itself. This is not the Shakespeare that we have been encouraged to regard as 'profoundly moving, or spiritually restoring, or simply strangely enjoyable', as recently proposed by Professor Boris Ford;[40] this carefully tailored brand of anti-intellectual prophylactic consumerism demands a kind of passivity that refuses to contemplate, among other things, the popular significance of that unsettling carnivalesque dance that closed the Globe performance of *Julius Caesar*. It subscribes tacitly to a teleological conception of Art not too far removed from the advice proffered by the Arts Minister, Richard Luce, as part of an argument in support of the suppression of modern 'popular' theatre: 'You should accept the political and economic climate in which we now live and make the most of it. Such an attitude could bring surprisingly good results.'[41] Of course, as we know from our own media representations of a crisis which is much nearer to us than Renaissance readings of the origins of Imperial Rome, no gun is ever naked.

Notes

1. See Geoffrey Bullough, *Narrative and Dramatic Sources of Shakespeare*, 8 vols (London and New York, 1977), vol. 5, pp. 58–211, for the full range of source material for *Julius Caesar*.

2. Thomas Heywood, *An Apology For Actors*, I. G., *A Refutation of The Apology For Actors, The English Stage: Attack and Defense 1577–1730* (New York and London, 1973), sig. E3v.

3. C. Suetonius Tranquillius, *The Historie of Twelve Caesars, Emperors of Rome*, trans. Philemon Holland (London, 1606), sig. c2v–3, and sigs. R4–4v. See also Suetonius, *The Twelve Caesars*, trans. Robert Graves (Harmondsworth, 1957), pp. 26ff. and pp. 219ff.

4. Roland Barthes, *Mythologies*, trans. Annette Lavers (St Albans, Herts., 1973), p. 109.

5. Ibid., p. 110.

6. William Shakespeare, *Julius Caesar*, ed. A. R. Humphreys (Oxford and New York, 1984), p. 1.

7. William Shakespeare, *Julius Caesar*, ed. J. Dover Wilson (Cambridge, 1941), p. ix.

8. Jonas A. Barish, *The Antitheatrical Prejudice* (Berkeley, Los Angeles, and London, 1981), p. 133.

9. See John Drakakis, *The Plays of Shackerley Marmion (1603–39): A Critical Old-spelling Edition*, 2 vols unpublished PhD thesis, University of Leeds (1988), vol. 1, pp. 494ff. for a full account of the controversial position of dancing during the late sixteenth and early seventeenth centuries.

10. Steven Mullaney, *The Place of the Stage: License, Play and Power in Renaissance England* (Chicago and London, 1988), p. 9.

11. Ibid., p. 31.

12. V.N. Volosinov, *Freudianism: A Marxist Critique*, trans. I.R. Titunik (New York, San Francisco and London, 1976), p. 88.

13. Ibid., p. 88.

14. Antony Easthope, *Poetry and Phantasy* (Cambridge and New York, 1989), pp. 36–7. For a fuller articulation of the debate to which Easthope responds, see Pierre Macherey, *A Theory of Literary Production*, trans. Geoffrey Wall (London, 1978), pp. 85ff., and Fredric Jameson, *The Political Unconscious: Narrative as a Socially Symbolic Act* (London, 1981), pp. 17–103.

15. Volosinov, *Freudianism*, pp. 89–90.

16. Ibid., p. 90.

17. Cf. Andrew Gurr, *Playgoing in Shakespeare's London* (Cambridge, 1987), pp. 51–7.

18. Volosinov, p. 89.

19. See John Drakakis, 'The Representations of Power in Shakespere's Second Tetralogy', *Cosmos: The Yearbook of the Traditional Cosmology Society*, vol. 2 (1986), ed. Emily Lyle, pp. 111–35.

20. Jonathan Dollimore and Alan Sinfield, 'History and Ideology: The Instance of *Henry V*', in John Drakakis, ed., *Alternative Shakespeares* (London, 1985), pp. 222–3.

21. Jacques Derrida, *Writing and Difference*, trans. Alan Bass (London, 1978), p. 280.

22. Ibid.

23. See Cornelius Castoriadis, *The Imaginary Institution of Society*, trans. Kathleen Blamey (Cambridge, 1987), pp. 146–56.

24. Robert Weimann, 'Towards a Literary Theory of Ideology: Mimesis, Representation, Authority', Jean E. Howard and Marion O'Connor, eds, *Shakespeare Reproduced: The Text in History and Ideology* (New York and London, 1987), p. 271.

25. Derrida, p. 279.

26. Cf. Richard Wilson, '"Is this a Holiday?": Shakespeare's Roman Carnival', *English Literary History*, 54, no. 1 (spring, 1987), 31–44. See also Mark Rose, 'Conjuring Caesar: Ceremony, History, and Authority in 1599', *English Literary Renaissance*, 19, no. 3 (autumn, 1989), 291–304. For a more general discussion of the anti-authoritarian notion of festivity, see also Mikhail Bakhtin, *Rabelais and His World*, trans. Hélène Iswolsky (Cambridge, Massachusetts, and London, 1968), pp. 21ff., and Peter Burke, *Popular Culture in Early Modern Europe* (London, 1979), pp. 182ff.

27. Sir John Davies, *The Poems of Sir John Davies*, ed. Robert Kreuger (Oxford, 1975), pp. 182ff.

28. I have followed the reading of 1.140 in *William Shakespeare: The Complete Works*, eds Stanley Wells, Gary Taylor, John Jowett, and William Montgomery (Oxford, 1986). However, the Folio reading of the line is: 'Men at sometime, are Masters of their Fates', and this is followed in A.R. Humphreys, ed., *Julius Caesar* (Oxford and New York, 1984), and T.S. Dorsch, ed., *Julius Caesar* (London, 1965). The use of the present tense of the verb lends greater immediacy to Cassius's machiavellian proposition to Brutus.

29. Ernest Schanzer, *The Problem Plays of Shakespeare* (London, 1963), p. 32.

30. Ibid., p. 6.

31. Cf. Christopher Marlowe, *The Jew of Malta*, ed. N.W. Bawcutt (Manchester, 1978), p. 63:

> Though some speak openly against my books,
> Yet will they read me, and thereby attain
> To Peter's chair; and when they cast me off
> Are poisoned by my climbing followers.

(Prologue: lines 10–13)

32. Michael Holquist, 'The Politics of Representation', in *Allegory and Representation*, ed. Stephen Greenblatt (Baltimore and London, 1981), p. 169.

33. Cf. Irving Ribner, *Patterns in Shakespearian Tragedy* (London, 1969), p. 60. See also Ernst Honigmann, *Shakespeare: Seven Tragedies: The Dramatist's Manipulation of Response* (London, 1976), p. 50; Alexander Leggatt, *Shakespeare's Political Drama: The History Plays and the Roman Plays* (London, 1988), p. 144; and Vivian Thomas, *Shakespeare's Roman Worlds* (London, 1989), p. 76.

34. For a more negative view, see Robert S. Miola, *Shakespeare's Rome* (Cambridge, 1983), p. 93, where it is suggested that 'Brutus's words reveal the savagery of the impending Roman ritual; in addition they expose the self-delusion of the conspirators.'

35. A.R. Humphreys, ed., *Julius Caesar*, pp. 80–81. I am also grateful to Professor Gunther Walch for having drawn this possibility to my attention in his unpublished paper '"Caesar did never wrong, but with just cause": Interrogative Dramatic Structure in *Julius Caesar*'.

36. Thomas Beard, *The Theatre of God's Judgements* (London, 1957), p. 249, *Short Title Catalogue (STC)* 1659.

37. William Fulbecke, *An Historicall Collection of the Continuall Factions, Tumults, and Massacres of the Romans and Italians* (London, 1601), p. 170, *STC* 11412.

38. See John Drakakis, 'Writing the Body Politic: Subject, Discourse, and History in Shakespeare's *Coriolanus*', *Shakespeare Jahrbuch*, ed. Gunther Klotz (1992), pp. 62–8.

39. Anne Righter, *Shakespeare and the Idea of the Play* (Harmondsworth, 1967), p. 141.

40. Boris Ford, 'Bardbiz', *Letters: The London Review of Books*, vol. 12, no. 14 (2 August 1990).

41. John McGrath, *The Bone Won't Break: On Theatre and Hope in Hard Times* (London, 1990), p. 161.

14

Henry V and the Paradox of the Body Politic

Claire McEachern

The ambivalent practice and effect of Shakespeare's *Henry V* is by now a critical commonplace. In Norman Rabkin's definitive characterization, the play's shifting portrayal of political power provides the fulcrum of its affective structure: the state appears alternately as beneficent or coercive, displaying 'the simultaneity of our deepest hopes and fears about the world of political action'.[1] Ambivalence about the stance of the play (and, by implication, those of its author and the Elizabethan theatre) with regard to the imperatives of the Elizabethan state persists in more recent critical evaluations. Arguments that the play presents an ideal portrait of state power emphasize the comic rhythm of the ending or perspectives such as that of the Chorus; evidence to the contrary includes Henry's denial of his former tavern companions, his insensitivity to the common soldiers, and his rapacious wooing of Katharine of France. Historicist critics phrase the play's representation of power in a vocabulary of subversion (the suspension of hegemonic interest) or mystification (the state's canny occlusion of its coercive nature),[2] tending to resolve the play's ambivalence in the direction of the ultimately coercive nature of the state (hence the bleak fashion, in many current arguments, for subversion to become mystification).[3] Feminist critics, too, have recently underscored the pejorative nature of the play's representation of power as it manifests itself through the patriarchy. Karen Newman writes, for instance, that Henry 'domesticates [Katharine's] difference, refashioning the other as the same.... Katharine is not only "englished" but silenced as well'.[4]

What is of most interest to me is the terminology invoked in such evaluations of hegemony. Changes in critical fashion notwithstanding, discussion of *Henry V*'s ambivalence frequently takes place in terms of Henry's character, a process in which the fleeting appeal of the state is that of its chief officeholder. As Rabkin observed, the play orchestrates our feelings about power through its depiction of Henry's personality, a personality coded as interiority: 'Shakespeare reveals the conflicts between ... our longing that authority figures can be like us and our suspicion that they must have traded away their inwardness for the sake of power.'[5] Despite current attempts to denaturalize notions of human subjectivity, *Henry V* frames response as a referendum on the fluctuating personableness of the king. Whether seen as a function of generic miscegenation or of the contradictions of social context, the play's ambiguity often surfaces in critical discourse in the terminology of personality. Whether they portray Henry as an 'amiable monster', 'an imperfect man', or 'the man placed at a disadvantage in the sphere of personal relations by the fact of a corporate self',[6] discussions of the character typically gauge his appeal in terms of his relative 'humanity', as if such a quality were a matter of degree.[7]

That we persist in discussing dramatic constructs as people – in Catherine Belsey's terms, 'unified, knowing and autonomous'[8] – perhaps testifies to our inheritance of novelistic notions of character (and no doubt owes more to our tendency to consider people as people). In the case of *Henry V*, modern narratives of the liberal subject are reinforced by Shakespeare's provision, in the second tetralogy, of a narrative of psychological maturation for this mirror of all Christian kings. Such personability is also a function of the phenomenology of acting: not only an actor's ability to embody the lines he speaks but our own affinity with the character who graces us with the intimacy of soliloquy – 'to identify with the "I" of an utterance, to be the agent of the action inscribed in the verb'.[9]

I would like to shift the discussion away from the personability of Henry V to the question of why the play and its location in Elizabethan culture so repeatedly generate *personableness* as the currency of our response. I will argue that discussion of the play's representation of power in terms of personhood derives from a similar inflection in Elizabethan discourses of communality. I wish, then, to examine the 'person-ality' of Henry as sharing in the Elizabethan personification of the crown, sharing not so much in a discourse of personal subjectivity as in the tropes of subjectivity used to produce a particular Elizabethan political affect – that of corporate identity, of what we might call 'the nation'.[10]

By *personification* I mean in part the anthropomorphic imagining of political process in terms of human agency, or what Phyllis Rackin has described as the Elizabethan humanist's secularizing attention to the 'second causes' of historical process, 'that is, ... [to] human actions and their consequences'.[11] Such personification, like the medieval theory of the monarch's two bodies, attempts to describe the relationship between the respective claims and longevities of individual interest and state power; it is also indebted to John Foxe's *Actes and Monuments*, arguably the first English 'popular' history, in imagining historical agency not merely as the property of human rulers but of ordinary (if elect) people. But in addition to this 'population' of political terminology, I would like to examine the affective or interpellative ramifications of the Elizabethan deployment of a vocabulary of the monarch's private identity in the service of corporate identity: what, in other words, are the consequences of imagining the state as if it were a person? Admittedly, to consider the symbolic evocation of personhood as a function of political identity may work only to denaturalize identity at the expense of mystifying power. The formulation may also seem overweening, since in early modern England, state power was largely concentrated in – or at least symbolically configured by – a person. Yet what I wish to explore is the way this discourse of personhood animates corporate identity.

Literary personification operates through a range of techniques, from denotations of psychological interiority (Rabkin's 'inwardness') to the more material portrait of a body (itself often a trope of affect) or of the passions. Tudor rhetorician George Puttenham describes personification as the 'attribut[ion of] any humane quality ... to dombe creatures or other insensible things, ... to giue them a humane person'. Henry Peacham defines it as 'the fayning of a person, that is, when to a thing senseless or dumme, wee fayne a fit person', giving as an example: 'an Oratoure by this figure maketh the common wealth to speak'.[12] Like many rhetorical operations, prosopopoeia depends on the construction of a similitude in which certain attributes of one term are conferred on another – 'to borrow the name of one thing, to expresse another, that did in something much resemble it'.[13] Indeed, personification literalizes this similitude; the endowment of an abstract ideal with human aspect typically relies for its effect on the attribution of speech to the 'dumme', speech that then produces the transactions of empathic identification or a kind of fellowship. As Peacham explains, 'The vse of this figure is very profytable in perswading, chyding, complayning, praysing, and pittying.'[14] Not surprisingly, among the responses attendant on dramatic characterization is a recognition between auditor and character of a common affect, as when a character seems to speak one's own thoughts – for example, Coleridge's smack of Hamlet – or in the milder acknowledgement that 'he' or 'she' may be measured against one's own image: like or unlike, the important fact is that the auditor entertains the possibility of a shared identity. Tellingly, discussions of Henry V's 'humanity' often index its presence as 'fellow feeling' or a consciousness of mutuality. Rabkin, for example, asks: 'can [the king's] political resourcefulness be combined with qualities more like those of an audience *as it sees itself*?'[15] Or as Richard Helgerson observes, 'Shakespeare's play unequivocally denies [a dream of commonality].... King Hal ... scarcely remembers his own humanity, which is squeezed almost to nothing by the burden, as he likes to think of it, of his office.'[16]

As these two formulations indicate, the transactions of audience-character identification in a history play, or even the alliances among characters within a play (the two may be intimately related), are instrumental to political identities. Personification's animating correspondences are perhaps especially relevant to a modern, democratic notion of popular sovereignty, given its assumptions about the state's obligation to elide differences between power and people, between 'office' and 'an audience as it sees itself'. However, as Rabkin and Helgerson also indicate, modern apprehensions of Henry's personhood tend to imagine an antipathy between hegemonic power and fellow feeling, a binary in which Henry's humanity exists in an inverse proportion to 'his' accommodation of state interests. In other words, we attribute variations in how we feel about power in *Henry V* to the mutability of character rather than of power. Such an antipathy is typical (if paradoxically so) of our own democratic imagination, which, while it holds to the ideal that common feeling may coexist with state power, more often betrays scepticism about this possibility, especially with regard to earlier state formations.[17] The now-commonplace consideration of the early modern state as ultimately hegemonic exacerbates such scepticism; any apprehension of early modern democratic impulses, we are told, is anachronistic – a false recognition, so to speak, of fellowship between past and present, monarchy and democracy (anachronism being a habit for which nationalism is also notorious). Such efforts to adjudicate historical difference have rightly served to estrange Shakespeare, whether out of an effort to denaturalize hegemony (while affirming its persistence) or, more wistfully (even Whiggishly), in order to argue some difference between Elizabethan state power and the state power of democracy.

While I acknowledge the dangers of anachronism, as well as the naivety of the hope that hegemony could be other than sinister, my chief target is the assumption that the exercise of state power stands in an unequivocally negative relation to human bonds, the position that reads fluctuation in *Henry V*'s portrait of hegemony as deriving not from any variant depredations of state power but from Henry's intermittent allegiance to its unvarying coercive interests. In discussions of Henry V's character, this position generates the nonsensical diagnosis of a flickering presence of Henry's personhood or humanity. In other words, it produces a discourse of relative human-ness, when, taxonomically speaking, either one is human or one is not. Apprehensions about the shifting appearances of Henry's fellow feeling owe less, I suspect, to the stringency of a postmodern ethos of discontinuous subjectivity than to a pious attempt to purge the terms *human* and *humanity* of what we would like to believe are non-human (or, conversely, all-too-human) tendencies: self-interest, for instance, or the will to power. In what follows I hope to demonstrate that such a segregation of personhood and power was not the habit of the Elizabethan discourse of social identity in which *Henry V* participates, and that social mutuality and tyranny were alike described in terms of monarchic personhood. In so doing, I hope to reveal that the Elizabethan vocabulary of corporate identity did not imagine the relationship between fellowship and hegemony to be an exclusively antithetical one. Rather, much as personhood figures both fellowship and hegemony, so are they complicit forms of social existence. I would like then to argue for the location of the source of the play's multivalent portrait of state power as within neither Shakespeare's ambivalent attitude toward state power nor his text's ambivalent representation of it but within the coincidental nature of state power itself as imagined by Elizabethan terminologies. I will approach this vocabulary by way of one of the major discourses available to us in which monarchic personhood and corporate identity intersect, namely, that of the social practice of the Elizabethan theatre.

For the most part, the contest for control of the Tudor theatre was curiously predictable. London authorities repeatedly insisted on the need for civic order and argued for the unruly potential of plays; and the Privy Council replied, somewhat coyly, in terms of the need to provide royal 'solace':

> the vse and exercise of suche plaies, not beinge euill in yt self, may with a good order and moderacion be suffered in a well gouerned estate, and … hir Maiestie beinge pleased at some times to take delighte and recreacion in the sight and hearinge of them, some order is fitt to bee taken for the allowance and mainteinance of suche persons, as are thoughte meetest in that kinde to yeald hir Maiestie recreacion and delight.[18]

The Privy Council defended playing as compatible with civic order, while London authorities attacked royal prerogative as a defence both of municipal order and, in 1592, of 'a Christian Common wealthe'. In 1594 players became, for city authorities, 'the very sinck & contagion not only of this Citie but of this whole Realm'. And in 1595 and 1597 the authorities' concern for 'the good government of this Cytie' produced the conviction 'that neither in policye nor in religion [plays] ar to be permitted in a Christian Common wealthe'.[19]

The escalation of stakes from the local 'good government of this Cytie' to the entirety of the 'Christian Common wealthe' may have been no more than a sign of mayoral desperation, the 'Common wealthe' becoming the highest rhetorical ground in a turf fight that was, as Steven Mullaney's work makes clear, both literal and symbolic.[20] But even if the 'real' argument concerned the place of the stage within the city of London, its terms were more than local: city authorities, Privy Council, queen, and players alike increasingly insisted that the issue was the place of theatre in the social whole.[21] Though the respective interests of the disputants may indeed have been merely partisan – the aldermen concerned only with civic order, the Privy Council with aristocratic allegiance, the queen with royal prerogative, and the players with private enterprise – the issue at stake, and the term of its expression, is corporate.

Whereas municipal authorities emphasized the common good that flows from comprehensive order, Elizabeth's formulation placed the pleasure of plays quite literally in a *common* weal. For the monarch, plays existed 'as well for the recreacion of our loving subjects, as for our solace and pleasure'.[22] The royal rhetorical disingenuity about the shared pleasure of ruler and ruled momentarily suspends the strata of the social order; the myth of royal munificence as the origin of public recreation not only licenses theatre but portrays the monarch as the bountiful source of and participant in a common feeling.[23] As theatrical pleasure originated with the monarch, so her sponsorship of theatre produced the potential congregation within the theatre. Royal rhetoric nonchalantly uses theatre as a trope for an idealized monarch–subject relationship. Elizabeth's subjects are 'loving', not least because they have been given theatre.[24] In the royal formulation, theatre stands as an index of the monarch–subject bond.

The survival of theatre companies had no doubt more to do with private enterprise than with royal protection and depended less on a queen's appetite than on a commodified taste for entertainment. Further, Elizabeth's 'permission' of this communal activity may be an instance of a state's attempt to regulate what it cannot thoroughly prohibit, and the ease with which the royal voice acknowledged the theatre's existence may have been the result of a studied nonchalance rather than an indulgence. Yet however heterogeneous the social practice, the royal position elaborates a rhetoric of mutuality, of a political identity founded in common feeling. Indeed, as has been well noted in recent criticism, much of the anti-theatrical literature takes as its principal grievance the theatre's potential construction of a 'common' identity in its suspected erosion of social distinctions, both by means of its representational content and through the effects of its material practice.[25] Perhaps most threatening was the literal congregation produced by the theatrical occasion: 'the assemblies of multitudes of the Queenes people' was a fact alluded to in many a mayoral complaint.[26] The description of theatre's public availability as a function of royal munificence, the queen's conflation of allegiance and common-ality, suggests a mystification of order in which the city fathers were loath to concur.

Elizabeth of course did not literally share her subjects' pleasure, or vice versa: public players attended the queen, but the queen herself never attended public theatre. But what in fact the aldermen objected to was the extrapolation of public theatre from Elizabeth's private appetite, the assumption that the latter in some sense occasioned and excused the former. Whereas the queen's voice emphasized the innocence of a common pleasure, resistance to theatrical practice sought to construe innocence as corruption, corporateness as corporeality. Anti-theatrical discourse casts Elizabeth's penchant for plays and aristocratic sponsorship of theatre companies as a wilful exercise of private appetite at the expense of corporate order. As one opponent bemoaned, 'Alas, that priuate affection should so raigne in the Nobilite, that to pleasure, as they thinke, their seruants ... they should restraine the Magistrates from executing their office'.[27] Another critic focused on the theatre's transgression of the boundaries of monarchic affect and the subsequent effect upon social hierarchies: 'there is no passion wherwith the king, the soueraigne maiestie of the Realme was possest, but is amplified, and openly sported with, and made a May-game to all the beholders'.[28] If such a statement censures the violation of social decorum in the translation of royal 'passion' to 'May-game', another complaint contends that the commonly carnal nature of theatrical pleasure itself dissolves another hierarchical boundary – that between humans and animals: 'Tragedies and Commedies stirre vp affections, and affections are naturally planted in that part of the minde that is common to vs with brute beastes'.[29] The same writer objected to the effects of theatrical practice on the borders between private and public: 'in a commonweale, if priuat men be suffered to forsake theire calling because they desire to walke gentleman like in sattine & velvet, with a buckler at theire heeles, proportion is so broken, vnitie dissolued, harmony confounded, that the whole body must be dismembred and the prince or the heade cannot choose but sicken'.[30] And, as the final phrase of this statement suggests, the ultimate recourse was that of the queen's body itself:

> Where [players] pretend that they must haue exercise to enable them in their seruice before her maiestie:
>   It is to be noted that it is not conuenient that they present before her maiestie such playes as haue ben before commonly played in open stages before all the basest assemblies in London and Middlesex.... [I]t lyeth within the dutiefull care for her Maiesties royal persone, that they be not suffred, from playeing in the throng of a multitude and of some infected, to presse so nere to the presence of her maiestie.[31]

As plays originate with Elizabeth, so her body becomes the terrain of last resort. The communal nature of playing is confirmed, ultimately, by its ability to communicate plague to the 'royal persone' of Elizabeth.[32] Theatrical activity and appetites are literally corporeal threats: both originate from, and return to, the body. Whereas in royal discourse a common appetite for theatrical pleasure links the monarch with her subjects, the discourse of order emphasizes a far greater leveller, the common vulnerability to mortality.

The representation of social mutuality as unruly corporeality was not limited to anti-theatrical discourse; on the contrary, such representation was a commonplace of political theory. The Homily of Obedience, for instance, portrays the erosion of social hierarchy as resulting in (and from) 'carnal liberty, enormity, sin, babylonical confusion ... no man shall keep his wife, children, possession in quietness, *all things shall be common*'.[33] Or, as Thomas Elyot warns, 'they which do suppose [commonwealth] so to be called for that ... euery thinge shulde be to all men in comune without discrepance of any estate or condition, be thereto moued more by sensualitie than by any good reason or inclination to humanitie'.[34] Both of these texts imagine social commonness as a comprehensive pursuit of individual interests, not (as we tend to) as a collective sacrifice of them. Yet as such a warning reveals, the labile quality of theatrical congregation (was it innocent fellowship or corrosive leveller?) is less a problem with theatre than with the body, the metaphor used to defend order.

Commonwealth can be, on the one hand, a fairly staid image of corporate welfare. But on the other, of course, it can connote a shared public space of universal welfare potentially contradictory to order and degree. Even though hardly an actual social possibility, the connotation was, not surprisingly, one that contemporary theorists wished to eradicate. Writing in 1606, Edward Forset punctiliously curtails the utopian promise of 'common weale' by collating the image with another that denies the possibility of a society without distinctions:

> It is not therefore called a Commonwealth, that all the wealth should be common; but because the whole wealth, wit, power, and goodnesse whatsoeuer, of euery particular person, must be conferred and reduced to the common good: and that same sort and semblance, as the distinct members of the bodie, being ordained to different vses, do yet concurre in this consonance of intention ... for the procuring and preseruing of the comfort and continuance of this one bodie.[35]

Forset limits the impulse toward a literal distribution of property among individuals and instead defines commonwealth as the collective well-being that results from the subordination of local interests. Whereas municipal authorities would compare social disorder to an unruly body, the 'common good' emerges from a singular 'consonance of intention'. For, as Forset continues, 'there must be a proportionablenesse and a kind of vnanimitie of the members, for the aiding and adorning of the publike comprehending all: so that foule daughter of darknesse and Chaos confused and all disturbing Anarchie, is to be exiled, or rather excluded out of this compaction of the bodie politique'.[36] This body thus excludes the possibility of a 'horizontal' social community in favour of a 'vertical' one, the assumption being, of course, that the 'comfort and continuance of this one bodie' depends on the denial of wealth equally shared. A community imagined in terms of a body appeals because it is bounded, cohesive, and hierarchically organized: the image lends selfhood and a single intention to a political totality that is multifarious in desire.[37]

The image of a centralized 'bodie politique', much like the etymologically labile 'common wealth', is invoked expressly because it contains this levelling potential. But it, too, possesses an inherent instability, an instability also phrased in terms of an excessive corporeality. For just as the possibility that 'all the wealth should be common' threatens the status quo, so, too, does the possibility that the single intention of 'vnanimitie' – an intention personified by the monarch – will rule in conflict with the 'comfort and continuance of this one bodie'. Thus discussions of the body politic describe the image as constraining not only the desires of a common will – 'carnal liberty, enormity, sin' – but also the potentially tyrannical power of the monarch, itself expressed as a disruptive private will.[38] Forset phrases this control as the regulation of corporeality: 'soueraignes through their naturall frailties, are subject as well to the imbecillitie of iudgement, as also to sensuall and irrationall mocions, rising out of the infectious mudd of flesh and bloud, ... do at the making of Statutes ... drawing supplies out of their politicall bodie ... make good what wanteth in their naturall'.[39] The image designed to stabilize and order an aggregate itself unfolds a potential source of (top–down) disorder in the social whole. In the political cosmology where a well-ruled body represents proper community, social disorder is a private, local, willful body – more body than politic. A well-ordered body should be a body only to a certain degree (so to speak). The metaphor employed to inscribe an orderly unity is itself in need of circumscription.

Tyranny is conventionally imagined as antithetical to utopian community; yet, as constructed by Tudor–Stuart texts, they are similar insistences on private interest at the expense of corporate welfare. Both forms of social disorder – the literal common weal and the wilful monarchic interest, the horizontal and vertical extremes of corporateness – collapse into unruly corporeality. 'Carnal liberty' meets 'the infectious mudd of flesh and bloud'. A similar conflation occurs in the intersection of theatre and its royal sponsorship. What in the royal defence of theatre is presented as a coincidence of monarch–subject mutuality – the production of 'loving subjects' – can only be imagined by municipal authorities as the product of a tyrannical 'private appetite'. Such imagination (or lack thereof) demonstrates the difficulty attendant on a monologic ideology of hierarchy in grasping the apparently paradoxical convergence of mutuality and allegiance. The reductive description of the extremes of social totality as corporeality suggests that, as an image of the simultaneity and compatibility of diverse interests, the Tudor–Stuart ideal of corporate identity was, while integrative, yet precariously balanced.[40]

The convergence of monarchic interest with mutuality in the dispute over theatre – the invocation of royal appetite as a trope of common fellowship – raises a related issue fundamental to the conduct of patriotic feeling: what distinguishes a comprehensive hegemonic allegiance from horizontal communion? As Forset's language reveals, the boundary between duty and pleasure is tenuous. A common obligation may unite a social body: 'this strong vnion ... instructeth all true subjects of any countrie to ... the firmest adherence against all opposing enmities ... remembring that a common daunger alike distresseth the lesse as the greatest'. He is yet at pains to warn that a common duty should not be interpreted as producing any equality of persons – 'but especially, to bee tenderly affected in the losse or harme likely to befall their choicest statesmen of the best account and qualitie, against whom the enemies of the state doe chiefly bend their malignant intentions'.[41] If the common pleasure of the theatre can elide categories of order and degree, so might a political identity based in collective loyalty, not to mention a theatre that produces the affect of a common political identity. I don't mean to imply that the experience of theatregoing (or the experience of the nation) is in any way uniform or homogeneous among its participants; 'gentles all' is (in both instances) always ever a fantasy. Nor do I infer that the congregating of play-viewers necessarily results in a feeling of social unity (it might well do the opposite). I would like to suggest, however, that the convergence of tyranny and fellowship exhibited in the terminology of personification – 'solace', 'delight', 'private appetite', 'pleasure' – perhaps reveals why hierarchical societies, despite exhortations to uniformity of allegiance among their citizenry, in fact depend for their survival on differential distributions of loyalty. Or, to imagine the problem differently, this convergence explains why order is best maintained not by comprehensive compliance with the law but by its transgression. As London's aldermen perennially realized, royal sponsorship of the theatre was threatening hierarchy precisely in its promise of a common allegiance. It is with the dual valence of the monarch's body in mind that I would like to turn to a reading of Henry V's personhood.

Critical conventions usually demand at this point (if not well before) a reading of the play which puts such 'backgrounds' to work and, if only proportionally, reestablishes the sovereignty of the literary text. Ideally such a reading would preface itself (having skirted temptations offered by coincidence and innuendo) with an explanation of its correlative mechanism, setting out the nature of the links to be forged between discourses of contexts and literary texts. With *Henry V* the problem of such parallel discourses is unusually difficult to finesse, given that, in the Chorus to Act V, the play itself insists on the act of correspondence between play and culture. 'As by a lower but by loving likelihood', Essex is allied, through comparison, with Henry V. As the phrase reveals, such contextual figurations are not simply mimetic or fully identical but exist in some partial and tendentious relationship to each other. In the spirit of 'lower but loving', I would like then to suggest the congruences and contradictions of a common language, in which Shakespeare's play joins the lexicon of monarchic corporeality to explore the paradox of a space of selflessness imagined as a person.

Perhaps the most evident personification of the coincidence of hegemony and collectivity is that of 'Britain' constructed in the four persons of Captains Fluellen, Gower, Jamy, and Macmorris. The four parts of Britain have unified in a fight against the greater evil of France; individual wills and Britain's traditional regional feuding are subsumed to greater purpose within a fantasy of national (male) bondedness; however, as Jonathan Dollimore and Alan Sinfield put it, 'the Irish, Welsh and Scottish soldiers manifest not their countries' centrifugal relationship to England but an ideal subservience of margin to centre'.[42] Despite the unanimity, a pecking order remains.[43] Caricature functions to isolate Macmorris, but in Fluellen's leek-wearing it serves to assimilate cultural chauvinism to the totality of Britain via tolerance for a bit of quaintness. Although Fluellen is 'a little out of fashion' (IV.i.84),[44] as Henry puts it, he clearly ranks as the favoured subcultural exponent, with an authority both guaranteed and subordinated by ethnic kinship to Henry himself. 'I am Welsh, you know, good countryman', Henry tells Fluellen, who replies, 'All the water in Wye cannot wash Your Majesty's Welsh blood out of your body, I can tell you that' (IV.vii.104–7). Henry's blood secures his corporeal link to his subjects, his intransigently common body, as it were.

But if Henry's blood is Welsh, it is also blue. Henry offers both the most powerful fantasy of collectivity in the play and the most hierarchical denial of common will. Like the salutation of the Chorus – 'gentles all' – the rousing speech before Agincourt explicitly suspends social distinctions in a fantasy of familial harmony: 'We few, we happy few, we band of brothers. / For he today that sheds his blood with me / Shall be my brother; be he ne'er so vile, / This day shall gentle his condition' (IV.iii.60–63).[45] Yet, as if to check the levelling potential of this erasure of social hierarchy,

Henry's closing words on the battlefield displace the promised kinship with a hierarchical ordering: 'Where is the number of our English dead?/ Edward the Duke of York, the Earl of Suffolk, / Sir Richard Keighley, Davy Gam, esquire; / None else of name, and of all other men / But five-and-twenty' (IV.viii.102–6). By naming them in rank order – unless they have no 'name' – this enumeration of the dead reinscribes social divisions, the link between blood and power. Blood and power were, of course, linked within the hierarchical entity of the Elizabethan family, which organized power according to gender and priority of birth. Henry, too, links blood and power in his rallying cry before the gates of Harfleur, when he urges the transformation of body into an instrument of war:

> Stiffen the sinews, conjure up the blood,
> . . .
> Then lend the eye a terrible aspect:
> Let it pry through the portage of the head
> Like the brass cannon. . . .
>
>   (III.i.7–11)

At the same time, Henry punctiliously insists on differences among his 'dear friends', between 'you noblest English, / Whose blood is fet from fathers of war-proof' (III.i.17–18), and 'you, good yeomen, ... Let us swear / That you are worth your breeding ... For there is none of you so mean and base / That hath not noble luster in your eyes' (ll. 25–30).

The play is as vigilant in limiting the scope of common feeling as it is in encouraging it. Henry's body becomes the chief site of this contest. It is precisely the corporeality of the monarchic body that is resisted as the trope is turned into a metaphysics of power. '[H]aving given [him]self over to barbarous license' in the past, he has, on becoming king, 'whipped th' offending Adam out of him, / Leaving his body as a paradise' (I.i.30–31). In Henry's transformation into the head of the unitary body politic (Forset's 'consonance of intention'), 'Hydra-headed willfulness ... soon did lose his seat' (ll. 36–7). Instead of a personable prince, Henry is a collective symbol that denies what he did affect: 'His companies unlettered, rude, and shallow, ... And never noted in him any study, / Any retirement, any sequestration / From open haunts and popularity' (ll. 56–60). In the course of the play, all evidence of his former 'addiction' (l. 54) either dies, is executed, or, like Pistol, 'steals' away (V.i.86). The king who moments before advocated an orgiastic plundering of Harfleur justifies Bardolph's 'cutting off' for the theft of a pax by invoking a modulated conquest: 'we give express charge that, in our marches through the country, there be nothing ... taken but paid for, none of the French upbraided or abused in disdainful language; for when lenity and cruelty play for a kingdom, the gentler gamester is the soonest winner'

304 MATERIALIST SHAKESPEARE

(III.vi.107–13). Thus to 'gentle' is both to erase social division and to reinstate it by turning conquest into a 'noble' sport.

The purification of the body is, of course, nowhere more evident than in the death of Falstaff. Excessive, voracious in its appetites, Falstaff's corporeality appears only in its absence from the play. Henry's 'right wits' and 'good judgments' replace 'the fat knight with the great-belly doublet' (IV.vii.46–7) at the heart of the body politic. Falstaff's death would seem to prove the coercive rather than communal nature of Henry's personification of the body politic: 'the King has killed his heart' (II.i.88). Hostess Quickly's report of Falstaff's demise makes clear the death of corporeality and of the disorder corporeality breeds: 'So 'a bade me lay more clothes on his feet. I put my hand into the bed and felt them, and they were as cold as any stone; then I felt to his knees, and so upward and upward, and all was as cold as any stone' (II.iii.22–5). The cold of Falstaff's genitals tempers the bawdy of this statement, and nostalgia replaces the carnivalesque that Falstaff had embodied. Unassimilable to a geographic typology, Falstaff's boundless body is less a place than a time – as Orson Welles puts it, 'Falstaff is a man defending a force – the old England – which is going down. . . . the death of Merrie England. . . . the age of chivalry, of simplicity, of Maytime and all that'.[46] Libidinal energy and the body are exiled to the margins as the play constructs community in the exclusive image of state power. Falstaff dies offstage.

The preceding account recapitulates conventional response to the second tetralogy, which typically narrates a transformation in the character of Henry, from a personable prince (who can 'drink with any tinker in his own language') to an unfeeling embodiment of state power, and a concomitant affective shift from fellowship to estrangement. However, analysis of *Henry V* also reveals that the opposition between hegemony and mutuality, between power and personhood, is unstable, even anachronistic. For, from his father's vantage point, Hal – 'young wanton and effeminate boy' (*Richard II*, V.iii.10) – cultivates his tavern-founded fellowship in an act of personal wilfulness at the expense of corporate welfare. As Bardolph's transgression reveals, rousing exhibitions of state power have the capacity to break rank: 'What rein can hold licentious wickedness / When down the hill he holds his fierce career?' (III.iii.22–3). More tellingly, *Sir* John Falstaff, if usually described as an embodiment of carnivalesque subversion, also represents an excess of aristocratic prerogative. Necessity as well as nostalgia attend his passing. Tyranny and fellowship are compounded in each instance. Their conjunction suggests that hegemony is not antithetical to collectivity but constitutive of it. Indeed it is arguable that the monarch's less 'personable' qualities, his denial of a common body, only serve to idealize the bonds of allegiance. For instance, in response to Sir Thomas Erpingham's willing embrace of a shared physical discomfort – 'This lodging likes me better, / Since I may say, "Now lie I like a king"' (IV.i.16–17) – Henry concurs with an apocalyptic description of how the denial of physical presence leads to a reincarnation of sorts: 'Tis good for men to love their present pains ... so the spirit is eased. / And when the mind is quickened, out of doubt / The organs, though defunct and dead before, / Break up their drowsy grave and newly move' (ll. 18–22). Similarly, Falstaff's death invokes the eros of sacrifice: we relinquish him as a condition of our willingness to suffer loss for inclusion in the corporate good. A death for your country – the exchange of body for state, of private for public – is, after all, the supreme commerce of social belonging.

The language of the monarch's body, with its punning conflation of both power and pleasure, is also present in the final scene. In his role as the fumbling lover, the king repudiates his private appetites by insisting on the sheerly powerful function of his person. He denies his ability to dance – 'I have no measure in strength' – but affirms his prowess on the battlefield: 'If I could win a lady at leapfrog, or by vaulting into my saddle with my armour on my back, under correction of bragging be it spoken, I should quickly leap into a wife' (V.ii.138–41). Unlike the model lover, Henry shuns his person, describing himself as one 'whose face is not worth sunburning, that never looks in his glass for love of anything he sees there' (ll. 148–50). His claims to Katharine's affection are based on the corporeality of power alone: 'my blood begins to flatter me that thou dost [love me], notwithstanding the poor and untempering effect of my visage' (ll. 223–5). Even at the moment of his conception, he argues, coercion upstaged communion: 'Now beshrew my father's ambition! He was thinking of wars when he got me; therefore was I created with a stubborn outside, with an aspect of iron, that, when I come to woo ladies, I fright them' (ll. 226–9).

However, if Henry's 'blood' reassures him of Katharine's favour (and she is, we must remember, a spoil of war), the affective power of a common body, with its shared vulnerability, is also on his side: 'A good leg will fall, a straight back will stoop, a black beard will turn white, a curled pate will grow bald, a fair face will wither. . . . But in faith, Kate, the elder I wax, the better I shall appear. My comfort is that old age, that ill layer-up of beauty, can do no more spoil upon my face' (ll. 160–63; 229–32). He ends on a typically punning conjunction of tyranny and mutuality:

> take me by the hand, and say, 'Harry of England, I am thine.' Which word thou shalt no sooner bless mine ear withal, but I will tell thee aloud, 'England is thine, Ireland is thine, France is thine, and Henry Plantagenet is thine' – who, though I speak it before his face, if he be not fellow with the best king, thou shalt find the best king of good fellows.
>
> (ll. 237–44)

In this oddly theatrical, disembodied moment – 'though I speak it before his face' – Henry resuscitates his claim to fellow feeling. As with most demonstrations of disingenuity, the effect is at once repellent and appealing. In the symbolic economy where tyranny and fellowship are alike corporeal, denial of one – in this case, the body of pleasure, or of affective union – is at once a denial of the other – the body of tyrannic coercion.

For all of its claims to convergent meanings, the notion of a common language must, in all honesty, acknowledge lapses in convergence; some likelihoods, are, so to speak, lower than others. Any argument for the participation of Shakespeare's play in the Elizabethan language of royal personhood must acknowledge the most glaring instance in which the representation of power in the play differs from its representation in the culture: namely, in the fact of gender difference. In other words, what and how does it matter that the monarch of the history play is male while the then monarch of the Elizabethan state was not? Does the play's representation of a tyrannical appetite as male divertingly idealize Elizabethan monarchy? Does its imagination of monarch–subject mutuality as male alliance suppress cultural anxieties about a female monarch?

In materialist criticism similar questions about contradictions between play and world have produced an evolution in the vocabulary that describes their interplay, a process in which the older language of text-context reflectionism has been replaced by the more sophisticated terms of subversion and containment, mystification and mask. Yet oddly, while we have complicated our notions of aesthetic practice and have even affirmed the textuality of all ideological production, we have yet to apply a similar pressure to the state, except occasionally to point out its internal contradictions. These contradictions function then as signs of ideological incoherence that the state presumably would, if it could, stamp out. In arguing to the contrary that the play's representation of the paradox of monarchic personhood shares in the labile terms of Tudor–Stuart ideology generally, I am arguing in some sense for a return to a kind of reflectionism. I would urge the rehabilitation of ideology as the enabling medium of collectivity as well as that which 'legitimate[s] inequality and exploitation by representing the social order which perpetuates these things as immutable and unalterable'.[47] In other words, I would suggest we might imagine that among the state's interests, the production of an integrated and beneficent social unity is as authentic as any other.

Among the results of our perceived antagonism between fellow feeling and hegemony has been its inability to account for the emotional power of the play's ending, in which the consummation of state interest is attended with all affections of charismatic fellowship. Perhaps the most potent

fantasy of unity and, simultaneously, the most violent purification of the
body from the body politic are proposed in the unification of England and
France through the union of Henry and Katharine: 'the paction of these
kingdoms', as the Queen of France puts it, in 'the bed of blessèd marriage'
(V.ii.263–4). In order more fully to evaluate the play's closing gesture
toward a powerful and pleasurable fellowship, as well as the contradiction
between play and world, I would like to return to the discourse of
monarchic pleasure and its relations to gender.

Where does pleasure reside in the body politic? This question is mostly
avoided by contemporary descriptions of the figure. While internal organs
are given their legislative function, the limbs a juridical purpose, the mind
or soul the chief office, the analogy of function is never pushed to its limits,
its margins, its orifices. Forset allows that a monarch should have some
fun:

> There is nothing that is either more gracefull for seemelinesse of shew,
> or more auaileable to any man for his health, than to haue alwayes a light
> and chearfull heart: and it was yet neuer seene that any part of the body
> cuer grudged at or repugned, but rather willingly furthered the well-
> pleasing delights of the heart. From hence good people will learne this
> well-resembling inference, That the recreating sports and pleasures of
> Soueraignes (in whom is the heartbloud of the ciuill bodie) be not
> dislikingly crossed or repyned at, but rather entertainingly allowed, and
> comfortably affoorded vnto them.[48]

If the monarch-as-heart seems an innocent locus of 'light and chearfull'
pleasure, the heart's morphology confirms the uncontroversial nature of
recreation, for, as Forset continues,

> The figure of the hart is shaped sharpe poynted at the lower end, and
> vpward it is more widely spread abroad: To this forme the best princes
> doe conforme, they open their hearts with a full spread towards vertue,
> goodnesse, and heauenly things, but do make narrow and close the same
> against all base appetites of this vnhallowed flesh.[49]

Forset is writing in 1606 for a male monarch for whom, as Leeds Barroll
reminds us, 'hunting, not plays, was the approved solace',[50] and whose
hips were ideally narrower than his shoulders. Elizabeth's 'full spread',
however, was downward, as the Ditchley portrait makes clear: she held all
of England in her skirts.

Some Elizabethans were more wary of princely pleasure. Hence Thomas
Floyd, writing 'Of pleasures and Delight' in his *Picture of a perfit Common
wealth*, decrees that when properly executing their duty,

governours ... are always to be emploied in matters of great consequence, whereof the charge is such, that if they discharge their duty,
they shall hardly have so much leasure, as to eat their meat, and take their
rest, unlesse they omit some of that time which should be emploid in
publicke affairs.[51]

Floyd envisions a ruler's schedule as containing leisure for only the most
basic of physical appetites. He expresses an opinion probably dear to
London authorities, who, short of foreclosing monarchic pleasure, tried to
limit it, and to isolate it from the common weal. The lord mayor writes in
1592 to the archbishop of Canterbury to request – 'bycause wee vnderstand
that the Q. Maiestie is & must bee served at certen times by this sort of
people [i.e., actors]' – that 'if by any means it may bee devised that hir
Maiestie may bee served with these recreations ... by the privat exercise
of hir Maiesties own players in convenient place'.[52] These words at once
acknowledge the appetitive origin of theatre ('must bee served') and urge
that that appetite be privatized.

   Theatre: 'well-pleasing delights of the heart' or 'base appetites of this
vnhallowed flesh'? The answer may well depend on the gender of the
desirer in question. Anthony Munday's lurid (and possibly parodic)
instance of anti-theatrical discourse underscores the link between the
effects of theatre and a specifically female corporeality. *A second and third
Blast of retrait from plaies and Theaters* locates the pernicious effects of
playing and the 'force ... [of] their inchantments of pleasure' specifically
in the bodies of women:

> they haue receiued at those spectacles such filthie infections, as haue
> turned their minds from chast cogitations, and made them of honest
> women light huswiues; by them they haue dishonored the vessels of
> holines; and brought their husbandes into contempt, their children into
> question, their bodies into sicknes, and their soules to the state of
> euerlasting damnation.[53]

Here the subversive effect of plays is linked to the sexual appetites of
women, always potentially wayward and threatening to exceed the legal
and physical boundaries of home and hearth. As female bodies are the
vehicles of uncorrupted inheritance, their control provides the cornerstone
of patriarchal order and the property it guards. Certain plays erode both the
boundaries that contain female sexual appetites and the material property
that their chastity is designed to consolidate and keep within the family.
'Credite me', urges Munday,

> there can be found no stronger engine to batter the honestie as wel of
> wedded wiues, as the chastitie of vnmarried maides and widowes, than

are the hearing of common plaies. There wanton wiues fables, and pastorical songes of loue, which they use in their comical discourses (al which are taken out of the secret armorie of Venus, & practicing bawderie) turne al chastitie vpside downe, ... insomuch that it is a miracle, if there be found anie either woman, or maide, which with these spectacles of strange lust, is not oftentimes inflamed even vnto furie.[54]

'Inflamed' by plays, female desire is both source and metaphor of civil disorder. In particular, representations of the trajectories of libidinal desire – 'wanton wiues fables, and pastorical songes of loue' – urge unruly union at the expense of order; this is not corporateness but corporeality. Theatre, itself the product of a female (monarch's) appetite, represents and elicits a form of feeling that threatens the nucleus of social order, producing a behaviour 'common' in its sexual and material effects. For where lies the security of property if not in female chastity?

The feminized terminology of political disorder is not unique to an anti-theatrical location. Recall, for instance, that Forset imagines order's antithesis as a 'foule daughter of darkeness'. The traditionally gendered binary of passion and reason associates women with appetite, and, so constructed, women are more susceptible to the corporeality solicited and produced by affect. Richard Hooker, for instance, identifies female affective penetrability in another domain as the susceptible target of religious radicals' infiltrations:

[M]ost labor hath been bestowed to win and retain towards this cause them whose judgements are commonly weakest by reason of their sex.... Apter they are through the eagerness of their affection, that maketh them which way soever they take, diligent in drawing their husbands, children, servants, friends and allies the same way; apter through that natural inclination unto pity which breedeth in them a greater readiness than in men, to be bountiful towards their Preachers who suffer want ... finally, apter through a singular delight which they take in giving very large and particular intelligence how all near about them stand affected as concerning the same cause.[55]

Given their domestic location – as mothers, lovers, and gossips – women are the first line of defence against the seductions of zeal, 'diligent in drawing' others along with them. Such a combination of centrality and vulnerability also provoked the cautionary tones of domestic conduct books. Whether recommending the choice of a wife, or suggesting methods for securing the consciences of children and servants, such texts recommend that the patriarch police the boundaries and purify the interior. As Henry Smith's *Preparative to Marriage* recommends, 'he which chuseth of [women], had neede ... make an Anatomie of their bodies and mindes by squire and rule, before he say, This shall be mine.... [S]o our Spouse should bee holy, vndefiled, and faire within'.[56] Elizabeth's 'solace', then, both originates in and strikes at female appetites, strikes at the foundation of the consolidation of property and order that is England.

As it was inscribed at the local level, so the dependence of political integrity on that of the female body was also inscribed at the broadest level. As critics have noted, Elizabeth's body was the compass and synecdoche of England's ideological insularity and coherence; her physical self and physical boundaries – namely, her much-touted virginity – was the guarantor of English ideological purity.[57] This dependence of the body politic on the body natural emerges most clearly in the objections to the marriage negotiations with Alençon in 1580. In *A Gaping Gvlf*, John Stubbs warned that the threat to English insularity was 'the old serpent in the shape of a man, whose sting is in his mouth, and who doth endeavor to seduce our Eve, that she and we may lose this English paradise'.[58] Sir Philip Sidney likewise warns against the ardent Frenchman who would '[thrust] him self into the low countrey matters, he sometime seeking the king of Spaine daughter somtime your Majesty ...'[59] Sidney's pun registers the particular association of English ideological integrity with Elizabeth's physical inviolability. Both of these Protestant writers imagine Elizabeth's alliance through marriage with an international elite to be in conflict with English religious insularity; they thus cast her marriage as the double loss of chastity and cultural purity. (These terms of isolationism and insularity are ones we have come to associate with nationalist propaganda or with the 'othering' of cultural difference.) In 1588 one writer generalizes this gendered vulnerability, applying it to a national context and urging militant self-defence in order to avoid seeing 'our Countrie ruinated, our Souereigne Princesse iniured, our wiues and virgins defiled, our infants tost on pikes, and our goods the greedie Spaniardes spoyle'.[60] This equation of geography and the body, of the security of territorial boundaries and female boundaries, necessarily envisions boundary altera-tions as the result of phallic aggression. Thus in 1593 we find Elizabeth excusing England's insularity – her failure 'to advance My Territories, and enlarge my Dominions' – as a corollary of her gender: 'I acknowledge my Womanhood and Weakness in that Respect'.[61] Whether passive or inviolable, Elizabeth's gendered physical identity is less the token of a transient 'natural' body than the bulwark of England's ideological integrity. Virginity literalizes insularity. But the vulnerability of such integrity – as with the 'huswiues'' susceptibility to theatrical pleasure – is particularly female in nature.

As the 1547 date of the Homily of Obedience makes clear, the associations of social regulation with corporal regulation are the inherit-ance rather than the invention of Elizabethan political discourse. By the

1590s it was not Elizabeth's virginity but her mortality on which English ideological intactness depended, and it was her successor, not her husband, who was the forbidden subject of public speculation. Yet the language of political integrity persists. Patriarchy's subordination of women is often the chief symptom of internal hierarchy as well as of cultural insularity – hence our common term for both: chauvinism. Thus both the internal threat to hegemony (that adulterous levelling erosion of the boundaries of private property) and the external threat (invasion, miscegenation, from without) are imagined pejoratively as loss of chastity via adultery or rape.

But what is the relevance to *Henry V* of these associations of political corruption with female corporeality? Does the play end pleasurably, with an image of compatible cultural difference and a promise of internal community; or does the betrothal between the factions of an international political elite reinforce hegemonic difference? Are indeed the two distinct? Questions about whether the ending of the play emphasizes pleasure or power are to a great extent related to those often applied to its formal category. *Henry V* has elicited a good deal of criticism that tries to isolate its governing genre. Negotiating the play's generic multiplicity and uncertain ideological valence alike, criticism has tried to impose formal coherence on what has been described variously as a history, a comical history, an epic, a romance, even a pastoral.[62] The most successful grounds for such taxonomy have been located in the play's resemblance, in its resolution, to romantic comedy: its representation of a marriage that secures the integrity of the English state.

Comedy is, formally, a conservative genre, usually predictable in its assignment of moral rewards. If female characters, for instance, are allowed articulate reign within the body of the Shakespearean comedy, it is only to be finally domesticated in marriage.[63] History plays, on the other hand, are held up by defenders of the theatre as productive of ideological stability: what, asks Thomas Nashe 'can be a sharper reproofe to these dangerous effeminate days of ours?' But they are notoriously indeterminate in their formal identity.[64] Thus it is significant that the aspect of comic form that *Henry V* appropriates is in fact *closure*: marriage. If the chastity of the female body is vulnerable to the invasion of plays, and the chastity of the Elizabethan state vulnerable alike to external invasion and common pleasure, it is perhaps appropriate that *Henry V* closes with containment of the 'effeminate'.

One reading of the ending as a conservative expression of the modes of power might be as follows: having rid itself of libidinal Falstaffian pleasures, the play reimagines corporate unity by means of an appropriation of comic form which subordinates female pleasure. The conversion of the politics of domination into a poetics of desire – of conquest into communion – is an awkward one. Henry's vacillation between the languages of power and of pleasure betrays the incongruity of configuring violence as romance. 'I love thee cruelly', he tells Katharine, as sex gives way to power (V.ii.203). The mutuality represented here is inherently dual; unity is suggested but in decidedly hierarchical terms, as the insistent pressure of gender politics qualifies the utopian movement of comedy.

The configuration of Katharine as an object of desire further circumscribes the romantic tenor of the scene. Less an affective than a political gain, she is 'our capital demand, comprised / Within the fore-rank of our articles' (V.ii.96–7). The figuring of Katharine's inaccessibility not as erotic resistance but as linguistic disadvantage exposes the Petrarchan fantasy as a strategy of male manipulation. The woman's silence here is made quite literal: 'I cannot speak your England' (ll. 102–3). Most Shakespearean comedy is dominated by a verbal woman, but here an articulate man determines the terms of courtship – however much he might deny verbal facility: 'I speak to thee plain soldier' (ll. 150–51).

The equation of woman and territory, with its insistence on the body-as-'politic', develops in the juxtaposition of scenes iii and iv of Act III. Henry's opening battle cry has urged the 'noblest English' to prove their mothers' chastity and aristocratic birth simultaneously: 'Dishonour not your mothers; now attest / That those whom you called fathers did beget you' (III.i.17, 22–4). In III.iii, Henry threatens to invade Harfleur with a speech that returns obsessively to images of rape, of 'the fleshed soldier . . . mowing like grass / Your fresh fair virgins' (ll. 11–14); 'pure maidens [fallen] into the hand / Of hot and forcing violation' (ll. 20–21). State power appears here as an excessive corporeality, and as Karen Newman observes, 'the expansionist aims of the nation-state are worked out [in these notorious lines] on and through the woman's body'.[65] In the following scene Katharine learns English and performs an anatomy of her body, laying herself open to semantic invasion as her innocent English words are transformed into French sexual slang: 'Le foot et le count! O Seigneur Dieu! Ils sont les mots de son mauvais, corruptible, gros, et impudique' (III.iv. 50–52).[66] Like most sexual joking, the linguistic play here occludes the violence of victimization: the pleasure of punning tempers the pressure of rape. If England's political integrity – her national chastity – is vulnerable as, and to, the female body, such fragility is here controlled by its representation as foreign. Tellingly, while Henry's body can be purified, the only Englishwoman in the play, the bawdy and common Hostess Quickly, is dead 'of a malady of France' (V.i.81).[67] The play converts the Elizabethan fear of subversion from within the (female) body of the state – whether from monarchic willfulness or unruly communion – into a foreign vulnerability that is then subject to phallic aggression. By means of the body of the French maid, Henry names himself 'Héritier de France' (V.ii.339).

However, romantic comedy, we recall, is an 'inflamer' of (female) desire and was singled out by anti-theatrical Elizabethans as the genre most disruptive of political harmony, in its potential production of unruly corporeal unity among its audiences. As Stephen Gosson put it, 'when Comedie comes vpon the stage, *Cupide* sets vpp as Springe for Wood-cockes'.[68] Such plays violate the boundaries of the platform stage and the body alike: 'the gesturing of a plaier, which Tullie termeth the eloquence of the bodie ... prepare[s] a man to that which is il.... There cometh much euil in at the eares, but more at the eies, by these two open windowes death breaketh into the soule'.[69] And if plays threaten the body's orifices, they violate the state's as well: 'vnchast fables, lascivious devises, shifts of cozenage ... ar so framed & represented by them, that such as resort to see & hear the same, beeing of the base & refuse sort of people ... draue the same into example of imitation & not of avoyding the sayed lewd offences'.[70] If comedy is ostensibly conservative in its decorous assignment of moral rewards and marital partners, it is also, in utopian reconciliation of desires and satisfactions, non-determinative. As anti-theatrical opponents realized, affect exceeds boundaries, and the ostensible messages of social control are not always sufficient to contain the disorder they conclude. Furthermore, if most comedies end with the promise of marriage, they do not often end with its accomplishment; their affect, as it is apocalyptic in structure, is also in feeling wholly anticipatory or open-ended.

Henry may claim that love tempers his power interests, that he 'cannot see many a fair French city for one fair French maid that stands in my way' (V.ii.318–20). The King of France points out that the two are identical: 'my lord, you see them perspectively, the cities turned into a maid; for they are all girdled with maiden walls that war hath never entered' (ll. 321–3). Appropriately enough, her image through a perspectival illusion is double, complicit: Katharine is simultaneously an object of affection and of political interest. While she may recoil at the English perversion of the French terms for her body, the slang does allow Katharine a sexual voice, as her repetition of terms displays: 'Foh! Le foot et le count! Néanmoins, je réciterai une autre fois ma leçon ensemble: d'hand, de fingre, de nailes, de arm, d'elbow, de nick, de sin, de foot, le count' (III.iv.54–7). Katharine's titillating recitation is indeed a male-authored ventriloquist fantasy of female eroticism, but she also performs what patriarchy most fears. In the following scene the Dauphin dreads just such an articulate female libidinousness: 'Our madams mock at us and plainly say ... they will give / Their bodies to the lust of English youth / To new-store France with bastard warriors' (III.v.28–31). The final love scene reinscribes the violent confrontation of cultural difference but in a gentler form. 'Is it possible dat I sould love de *ennemi* of France?' (V.ii.170–71), asks

Katharine pointedly. 'No, it is not possible you should love the enemy of France, Kate,' responds Henry; 'but in loving me you should love the friend of France, for I love France so well that I will not part with a village of it. I will have it all mine. And, Kate, when France is mine and I am yours, then yours is France and you are mine' (ll. 72–7). Henry's verbal confusion – of pronouns, of political and sexual desires, indeed, of territorial boundaries – forges an accommodation between power and affect, political possession and sexual possession, which accommodates the body to hegemony and vice versa. The joke results not so much from linguistic disadvantage as from the beginnings of a common language: 'thy speaking of my tongue, and I thine, most truly-falsely, must needs be granted to be much at one' (ll. 191–3). Henry urges the combination of pleasure with power and gives the body a utility for the state: 'I get thee with scambling, and thou must therefore needs prove a good soldier-breeder. Shall not thou and I, between Saint Denis and Saint George, compound a boy, half French, half English, that shall go to Constantinople and take the Turk by the beard?' (ll. 205–10). The brute exercise of a sovereign will (albeit directed on an even more foreign territory) is rehabilitated into an ideologically useful corporeality, the biological reproduction of dynastic power. On the one hand, the play's closure offers an image of the alliance of an international aristocracy secured through the exogamous exchange of a woman. On the other, it offers an image of the apocalyptic eventuality of a mutual alliance in which difference, whether of culture or gender, is collaborative rather than coercive, suspended rather than suspect.

It is no coincidence that the terms of the debate about the status of early modern representations of Protestant marriage (egalitarian or hierarchic) are the same as those that have governed consideration of its political formations.[71] Both debates concern the potential accommodation of difference, whether of gender or status, within a social totality. Yet to concede the victory of a hegemonic organization of such difference is to relinquish the promise and pressure of an alternative ideal. Our tendency to segregate (often chronologically) power and fellowship denies not only the extent to which ostensibly democratic state formations are hegemonically inflected but also the extent to which community takes place in and through institutions, rather than in some sentimentalized *locus amoenus* beyond power's reach. The ambivalence that characterizes *Henry V* is an ambivalence fundamental not to his personality but to a fantasy of social union which employs the tropes of personhood as a means to its realization. *Henry V* might have pleasure serve the body politic. But Elizabeth herself, as tradition has it, requested that Falstaff be resuscitated, excerpted, and in love.

Notes

I would like to thank those people whose generous responses helped shape this essay, especially David Bevington, James K. Chandler, Janet Coit, Julie Mazman, Janel Mueller, and David Scott Kastan, who chaired the 1988 MLA panel of the Division on Shakespeare where the earliest version of this paper was presented.

1. 'Rabbits, Ducks, and *Henry V*', *Shakespeare Quarterly* 28 (1977): 279–96, esp. 296.

2. For a range of opinions on the subversive potential of the Elizabethan theatre relative to ideology, see, for instance, Walter Cohen, *Drama of a Nation: Public Theater in Renaissance England and Spain* (Ithaca, NY, 1985): Jean E. Howard, 'Renaissance Antitheatricality and the Politics of Gender and Rank in *Much Ado About Nothing*' in *Shakespeare Reproduced: The Text in History and Ideology*, Jean E. Howard and Marion F. O'Connor, eds (New York, 1987), 163–87; and Robert Weimann, 'Bifold Authority in Shakespeare's Theatre', *Shakespeare* 39 (1988): 401–17, esp. 413–14.

3. See, for example, Richard Helgerson's discussion of the play in chap. 5 of *Forms of Nationhood: The Elizabethan Writing of England* (Chicago, 1992): 'The exposure of kingship in a narrative and dramatic medium that not only displayed power but revealed the sometimes brutal and duplicitous strategies by which power maintained itself might be thought to subvert the structure of authority it ostensibly celebrated. But though the plays do bear a subversive potential, neither it nor their festive power of inversion have in fact made themselves felt in any historically disruptive way.... Shakespeare ... gave that genre a singularity of focus that contributed at once to the consolidation of central power, to the cultural division of class from class ...' (pp. 244–5). Also see Jonathan Dollimore and Alan Sinfield, 'History and Ideology: The Instance of *Henry V*' in *Alternative Shakespeares*, John Drakakis, ed. (London, 1985), pp. 206–27; and Leonard Tennenhouse, *Power on Display: The Politics of Shakespeare's Genres* (London, 1986), pp. 68–70.

4. See 'Englishing the Other: "le tiers exclu"' and Shakespeare's *Henry V*', *Fashioning Femininity* (Chicago, 1991), pp. 95–108, esp. 104.

5. Rabkin, p. 296.

6. See, respectively, William Hazlitt, '*Henry V*' in 'The Characters of Shakespear's Plays' in *The Complete Works of William Hazlitt*, ed. P.P. Howe, 21 vols. (London, 1930–34), 4: 286; Paul Dean, 'Chronicle and Romance Modes in *Henry V*', *SQ* 32 (1981): 18–27, esp. 27; and Anne Barton, 'The King Disguised: Shakespeare's *Henry V* and the Comical History' in *The Triple Bond: Plays, Mainly Shakespearean, in Performance*, Joseph G. Price, ed. (University Park, PA, 1975), pp. 92–117, esp. 107.

7. For example, Joanne Altieri in 'Romance in *Henry V*' (*Studies in English Literature* 21 (1981: pp. 223–40) states that in IV.i 'Henry is humanized for us to a greater degree than anywhere else in the play' (p. 228). Similarly, Rabkin asks, 'can the manipulative qualities that guarantee political success be combined in one man with the spiritual qualities that make one fully open and responsive to life and therefore fully human?' (p. 281). This terminology of subjectivity exerts a pull on even those efforts that attempt to account for the play's contradictions within the contingencies of social context. Most recently, Joel Altman, in an analysis of the play's rhetoric, attempts to locate this duality in the ambivalence Elizabethans manifested in regard to the Irish wars. Yet he, too, examines the duality as a function of character: his phrase 'participating the king' (i.e., 'not only sharing his presence with others but absorbing in return their private thoughts and words') attempts to measure our relative kinship to or estrangement from what – or, rather, whom – we inevitably relate to as a person; see his '"Vile Participation": The Amplification of Violence in the Theater of *Henry V*', *SQ* 42 (1991): 1–32, esp. 7.

8. *The Subject of Tragedy: Identity and Difference in Renaissance Drama* (London, 1985), p. 8. Also see Harry Berger, Jr., '"What Did the King Know and When Did He Know It?": Shakespearean Discourses and Psychoanalysis' in *South Atlantic Quarterly* 88 (1989): 811–62.

9. Belsey, p. 15.

10. I use the term *nation* advisedly but emphatically. Most current political theory limits national identity to a post-nineteenth-century location, a product of the presumed social

homogeneity produced by industrialism; see, e.g., Benedict Anderson, *Imagined Communities: Reflections on the Origin and Spread of Nationalism*, rev. ed (London, 1991); Ernest Gellner, *Nations and Nationalism* (Ithaca, NY, 1983); E. J. Hobsbawm, *Nations and Nationalism Since 1790: Programme, Myth, Reality* (Cambridge, 1990). I would argue for an early modern political consciousness shaped, among other things, by the state institutionalization and centralization of religious practices. Criticism typically treats *Henry V*'s nationalism as a synonym for state ideology (hence as propagandistic) and invariably considers its operations repressive; see Altman, p. 8; and Dollimore and Sinfield in Drakakis, ed., p. 211.

11. *Stages of History: Shakespeare's English Chronicles* (Ithaca, NY, 1990), p. 6.

12. Puttenham, *The Arte of English Poesie* (London, 1589), p. 200; Peacham, *The Garden of Eloquence* (London, 1577), sig. O3^r.

13. Peacham, sig. B1^v.

14. Peacham, sig. O3^v. It could be argued that the construction of simile mimics the formational processes of group identity: some valences are held in common, while others are excluded.

15. Rabkin, p. 281 (emphasis added).

16. Helgerson, p. 232.

17. Quentin Skinner observes that such an antipathy – 'the idea that the confrontation between individuals and states furnishes the central topic of political theory' – is relatively recent in conception, dating from Hobbes's elaboration of a notion of a state independent of charismatic personal occupation; see 'The State' in *Political Innovation and Conceptual Change*, Terence Ball, James Farr, and Russell L. Hanson, eds (Cambridge, 1989), pp. 90–131, esp. 90.

18. 'Order of the Privy Council', 22 June 1600, reprinted in E.K. Chambers, *The Elizabethan Stage*, 4 vols (Oxford, 1923), 4:329–31, esp. 330.

19. Chambers, 4:317, 318, 321, and 330. The term *commonwealth* makes its initial Elizabethan appearance in this context in a royal proclamation of 1559 forbidding public representation of political matters: 'also some [plays] that haue ben of late vsed, are not conuenient in any good ordred Christian Common weale to be suffred' (Proclamation 509, reprinted in Chambers, 4:263).

20. See *The Place of the Stage: License, Play, and Power in Renaissance England* (Chicago, 1988), pp. 1–88.

21. While my discussion is limited to the London context of theatre relations, the touring existence of theatre companies in this period provides another possible practice of (or at least metaphor for) the unification of diverse communities in a common cultural lexicon. For a discussion of the effects of national consolidation on provincial theatre see Peter Womack, 'Imagining Communities: Theaters and the English Nation in the Sixteenth Century' in *Culture and History 1350–1600: Essays on English Communities, Identities and Writing*, David Aers, ed. (Detroit, 1992), pp. 91–146.

22. 'Privy Seal of Queen Elizabeth, May 7, 1574, granting a Licence for Dramatic Performances to James Burbage and others,' reprinted in *The English Drama and Stage under the Tudor and Stuart Princes, 1543–1664*, ed. William Carew Hazlitt (1869; rpt. New York, 1964), pp. 25–6. The scope of this response was, as Annabel Patterson remarks, 'totally inadequate to the scale on which the theaters were tolerated, indeed encouraged' ('The Very Age and Body of the Time His Form and Pressure': Rehistoricizing Shakespeare's Theater', *New Literary History* 20 [1988]: 83–104, esp. 91). The coy or nostalgic quality of the justification's image of the relation between sovereign and subjects (and the innocent mutuality of theatrical pleasure) is perhaps corroborated by another stock defence of the theatre's origins, the citation of a medieval precedent of a pleasure-loving king: Edward IV is variously cited as having liked to see plays (e.g., Thomas Heywood, *Apology for Actors* [London, 1608], sig. E1^v).

23. The theatrical experience is not, of course, necessarily pleasurable, any more than it is homogeneous; or, rather, pleasure (like pain) is notoriously difficult to generalize, as are its effects. Robert Weimann defines theatrical pleasure as subversive: 'one of the ways by which the Elizabethan theater appropriated power was to challenge the representation of authority by an alternative authority of theatrical representation which derived at least part

of its strength from vitalizing and mobilizing a new space for *Spass* [fun, pleasure], with all its irreverent and equalizing implications in the social process' ('Towards a Literary Theory of Ideology: Mimesis, Representation, Authority' in Howard and O'Connor, eds, pp. 265–72, esp. 272).

24. The question of whether the product of theatre was a community unified in support of order or a community unified in opposition to it informed to some extent the earliest Tudor discussions of the place of the stage. Defences of the theatre struggle to argue its relevance to the health of the common weal, with strategies that ranged from the naively homiletic to the cynically repressive. Henry VIII proclaimed in Acts 34 and 35 of 1543 that it is 'lawfull to all and euery persone and personnes, to sette forth songes playes and enterludes, to be vsed and exercised within this realme, & other the kynges dominions, for the rebukyng and reproching of vices, & the setting forth of vertue' (reprinted in Hazlitt, ed., pp. 2–6, esp. 5). While this defence would not be forthcoming from a royal quarter again in the Tudor age, a similar tactic harnessed the pleasure of plays for purposes of social control: 'the people must haue soom kynd of recreation' was the (sceptical) paraphrase of the municipal authorities' 'and that policie requireth to divert idle heads and other ill disposed from other woorse practize' ('The Lord Mayor to Lord Burghley', 3 November 1594, reprinted in Chambers, 4:316–17).

25. See, for instance, chaps. 1 and 2 of Jean E. Howard's *The Stage and Social Struggle in Early Modern England* (New York and London, 1994). Actors' violation of sumptuary laws, their impersonation of authoritative and gendered figures, and the physical mingling of social and gender hierarchies in theatre audiences are alike cited as evidence of the theatre's disorder. Stephen Gosson in *Playes Confuted in fiue Actions* (London, 1582) observes: 'for a boy to put one the attyre, the gesture, the passions of a woman; for a meane person to take vpon him the title of a Prince with counterfeit porte, and traine, is by outwarde signes to shewe them selues otherwise then they are, and so with in the compasse of a lye' (sig. E5).

26. See 'Lord Mayor and Aldermen of London to Lord Chamberlain Sussex', 2 March 1574, reprinted in Chambers, 4:271–72 and passim. Congregation is described throughout in pejorative terms: 'the inordynate hauntyinge of greate multitudes of people' and 'such conventicles of people by such meanes called together whereof the greater number is the meanest sort' (pp. 273, 269).

27. Anthony Munday, *A second blast of retrait from plaies and Theaters* (1580), reprinted in Chambers, 4:210.

28. Henry Crosse, *Vertues Common-wealth, or the High-Way to Honour* (London, 1603), sig. P3.

29. Gosson, *Plays Confuted*, sig. F1.

30. Gosson, *Plays Confuted*, sig. G7.

31. 'Answer of the Corporation of London' to the 'Petition of the Queen's Players to the Privy Council', November 1584, reprinted in Chambers, 4:299–302, esp. 300.

32. Elizabethans suspected that plague was communicable through the air and by means of physical contact, but also that frequenting theatres could occasion plague for moral rather than physical vulnerabilities, interpreting plague as an instrument of divine vengeance for playgoing. 'To play in plagetime is to encreasce the plage by infection: to play out of plagetime is to draw the plage by offendinges of God vpon occasion of such playes' ('Answer of the Corporation of London', Chambers, 4:301). It should, however, be observed that while the physiological explanation of plague was invoked to censure theatres, other sites of congregation, such as churches, escaped like censure. See also Paul Slack, *The Impact of Plague in Tudor and Stuart England* (London, 1985); and J. Leeds Barroll, *Politics, Plague, and Shakespeare's Theater: The Stuart Years* (Ithaca, NY, 1991).

33. 'An Exhortation Concerning Good Order and Obedience to Kings and Magistrates' (1547), reprinted in *Certain Sermons or Homilies, Appointed to be Read in Church* (Oxford, 1840), pp. 55–56 (emphasis added).

34. *The boke named the Gouernour* (London, 1531), sig. A1ᵛ.

35. *A Comparative Discourse of the Bodies Natvral and Politique* ... (London, 1606), p. 48. Also see Sir Thomas Smith, *A Discourse of the Commonwealth of this Realm* (London, 1570); and Thomas Wilson, *A Discourse on Usury* (London, 1563).

36. Forset, pp. 49–50.

37. As Thomas Floyd noted in 1600, 'If therefore the Common wealth be guided by the handes of one supreame gouernour, it is the rather mumified.... an uniuersall Common wealth, is nothing els sauing an imaginary, or artificiall perpolited bodie, seying that in such a naturall body, we do coniecture and see one head and many members: wherefore a Citie or Monarchie, if it be so gouerned, it farre exceedeth: because it more imitates & resembles nature'; see *The Picture of a perfit Common wealth* ... (London, 1600), sigs. C1^v–C2^r.

38. As Marie Axton's work demonstrates, far from being a disinterested and general cultural commonplace, the 'body politic' had quite a specific polemical life; see *The Queen's Two Bodies: Drama and the Elizabethan Succession* (London, 1977). See also, of course, Ernst H. Kantorowicz, *The King's Two Bodies: A Study in Mediaeval Political Theology* (Princeton, NJ, 1957). For a survey and bibliography of anthropological literature dealing with the metaphor of the body, see Jean Comoroff, 'Bodily Reform as Historical Practice: The Semantics of Resistance in Modern South Africa,' *International Journal of Psychology* 20 (1985): 541–67.

39. Forset, p. 16. It was this vocabulary that provided James I with the terms for a threat to a stubborn Parliament: 'I looked for no such Fruits at your Hands.... I am a Man of Flesh and Blood, and have my Passions and Affections as other Men: I pray you, do not too far move me to do that which my Power may tempt me unto' (*Journals of the House of Commons* [London, 1803–], 2 May 1607, 1:367–8. Ironically, the dispute in question concerned the union of Great Britain.

40. Even the order-mongering Homily of Obedience affirmed to different degrees that 'everyone hath need of other'.

41. Forset, p. 49.

42. See Drakakis, ed., p. 217. They also make the instructive observation that 'the play's obsessive preoccupation is insurrection' (p. 216).

43. As the work of Brian P. Levack on the British union demonstrates, such unity would soon be a highly contested construct; see *The Formation of the British State: England, Scotland, and the Union, 1603–1707* (Oxford, 1989).

44. Shakespeare quotations are from *The Complete Works of Shakespeare*, ed. David Bevington, 4th ed. (New York, 1992).

45. For a reading that suggests some of the popularizing effects of the Chorus's participatory invitations, see Weimann in Howard and O'Connor, eds. p. 272.

46. See *Chimes at Midnight*, ed. Bridget Gellert Lyons (New Brunswick, NJ, 1988), pp. 261–2.

47. Dollimore and Sinfield in Drakakis, ed., p. 212.

48. Forset, pp. 31–32.

49. Forset, p. 30.

50. 'A New History for Shakespeare and His Time,' *SQ* 39 (1988): 441–64, esp. 461. *Coriolanus*, on the other hand, locates the governing body more in the region of the grotesque middle: see Zvi Jagendorf, '*Coriolanus*: Body Politic and Private Parts', *SQ* 41 (1990): 455–69.

51. Floyd, sig. M5^r. Floyd has a low opinion of pleasures generally, especially those 'which are superfluous & vnprofitable ... spending their time about nothing.... Moreouer there are other plasures which are lewd, & are termed by the name of carnall & worldly pleasures.... Conceale thy delights in thy heart, lest shamefully they be discouered. Delight is the brook of euils, quenching the light of the soule, & hindering counsell, turning men aside from the right way' (sigs. M4^v–M7^r).

52. 'The Lord Mayor to John Whitgift,' 25 February 1592, reprinted in Chambers, 4:308.

53. Hazlitt, ed., pp. 142 and 125, respectively. Significantly, Munday signs himself with a compound term of nation and affect: 'Anglophile'. Although the particular susceptibility of the female body figured as a trope for the sexual licence the theatre provoked – married women were frequently singled out as the group most in need of being prevented from going to the theatre – men were also targeted as vulnerable, and the theatre was thought to be a site for prostitution (see Chambers, 4:198, 203, 218, and 223). For a discussion of the relationship of the theatre and the categories of gender, see Jean E. Howard, 'Crossdressing, the Theatre, and Gender Struggle in Early Modern England', *SQ* 39 (1988): 418–40.

54. Hazlitt, ed., p. 143.

55. *Of The Laws of Ecclesiastical Polity* (1592), ed. Arthur Stephen McGrade (Cambridge, 1989), pp. 17–18.

56. (London, 1591), sigs. C4 and C5. See also Heinrich Bullinger, *The Christen state of Matrimonie*, trans. Myles Coverdale (London, 1541).

57. For a discussion of the identity of Elizabeth's body and political territory, see Peter Stallybrass, 'Patriarchal Territories: The Body Enclosed' in *Rewriting the Renaissance: The Discourses of Sexual Difference in Early Modern Europe*, Margaret W. Ferguson, Maureen Quilligan, and Nancy J. Vickers, eds (Chicago, 1986), pp. 123–42, esp. 129–33. For a discussion of Elizabeth's own manipulation of the fact of her gender, as well as its culturally contested quality, see Louis Adrian Montrose, 'The Elizabethan Subject and the Spenserian Text' in *Literary Theory/Renaissance Texts*, Patricia Parker and David Quint, eds (Baltimore and London, 1986), pp. 303–40; and Leah S. Marcus, 'Elizabeth', chap. 2 of *Puzzling Shakespeare: Local Reading and Its Discontents* (Berkeley, 1989), pp. 51–105.

58. *The Discoverie of a Gaping Gvlf whereinto England is like to be Swallowed by an other French Marriage* ... (1579), reprinted in *John Stubb's Gaping Gulf with Letters and Other Relevant Documents*, ed. Lloyd E. Berry (Charlottesville, VA, 1968), pp. 3–4.

59. 'A discourse of Syr, Ph. S. to the Queenes Majesty touching hir mariage with Monsieur' (1580), reprinted in *The Complete Works of Sir Philip Sidney*, 4 vols., ed. A. Feuillerat (Cambridge, 1922–26), 3: 51–60, esp. 54.

60. *An Oration Militarie to all naturall Englishmen, whether Protestants, or otherwise in Religion affected* ... (London, 1588), sig. A3^r.

61. *A Speech Made By Queen Elizabeth (Of Famous Memory) In Parliament, Anno 1593. ... concerning the Spanish Invasion* (London, 1688).

62. See, for example, essays of Altieri, Barton, and Dean, cited above; see also Tennenhouse, pp. 68–71.

63. For a discussion of the relative limits that certain genres impose on female energies, see Carol Thomas Neely, *Broken Nuptials in Shakespeare's Plays* (New Haven, 1985).

64. *Pierce Penniless his Supplication to the Devil*, reprinted in *The Renaissance in England*, ed. Hyder E. Rollins and Herschel Baker (Boston, 1954), p. 880. For a discussion of the generic location and assumptions of history plays, see Irving Ribner, *The English History Play in the Age of Shakespeare* (New York, 1957). See also David Scott Kastan, '"To Set a Form upon that Indigest": Shakespeare's Fictions of History', *Comparative Drama* 17 (1983): 1–16.

65. Newman, 101. See also Lance Wilcox, 'Katherine of France as Victim and Bride', *Shakespeare Studies* 17 (1985): 61–76.

66. The relative proficiencies in the King's English assigned to characters from Macmorris to Fluellen to Katharine provide a corroboration of the ranked membership of the British body politic; see David Cairns and Shaun Richards, *Writing Ireland: Colonialism, Nationalism, and Culture* (Manchester, 1988), p. 10. Henry V was the first king of England to institute the use of the English language (replacing French and Latin) in Chancery proceedings; see Malcolm Richardson, 'Henry V, the English Chancery, and Chancery English', *Speculum* 55 (1980): 726–50.

67. Even though Pistol refers to her as 'Doll', Bevington and other editors suggest this is a typographical error substituting for 'Nell'.

68. *The Ephemerides of Phialo ... and a short Apologie of the Schoole of Abuse* (1579), reprinted in Chambers, 4:207. The sentiment is seconded by the lord mayor and aldermen in a 1597 letter to the Privy Council: '... they impresse the very qualitie & corruption of manners which they represent, Contrary to the rules & art prescribed for the makinge of Comedies eaven amonge the Heathen' (Chambers, 4:322).

69. Munday, reprinted in Hazlitt, ed., p. 141.

70. 'The Lord Mayor to Lord Burghley', Chambers, 4:317.

71. See, for instance, William and Malleville Haller, 'The Puritan Art of Love', *Huntington Library Quarterly* 5 (1942): 235–72; and Linda T. Fitz, '"What Says the Married Woman?": Marriage Theory and Feminism in the English Renaissance', *Mosaic* 13:2 (1980): 1–22.

15

Radicalizing Radical Shakespeare: The Permanent Revolution in Shakespeare Studies

Fredric Jameson

In a theoretical age, it comes to be recognized that the encounter between Shakespeare and radical (or Marxist) criticism and theory is a two-way street: we find ourselves asking not merely what such critical theory has to tell us about Shakespeare (and has to tell us with an originality that transcends Marx's well-known taste for Shakespeare over Schiller, and the gold quotes from *Timon of Athens*, etc., etc.), but also what Shakespeare has to tell us about radical criticism.

This reversal acknowledges two presuppositions: first, that all of criticism and theory today is part and parcel of its own historical evaluation, and is also (alongside the immediate polemic aim of this or that interpretation or intervention) bound up with a more general theoretical claim about the superiority and advantages of its own 'method' over the rival ones. But also, second, that the signals given off by 'Shakespeare' today – although carefully laundered of all the 'genius' ideology of the bourgeois era – still assure us that the named textual corpus in question is more interesting because more complicated and multi-dimensional than even the most complicated single-shot structure of a printed text for individual reading, for example (a novel, a lyric poem). The advantage of this particular critical pretext or occasion is therefore that its poles largely transcend what bourgeois forms and genres allow as problems: from the radical generic difference of the play form as such all the way to the extraordinary syntactical freedoms and metamorphoses of Shakespeare's language. It would be too simple to say that what is at stake in this enlargement is a view of culture and the text that at once transcends or excludes problems of the individual subject and the individual author, although that is also true, and the new pre- or post-individualistic perspective allows the very problem of the subject and the signature to be posed more dramatically than in any of the forms of an individualistic age. This, then, is the place at which we encounter Margreta de Grazia's work on the very construction (by his eighteenth-century editors) of a unified subject-signature called Shakespeare, from out of a welter of texts which are also the traces of an ineradicably collective acting and stage-managing praxis.[1]

Proust's method of transcending the individual subject – by an insistence on what we can now in hindsight identify as the situation – passed through a deeply held metaphoric conviction as to the kinship between cultural production and warfare, or the art of military strategy: the 'writer' (or whatever we want to call this subject-position today) is like the great general:

> Hindenburg is profoundly infused by the Napoleonic spirit. His rapid troop displacements, his bluffs and feints . . . his withdrawals, analogous to those with which Austerlitz, Arcole, Eckmühl began – everything in him is Napoleonic, and that's not the half of it. I would also want to add, should in my absence [Robert de Saint-Loup is speaking to the narrator] you try to make your own interpretation of the events of this war [World War I], that you had better not rely exclusively on this particular manner so characteristic of Hindenburg in order to discover the meaning of what he does, or the key to what he will do in the future. A general is like a writer who means to construct a certain play, a certain book, and who is forced to deviate in the extreme from that preconceived plan by the book itself, with the unexpected resources it yields up at this particular moment, or the dead-ends and contradictions it confronts him with in that. As for example in the case of a diversion that bears on a point necessarily of some strategic significance in its own right, which then has as its consequence, the diversion succeeding beyond anything that might have been expected, that the principal operation meets with failure while it is the diversion itself that becomes the principal operation in its turn . . .[2]

Thus a Proustian Shakespeare would be a Napoleon–Hindenburg for whom 'intention' is not some subjective, individual, bourgeois matter, but rather a practical engagement then itself modified in course by the unexpected realities and contingencies of its object situation – in the case of the work of art, of its concrete content, of the deeper form of its social content and what that enables of form-production, of narrativity, or on the contrary what in it resists narrativity. This holds for all literary production, to be sure, but the Shakespearean proviso suggests that such problems are more interesting and complicated, among other things, because 'Shakespeare' is a name for collective agency, on the one hand (and not for the private author writing up his novel in a closed room somewhere), and also that his content, at this supremely 'transitional' moment of the emergence of modern secular society, offers many more form possibilities than the relatively 'contained' and specialized, respectabilized content that confronts the great nineteenth-century (bourgeois) novelists.

But such a critical occasion is also the place in which the older modernist discovery of language – or better still, like Galileo's telescope, of the instruments for its newly microscopic analysis – is fulfilled and transcended all at once: Shakespeare's language no longer being an individual style in any of the modernist or New Critical senses, but rather a kind of objective moment or situation in which English (now characterized, as Gertrude Stein puts it, by a fundamental 'choosing ... you have an infinite variety of length and shortness of words chosen of vowels and consonants of words chosen ... things could be long that is words next to each other could be long and go on and very often they were short', etc.,[3]) deploys an extraordinary array of connectives and syncategoremic categories that all get arthritically concentrated and frozen in the sequel, a Shakespearean sentence reinventing itself from present to present, from clause to clause, in ways that will no longer be possible when the sentence becomes a completed thing whose parts must be interrelated in a spatial way (Eliot's notes, his Elizabethan draft-essays, convey this kind of approach to Shakespearean language-production without theorizing the new method thereby required or incorporating the newly discovered fact into emergent New Critical ideology, into the modernist paradigm as such). At this point, linguistic or stylistic analysis is at one with historical or social analysis: criticism and theory stand before the great divide, and precede the moment of the fall at which subject is sundered from object and style from content. Such criticism then ought to enjoy as privileged a moment as does Shakespeare's own production with respect to language and culture itself: the problem lying in that nagging sense we have of having overcome the dilemma because we follow its supercession historically, whereas 'Shakespeare' precedes its happening in the first place.

Radical Shakespearean criticism thus ought to offer a privileged occasion for taking an inventory of what contemporary theory and analysis is capable of doing more generally: but such an inventory requires us to note, at the outset, the distinction between a restricted and a generalized sense of the notion of a 'Marxist' criticism. The latter can then be one specialized area in a whole array of possible radical reversals (an attention to social class issues, for example, as opposed to gender and race); or it can be the code word for a whole systematic perspective of reversal across the board, and a designation of the place in which a whole radically other view of culture and literature can be expected slowly to emerge (along with the emergence of a whole radically other way of living and of organizing ourselves as social and collective beings): in that case all the radical themes, very much including the limited ones of class and economics, are subsumed by some vaster transcendent Utopian vision or horizon of interpretation.

In either case, Marxist or radical criticism (or theory) necessarily

involves reversal: intervention into pre-existing critical values and problematics, and a moment in which those are materialistically regrounded,
rewritten in terms of a more concrete context. That ought to be enough to
mean that the problems and values dear to an aestheticizing criticism are
scarcely abandoned en route: rather they are *aufgehoben*, carried along,
cancelled and transcended all at once. The problems are retained but are
themselves problematized, and made more complicated and more interesting, by a larger and more complex frame than the one offered by
'spirituality' or 'high cultural values', by 'ethics' or 'metaphysical world-
views'. For a Marxist criticism must ask questions about spirituality or
metaphysics, about ethics or cultural values: it must also grapple with the
issue of why such ideological mystifications exist and have their own
'reality of the appearance', their own objectivity; whereas a spiritual or
aestheticist criticism feels itself exempt from the need to account for such
rival concern with daily life, money, inequality or exploitation in the
context of the 'great work' or literary 'masterpiece'. It is all the more
crucial to make this point again today when, along with market rhetoric,
a resurgence of the classically aesthetic concerns and a repudiation of the
bad 1960s political perspective on art and culture (which very much
includes just such critical approaches to Shakespeare as we are concerned
with here) have everywhere slowly offered to become a new doxa, which
really needs no defence. Marxist approaches to Shakespeare today thus
need to be argued rather differently than in the period in which, concurrent
with an enormous wealth of new and radical theatrical stagings of the
plays, and with a general consensus among intellectuals and youth as to the
burning need for social change generally, they came as beachheads and as
the exciting opening up of new territory (or its conquest from the enemy).
Today Marxist (and other radical) approaches to Shakespeare are staged by
what we may call Reaganite and Thatcherite literary criticism as a kind of
cultural Soviet Union, whose collapse is evident to everybody. Conservatives thus need not argue their case, but take it for granted; while by
the same token the Left must offer theirs on both levels at once, as the
defence of new local interpretations which is at one and the same time a
whole social and cultural programme, a whole new defence of the radical
agenda as such. (To which it may be added that all kinds of differences
within that Left have had the result of discrediting a great many features
of that very radical tradition in advance, including the totalizing one which
insists on absolute systemic change and on an approach to literary and
cultural texts that posits the ultimate interrelationship of all their features
and properties.)

The idea that there is something unified that can be called a Marxist
criticism is a hangover from older modes of explanation that have now
entered into crisis: Wittgenstein's very account of explanation itself is a

useful way of grasping this crisis – that point, or that code, with which we are content to stop. It then becomes easier to understand how new places to stop explaining, to be content with what has thus far been explained, get substituted historically for older ones: the gradual shift from diachronic stopping points to synchronic or systemic ones is only the most famous of such shifts in recent times, while the Derridean attack on the temptations of 'truth' in general reflects the consequences of an acceptance of the new situation, in which there are any number of such stopping points, and no particular reason to feel passionate about the priority of one over all the others. Meanwhile the term 'pluralism' still remains a little too complacent about what used to be a scandal for thought, and presumes what is yet to be demonstrated, namely that all these various explanatory codes can non-antagonistically coexist, whether in a well-behaved parliamentary or an orgiastic Bakhtinian way. This collection picks up 'Marxist criticism' after the point at which it has entered this world of multiple causalities, and offers a useful laboratory situation for studying those multiplicities themselves (fully as much as Marxism's possibilities of response to them).

But it should not be thought that the construction of the object of study – here loosely termed 'Shakespeare' – is exempt from such modifications either; and given the notorious difficulties in describing methodological operations, it would seem more practical and manageable to start with those multiple constructions, which can range from a single play (a unity itself subject to perceptual modifications) or a few lines of verse supposed to correspond to a style or linguistic structure, all the way to various metaphysics or personified institutions. False problems can be eliminated by specifying the type of object constructed by this or that approach (so that there turns out to be no particular quarrel about a 'Shakespeare' under which two very different objects are designated): new and more interesting problems are thereby produced by precisely this multiplicity of 'object-positions', so to speak (a term whose possible relations to the various 'subject-positions' it might also be interesting to explore).

In *The Political Unconscious*[4] I suggest a loose ordering of such analytic possibilities that can be usefully tested against the practical criticisms, the critical practices, at work in the particular continent marked Shakespeare. According to this threefold schema, a cultural object finds itself (re)constructed according to Braudel-like parameters, depending on whether its temporality is that of the rush of immediate current events (the shorthand here would be the 'political' in the most commonsensical acceptation, if this does not lead to misunderstandings); or that of the larger and slower struggles between general class ideologies (something like the level of history of ideas in any period, or the content of the period epistemes, at least when those are viewed functionally as being 'moves' in a strategic struggle between conservative and radical forces and ideologies); or finally the grandest and most abstract of all the levels, that of the mode of production itself, in which residual or emergent features of social structures in dissolution or yet to come survive on into the hegemonic present and introduce a noise there which the analyst will wish to rewrite in the form of systemic contradiction. And indeed on each of these levels the fundamental vocation of the Marxian analyst (as opposed to most of the others, which often share a general Marxian thematics) lies in the commitment to rewrite various types of content analysis in the strong form of the contradiction as such: it is something of a narrative vocation, which calls for the translation of various forms of received data (the empirical, the history of ideas, the antinomy, the tension, the simple contingency or coexistence) into that essentially narrative form which is the dual structure of 'the way people become conscious of such struggles and fight them out.'[5] It may be suggestive, if a little overhasty, to recharacterize these three levels as those of fashion (the political), of ideology (that of class conflict), and of commodification (this feature being perhaps the most insistent marker of the originality of the new mode of production, and one only recently underscored again by Richard Halpern's path-breaking *Poetics of Primitive Accumulation*).[6]

In Shakespeare criticism, this ultimate level is perhaps the most accessible, since it is here that a certain more 'traditional' Marxian approach – beginning with Marx and Engels themselves, codified by Paul N. Siegel,[7] and here brilliantly exemplified in Paul Delany's contribution – staked out its claim to distinctiveness: Shakespeare would thus be the name for the space and locus of transition as such – the immense historical dislocations and sufferings of an incomprehensible and seismological shift from the feudal to the commercial and later on the capitalist. How this shift is identified in the texts is a good deal more various and optional than such a description might suggest: for in such cases superstructure may well precede base, and anticipate forms not yet realized in the economic structures. Or, particularly in the English case which is both first and non-paradigmatic all at once, the emergence of the new forms of business may go hand in hand with a strengthening of older feudal institutions and social survivals (as a merchant class buys land and tries to wear aristocratic trappings, etc.). *King Lear* is evidently one of the crucial texts in which such multiple x-rays are to be taken and then compared among themselves.

The first level of event and of the local or immediate public sphere (rumour, gossip, 'current events') is also not without its relationship to more traditional source analysis: but it has exciting modern (and postmodern) analogues, for example, in Annabel Patterson's juxtaposition of *Coriolanus* with the Midland riots of 1607;[8] in Frances Yates's reinterpretation of the romances in terms of the dynastic hopes pinned on James I's older children;[9] or, in the present collection, in Alan Sinfield's rereading of the echoing resonance in *Macbeth* of ideological debates within Jacobine court space. I believe that the 'current events' of form and theatrical history ought also to be included here: the changes of fashions in the drama itself, the lag in the prestige of this or that genre, indeed the very significance of what has been called Shakespeare's own *coupure* of 1594, the abandonment of high-cultural verse forms and the commitment to what we will later on call mass culture. But the very interpretation of such a break has clearly already slipped significantly in the direction of our second level, that of class ideology and symbolic class struggle, and admonishes us above all – on all three levels – to take a postmodern and a problematic view of the categories in play here. In other words, if you want to correlate the text with the coexistence of various modes of production, or with the force of 'current events', you have to begin by complexifying the very category of the event or of such 'coexistence': you have to explore a far more multiple and textual model for what holds as synchronous, as well as what holds for the intervention of a mode of production into daily life, and thereby into daily speech and the symbolic functioning of culture itself.

But it will clearly be our second level which will pose the greatest problems for contemporary analysis, for not only does it deploy the universally decried and stigmatized category of social class, about which I would wish to argue that it must be at least as internally conflicted and non-self-identical as other more popular post-contemporary ones; but is also redolent of the oldest 'popular front' debates about Shakespeare (and about culture in general) on an older Left, namely the matter of his 'rich progressive humanism' or on the other hand of his reactionary infeudation to all kinds of 'Elizabethan world-views' or great and aristocratic chains of being and the status quo of bourgeois as well as aristocratic values, perhaps all together at the same time (since Shakespeare himself was an investor, particularly in land, who aimed at a coat of arms and at the aristocratic consolidation of his holdings by way of primogeniture). Once again, such old-fashioned questions are scarcely outmoded, but demand the problematization of their starting point – not only that of social class, but that of the individual ideological subject as well. If what is suggested here is the old notion of a unified subject that 'adheres' to this or that class determination, then the questions and problems raised are not complicated enough, particularly for this theatrical moment of a still pre-bourgeois mode of language and expression. One would prefer to suggest that, whatever the multiple subjectivities of a 'Shakespeare himself' (clearly an ideological construct in its own right), the play form imposes a model in which the subject does not so much 'have' this or that ideology as it constitutes an opening onto multiple objective ideologies at play in the emergent public sphere: this is the sense in which Shakespeare's forms and representational apparatuses can detect a number of distinct and mutually contradictory ideologies in struggle all at once, and in terms of which it becomes no longer particularly significant to decide which one of them 'he' adheres to. Still, Annabel Patterson's recent book (mentioned above) suggests that the issue of Shakespeare's social sympathies is by no means a dead one, even at the present time and in the present 'end of history': her argument is primarily, I believe, directed against a certain Left consensus for which it goes without saying that 'Shakespeare' (whatever he or it might be) was obviously locked into the force-field of hegemonic values (either of commercial or aristocratic varieties, or of all those all together). We might here, however, want to reinvoke notions of repression, occultation, and the like, to suggest that ideology is not so much 'believing' something as it is being capable of registering or representing something: thus even the most reactionary treatment of the London city mobs, for example, is at least a significant blip on the ideological radar-screen, and preferable to the later modes whereby the 'stinking' populace is banished from cultural representation altogether.

An even more serious methodological problem arises, however, when on this second general level of struggle and ideology, of class value and social agency, we encounter the general problematics of power, something characteristic of a whole span of 'radical' Shakespeares from the English 'cultural-materialist' ones to those of American 'new historicism'. For a long time this Foucauldian gesture served its purpose, which was to scandalize the remnants of a high-cultural Shakespearean tradition (very much in the process of reformation and 'moral rearmament' today, as has been suggested above): the establishment aesthetes in Britain or the US, whatever else they failed to have in common, could at least be identified by their mutual allergy to notions that Shakespearean 'greatness' had anything to do with the nastier features of the Elizabethan police-state, with torture, with surveillance, with reason-of-state religious enforcement, and so on. And indeed it seems to me that the majority of the present offerings fall into this general heading, but in an impressive variety of modes.

Perhaps then it is time to suggest that here too the fundamental category – 'power' – needs itself to be problematized in some thoroughgoing postmodern way. First of all, clearly enough, the 'object of study', the constructed 'Shakespeare', needs to be opened up: in this context it is clear that it splits open into some allegedly real 'historical' Shakespeare (what kind of investments did he make, etc., along the lines of Edward Bond's *Bingo*), and the historical ideologies about Shakespeare, which now demand histories and analyses of their own, and are in the process of richly receiving them, from Hugh Grady's superbly theoretical *Modernist*

Shakespeare to Michael Bristol's rich case studies.[10]

As for power in general, however, is it too radical to suggest that it has itself become the 'space of discursive struggle' between base and superstructure today? The tugging of power in some purely cultural direction opens up a space of multiple alliances in which the new social movements can all participate; the drawing back in the other direction (as in the Halpern book mentioned above) incites us to new and more complex explorations of the relationship between capitalist production and power (both exploitation and domination) as such: in other words it also leads on to the mysteries of commodification – mysteries which can be expected to be significantly intensified within the originality of our own postmodern or world-systems moment of present history. The politics of the sign so admirably explored here by Robert Weimann itself stands as an intriguing signpost to this whole new terra incognita.[11] We do not need to return to the pieties of greatness and the affirmation of Shakespeare's 'inexhaustible relevance' to future generations and indeed to Posterity as such, in order to suggest that it is political commitment to the historical originality of late capitalism which is most likely to spur contemporary readers of 'Shakespeare' in new and exciting directions.

Notes

1. Margreta de Grazia, *Shakespeare Verbatim: The Reproduction of Authenticity and the 1790 Apparatus* (Oxford: Oxford UP, 1991).

2. Marcel Proust, *Le temps retrouvé. A la recherche du temps perdu*, Editions de la Pléiade, vol. 4 (Paris: Gallimard, 1989), pp. 340–41.

3. Gertrude Stein, 'What Is English Literature?', *Lectures in America* (Boston: Beacon Press, 1957), p. 31.

4. Fredric Jameson, *The Political Unconscious: Narrative as a Socially Symbolic Act* (Ithaca, NY: Cornell UP, 1981).

5. Karl Marx, 'Preface', *A Contribution to the Critique of Political Economy*, trans. N.I. Stone (Chicago: Kerr, c. 1904).

6. Richard Halpern, *Poetics of Primitive Accumulation: English Renaissance Culture and the Genealogy of Capital* (Ithaca, NY: Cornell UP, 1991).

7. Paul N. Siegel, 'Marx, Engels, and the Historical Criticism of Shakespeare', *Shakespeare Jahrbuch*, 113 (1977): 124–34.

8. Annabel Patterson, *Shakespeare and the Popular Voice* (Oxford: Blackwell, 1989), pp. 135–46.

9. Frances Yates, *Shakespeare's Last Plays: A New Approach* (London: 1975).

10. Hugh Grady, *Modernist Shakespeare: Critical Texts in a Material World* (Oxford: Clarendon Press, 1991); Michael Bristol, *Shakespeare's America, America's Shakespeare* (London and New York: Routledge 1990).

11. See also Robert Weimann, *Shakespeare and the Popular Tradition in the Theater: Studies in the Social Dimension of Dramatic Form and Function*, trans. Robert Schwartz (Baltimore: Johns Hopkins UP, 1978).

Notes on Contributors

James R. Andreas is the Director of the Clemson Shakespeare Festival and Professor of English at Clemson University. He has been the editor of *The Upstart Crow: A Shakespeare Journal* for ten years. His most recent articles have dealt with the rhetoric of the links in the *Canterbury Tales* and oral, 'vulgar' elements in the works of Chaucer and Shakespeare. 'Othello's African American Progeny' won the SAMLA prize as outstanding article in the *South Atlantic Review* for 1992/93. He is at work on books dealing with the subjects of 'Shakespeare and the Black Experience' and 'Dialogical Chaucer'.

Lynda E. Boose is Associate Professor of English and Women's Studies at Dartmouth College. She has published articles in such journals as *Shakespeare Quarterly, English Literary Renaissance*, and *Renaissance Quarterly*. With Betty S. Flowers she is the co-editor of *Daughter and Fathers* (1989).

Michael D. Bristol is Professor of English at McGill University. His most recent books are *Carnival and Theater: Plebeian Culture and the Structure of Authority in Renaissance England* (1985) and *Shakespeare's America, America's Shakespeare* (1990).

Walter Cohen is Professor of Comparative Literature and Dean of the Graduate School at Cornell University. The author of *Drama of a Nation: Public Theater in Renaissance England and Spain*, he is currently co-editing the Norton Shakespeare and writing a book on the history of European literature.

Paul Delany teaches modern British literature and literary theory at Simon Fraser University, where he is Professor of English. His books include *D.H. Lawrence's Nightmare* (1978) and *The Neo-Pagans* (1987); and, as editor or co-editor, *Hypermedia and Literary Studies* (1991), *Digital World* (1993), and *Vancouver: Representing the Postmodern City* (1994).

John Drakakis is Reader in English Studies at the University of Stirling. He is the editor of *British Radio Drama* (1981), *Alternative Shakespeares* (1985), *Shakespearean Tragedy* (1992), and the New Casebook *Antony and Cleopatra* (1994). He is currently completing a book on *Shakespearean Discourses*, and is editing *The Merchant of Venice* in the New Arden Series, and *Richard III* in the Shakespeare Originals Series.

Stephen Greenblatt is the Class of 1932 Professor of English Literature at the University of California, Berkeley. Among his many books are *Renaissance Self-Fashioning: From More to Shakespeare* (1980), *Shakespearean Negotiations: The Circulation of Social Energy in Renaissance England* (1988), *Learning to Curse: Essays in Early Modern Culture* (1991), and *Marvelous Possessions: The Wonder of the New World* (1992).

Graham Holderness is Professor of English and Dean of the School of Humanities and Education at the Watford Campus of the University of Hertfordshire. He is the author of *Shakespeare's History* (1985), *The Taming of the Shrew* in the Shakespeare in Performance Series, and co-author of *Shakespeare: The Play of History* (1988). He has edited *The Shakespeare Myth* (1988).

Fredric Jameson is the Director of the Literature Program at Duke University and the editor of *South Atlantic Quarterly*; his most recent books are *The Geopolitical Aesthetic* (1993) and *The Seeds of Time* (1994).

Ivo Kamps is Assistant Professor of English at the University of Mississippi. He is the editor of *Shakespeare Left and Right* (1991), and the author of a forthcoming book *Staging History: Historiography, Ideology, and Literary Form in the Stuart Drama*. With Deborah Barker he has edited *Shakespeare and Gender: A History* (1995). He has co-edited with Lawrence Danson *The Phoenix* for the Oxford complete works of Thomas Middleton (1995).

Katharine Eisaman Maus is Associate Professor of English at the University of Virginia. She has written *Inwardness and Theater in the English Renaissance* (1995), *Ben Jonson and the Roman Frame of Mind* (1985), and many essays for scholarly journals. She is the editor of *Four Revenge Tragedies of the English Renaissance* (1995) and (with Elizabeth Harvey) *Soliciting Interpretation: Literary Theory and English Seventeenth-Century Poetry* (1990). She is a member of the editorial team for *The Norton Shakespeare*, forthcoming in 1996, and will be writing the 1603–1660 volume of *The Oxford English Literary History*.

Claire McEachern is an Assistant Professor of English at the University of California, Los Angeles. She is currently working on a study of the Tudor–Stuart nation and its literature.

Louis Adrian Montrose is Professor of English Literature and Chairman of the Department of Literature at the University of California, San Diego. He has published widely on Elizabethan culture and on theory and method in the historical analysis of literature, and has recently completed a book on the cultural politics of the Elizabethan theatre.

Alan Sinfield is Professor of English at Sussex University. He is the author of several books on Renaissance literature, most recently *Faultlines: Cultural Materialism and the Politics of Dissident Reading* (1992). He is the co-editor (with Jonathan Dollimore) of *Political Shakespeare: New Essays in Cultural Materialism* (1985).

Robert Weimann is Professor of English at Forshungsschwerpunkt Literaturwissenschaft, Wiss. Neuvorhaben (Berlin/Munich) and is Professor of Drama and Performance Theory at the University of California, Irvine. He is the author of numerous works on Renaissance drama and literary theory, including *Shakespeare and the Popular Tradition in the Theater: Studies in the Social Dimension of Dramatic Form and Function* (1978). He is presently engaged in a project on Authority and Representation in early modern discourse, of which a first part on Reformation writings and sixteenth-century fiction will be published shortly.

Index